China's Use of Military Force in Foreign Affairs

This book explains why China has resorted to the use of large-scale military force in foreign affairs.

How will China use its growing military might in coming crises and existing conflicts? This book contributes to the current debate on the future of the Asia-Pacific region by examining why China has resorted to using military force in the past. Utilizing fresh theoretical insights on the causes of interstate war and employing a sophisticated methodological framework, the book provides detailed analyses of China's intervention in the Korean War, the Sino-Indian War, China's border clashes with the Soviet Union and the Sino-Vietnamese War. It argues that China did not employ military force in these wars for the sake of national security or because of material issues under contestation, as frequently claimed. Rather, the book's findings strongly suggest that considerations about China's international status and relative standing are the principal reasons for China's decision to engage in military force in these instances. When reflecting the study's central insight back onto China's contemporary territorial conflicts and problematic bilateral relationships, it is argued that the People's Republic is still a status-seeking and thus highly status-sensitive actor. As a result, China's status ambitions should be very carefully observed and well taken into account when interacting with the PRC.

This book will be of much interest to students of Chinese foreign policy, Asian politics, military and strategic studies and IR in general.

Markus B. Liegl is a PhD candidate at the Goethe-University Frankfurt, Germany.

Asian Security Studies

Series Editors: Sumit Ganguly, *Indiana University, Bloomington*, Andrew Scobell, *Research and Development (RAND) Corporation, Santa Monica*, and Joseph Chinyong Liow, *Nanyang Technological University, Singapore*.

Few regions of the world are fraught with as many security questions as Asia. Within this region it is possible to study great power rivalries, irredentist conflicts, nuclear and ballistic missile proliferation, secessionist movements, ethnoreligious conflicts and inter-state wars. This book series publishes the best possible scholarship on the security issues affecting the region, and includes detailed empirical studies, theoretically oriented case studies and policy-relevant analyses as well as more general works.

Power Transition and International Order in Asia
Issues and Challenges
Edited by Peter Shearman

Afghanistan, Pakistan and Strategic Change
Adjusting Western Regional Policy
Edited by Joachim Krause and Charles King Mallory, IV

The Arms Race in Asia
Trends, Causes and Implications
Andrew T.H. Tan

Globalization and Security Relations across the Taiwan Strait
In the Shadow of China
Edited by Ming-chin Monique Chu and Scott L. Kastner

Multilateral Asian Security Architecture
Non-ASEAN Stakeholders
See Seng Tan

Chinese Foreign Relations with Weak Peripheral States
Asymmetrical Economic Power and Insecurity
Jeffrey Reeves

Democratic Transition and Security in Pakistan
Edited by Shaun Gregory

China's Use of Military Force in Foreign Affairs
The Dragon Strikes
Markus B. Liegl

China's Use of Military Force in Foreign Affairs
The Dragon Strikes

Markus B. Liegl

LONDON AND NEW YORK

First published 2017 by Transaction Publishers

2 Park Square, Milton Park, Abingdon, Oxfordshire OX14 4RN
711 Third Avenue, New York, NY 10017

Routledge is an imprint of the Taylor & Francis Group, an informa business

First issued in paperback 2018

Copyright © 2017 Markus B. Liegl

The right of Markus B. Liegl to be identified as author of this work has been asserted by him in accordance with sections 77 and 78 of the Copyright, Designs and Patents Act 1988.

All rights reserved. No part of this book may be reprinted or reproduced or utilised in any form or by any electronic, mechanical, or other means, now known or hereafter invented, including photocopying and recording, or in any information storage or retrieval system, without permission in writing from the publishers.

Notice:
Product or corporate names may be trademarks or registered trademarks, and are used only for identification and explanation without intent to infringe.

British Library Cataloguing-in-Publication Data
A catalogue record for this book is available from the British Library

Library of Congress Cataloging-in-Publication Data
Names: Liegl, Markus B., author. Title: China's use of military force in foreign affairs : the dragon strikes / Markus B. Liegl.
Description: Abingdon, Oxon ; New York, NY : Routledge, 2017. |
Series: Asian security studies | Includes bibliographical references and index.
Identifiers: LCCN 2016044284| ISBN 9781138693838 (hbk) |
ISBN 9781315529332 (ebk)
Subjects: LCSH: China--History, Military--20th century. | China--Military policy--History--20th century. | China--Foreign relations--1949-
Classification: LCC DS777.65 .L55 2017 | DDC 355.02/095109045--dc23LC record available at https://lccn.loc.gov/2016044284

ISBN: 978-1-138-69383-8 (hbk)
ISBN: 978-1-138-38905-2 (pbk)

Typeset in Bembo
by Fish Books Ltd.

To my parents,
Agnes and Josef Liegl,
for their never-ending encouragement and facilitation

Contents

List of illustrations viii
List of abbreviations ix
Acknowledgements x

1 Introduction 1

2 Why nations go to war 25

3 China's Korean War, 1950–1953 57

4 The Sino-Indian War of 1962 106

5 The Sino-Soviet border clashes of 1969 149

6 China's Vietnam War, 1979 190

7 Conclusion 227

Index 248

Illustrations

Tables

2.1	Overview: realist explanations for war	26
2.2	Overview: motives and implications	33
2.3	Expectations: *spirit*	41
2.4	Expectations: *fear*	42
2.5	Expectations: *rationalist model*	43

Figures

2.1	The 'social contract' of spirit-worlds	35
2.2	Overview: competing causal paths	45

Abbreviations

APC	Armored personnel carrier
CCP	Chinese Communist Party
CMC	Central Military Commission
CPSU	Communist Party of the Soviet Union
CPV	Chinese People's Volunteers
CPVEF	Chinese People's Volunteer Engineer Force
CSSR	Czechoslovak Socialist Republic
DMZ	Demilitarized Zone
DPRK	Democratic People's Republic of Korea
DRV	Democratic Republic of Vietnam
GMD	*Guomindang*
IR	International Relations
KIA	Killed in Action
KPA	Korean People's Army
KWP	Korean Workers' Party
MDL	Military Demarcation Line
MR	Military Region
NEFA	North Eastern Frontier Agency
PAVN	People's Army of Vietnam
PLA	People's Liberation Army
PLAAF	People's Liberation Army Air Force
POW	Prisoner of War
PRC	People's Republic of China
ROK	Republic of Korea
SRV	Socialist Republic of Vietnam
UN	United Nations
USPACOM	United States Pacific Command
USSR	Union of Socialist Soviet Republics
WIA	Wounded in Action

Acknowledgements

This book could not have been completed without the personal, institutional, and financial support I have received in the past few years. During the process of research, writing, and rewriting the manuscript, I have benefitted extensively from the help of many friends and scholars.

In particular, I want to thank Professor Reinhard Wolf and Professor Gunther Hellmann (Goethe-University Frankfurt am Main) for their guidance, advice, and patience with me as student, research assistant, and PhD candidate.

I am especially indebted to Professor Sven Bernhard Gareis (George C. Marshall Center for European Security Studies, Garmisch-Partenkirchen) for encouraging me to write this book, for his counsel during the first stages of this project, and for his assistance when it came to realizing my journey to China, despite many difficulties. I have been able to count on Sven's advice and profit from his academic experience for many years now, and I am glad that he is among my friends. My journey to China and the conclusion of the manuscript would not have been possible without the financial support I have received from the Hanns-Seidel-Foundation in the past years, for which I am indebted to Professor Hans-Peter Niedermeier and Professor Reinhard Meier-Walser.

At the George C. Marshall Center, my thanks goes to the staff of the research library and to Lt.-Col. Jan Kars for hours of discussion of the challenges and difficulties of military combat at high altitudes. During my time at the German Embassy in Beijing, I found an inspiring working environment and gained many insights, from which this book definitely profits. For that, I want to thank Col. Carlo Schnell, Lt.-Col. Daniel Schneider, and Lt.-Col. Thomas Siegel. I also owe thanks to Gudrun Wacker (SWP, German Institute for International and Security Affairs) for providing me with a stimulating workplace during my summer in Berlin, and for our many phone conversations since then.

At Routledge, my thanks go to Emily Ross, Hannah Ferguson, and Andrew Humphrys for their support and personal assistance. I am also deeply indebted to the series editors, Professors Andrew Scobell, Sumit Ganguly, and Joseph Chinyong Liow, for considering my piece for publication in this great book series, and I want to thank the two anonymous reviewers for their helpful comments.

I owe special thanks to my colleagues and friends Carsten Rauch, Lena Jaschob, Charlotte Dany, Sebastian Biba, and Iris Wurm (Goethe-University Frankfurt am Main), for being the best workmates I can imagine, for taking me by the hand during my first steps into academia, and for long evenings and entire nights full of great discussions. For their in-depth reading and very helpful and motivating comments on earlier versions of the manuscript, I am more than indebted to Iris Wurm, Carsten Rauch, Ai Noguchi, and especially Klaus Roscher.

Finally, I want to thank a number of exceptional people that may not have directly contributed to this publication but are of vital importance to its author. I owe more than I can ever return to my parents Agnes and Josef, and to my brother Johannes, for being such a great family. I want to thank my friends Sebastian Nieke, Steffen Horn, and Uli Pauluschke, and my best friend, Tom Eichinger, for their friendship over many years. I am really proud to have such fine friends. Lastly, my biggest thanks goes to my love, Iris, for deeply enriching my life since I met her, for encouraging me to start this book, and for her crucial support during its realization. Without her, this book would not have been concluded.

Any flaws and shortcomings readers may find in this volume are the responsibility of the author alone.

1 Introduction

> So it is said that if you know your enemies and know yourself, you will not be put at risk even if you have a hundred battles. If you only know yourself, but not your opponent, you may win or may lose. If you know neither yourself nor your enemy, you will always endanger yourself.
>
> Sun Tzu, *The Art of War*

East Asia is steering toward an uncertain future. In the South China Sea, tensions are on the rise as the People's Republic of China (PRC) is unilaterally bolstering its extensive territorial claims by building a 'Great Wall of Sand.' In the East China Sea, the simmering conflict between China and Japan over Senkaku/Diaoyu intensified when Tokyo decided to re-nationalize the islands in 2012. On the Korean Peninsula, tensions increased markedly after China's client and ally North Korea sank a South Korean frigate in 2010, declared re-entry into the state of war at the height of the Korea Crisis in 2013, and conducted its fourth nuclear weapons test in January 2016. All these regional hotspots inherit a decent potential to escalate into militarized conflicts and could do so with dramatic implications, as any confrontation in this globally important region will have extensive consequences for other regions, too.

It is thus the more worrisome that all of these conflicts are affected and even fueled by the direct or indirect involvement of China and the United States. Unfortunately, the relationship between the two most powerful nations of the current international system, often characterized as the most important dyad in the twenty-first century, has taken a turn for the worse and is now heading toward a great-power rivalry that "continues to unfold across geopolitical, economic, and even cultural realms and is now extant in all corners of the globe."[1] This situation not only harbors the prospect for a Cold War-like standoff between Washington and Beijing in Asia, which is – according to a recent Carnegie study – the second most likely outcome of current trends by the year 2030,[2] but also raises the potential for an actual military confrontation through increasing the number of latent cleavages and actual issues under contestation between Beijing and Washington. The concomitant risks and costs of such a collision are hard to underestimate, given the military strength and global significance of both powers. Currently, it seems that such a catastrophic outcome is fortunately far from inevitable, as there still exist stabilizing patterns in U.S.–China relations and sufficient prudence and political leeway on both sides of the Pacific;[3] even so, a further intensification of tensions between China and the United States is nonetheless looming on the horizon.

Besides attention and admiration, China's unprecedented rise has generated serious concerns, too. While Beijing, anxious not to be perceived as a revisionist or aggressive actor, traditionally emphasizes its peaceful intentions and cultivates the narrative of 'China's peaceful development' based on soft power, diplomacy and a 'new type of great power relations,'[4] scholars and practitioners alike point to the worrisome increase in the PRC's hard-power capabilities. Since the early 1990s, the People's Liberation Army (PLA) has undergone an intense modernization and armament program, which has transformed the PLA from an outdated peasant army into a modern, three-dimensional military force. As Beijing steadily expands the operative reach and effectiveness of its assertive capabilities, China's future global role does not necessarily seem limited to that of the 'world's workbench' or an economic powerhouse; on the contrary, the PRC aspires to become a first-class military power with the capacity to project military force by land, air, sea, and cyberspace well beyond its immediate peripheries.[5] At the same time, observers have found that Beijing now opts for a more comprehensive, self-confident, proactive and tougher, occasionally assertive approach in its foreign policy.

The obvious discrepancy in China's words and deeds worries policymakers in Washington and Asia–Pacific, and gives rise to more than just doubts about the strategic orientation of an economically prosperous and militarily ever more capable 'Middle Kingdom.' Will China emerge as a profound challenge to the existing regional and international order, or will it be possible to peacefully integrate China as a stakeholder and thereby manage a non-violent power transition? These questions dominate the current debate on China's rise, and proponents of the neorealist-inspired 'China threat' theory provide us with the most straightforward answers: according to this school of thought, it is inconceivable for China's rise to be peaceful because history has shown that growing economic power will translate into military capabilities that in turn awaken the desire for regional dominance and expansion.[6] China's 'new assertiveness' in foreign affairs and Beijing's strategy to erect and militarize artificial islands in the South China Sea might indeed be regarded as the first proof of this line of reasoning.[7] Moreover, the empirical record of non-peaceful power transitions also leads to the conclusion that a rising China will follow the unambiguous example set by its historical predecessors and inevitably, sooner or later, will collide with the most powerful state in the international system.[8] While some observers already predict a military confrontation between China and the United States, others emphatically urge the U.S. government to do everything it can to contain China now in order to preserve regional peace and stability in the future.[9]

While "the view of an all-menacing China is often exaggerated by academics, pundits and politicians,"[10] these warnings do not appear to have fallen on deaf ears in Washington, as China is increasingly perceived as a strategic challenge to the United States' military dominance and political leadership in East Asia.[11] In view of this, it should not come as a surprise that despite numerous public statements by U.S. government officials encouraging China to seek a more active role in regional and global affairs, "the majority of the foreign policy community in Washington is more likely to see China as a threat to American power that needs to be actively contained."[12] As strategic trust has become a scarce resource in U.S.–China relations, Washington's 'pivot to Asia' – unambiguously perceived by Beijing as targeted on the PRC – will almost certainly add its share to the further aggravation of tensions.[13] This is exactly what might lead to a dangerous conflict situation with all the prerequisites for a substantial security dilemma, plus all associated risks.

Aim of the book

In the decades to come, peace and stability in East Asia will increasingly depend on how China uses its growing military power in coming crises and conflicts, which already today characterize the volatile security environment of the region. China is presently involved in virtually every major regional hotspot, from the maritime territorial disputes in the East and South China Seas over the situation on the Korean Peninsula and the still unresolved Sino-Indian territorial dispute to the Taiwan Question. With intensifying competition between China and the United States over power, status, and influence as a background condition, this makes for a highly delicate setting in which China as a rising power is emerging as a challenge to the regional status quo by demanding a greater say in world politics and by expecting greater deference to its interests and wishes in the region.[14]

A brief look back at the history of modern China confirms that worries about a potentially aggressive 'Middle Kingdom' might indeed be reasonable. Since the proclamation of the People's Republic in 1949, China has demonstrated on several occasions that it will not refrain from the proactive use of large-scale military force in order to safeguard its interests and to force others into obedience. Despite its self-proclaimed 'principles of peaceful coexistence' and during the seemingly stable bipolar setting of the Cold War, China challenged the United States in Korea, resorted to force against its former friend India, provoked armed clashes with the Soviet Union, and went to war against its socialist sister state and long-standing ally, Vietnam.

This book is about these four cases of China's use of force in foreign affairs. Specifically, I am interested in answering the question of why China resorted to the use of military force in these four instances. Examining the concrete causes for China's use of force is appropriate, meaningful, and relevant for at least three reasons. First, all four cases of China's use of force reveal specific characteristics and patterns that cannot or can only poorly be explained by the well-established and broadly accepted theories for interstate warfare in International Relations (IR) based on the rational-choice assumption. As this dominant strand of theorizing on the outbreak of war between states fails to provide us with comprehensive and accurate rationalizations for the cases at hand, we do not know for sure why China has used military force in the past. This deficit in knowledge is more than worrisome, especially with regard to the current developments in East Asia. Second, providing more specified and precise explanations for these "outlier cases"[15] is highly relevant, and not only with regard to historical or theoretical perspectives. In order to assess the inherent potential for conflict in the emerging structure of East Asia, a promising line of inquiry starts by identifying the specific issues and concrete reasons China regarded as valuable enough to fight for in previous instances. If these issues and interests reveal trans-epochal relevancy and are thus of significance for today's China, their identification allows for more accurate assessment of the escalatory potential of ongoing conflicts involving the PRC.[16] In doing so, the findings of my analysis might be of help for avoiding the unnecessary repetition of history. Third, as policy-makers in Washington apparently frame China's rise predominantly through a neorealist prism and react to it with policies that are well known from the Cold War era, a look back at China's strategic behavior during the actual Cold War not only appears reasonable, but gains even more relevancy when cast through an alternative theoretical lens that allows for a critical re-reading and evaluation of well-established and broadly accepted findings on the causes of China's use of force in foreign affairs.

Taking these three arguments as the starting point for my project, this book attempts to contribute to the ongoing debate on the future of the Asia-Pacific region by digging into China's past. In doing so, I seek to identify the concrete motives behind China's proactive use of force as my primary research interest. Approaching the inquiry from this perspective appears particularly promising, as the analysis of motives provides direct insights into the immediate causes of a specific conflict escalation, rather than just disclosing underlying or enabling conditions as the permissive causes.[17] Focusing on motives as an analytical category also encourages me to take into account non-material incentives such as con-siderations about social status or the role of emotions, which are basically neglected by existing theories that focus predominantly on material incentives and/or security as the principal causes of interstate war. However, as states "frequently go to war for reasons that have little, if anything, to do with security,"[18] any analysis of interstate warfare would thus be well advised to also take these non-material incentives into account. For that reason, I utilize Ned Lebow's Cultural Theory of International Relations as the theoretical framework that will guide my empirical analysis. In contrast to other approaches, Lebow focuses decidedly on motives as explanations for political behavior and systematically integrates material and ideational variables in an encompassing explanatory model for collective action such as national foreign policy.

In the universe of theorizing about international relations, Lebow's Cultural Theory is still a relatively new approach and – at least to my knowledge – has not yet demonstrated its explanatory capacity for empirical cases beyond those used for its development. This provides me with a unique opportunity to test the theory's logical coherence and explanatory power under live-fire conditions as my secondary research interest. Lebow's stated goal is the construction of a grand theory of inter-national relations, which is distinguished from medium- or small-range models "by the generalizations it makes across cultures and epochs."[19] However, by utilizing the ancient Greek "storehouse of insights and ideas … relevant to international relations"[20] as his fundament, Lebow builds his theory upon the nucleus of occidental culture and Western civilization.[21] While he justifies this approach by arguing that the concepts and insights borrowed from Greek philosophy "capture universal attributes of human nature that find expression in all cultures at all times,"[22] Lebow does not offer a comprehensive test for the validity of this ambitious hypothesis.[23]

Even though he draws upon an impressive number of empirical cases to develop, specify, and validate his Cultural Theory, the evidence provided substantiates his argument only in part: while the cases indeed reveal variance across epochs, they do not do so across cultures. With Imperial Japan as the single exception, Lebow focuses exclusively on political relations in the Western world, and there is good reason to also categorize Imperial Japan – due to its societal and political characteristics as well as its self-conception – as Western rather than as a genuine Asian actor.[24] Consequently, the Cultural Theory has yet to demonstrate its applicability and validity across cultural and epochal boundaries in order to qualify as a genuine grand theory of IR, according to Lebow's self-set criteria. For doing so, Lebow passes the baton by stating the hope "that others will extend my analysis to the non-Western world and use their findings to reflect back"[25] upon the theory. Taking this invitation as the second starting point for my project, I hope that my findings will contribute a modest share to the further vitalization of the innovative theoretical paradigm inspired and sketched out by Ned Lebow. By testing his theory's coherence and explanatory capacity for the four cases investigated in this book, I confront Lebow's model with an Asian actor that furthermore positioned itself within the anti-Western bloc at the onset of the Cold War. This should pose a tough test for Lebow's Western-centered Cultural Theory.

The puzzle of China's use of military force

Why are the four cases of China's use of military force I investigate in this book still in need of explanations? My answer is that none of them can be adequately addressed or sufficiently explained by those explanatory models for interstate warfare that are ontologically based on the rational-choice assumption (i.e. the logic of consequences).[26] Even at first glance, this dominant strand in theorizing the outbreak of war faces difficulty when taking into account the specific circumstances and characteristics inherent in China's use of military force: Beijing's seemingly 'irrational' decisions to proactively go to war against highly militarily superior, and even nuclear-armed, opponents such as the United States and the Soviet Union greatly overstretches the explanatory capacity of these models. In both cases, Beijing did not command a nuclear capability that may have allowed for such a bold move by functioning, according to the logic of rational deterrence theory, as an ultimate guarantee for China's security and survival in the case of follow-up escalations and large-scale retaliations. Moreover, as even the conventional military balance unfolded to China's disadvantage, Beijing's leadership could by no means start from the premise that victory on the battlefield could be accomplished with a decent certainty of likelihood when deciding to resort to force against the United States in Korea or to ambush Soviet forces at Zhenbao Island. High-risk calculations of that kind greatly contradict the postulation of rationalist theories for interstate war as these models regard "the premeditation of war [as a] rational process consisting of careful and deliberate calculations,"[27] with the aim of identifying, evaluating, and controlling the inherent risks of an upcoming confrontation.

In the same way, this class of theories also appears incapable of rationalizing China's war objectives and conduct of warfare against India and Vietnam. As even the most cursory survey of the existing literature indicates, both offensives were hardly motivated by security considerations or aimed at gaining control over territory under dispute.[28] Rather, it seems as if these campaigns were primarily intended to punish or humiliate these nations and their leaderships by teaching them some 'bitter lessons': as Deng Xiaoping tellingly explained to U.S. President Carter shortly before China went to war against Vietnam, "children who do not listen have to be spanked."[29] In both instances, Chinese forces gained control over fiercely defended territory at a considerable toll of blood, but instead of realizing China's territorial demands, the PLA voluntarily withdrew from these hard-won areas shortly afterwards. As Beijing obviously did not aim at conquering the territory under dispute, theories focusing exclusively on material and/or security-related incentives for interstate warfare are unable to explain China's obviously non-material war objectives in these two instances. Besides, Alastair Johnston has demonstrated that other well-established explanatory models such as diversionary theories of conflict and crisis behavior, theories focusing on the foreign policy of revolutionary states, or Neorealism's balance-of-power logic fall short of developing sufficient explanatory power to account for the four cases of China's large-scale use of military force in foreign affairs.[30] As none of them can be comprehensively explained by existing theories, these cases cannot be regarded as closed chapters in scholarly writing. Consequently, the phenomenon of China's large-scale use of military force in foreign affairs commands further analytical attention and explanatory efforts in order to disentangle the empirical puzzle and overcome the corresponding explanatory deficit of established theories.

Core argument and central findings

If China did not resort to military force for reasons that are related to security, territory, or any other material incentive, what did motivate Beijing to proactively engage in four costly and risky wars? In a nutshell, my answer to this question reads as follows. As I will demonstrate in more detail in the remainder of this book, China fought the United States in Korea in order to increase its international status by fulfilling its obligations toward the international socialist society, and resorted to force against India, the Soviet Union, and Vietnam in order to enforce its self-claimed status rank *vis-à-vis* New Delhi, Moscow, and Hanoi. According to my findings, China's international status rank and its associated social implications are thus the predominant issues that Beijing regarded as valuable enough to fight for, at great risk and cost, in the past. I am certainly not the first to argue that colliding claims about status rank can result in interstate conflict and violence.[31] Neither am I the first to emphasize China's specific sensitivity when it comes to matters of status and standing.[32] The unique value of this contribution lies in the combination of both perspectives to identify and explain the reasons why China resorted to the use of military force in the four cases I investigate.

In international politics, the actions of states do not only reflect the interests of seeking security (Neorealism) or maximizing wealth (Liberalism). States also strive for status, defined as an actor's relative rank within a group-specific hierarchy, and its appreciation among peers.[33] Underlying this pursuit is the universal human need for self-esteem and the desire for social recognition, which both can very easily be transferred from the individual to the international level. States are not 'black boxes' with pre-fixed preferences but hierarchically organized groups of emotional people, who saturate their basic need for social esteem by identifying with the accomplishments of their collective.[34] This insight holds especially true for the elites of a political unit, as these individuals identify themselves particularly extensively with the achievements and the reputation of their collective due to their exposed political or military functions. In doing so, these elites reflect their psychological needs outward, and thus into the sphere of international relations.[35] Accordingly, status-seeking and its associated emotional effects are not only limited to interpersonal relations. Status-seeking is also an observable phenomenon in the interactions between political units across cultures and epochs, with specific implications for cooperation, risk behavior, and conflict.

While neighboring fields such as social psychology, sociology, and philosophy have long acknowledged and fruitfully utilized these insights, they were only recently picked up and systematically addressed by IR as a discipline. The reasons for this can be attributed to the supposed incompatibility of social factors with the dominant rationalist ontology in IR theorizing, to the challenges of semantics and concept-building, and to developments within the discipline itself, as "[r]esearch on the international politics of status-seeking simply did not fit the field-shaping debates of the 1980s and 1990s."[36] Even so, the social dimension of international relations should actually not be seen as a new analytical category for IR, because important concepts have already been present in and were reflected by central IR theories.[37] IR still, nevertheless, lacks a coherent paradigm that focuses decidedly on the independent explanatory power of social status – but it seems as if compensation for this deficit is imminent due to the fresh theoretical impetus generated in the wake of IR's recent 'turn to emotion.'[38] Since this turn, research on status in international politics has shown that the quest for social status has profound material consequences, as a high-status rank

> brings with it deference to a state's interests and concerns. A great power is considered to have a *droit de regard* in neighboring areas. The assurance that others will acknowledge, respect, and defer to a state's special interest, not only in crises but in everyday interactions, is highly valued among major powers.[39]

If other states fail to defer to the wishes and interest of a high-status actor, however, this can result in highly emotionalized conflicts: such an affronted actor may be perfectly secure but nonetheless feel the need to put others in their place through the use of military force in order to demonstrate its superior status. Conflicts of that kind thus have a high tendency to escalate into violence and are, because of inherent emotions, much harder to deter by conventional means.

The intensified scholarly interest in status in IR has resulted in a minimal consensus on the phenomenon itself. Most scholars agree that status in international politics has collective, subjective, and relative dimensions. First, it is a collective social construction and thus necessarily requires a social framework to function because status "cannot be attained unilaterally; it must be recognized by others."[40]

The respective social framework also determines what specific material, symbolic, or cultural attributes are regarded as prestigious and thus convey status. Second, this makes status a profoundly subjective category in which self-perception and external attribution are prone to diverge. Rising states in particular frequently claim a higher status rank for themselves than the established actors are willing to concede. Last, status describes a positional commodity in an asymmetric social order and thus has a relative character.[41] Thereby, an actor's specific status rank functions as the point of reference to determine the higher or lower rankings of other actors. While these characteristics can turn status hierarchies into stabilizing patterns on the international level when the ranks are known and respected, they can also become conflict-prone battlegrounds, especially when it comes to the concrete delineation of ranks between two states.

Current state of research and debate and relevancy of this contribution

As the current debate focuses predominantly on China's future, it seems as if I am pursuing a rather acyclic research project by looking at China's past. The overwhelming majority of contributions to the contemporary debate focus on the future of Asia-Pacific, the relationship between China and the United States, and the question of the kind of social structure that will likely develop between these two important actors. The emergence of a true Sino-American friendship is considered the least likely outcome.[42] Following Alexander Wendt's triadic model, this leaves the options of enmity and rivalry on the table.[43] The formation of a genuine enmity, however, can currently be ruled out due to the unprecedented degree of economic interdependence between China and the United States, which strongly affects the fate of both nations for better or worse. Even so, this stabilizing pattern appears incapable of preventing the emergence of a political rivalry. As outlined above, such a rivalry is currently unfolding and present developments do not indicate any reversal of this trend, as the PRC is increasingly perceived as a potential competitor and strategic challenge to U.S. security interests in the Asia-Pacific region. Over the course of Barack Obama's 'pacific presidency', the United States not only enlarged its existing military and political footprint in Asia, despite profound budgetary restrictions, but, with the 'pivot to Asia,' comprehensively shifted its strategic focus toward the region, and thus on China.[44] The extent and comprehensiveness of Washington's intensified engagement in Asia nurture the perception in Beijing that the United States has abandoned the policy of strategic engagement, which had been the cornerstone of U.S.–China relations since the end of the Cold War, and now opts instead to contain China.[45] As the United States is apparently reacting to China's rise with strategies that are well known from the Cold War era, it should not come as a surprise that scholars suggest a 'new Cold War' over spheres of influence, bases, and resources is already looming on the horizon, because "U.S.–China relations are becoming increasingly militarized and assume the character of a zero-sum game."[46] Containment, balance-of-power logic, and zero-sum competition comprise the home turf of neorealist theory in IR – a paradigm that enjoys questionable popularity among political practitioners.

Regarding the latter, it is highly interesting that the available – for the most part, Western – literature on specific cases of China's use of force unfolded in two distinct 'waves' of interpretations, and both could be regarded as products (or at least byproducts) of the respective *zeitgeist*. In a nutshell, while the first wave aimed somewhat at demonizing China by emphasizing the evilness and ideological radicalism of Mao's Red Middle Kingdom as the principal sources for China's aggressive behavior, subsequent studies regularly revised these findings comprehensively in order to provide more scientifically grounded, primarily neorealist-inspired explanations.[47] It may only be a coincidence, but the watershed between these two waves seems to be marked by the Sino-American rapprochement of the late 1970s. When viewed against this background, one could be tempted to assume that changes in the structural setting of the international system have not only affected the foreign policy of states, as Neorealism postulates, but may also have subcutaneously framed the analytical perspectives of scholarly research on China's foreign policy.[48] Tellingly, the relatively few analyses of China's punitive campaign against Vietnam in 1979, published after the United States and China had established diplomatic relations in December 1978, reveal themselves as single exceptions to that tidal pattern in Western interpretations of China's use of military force.

Neorealism's principal analytical categories – security and power – are indeed attractive research tools, as they are relatively easy to apply and lead to intuitively convincing findings. These advantages may explain the obvious predominance of neorealist interpretations in explaining the use of force in international relations. However, reducing the analytical focus to security-relevant aspects only is strikingly problematic, because this research strategy deliberately circumvents the complexity of social and political processes. In turn, this can lead to two highly precarious results. On the one hand, policy guided by research of this kind can unintentionally and unnecessarily stimulate the emergence of a problematical security dilemma that typically leads to spirals of self-fulfilling prophecies. As the recent developments in Asia-Pacific indicate, such a situation is currently emerging, and its effects are already straining the relationship between the United States and China.[49] On the other hand, such parsimonious but reductionist models provide futile grounds for the establishment of myths – such as the 'security myth' – in seeking to explain escalations of military violence.[50] Narrowing the focus to security-related issues only pushes to the background less prominently postulated causes of conflict that contain the same, or even increased, potential for escalation. While largely disregarded due to the lack of systematic theorizing, these causes and their specific effects have nonetheless been efficaciously present in the cases of China's use of force, and occasionally even reveal themselves in the subtext of the available literature. In view of that, the four cases of China's use of military force investigated in this study cannot be regarded as closed chapters. Analysis of the respective causes of China's resorting to military force is therefore appropriate, relevant, and meaningful, especially when guided by an alternative theoretical model that allows for the identification of potential 'research myths' by encouraging a critical re-reading of well-established and broadly accepted findings.

Designing research

My analysis unfolds as a theory-guided, small-*n* case-study design, covering a period of investigation from the foundation of the People's Republic of China on October 1, 1949 until the time of writing (2016). This approach appears particularly suitable as it enables me to pursue both of my research objectives simultaneously and also allows for stronger tests than large-*n* methods could provide.[51] The reasons for this, as Christopher Achen and Duncan Snidal argue, are apparent, as

> only case studies provide the *intensive empirical analysis* that can *find previously unnoticed causal factors* and historical patterns. ... Because they are *simultaneously sensitive to data and theory*, case studies are more useful for [theory construction and testing] than any other methodological tool.[52]

As my primary research objective consists in identifying the concrete motives for China's use of force through a critical re-reading of established findings, approaching the inquiry via a theory-informed case-study design thus promises to serve as an especially capable method for discovering previously unnoticed, overlooked, or misinterpreted data.[53]

Moreover, organizing my analysis into distinct, self-contained cases also allows for a cross-case comparison to detect potential variation in China's motivations over time.[54] As Arend Lijphart has observed, case-study designs and the comparative method should be closely connected because of the reciprocal advantages provided by the combination of both methods.[55] With regard to the case studies themselves, I will utilize process tracing and within-case congruence tests as the principal methods of investigation.

In order to delineate the universe of cases, I first need to clarify more precisely which phenomenon I want to investigate. As the book's title indicates, my explanadum (or dependent variable) is China's use of military force in foreign relations, which I define as the proactive use of organized force as a political instrument in the external affairs of the People's Republic of China. In order to eliminate any potentially remaining ambiguity, the several components of this definition merit some further specification: I understand 'the proactive use of organized force' as the deployment to battle of the PRC's regular armed forces (i.e. the PLA), whereby this deployment should constitute a new level of violence escalation in a given situation or conflict. In order to be regarded as a 'political instrument,' the escalation from non-combat to combat needs to be authorized by the PRC's relevant political decision-making institutions, such as the CCP Politburo and the Central Military Commission (CMC). In order to affect an 'external affair,' the PLA has to be deployed to battle on the territory and/or against regular armed forces of another state. It also appears essential to differentiate between politically intended and spontaneous (i.e. non-authorized or accidental) escalations of military violence. In order to preserve the study's focus on the former, an instance has to meet the following requirements: I only take those cases into account in which a minimum of one PLA regiment (around 1,500–3,000 troops) was deployed, resulting in a substantial number of battle-related casualties on behalf of the PLA (i.e. a minimum of 500 Chinese soldiers killed in action, KIA, or wounded in action, WIA). I chose the regiment as a benchmark because the deployment of this formation requires the pooling of several battalions from different military branches, which should clearly exceed the level of competence of local PLA commanders, thus making an unauthorized resort to force less plausible. In the same way, the benchmark of 500 battle-related PLA casualties should exceed by far the losses resulting from spontaneous skirmishes and accidental clashes, which are usually much lower, and thus functions as a clear indicator for high-intensity combat resulting from a deliberate decision to resort to organized force on the part of Beijing's political leadership.

With this definition at hand, I can now explain my case selection. In principle, I can draw on all cases that meet the definition of my dependent variable during the period of investigation. In order to avoid confusion and potential distortion of my research results, I follow the PRC's officially stated distinction between internal and external issues. Consequently, I exclude China's annexation of Tibet in 1950 and the PLA's offensive operations during the first two Taiwan Crises (1954–5/1958), because Beijing regarded and still regards Tibet and Taiwan as decidedly domestic affairs. Based on the same argument, I also exclude the PRC's naval engagements with the Republic of Vietnam in 1974 and the Socialist Republic of Vietnam in 1988.[56] The following four cases comprehensively fulfill the pre-set criteria and thus constitute my case sample: China's intervention in the Korean War (1950–3); the Sino-Indian War of 1962; China's border clashes with the Soviet Union in 1969; and the Sino-Vietnamese War of 1979.[57]

I am aware that my case selection may invite criticism from at least two directions. First, empirical critique might arise because of the inclusion of the Sino-Soviet border clashes even though the proactive character and the adequate extent of China's use of force is not as unambiguously acknowledged in the existing literature here as it is for the three other cases. This makes it essential to put forward a convincing argument for the inclusion of the Sino-Soviet clashes, which I will provide in the case study itself. Second, I am aware that the case selection may well face criticism from a methodological perspective because I deliberately 'sample on the dependent variable' and thereby violate the "basic and obvious rule [that] selection should allow for the possibility of at least some variation on the dependent variable."[58] Gary King, Robert Keohane, and Sidney Verba (KKV) explicitly attest a 'selection bias' for "research that tries to explain the outbreak of war with studies of only wars" and advise strict avoidance of such 'no-variance' designs because "we will not learn anything about causal effects from them."[59] In contrast to this drastic judgment, other scholarly opinions differ greatly in their assessment on the heuristic value of no-variance designs.[60] Positioning myself in support of this more optimistic group, I argue that even though my cases are sampled in disregard of KKV's basic rule, this does not necessarily translate into constant values on my dependent variable. In fact, the dichotomous nature of the phenomenon under investigation allows for a clear-cut differentiation whether it is present or not. Accordingly, my dependent variable not only reveals variation over the course of one case, but does so by taking on two extreme values (i.e. non-combat vs. combat).[61] This allows the separation of two distinct phases in each case, which in turn provides me with at least two observation points for a within-case comparison.[62] As the dependent variable actually varies within each of my cases, a selection bias should thus not distort my research results.[63]

Plan of the book

The remainder of this book is organized as follows. In Chapter 2, I first present, evaluate, and discuss the explanatory repertoire of realist theories for the four empirical cases investigated in this book. This evaluation has two central aims: on the one hand, I demonstrate that these well-established and broadly accepted theories fail to develop sufficient explanatory power to account for China's past uses of military force in foreign affairs; on the other, I use the insights gained through this theory test to formulate requirements for a more capable explanatory model, on the basis of which I explain and justify my choice to use Ned Lebow's Cultural Theory of International Relations. I then explicate the theory and operationalize its variables for my subsequent case-study analyses. As the "plausibility of an explanation is enhanced to the extent that alternative explanations are considered less consisted with the data, or less supportable by available generalizations,"[64] I introduce James Fearon's 'rationalist explanation for war' as my alternative (or controlling) explanatory model. In the last part of the chapter, I explicate my research strategy and my methodological approach.

The main part of the book consists of the four case studies, in which I put the theoretically deduced expectations and the explanatory capacity of the two competing models to the empirical test. In the first case study, I analyze the motivation for China's intervention in the Korean War (1950–3), which reveals itself as the book's most data-rich case, allowing for in-depth analysis and also for conclusive results. My findings strongly disagree with the well-established and broadly accepted narrative of a security-motivated Chinese intervention, triggered by the United States' amphibious landing at Inchon and the materializing threat to China's northeastern provinces. Instead, the results of all my partial analyses unambiguously depict the motive *spirit* and its effects as the immediate cause for the PRC's intervention. Almost ideal-typically, the decisions of Beijing's leadership, and China's actions, reflected the execution of the theoretically postulated social responsibilities arising from the inherent logic of Lebow's spirit-worlds.

Following on from that, I investigate the causes of China's war against India in 1962 and analyze the central developments that turned the Sino-Indian friendship into hostility. Thereby, competing interpretations of the course of the bilateral border are revealed as the central cleavage in the relationship and the permissive cause for Beijing's resort to force. The immediate cause, however, is to be found in the Indian forward policy, with which New Delhi not only exaggerated Beijing's patience and forbearance but also highly affronted the Chinese leadership: in Beijing's perspective, the forward policy was the materialized peak of India's continuous disrespect for China's interests and an open belittling of the status and military power of the Middle Kingdom, which made drastic but limited punishment on the battlefield necessary.

In contrast to the other empirical cases, the Sino-Soviet border clashes of 1969 have received relatively little scholarly attention so far, although this instance reveals itself as a highly interesting case: to highlight the dramatic nature of the events taking place on the ice of the Ussuri River, just imagine the severe implications if American and Soviet soldiers had opened fire on each other in a similar standoff during the Berlin Crisis in 1961. Besides the scarcity of available literature, the analysis is further complicated by the fact that the concrete circumstances of the clashes have been subject to polarized discussions. Consequently, before the analysis of Beijing's motivation can be approached, I first have to verify whether China can be held responsible for the outbreak of hostilities by clarifying the proactive and deliberate character of China's resort to force. It will be shown that the declaration of the Brezhnev Doctrine, which was perceived by the Chinese leadership as a degradation of the People's Republic to the rank of a vassal by Moscow's grace, triggered this resort to force.

In the final case study, I examine the PRC's most recent use of large-scale military force against Vietnam in 1979. Only four years after Beijing and Hanoi had acted as close allies in the Second Indochina War, China and Vietnam fought each other in a short but bloody war. My analysis traces the metamorphosis of the bilateral relationship from brotherly comradeship into bitter enmity. In doing so, I disclose the interplay between emotional and material factors as drivers for this collapse, and show that a bitter sense of Vietnamese ingratitude for and disloyalty to Beijing's steadfast contributions to Hanoi lies at its heart. When Vietnam not only started to challenge the status of its former patron but also openly sided with the Soviet Union, these developments added furious anger to the sense of Vietnamese ingratitude felt in Beijing. Seeking revenge, the Chinese leadership made an emotionally induced decision to 'teach Vietnam a lesson' and put its ungrateful and arrogant little neighbor in its place.

Having completed my empirical analysis, I summarize the central findings in the concluding chapter. In a first step, I present an evaluation of the case studies' results and explicate the respective motives for China's resort to the use of military force. Following that, I reflect my findings back on the two competing theoretical models and assess their explanatory capacities. It will be shown that while Ned Lebow's Cultural Theory proves itself capable of explaining the four cases of China's use of force, James Fearon's rationalist model is unable to do so as it lacks the analytical sensitivity to take into account the crucial non-material dimension of international conflicts. Finally, I compare my central findings in order to cast a look forward from China's past onto the future of the Asia-Pacific region.

Notes

1   Goldstein, Lyle J., *Meeting China Halfway: How to Defuse the Emerging U.S.–China Rivalry* (Washington, D.C.: Georgetown University Press, 2015), 2.
2   See Swaine, Michael D. *et al.*, *Conflict and Cooperation in the Asia-Pacific Region: A Strategic Net Assessment* (Washington, D.C.: Carnegie Endowment for International Peace, 2015), 174–80.
3   See Glaser, Charles L., "A U.S.–China Grand Bargain? The Hard Choice between Military Competition and Accomodation," *International Security* 39, no. 4 (2015); Zhao, Suisheng, "China and America: Showdown in the Asia-Pacific?" in

Conflict and Cooperation in Sino-US Relations. Change and Continuity, Cause and Cure, ed. Blanchard, Jean-Marc F. and Shen, Simon (Milton Park/New York: Routledge, 2015).

4 See Shirk, Susan L., *China – Fragile Superpower* (New York: Oxford University Press, 2007), 108–09; Ding, Shen, "Analyzing Rising Power from the Perspective of Soft Power: A New Look at China's Rise to the Status Quo Power," *Journal of Contemporary China* 19, no. 64 (2010).

5 See Li, Nan, "China's Naval Modernization and Its Impact on Asian Security," in *Security and Conflict in East Asia*, ed. Tan, Andrew T. H. (Milton Park/New York: Routledge), 37; Li, Xiaobing, *A History of the Modern Chinese Army* (Lexington, KY: The University Press of Kentucky, 2007), 192–94; Wagener, Martin, "Grundlagen der Sicherheitspolitik Ostasiens: Mächte – Konflikte – Strukturen," in *Neue Dimensionen internationaler Sicherheitspolitik*, ed. Meier-Walser, Reinhard and Wolf, Alexander (München: Hanns-Seidel Stiftung, 2011), 245; Kamphausen, Roy, Lai, David, and Scobell, Andrew, *Beyond the Strait – PLA Missions Other Than Taiwan* (Carlisle: Strategic Studies Institute, U.S. Army War College 2009), 5. For overviews and assessments of China's military build-up and modernization, see Cliff, Roger, *China's Military Power. Assessing Current and Future Capabilities* (New York: Cambridge University Press, 2015); Wortzel, Larry M., *The Dragon Extends Its Reach. Chinese Military Power Goes Global* (Washington, D.C.: Potomac Books, 2013); Nathan, Andrew J. and Scobell, Andrew, *China's Search For Security* (New York: Columbia University Press, 2014), 278–316; Twomey, Christopher P. and Xu, Hui, "Military Developments," in *Debating China: The U.S.–China Relationship in Ten Conversations*, ed. Hachigan, Nina (Oxford/New York: Oxford University Press, 2014); Chase, Michael S. et al., *China's Incomplete Military Transformation. Assessing the Weaknesses of the People's Liberation Army (PLA)* (Santa Monica, CA: RAND, 2015).

6 See Roy, Denny, "The 'China Threat' Issue – Major Arguments," *Asian Survey* 36, no. 8 (1996); Hays-Gries, Peter, "Problems and Misperceptions in U.S.–China Relations," *Orbis* 53, no. 2 (2009): 225; Broomfield, Emma V., "Perceptions of Danger: The China Threat Theory," *Journal of Contemporary China* 12, no. 35 (2003); Callahan, William A., "How to Understand China: The Dangers and Opportunities of Being a Rising Power," *Review of International Studies* no. 31 (2005): 702–06.

7 See Yahuda, Michael, "China's New Assertiveness in the South China Sea," *Journal of Contemporary China* 22, no. 81 (2013); Friedberg, Aaron L., "The Sources of Chinese Conduct: Explaining Beijing's Assertiveness," *The Washington Quarterly* 37, no. 4 (2015); Chen, Yi-Hsuan, "South China Sea Tension on Fire: China's Recent Moves on Building Artifical Islands in Troubled Waters and Their Implication on Maritime Law," *Maritime Safety and Security Law Journal*, no. 1 (2015): 1–2, 11–12; Bräuner, Oliver, "'Wenn du einen Schritt machst, dann mache ich zwei' – Chinas maritime Strategie im Ost- und Südchinesischen Meer," *Zeitschrift für Außen- und Sicherheitspolitik* 7, no. 4 (2014): 446. For critical perspectives, see Johnston, Alastair I., "How New and Assertive Is China's New Assertiveness?" *International Security* 37, no. 4 (2013); Jerdén, Björn, "The Assertive China Narrative: Why It Is Wrong and How So Many Still Bought Into It," *The Chinese Journal of International Politics* 7, no. 1 (2014).

8 See Li, *A History of the Modern Chinese Army*, 3–4.

9 See Babbin, Jed and Timberlake, Edward, *Showdown – Why China Wants War with the United States* (Washington: Regnery Publishing, 2006); Bernstein, Richard and Ross, H. Munro, *The Coming Conflict with China* (New York: Knopf, 1997); Gertz, Bill, *The China Threat – How the People's Republic Targets America* (Washington, D.C.: Regnery, 2002); Mearsheimer, John J., *The Tragedy of Great Power Politics* (New York/London: W.W. Norton & Company, 2001), pp. 396–402; Ross, Robert S., "U.S. Grand Strategy, the

Rise of China, and U.S. National Security Strategy for East Asia," *Strategic Studies Quarterly* 7, no. 2 (2013): 24–25; Mearsheimer, John J., "The Gathering Storm: China's Challenge to US Power in Asia," *The Chinese Journal of International Politics* 3, no. 4 (2010); Friedberg, Aaron L., *A Contest for Supremacy: China, America, and the Struggle for Mastery in Asia* (New York: W.W. Norton, 2011).
10 Al-Rodhan, Khalid R., "A Critique of the China Threat Theory: A Systematic Analysis," *Asian Perspectives* 31, no. 3 (2007): 44.
11 See Ross, "U.S. Grand Strategy," 24–25; Dobbins, James, "War with China," *Survival* 54, no. 4 (2012): 7; Ross, Robert S., "The Problem with the Pivot: Obama's New Asia Policy is Unneccesary and Counterproductive," *Foreign Affairs* 91, no. 6 (2012): 73; Sutter, Robert G., *Chinese Foreign Relations: Power and Policy Since the Cold War* (Plymouth: Rowman & Littlefield Publishers, 2008), 172–75; Medeiros, Evan S., "Strategic Hedging and the Future of Asia-Pacific Stability," *The Washington Quarterly* 29, no. 1 (2005): 145–48; Rice, Condoleeza, "Promoting the National Interest – Life after the Cold War," *Foreign Affairs* 79, no. 1 (2000): 54–57.
12 Annen, Niels, "A Comeback in Asia? How China is Shaping U.S. Foreign Policy in the Pacific," *Perspectives – Friedrich Ebert Stiftung* (February 2011): 1.
13 See Ikenberry, G. John and Liff, Adam P., "Racing toward Tragedy? China's Rise, Military Competition in the Asia Pacific, and the Security Dilemma," *International Security* 39, no. 2 (2014); Ross, "The Problem with the Pivot"; Ling, Wei, "Rebalancing or De-Balancing: U.S. Pivot and East Asian Order," *American Foreign Policy Interest* 35, no. 3 (2013); Chase, Michael S., "Chinese Suspicion of U.S. Intentions," *Survival* 53, no. 3 (2011); Lai, David and Stevens, Cameron, "Fixing the U.S. Rebalance to the Asia-Pacific," *The Diplomat*, June 12, 2014.
14 See Holslag, Jonathan, *China's Coming War with Asia* (Cambridge: Polity, 2015), 4.
15 Van Evera, Stephen, *Guide to Methods for Students of Political Science* (Ithaca/London: Cornell University Press, 1997), 22.
16 See Li, Xaioting, "The Taming of The Red Dragon: The Militarized Worldview and China's Use of Force, 1949–2001," *Foreign Policy Analysis* 9, no. 4 (2013): 387.
17 "Since Thucydides, the origins of war have been framed in terms of their underlying and immediate causes. They are generally associated with necessary and enabling conditions. International relations has focused exclusively on underlying causes and has sought to develop general accounts of war. [However, in order to] understand the causes of war we need to start with motives and the foreign-policy goals to which they lead." Lebow, Richard N., *Why Nations Fight. Past and Future Motives for War* (Cambridge: Cambridge University Press, 2010), 13–14. See also Wendt, Alexander, "Anarchy is What States Make of It: The Social Construction of Power Politics," *International Organization* 46, no. 2 (1992): 395; Levy, Jack S. and Thompson, William R., *The Causes of War* (Chichester: Wiley-Blackwell Publishing, 2010), 10.
18 Lebow, *Why Nations Fight*, 12.
19 Lebow, Richard N., *A Cultural Theory of International Relations* (Cambridge: Cambridge University Press, 2008), 38.
20 Lebow, Richard N., "Motives, Evidence, Identity: Engaging My Critics," *International Theory* 2, no. 3 (2010): 486–94.
21 See Der Derian, James, "Reading Lebow: A Funny Thing Happened on the Way to the Oracles," *International Theory* 2, no. 3 (2010): 483.
22 Lebow, *A Cultural Theory*, p. 41. See the criticism brought forward by Patomäki, Heikki, "Back to Renaissance?" *International Relations* 23, no. 1 (2009): 155–59.
23 See Betts, Richard K., "Strong Arguments, Weak Evidence," *Security Studies* 21, no. 2 (2012): 345.

24 I owe this insight to Ai Noguchi (Keio-University, Japan). See also Kitaoka, Shinichi, "Japan's Identity and What It Means," in *Japan's Identity – Neither the West, Nor the East*, ed. Ito, Kenichi, Nishio, Kanji, and Kitaoka, Shinichi (Tokyo: Japan Forum on International Relations, 1999).

25 Lebow, Richard N., "Theory, Motives, and Falsification," *International Relations* 23, no. 1 (2009): 167.

26 "Rationality is a core assumption of all existing theories of war. It provides the necessary link connecting systemic opportunities and constraints, formulations of the national interest and specific foreign policies." *Why Nations Fight*, 44–45. For an overview of rational choice-based theories of interstate warfare, see Lindley, Dan and Schildkraut, Ryan, "Is War Rational? The Extent of Miscalculation and Misperception as Causes of War," University of Notre Dame [unpublished paper], 2005), 4.

27 de Mesquita, Bueno, *The War Trap* (New York: Yale University Press, 1981), 19. See further Fearon, James D., "Rationalist Explanation for War," *International Organization* 49, no. 3 (1995).

28 Even at first glance, the punitive character of these wars seems to be in conflict with purely security-based explanations: see Elleman, Bruce A., "China's 1974 Naval Expedition to the Paracel Islands," in *Naval Power and Expeditionary Warfare. Peripheral Campaigns and New Theatres of Naval Warfare*, ed. Elleman, Bruce A. and Paine, S. C. M. (Oxon: Routledge, 2011), 147–48; Garver, John W., "China's Decision for War with India in 1962," in *New Directions in the Study of China's Foreign Policy*, ed. Johnston, Alastair and Ross, Robert S. (Stanford: Stanford University Press, 2006), 109–10.

29 Cited in Annen, "A Comeback in Asia?", 5.

30 See Johnston, Alastair I., "China's Militarized Interstate Dispute Behavior 1949–1992: A First Cut at the Data," *The China Quarterly* no. 153 (1998): 18–23.

31 See Dafoe, Allan, Renshon, Jonathan, and Huth, Paul, "Reputation and Status as Motives for War," *Annual Review of Political Science* 17, no. 1 (2014); Lebow, *Why Nations Fight*; Wohlforth, William C., "Unipolarity, Status Competition, and Great Power War," *World Politics* 61, no. 1 (2009); "Status Dilemmas and Interstate Conflict," in *Status in World Politics*, ed. Paul, T. V., Welch-Larson, Deborah, and Wohlforth, William C. (Cambridge: Cambridge University Press, 2014); Wolf, Reinhard, "The Concept of Status in International Relations: Diversity and Integration." Paper presented at the World International Studies Conference, Frankfurt am Main, August 6–9, 2014.

32 See Deng, Yong, *China's Struggle for Status. The Realignment of International Relations* (Cambridge: Cambridge University Press, 2008); Wolf, Reinhard, "Auf Kollisionskurs: Warum es zur amerikanisch-chinesischen Konfrontation kommen muss," *Zeitschrift für Politik* 59, no. 4 (2012); Welch-Larson, Deborah and Shevchenko, Alexei, "Status Seekers: China and Russian Responses to U.S. Primacy," *International Security* 34, no. 4 (2010); Johnston, "China's Militarized Interstate Dispute Behavior," 25–27.

33 See Onuf, Nicholas, *World of Our Making: Rules and Rule in Social Theory and International Relations* (Columbia: University of South Carolina Press 1989), 278; Wohlforth, "Unipolarity, Status Competition, and Great Power War," 29; Lake, David A., "Status, Authority, and the End of the American Century," in *Status in World Politics*, ed. Paul, T. V., Welch-Larson, Deborah, and Wohlforth, William C. (Cambridge: Cambridge University Press, 2014), 117; Wolf, "The Concept of Status in International Relations: Diversity and Integration," 2; Welch-Larson, Deborah, Paul, T.V., and Wohlforth, William C., "Status and World Order," in *Status in World Politics*, ed. Paul, T.V., Welch-Larson, Deborah, and Wohlforth, William C. (Cambridge: Cambridge University Press, 2014), 3.

34 See Hymans, Jacques E., "The Arrival of Psychological Constructivism," *International Theory* 2, no. 3 (2010): 462; Welch-Larson, Paul, and Wohlforth, "Status and World

Order," 16–18; Lebow, *A Cultural Theory*, 17, 61–63; Kang, David, "Status and Leadership on the Korean Peninsula," *Orbis* 54, no. 4 (2010): 265.

35 See Dafoe, Renshon, and Huth, "Reputation and Status as Motives for War," 381; Wohlforth, "Unipolarity, Status Competition, and Great Power War," 37; Wolf, Reinhard, "Der 'emotional turn' in den IB: Plädoyer für eine theoretische Überwindung methodischer Engführung," *Zeitschrift für Außen- und Sicherheitspolitik* 5, no. 4 (2012): 612–13.

36 Welch-Larson, Paul, and Wohlforth, "Status and World Order," 3. See further Crawford, Neta C., "The Passion of World Politics: Proposition on Emotions and Emotional Relationships," *International Security* 24, no. 4 (2000): 117; Wolf, "Der 'emotional turn' in den IB," 677; Dafoe, Renshon, and Huth, "Reputation and Status as Motives for War," 379–81; Lake, "Status, Authority, and the End of the American Century," 246; Wohlforth, "Unipolarity, Status Competition, and Great Power War," 38.

37 Prestige, a socially constructed concept deeply linked to status, is already found in Hans Morgenthau's otherwise strictly materalistic conception of power. Proponents of the English School in IR emphasize the existence of social hierarchies in the society of states, as well as the relevancy of social recognition of an actor's specific rank within these orders: see Morgenthau, Hans J., *Politics among Nations: The Struggle for Power and Peace* (New York: Knopf, 1954), 84; Hurrell, Andrew, "Rising Powers and the Question of Status in International Society." Paper presented at the 50th International Studies Association Convention, New York, February 15–18, 2009, 4; Bull, Hedley, *The Anarchical Society* (London: Macmillan Publishers, 1977), 200–02; Watson, Adams, "Hedley Bull, States Systems and International Societies," *Review of International Studies* 13, no. 2 (1987): 149; Buzan, Barry, *The United States and the Great Powers. World Politics in the Twenty-First Century* (Cambridge/Malden: Polity Press, 2004), 63–69.

38 See Bleiker, Roland and Hutchinson, Emma, "Fear No More: Emotions and World Politics," *Review of International Studies* no. 34 (2008); Crawford, "The Passion of World Politics."

39 Welch-Larson, Paul, and Wohlforth, "Status and World Order," 18 [emphasis in original]. See further Lebow, *A Cultural Theory*, 64; Wolf, "The Concept of Status in International Relations: Diversity and Integration," 16; Dafoe, Renshon, and Huth, "Reputation and Status as Motives for War," 374–75.

40 Welch-Larson, Paul, and Wohlforth, "Status and World Order," 9.

41 See Wolf, "The Concept of Status in International Relations: Diversity and Integration," 3; Lebow, *A Cultural Theory*, 63.

42 See Foot's interesting argument about exceptionalistic identities' impediments to the development of the Sino-American relationship: Foot, Rosemary, "China and the United States: Between Cold War and Warm Peace," *Survival* 51, no. 6 (2009): 129–30.

43 See Wendt, Alexander, *Social Theory of International Politics* (Cambridge: Cambridge University Press, 2010), 247.

44 See Clinton, Hillary, "America's Pacific Century," *Foreign Policy* 189, no. 1 (2011): 57; Indyk, Martin S., Lieberthal, Kenneth G., and O'Hanlon, Michael E., *Bending History – Barack Obama's Foreign Policy* (Washington, D.C.: Brookings Institution, 2012), 58–61.

45 See Ross, "The Problem with the Pivot," 81.

46 Wolf, "Auf Kollisionskurs," 392 [own translation].

47 See Van der Mey, Leo, "The India–China Conflict: Explaining the Outbreak of War in 1962," *Diplomacy & Statecraft* 5, no. 2 (1994): 184–85; Chen, Jian, *China's Road to the Korean War – The Making of the Sino-American Confrontation* (New York: Columbia University Press, 1994), 2–3; Hunt, Michael H., "Beijing and the Korean Crisis, June 1950– June 1951," *Political Science Quarterly* 107, no. 3 (1992): 453–54. For a practical

example, see Fravel, Taylor M., "Power Shifts and Escalations: Explaining China's Use of Force in Territorial Disputes," *International Security* 32, no. 3 (2007/8). The study operates primarily with the balance of (military) power as an analytical category. In contrast to this third-level analysis, Bruce Elleman highlights the criticality of the domestic dimension and reaches the conclusion that the fundamental objective behind China's use of military force was "to preserve the unity of China": *Modern Chinese Warfare, 1795–1989* (Routledge: New York, 2001), 2.

48 Other factors that could have influenced this revision are the opening of archives and the emergence of Neorealist theory in IR.

49 See Ikenberry and Liff, "Racing toward Tragedy?" 58. Such a spiral of self-fulfilling prophecies already affects U.S.–China relations today: China is building up its military capabilities to prepare for the uncertainties of the future, whereby the U.S. strategy towards the PRC is arguably the most important element of uncertainty, as it reveals the greatest vulnerabilities for Beijing. The United States, on the other hand, perceives an increasingly powerful and potentially revisionist China as a challenge and employs a containment strategy in order to hedge for the uncertainties of the future. Abandoning this vicious circle of reciprocally constituted threat perceptions would require mutual strategic trust and deepened cooperation, including confidence and transparency-building measures in security and defense issues: see Dobbins, "War with China," 22; Wolf, "Auf Kollisionskurs," 404–05; Foot, "China and the United States," 124–34.

50 In his landmark study on China's intervention in the Korean War, Allen S. Whiting reached the conclusion that Beijing intervened only after measures of deterrence had failed and U.S. troops began to march northward toward the Yalu River, thus severely threatening China's territorial security: see *China Crosses the Yalu – The Decision to Enter the Korean War* (New York: Macmillan Publishers, 1960). Whiting's interpretation influenced generations of scholars, with following analyses regularly echoing his results by emphasizing that Beijing's decision to enter the Korean War was simply a reaction to an imminent threat to China's physical security. However, as Chen Jian found, there are good reasons to doubt the validity of purely security-based explanations of China's intervention in Korea, as these studies focus "more on the … environment in which the Beijing leadership made their decision … than on a close examination of the decision-making process": *China's Road to the Korean War*, 3. As Chen convincingly demonstrates in his own book-length argument, many reasons make it no longer possible to adhere to the established security-based explanation for China's inter - vention in Korea.

51 See Van Evera, *Guide to Methods*, 30.

52 See Achen, Christopher H. and Snidal, Duncan, "Rational Deterrence Theory and Comparative Case Studies," *World Politics* 41, no. 2 (1989): 167–68 [emphasis added].

53 See Van Evera, *Guide to Methods*, 54.

54 The comparison unfolds according to the *method of agreement*: see Mill, John Stuart, *A System of Logic, Ratiocinative and Inductive. Being a connected view of the Principles of Evidence, and the Methods of Scientific Investigation* (New York: Harper & Brothers, 1882), Chp. VIII: Of the Four Methods Of Experimental Inquiry; George, Alexander L. and Bennett, Andrew, *Case Studies and Theory Development in the Social Sciences* (Cambridge/London: MIT Press, 2005), pp. 152–79.

55 See Lijphart, Arend, "Comparative Politics and the Comparative Method," *American Political Science Review* 65, no. 3 (1971): 691.

56 See Elleman, "China's 1974 Naval Expedition," 141–43; Garver, John W., "China's Push Through the South China Sea: The Interaction of Bureaucratic and National Interest," *The China Quarterly* no. 132 (1992): 1002–03.

57 As I pursue a theory test as my second research objective, George and Bennett emphasize the importance of identifying whether the selected cases are most likely, least likely, or crucial tests for the theory under investigation: see *Case Studies and Theory Development*, 75. With regard to my case sample, and taking into account Lebow's profound skepticism concerning the predominance of the security motive in established explanations for interstate war, I classify China's intervention in the Korean War – almost unambiguously explained in available accounts as a result of a materializing threat to China's territorial security – as a *crucial test case*. In contrast to that, China's punitive wars against India and Vietnam appear as *most-likely* cases, while the Sino-Soviet border clashes can be categorized as a *least-likely* case because the majority of available studies rationalize China's use of force as preemptive action to dissuade a Soviet intervention.

58 King, Gary, Keohane, Robert O., and Verba, Sidney, *Designing Social Inquiry. Scientific Inference in Qualitative Reserach* (Princeton, NJ: Princeton University Press, 1994), 129 [emphasis in original].

59 Ibid., 130.

60 See Collier, David and Mahoney, James, "Insights and Pitfalls: Selection Bias in Qualitative Research," *World Politics* no. 49 (1996): 72; George and Bennett, *Case Studies and Theory Development*, 76; Geddes, Barbara, "How the Cases You Choose Affect the Answers You Get: Selection Bias in Comparative Cases," *Political Analysis* no. 2 (1990): 132; Van Evera, *Guide to Methods*, 43, 46–47.

61 See Collier, David, Mahoney, James, and Seawright, Jason, "Claiming Too Much: Warnings about Selection Bias," in *Rethinking Social Inquiry – Diverse Tools, Shared Standards*, ed. Collier, David and Brady, Henry E. (Lanham, MD: Rowman & Littlefield Publishers, 2004), 87.

62 "Controlled comparison can be achieved by dividing a single longitudinal case into two – the 'before' case and an 'after' case that follows a discontinuous change in an important variable. This may provide a control for many factors and is often the most readily available or strongest version of a most-similar case design": George and Bennett, *Case Studies and Theory Development*, 81.

63 See Collier, Mahoney, and Seawright, "The Quest for Standards," in *Rethinking Social Inquiry – Diverse Tools, Shared Standards*, ed. David Collier and Henry E. Brady (Lanham: Rowman & Littlefield Publishers, 2004), 38–39; Collier, Mahoney, and Seawright, "Claiming Too Much," 101.

64 George and Bennett, *Case Studies and Theory Development*, 91.

Bibliography

Achen, Christopher H., and Snidal, Duncan. "Rational Deterrence Theory and Comparative Case Studies." *World Politics* 41, no. 2 (1989): 143–69.

Al-Rodhan, Khalid R. "A Critique of the China Threat Theory: A Systematic Analysis." *Asian Perspectives* 31, no. 3 (2007): 41–66.

Annen, Niels. "A Comeback in Asia? How China is Shaping U.S. Foreign Policy in the Pacific." *Perspectives – Friedrich Ebert Stiftung* (February 2011). Accessed at http://library.fes.de/pdf-files/id/07865.pdf (September 1, 2016).

Babbin, Jed, and Timberlake, Edward. *Showdown – Why China Wants War with the United States*. Washington: Regnery Publishing, 2006.

Bernstein, Richard, and Ross, H. Munro. *The Coming Conflict with China*. New York: Knopf, 1997.

Betts, Richard K. "Strong Arguments, Weak Evidence." *Security Studies* 21, no. 2 (2012): 345–51.

Bleiker, Roland, and Hutchinson, Emma. "Fear No More: Emotions and World Politics." *Review of International Studies* no. 34 (2008): 115–34.

Bräuner, Oliver. "'Wenn du einen Schritt machst, dann mache ich zwei' – Chinas maritime Strategie im Ost- und Südchinesischen Meer." *Zeitschrift für Außen- und Sicherheitspolitik* 7, no. 4 (2014): 441–50.

Broomfield, Emma V. "Perceptions of Danger: The China Threat Theory." *Journal of Contemporary China* 12, no. 35 (2003): 265–84.

Bull, Hedley. *The Anarchical Society*. London: Macmillan Publishers, 1977.

Buzan, Barry. *The United States and the Great Powers: World Politics in the Twenty-First Century*. Cambridge/Malden: Polity Press, 2004.

Callahan, William A. "How to Understand China: The Dangers and Opportunities of Being a Rising Power." *Review of International Studies* no. 31 (2005): 701–14.

Chase, Michael S. "Chinese Suspicion of U.S. Intentions." *Survival* 53, no. 3 (2011): 133–50.

Chase, Michael S., Engstrom, Jeffrey, Cheung, Tai Ming, Gunness, Kristen A., Harold, Scott Warren, Puska, Susan, and Berkowitz, Samuel K. *China's Incomplete Military Transformation. Assessing the Weaknesses of the People's Liberation Army (PLA)*. Santa Monica: RAND, 2015.

Chen, Jian. *China's Road to the Korean War – The Making of the Sino-American Confrontation*. New York: Columbia University Press, 1994.

Chen, Yi-Hsuan. "South China Sea Tension on Fire: China's Recent Moves on Building Artifical Islands in Troubled Waters and Their Implication on Maritime Law." *Maritime Safety and Security Law Journal* no. 1 (2015): 1–15.

Cliff, Roger. *China's Military Power. Assessing Current and Future Capabilities*. New York: Cambridge University Press, 2015.

Clinton, Hillary. "America's Pacific Century." *Foreign Policy* 189, no. 1 (2011): 56–63.

Collier, David, and Mahoney, James. "Insights and Pitfalls: Selection Bias in Qualitative Research." *World Politics* no. 49 (1996): 56–91.

Collier, David, Mahoney, James, and Seawright, Jason. "Claiming Too Much: Warnings about Selection Bias." In *Rethinking Social Inquiry – Diverse Tools, Shared Standards*, edited by David Collier and Henry E. Brady, 85–102. Lanham, MD: Rowman & Littlefield Publishers, 2004.

Collier, David, Mahoney, James, and Seawright, Jason. "The Quest for Standards: King, Keohane, and Verba's Designing Social Inquiry." In *Rethinking Social Inquiry – Diverse Tools, Shared Standards*, edited by David Collier and Henry E. Brady, 21–50. Lanham, MD: Rowman & Littlefield Publishers, 2004.

Crawford, Neta C. "The Passion of World Politics: Proposition on Emotions and Emotional Relationships." *International Security* 24, no. 4 (2000): 116–36.

Dafoe, Allan, Renshon, Jonathan, and Huth, Paul. "Reputation and Status as Motives for War." *Annual Review of Political Science* 17, no. 1 (2014): 371–93.

de Mesquita, Bueno. *The War Trap*. New York: Yale University Press, 1981.

Deng, Yong. *China's Struggle for Status: The Realignment of International Relations*. Cambridge: Cambridge University Press, 2008.

Der Derian, James. "Reading Lebow: A Funny Thing Happened on the Way to the Oracles." *International Theory* 2, no. 3 (2010): 481–85.

Ding, Shen. "Analyzing Rising Power from the Perspective of Soft Power: A New Look at China's Rise to the Status Quo Power." *Journal of Contemporary China* 19, no. 64 (2010): 255–72.

Dobbins, James. "War with China." *Survival* 54, no. 4 (2012): 7–24.

Elleman, Bruce A. *Modern Chinese Warfare, 1795–1989*. Routledge: New York, 2001.

Elleman, Bruce A. "China's 1974 Naval Expedition to the Paracel Islands." In *Naval Power and Expeditionary Warfare. Peripheral Campaigns and New Theatres of Naval Warfare*, edited by Bruce A. Elleman and S. C. M. Paine, 141–51. Oxon: Routledge, 2011.

Fearon, James D. "Rationalist Explanation for War." *International Organization* 49, no. 3 (1995): 379–414.

Foot, Rosemary. "China and the United States: Between Cold War and Warm Peace." *Survival* 51, no. 6 (2009): 123–46.

Fravel, Taylor M. "Power Shifts and Escalations. Explaining China's Use of Force in Territorial Disputes." *International Security* 32, no. 3 (2007/8): 44–83.

Friedberg, Aaron L. *A Contest for Supremacy: China, America, and the Struggle for Mastery in Asia*. New York: W.W. Norton, 2011.

Freidberg, Aaron L. "The Sources of Chinese Conduct: Explaining Beijing's Assertiveness." *The Washington Quarterly* 37, no. 4 (2015): 133–50.

Garver, John W. "China's Push Through the South China Sea: The Interaction of Bureaucratic and National Interest." *The China Quarterly* no. 132 (1992): 999–1028.

Garver, John W. "China's Decision for War with India in 1962." In *New Directions in the Study of China's Foreign Policy*, edited by Alastair Johnston and Robert S. Ross, 86–130. Stanford, CA: Stanford University Press, 2006.

Geddes, Barbara. "How the Cases You Choose Affect the Answers You Get: Selection Bias in Comparative Cases." *Political Analysis* no. 2 (1990): 131–50.

George, Alexander L., and Bennett, Andrew. *Case Studies and Theory Development in the Social Sciences*. Cambridge/London: MIT Press, 2005.

Gertz, Bill. *The China Threat – How the People's Republic Targets America*. Washington, D.C.: Regnery, 2002.

Glaser, Charles L. "A U.S.–China Grand Bargain? The Hard Choice between Military Competition and Accomodation." *International Security* 39, no. 4 (2015): 49–90.

Goldstein, Lyle J. *Meeting China Halfway: How to Defuse the Emerging U.S.–China Rivalry*. Washington, D.C.: Georgetown University Press, 2015.

Hays-Gries, Peter. "Problems and Misperceptions in U.S.–China Relations." *Orbis* 53, no. 2 (Spring 2009): 220–32.

Holslag, Jonathan. *China's Coming War with Asia*. Cambridge: Polity, 2015.

Hunt, Michael H. "Beijing and the Korean Crisis, June 1950–June 1951." *Political Science Quarterly* 107, no. 3 (1992): 453–78.

Hurrell, Andrew. "Rising Powers and the Question of Status in International Society." Paper presented at the 50th International Studies Association Convention, New York, February 15–18, 2009.

Hymans, Jacques E. "The Arrival of Psychological Constructivism." *International Theory* 2, no. 3 (2010): 461–67.

Ikenberry, G. John, and Liff, Adam P. "Racing toward Tragedy? China's Rise, Military Competition in the Asia Pacific, and the Security Dilemma." *International Security* 39, no. 2 (2014): 52–91.

Indyk, Martin S., Lieberthal, Kenneth G., and O'Hanlon, Michael E. *Bending History – Barack Obama's Foreign Policy*. Washington, D.C.: Brookings Institution, 2012.

Jerdén, Björn. "The Assertive China Narrative: Why It Is Wrong and How So Many Still Bought Into It." *The Chinese Journal of International Politics* 7, no. 1 (2014): 47–88.

Johnston, Alastair I. "China's Militarized Interstate Dispute Behavior 1949–1992: A First Cut at the Data." *The China Quarterly* no. 153 (March 1998): 1–30.

Johnston, Alastair I. "How New and Assertive Is China's New Assertiveness?" *International Security* 37, no. 4 (2013): 7–48.

Kamphausen, Roy, Lai, David, and Scobell, Andrew. *Beyond the Strait – PLA Missions other than Taiwan*. Carlisle: Strategic Studies Institute, U.S. Army War College, 2009.

Kang, David. "Status and Leadership on the Korean Peninsula." *Orbis* 54, no. 4 (2010): 546–64.

King, Gary, Keohane, Robert O., and Verba, Sidney. *Designing Social Inquiry: Scientific Inference in Qualitative Reserach*. Princeton, NJ: Princeton University Press, 1994.

Kitaoka, Shinichi. "Japan's Identity and What It Means." In *Japan's Identity – Neither the West, Nor the East*, edited by Kenichi Ito, Kanji Nishio, and Shinichi Kitaoka, Chapter III. Tokyo: Japan Forum on International Relations, 1999. Accessed at www.jfir.or.jp/e/special_study/seminar1/conversation.htm (October 24, 2016).

Lai, David, and Stevens, Cameron. "Fixing the U.S. Rebalance to the Asia-Pacific." *The Diplomat*, June 12, 2014. Accessed at http://thediplomat.com/2014/06/fixing-the-u-s-rebalance-to-the-asia-pacific/ (October 24, 2016).

Lake, David A. "Status, Authority, and the End of the American Century." In *Status in World Politics*, edited by T.V. Paul, Deborah Welch-Larson, and William C. Wohlforth, 33–57. Cambridge: Cambridge University Press, 2014.

Lebow, Richard N. *A Cultural Theory of International Relations*. Cambridge: Cambridge University Press, 2008.

Lebow, Richard N. "Theory, Motives, and Falsification." *International Relations* 23, no. 1 (2009): 167–71.

Lebow, Richard N. "Motives, Evidence, Identity: Engaging My Critics." *International Theory* 2, no. 3 (2010): 486–94.

Lebow, Richard N. *Why Nations Fight. Past and Future Motives for War*. Cambridge: Cambridge University Press, 2010.

Levy, Jack S., and Thompson, William R. *The Causes of War*. Chichester: Wiley-Blackwell Publishing, 2010.

Li, Nan. "China's Naval Modernization and Its Impact on Asian Security." In *Security and Conflict in East Asia*, edited by Andrew T.H. Tan, 37–50. Milton Park/New York: Routledge.

Li, Xiaobing. *A History of the Modern Chinese Army*. Lexington, KY: The University Press of Kentucky, 2007.

Li, Xaioting. "The Taming of the Red Dragon: The Militarized Worldview and China's Use of Force, 1949–2001." *Foreign Policy Analysis* 9, no. 4 (2013): 387–407.

Lijphart, Arend. "Comparative Politics and the Comparative Method." *American Political Science Review* 65, no. 3 (1971): 682–93.

Lindley, Dan, and Schildkraut, Ryan. "Is War Rational? The Extent of Miscalculation and Misperception as Causes of War." University of Notre Dame [unpublished paper], 2005.

Ling, Wei. "Rebalancing or De-Balancing: U.S. Pivot and East Asian Order." *American Foreign Policy Interest* 35, no. 3 (2013): 148–54.

Mearsheimer, John J. *The Tragedy of Great Power Politics*. New York/London: W.W. Norton & Company, 2001.

Mearsheimer, John J. "The Gathering Storm: China's Challenge to US Power in Asia." *The Chinese Journal of International Politics* 3, no. 4 (2010): 381–96.

Medeiros, Evan S. "Strategic Hedging and the Future of Asia-Pacific Stability." *The Washington Quarterly* 29, no. 1 (2005): 145–67.

Mill, John Stuart. *A System of Logic, Ratiocinative and Inductive. Being a connected view of the Principles of Evidence, and the Methods of Scientific Investigation*. New York: Harper & Brothers, 1882. Accessed at www.gutenberg.org/files/27942/27942-h/27942-h.html#toc103 (September 1, 2016).

Morgenthau, Hans J. *Politics among Nations. The Struggle for Power and Peace*. New York: Knopf, 1954.

Nathan, Andrew J., and Scobell, Andrew. *China's Search For Security*. New York: Columbia University Press, 2014.
Onuf, Nicholas. *World of Our Making: Rules and Rule in Social Theory and International Relations*. Columbia, SC: University of South Carolina Press 1989.
Patomäki, Heikki. "Back to Renaissance?" *International Relations* 23, no. 1 (2009): 155–59.
Rice, Condoleeza. "Promoting the National Interest – Life after the Cold War." *Foreign Affairs* 79, no. 1 (2000): 45–62.
Ross, Robert S. "The Problem with the Pivot: Obama's New Asia Policy is Unneccesary and Counterproductive." *Foreign Affairs* 91, no. 6 (2012): 70–82.
Ross, Robert S. "U.S. Grand Strategy, the Rise of China, and U.S. National Security Strategy for East Asia." *Strategic Studies Quarterly* 7, no. 2 (2013): 20–40.
Roy, Denny. "The 'China Threat' Issue – Major Arguments." *Asian Survey* 36, no. 8 (1996): 758–71.
Shirk, Susan L. *China – Fragile Superpower*. New York: Oxford University Press, 2007.
Sutter, Robert G. *Chinese Foreign Relations: Power and Policy since the Cold War*. Plymouth: Rowman & Littlefield Publishers, 2008.
Swaine, Michael D., Eberstadt, Nicholas, Fravel, Taylor M., Herberg, Mikkail, Keidel, Albert, Revere, Evans J. R., Romberg, Alan D., Freund, Eleanor, Esplin Odell, Rachel, and Wong, Audrye. *Conflict and Cooperation in the Asia-Pacific Region: A Strategic Net Assessment*. Washington, D.C.: Carnegie Endowment for International Peace, 2015. Accessed at http://carnegieendowment.org/files/net_assessment_2.pdf (September 1, 2016).
Twomey, Christopher P., and Xu, Hui. "Military Developments." In *Debating China: The U.S.–China Relationship in Ten Conversations*, edited by Nina Hachigan, 152–75. Oxford/New York: Oxford University Press, 2014.
Van der Mey, Leo. "The India–China Conflict: Explaining the Outbreak of War in 1962." *Diplomacy & Statecraft* 5, no. 2 (1994): 183–99.
Van Evera, Stephen. *Guide to Methods for Students of Political Science*. Ithaca/London: Cornell University Press, 1997.
Wagener, Martin. "Grundlagen der Sicherheitspolitik Ostasiens: Mächte – Konflikte – Strukturen." In *Neue Dimensionen internationaler Sicherheitspolitik*, edited by Reinhard Meier-Walser and Alexander Wolf, 243–56. München: Hanns-Seidel Stiftung, 2011.
Watson, Adams. "Hedley Bull, States Systems and International Societies." *Review of International Studies* 13, no. 2 (1987): 147–53.
Welch-Larson, Deborah, Paul, T.V., and Wohlforth, William C. "Status and World Order." In *Status in World Politics*, edited by T.V. Paul, Deborah Welch-Larson, and William C. Wohlforth, 3–32. Cambridge: Cambridge University Press, 2014.
Welch-Larson, Deborah, and Shevchenko, Alexei. "Status Seekers: China and Russian Responses to U.S. Primacy." *International Security* 34, no. 4 (2010): 63–95.
Wendt, Alexander. "Anarchy is What States Make of It: The Social Construction of Power Politics." *International Organization* 46, no. 2 (1992): 391–425.
Wendt, Alexander. *Social Theory of International Politics*. Cambridge: Cambridge University Press, 2010.
Whiting, Allen S. *China Crosses the Yalu – The Decision to Enter the Korean War*. New York: Macmillan Publishers, 1960.
Wohlforth, William C. "Unipolarity, Status Competition, and Great Power War." *World Politics* 61, no. 1 (2009): 28–57.
Wohlforth, William C. "Status Dilemmas and Interstate Conflict." In *Status in World Politics*, edited by T.V. Paul, Deborah Welch-Larson and William C. Wohlforth, 115–40. Cambridge: Cambridge University Press, 2014.

Wolf, Reinhard. "Auf Kollisionskurs: Warum es zur amerikanisch-chinesischen Konfrontation kommen muss." *Zeitschrift für Politik* 59, no. 4 (2012): 392–408.

Wolf, Reinhard. "Der 'emotional turn' in den IB: Plädoyer für eine theoretische Überwindung methodischer Engführung." *Zeitschrift für Außen- und Sicherheitspolitik* 5, no. 4 (2012): 605–24.

Wolf, Reinhard. "The Concept of Status in International Relations: Diversity and Integration." Paper presented at the World International Studies Conference, Frankfurt am Main, August 6–9, 2014.

Wortzel, Larry M. *The Dragon Extends Its Reach: Chinese Military Power Goes Global.* Washington, D.C.: Potomac Books, 2013.

Yahuda, Michael. "China's New Assertiveness in the South China Sea." *Journal of Contemporary China* 22, no. 81 (2013): 446–59.

Zhao, Suisheng. "China and America: Showdown in the Asia-Pacific?" In *Conflict and Cooperation in Sino-US Relations: Change and Continuity, Cause and Cure*, edited by Jean-Marc F. Blanchard and Simon Shen, 68–88. Milton Park/New York: Routledge, 2015.

2 Why nations go to war

Why do states at some times collide in wars, while at other times they cooperate and pursue peace? This crucial question has been at the forefront of the study of international politics ever since Thucydides put forward his account of the outbreak of the Peloponnesian War.[1] In various explanations, observers have identified the causes of war and peace in human nature, in the characteristics of societies and types of government, and in the properties of the international system. Over the centuries, the intensive scholarly interest in interstate warfare as a recurring phenomenon in world politics has resulted in a volume of publications that could easily fill entire libraries. It is thus clearly beyond my capacity to provide a comprehensive survey of the current state of research on the causes of war, as such an endeavor already demands book-length arguments on its own.[2]

Instead, in the first part of this chapter I will focus on explanations provided by the realist theories of International Relations (IR). This selection appears justifiable for at least three reasons. First, Realism is arguably the most influential theoretical paradigm of IR, which, furthermore, has been able to establish interpretational sovereignty over the phenomenon of interest.[3] Second, proponents of this school of thought not only posit that Realism "is (arguably) the most reliable theory of international politics,"[4] but highlight that many scholars have found Realism a useful framework to investigate world politics, too. As Joseph Grieco argues, "[t]his is because realist theory adresses the key question in international relations: What are the causes of conflict and war among nations, and what are the conditions for cooperation and peace among them?"[5] It thus seems highly appropriate to put this confidently postulated usefulness of realist theory to the test by confronting the paradigm's three most prominent variants (Classical Realism, Structural Neorealism, and Offensive Neorealism) with the specific characteristics of China's use of force in foreign relations. Third, and most importantly, this also allows for evaluating the viability of rational choice-based theories in general, as Realism and other well-established theories on the causes of war share the same assumptions about the logic of consequences determining an actor's behavior.[6] Ontologically, these theories constitute one distinct 'class' and can thus be tested as such: if no realist explanation for war is theoretically or empirically tenable, then neither is rationalism, and vice versa.[7]

Readers adhering to the realist paradigm might prepare for some bad news: my survey shows that none of the realist approaches proves capable of developing sufficient explanatory power to comprehensively account for the four empirical cases I investigate in this book. Furthermore, serious criticism emerged even inside the rationalist camp, as James Fearon found that existing realist explanatory models are generally incapable of explaining the occurrence of warfare in international relations. According to Fearon, established rational choice-based explanations fall short of addressing the phenomenon's central puzzle, which he identified in the '*ex post* inefficiency' of wars. In order to overcome this deficit, he thus outlines two alternative causal paths, which I will present as the fourth realist model.

Based on the findings of my theoretical survey, and by comparing Fearon's more sophisticated approach with Classical Realism, Structural Realism, and Offensive Neorealism, I then outline several requirements for an explanatory model capable of comprehensively rationalizing the occurrence of war in general, and explaining the four cases of China's use of force in foreign affairs in particular. The formulation of these requirements allows me to explain and justify my choice of Ned Lebow's Cultural Theory of International Relations as the theoretical framework that will guide my empirical analysis. The theory and its operationalization for my subsequent case-study analyses are presented in the third and fourth sections of this chapter.

Realist explanations for war

Inside the realist paradigm of IR, the various approaches to the study of war can be categorized due to their respective level of analysis, i.e. where the theories identify the causal variable for the phenomenon to be explained: the individual, the state, or the system level (see Table 2.1).[8]

The individual level: Classical Realism

Classical Realism posits that international politics, like all politics, is driven by a competitive struggle for power.[9] Hans Morgenthau, arguably the most prominent and most influential realist scholar, refers to a negative anthropology as the underlying cause and emphasizes the effects of the immutable *animus dominandi*, a universal human lust for power.[10] Accordingly, human nature is also identified as the source of aggressive behavior and warfare between states, because in the anarchical international system all statesmen "think and act in terms of interest defined as power."[11]

Table 2.1 Overview: realist explanations for war

Level of analysis	Proponent	Motive/Explanatory variable
Individual	Classical Realism (Hans Morgenthau)	Lust for power: *animus dominandi*
State	Rationalist explanation for war (James Fearon)	Private information Commitment problem
System	Structural Neorealism (Kenneth Waltz) Offensive Neorealism (John Mearsheimer)	Maximizing security Maximizing power

Source: author.

This assumption is of critical importance as it enables Morgenthau to theorize international politics as a bounded domain.[12] However, it also turns out to be problematic, because if Morgenthau's pessimistic anthropology is a universal constant over time and space, how can it account for the obvious variance of war and peace in the international system? In order to overcome this problem, Morgenthau introduces two intervening variables: the robustness of sub-systemic societies, and the configuration of the balance of power.[13]

Even so, Morgenthau has to admit that not all statesmen, at all times, follow his proposed ideal-type of rational power politics and carefully balance available policy options in accordance with the national interest. Rather, some states' actions can indeed be affected by the 'subjective interests' of domestic groups, or are even the result of popular emotion. Expecting actors to always behave in an unemotional manner reveals itself to be quite unrealistic.[14] Unfortunately, Classical Realism is thus unable to generate explanatory power in any cases in which actors choose to disobey the guidance and rules outlined in Morgenthau's 'mirror for princes' of responsible power politics. As a result, Morgenthau's theory seems to be of limited help and relevancy for the realization of my research objective, which consists in providing an explanation for exactly such outlier cases.

The system level: Neorealism

Conflict and competition in the international arena are the undisputed home turf of neorealist theories.[15] Two variants, Kenneth Waltz's Structural (Neo)Realism and John Mearsheimer's Offensive (Neo)Realism, qualify as clear-cut system-level approaches.[16] Both theories also depart from the same premises on the components and properties of the international system: here, rational-acting nation-states are doomed to coexist under the structural condition of anarchy, can never be assured about the intentions of others, and thus can only rely on themselves to ensure their survival by maximizing either security (Structural Neorealism) or power (Offensive Neorealism). Both strategies, however, give rise to a competitive security dilemma "wherein measures that enhance one state's security typically diminish that of others."[17] Based on these assumptions, the conclusion is drawn that warfare *in general* occurs because there exists no central authority in the international system to punish states that proactively wage war against others:

> Among states, the state of nature is a state of war. This is meant not in the sense that war constantly occurs, but in the sense that, with each state deciding for itself whether or not to use force, war may at any time break out.[18]

This quotation highlights two important but also problematic aspects of neorealist thinking about interstate war.

First, even though anarchy is regarded as an ultimate constant, there exists observable variance in the occurrences of war and of peace. In order to account for this variation, Waltz and Mearsheimer introduce the structural component of the systemic distribution of power, so-called 'polarity,' as their key explanatory variable.[19] Conversely, this makes it essential to determine how many powers actually make up the polarity of a given system. According to Waltz, this challenge can be accomplished by utilizing 'common sense' when ranking states roughly according to their military capabilities.[20] However, in the absence of universally accepted definitions of capability or power, even Neorealists disagree on the polarity of the contemporary international system, not to speak of defining the concrete configurations of specific (historical) subsystems.[21] While this problem could be overcome with further conceptual work, another one cannot be dismissed so simply: as Neorealism's core variable refers to a comparatively static condition, it does not reveal enough variation to account for the outcomes it attempts to explain. This is a striking problem for the empirical applicability and explanatory power of neorealist theory.

Second, the quotation clarifies that warfare is regarded as a goal-directed strategy: "Whether or not to use force, each state plots the course it thinks will best serve its interests."[22] It remains unclear, however, when and especially why states think warfare will best serve their interests. These crucial questions are left unanswered by Structural Realism, as Waltz's theory focuses exclusively on international politics at the system level and is thus unable to explain sub-systemic issues such as specific foreign-policy decisions. While Waltz is convinced that his model "does explain war's dismal recurrence through the millennia," he has to admit that it "does not explain why particular wars are fought,"[23] because neither anarchy as constant nor polarity as variable can provide specific explanations for why nations decide to go to war.[24] Because of that, it is now on Mearsheimer's Offensive Realism to hold high the banner of neorealist theory.

Offensive and Structural (or Defensive) variants of Neorealism differ eminently in their respective assessments of how states best achieve their primary goal of survival. While Defensive Realists argue that states' first concern is to maintain their position within the system (i.e. achieving security by conserving the status quo),[25] Offensive Realists postulate the opposite: for Mearsheimer, power maximization (i.e. achieving security by overthrowing the status quo in one's favor) is the only rationale for actors that have to coexist in an anarchical environment and want to survive.[26] Among the various strategies of direct and indirect power-acquisition, warfare serves as "the principal way of gaining power."[27] Armed aggression can enhance an actor's power position by conquering territory and resources, as well as by weakening or eliminating rivals.[28] Especially in multipolar settings, war becomes a viable option, and gains even more in attractiveness the more the military capabilities are unequally distributed.[29] Though the universe of Offensive Realism is thus populated with latent predators, states do not necessarily act as mindless aggressors:

> On the contrary, before great powers take offensive actions, they think carefully about the balance of power and about how other states will react to their moves. They weigh the costs and risks of offense against the likely benefit. If the benefits do not outweigh the risks, they sit tight and wait for a more prosperous moment.[30]

In essence, Offensive Realism assumes that warfare is a structurally induced, rational strategy of power maximization, and is chosen by militarily superior actors in multipolar settings on the basis of strategically calculated assessments of the expected material benefits versus costs and risks.

The empirical record of China's uses of force, however, contradicts this postulate *prima facie*. First, changes in the structure of the Asia-Pacific subsystem did not translate into changes in China's strategic behavior, as postulated by Mearsheimer's theory: China acted in a considerably aggressive manner and even fought a great-power war during the seemingly stable phase of regional bipolarity.[31] Since the PRC emerges as the dominant power in a multipolar Asia-Pacific region, Beijing behaves in a significantly more prudent fashion and has refrained from the large-scale use of military force. Second, in all four cases investigated in this book, China did not conquer foreign territory in order to establish permanent control; nor did the PRC significantly weaken the capabilities of a rival power when resorting to military force. As will be shown in the respective case studies, whenever territory played a role in a conflict, the contested area itself revealed no or only minor significance regarding resources or strategic positioning. With the single exception of 0.74 square kilometers (Zhenbao Island) that remain under Beijing's control to date, Chinese troops withdrew from all areas they had occupied by force after the fighting ceased. When viewed against this background, there is good reason to conclude that China's resort to force consumed the power resources of the People's Republic rather than actually increasing them in relation to China's respective opponents. Third, and arguably most strikingly, China was by no means the militarily superior actor when Beijing decided to challenge the United States and the Soviet Union on the battlefield. In both occasions, China had just undergone dramatic phases of domestic instability, and the PLA was definitely not in a state of preparedness to wage warfare against the two superpowers of the Cold War era with confidence in its chances of military success.

Taken together, the empirical balance strikingly confutes the postulates of Neorealism. As a result, neither Waltz's Structural nor Mearsheimer's more specified variant of neorealist theory can develop sufficient explanatory power to make sense of the apparent 'outliers' presented by China's use of military force in foreign affairs for neorealist theory.

The second image: rationality and warfare

Does the non-applicability of rational choice-based realist theories imply that China cannot be regarded as a rational actor? This would devalue all explanatory models which share the ontological assumption that agents adhere to the logic of consequences and strategically calculate their actions by weighing arising costs against expected benefits. According to James Fearon, this is not the case, although he admits that when evaluated from a rigorous rationalist perspective, existing realist explanations for interstate warfare fail to comprehensively explain the occurrence of the phenomenon:

> [I]t is not enough to say that under anarchy nothing stops states from using force, or that anarchy forces states to rely on self-help, which engenders mutual suspicion and (through spirals or the security dilemma) armed conflict. Neither do diverse references to miscalculation, deterrence failure because of

inadequate forces or credible threats, preventive and preemptive considerations, or free-riding in alliances amount to theoretically coherent rationalist explanations for war.[32]

Established approaches overlook the crucial puzzle of the phenomenon, which Fearon identifies in the so-called '*ex post* inefficiency' of wars: from a rationalist's point of view, waging a war to decide a conflict appears unreasonable, because the use of force usually goes along with much higher costs for all parties involved than would be found in a negotiated solution.[33] Consequently, any explanation based on the stringent implementation of the rational-choice assumption has to show why states cannot achieve this preferable outcome *ex ante*. As Fearon demonstrates, such *ex ante* bargaining ranges exist in principle for all international conflicts to which the following assumptions apply: first, all parties involved need to be aware *ex ante* that only one of them will prevail in the armed struggle *ex post*. Second, actors should behave in a risk-averse or at least risk-neutral manner with regard to the issue under contestation and their choice of strategy. Third, the basic potential for a non-violent and mutually acceptable resolution needs to exist.[34] Whenever these three assumptions are met, there should be not only the potential but also strong incentives to strive for effective resolution of a conflict by non-violent means. Even then, however, rationally acting states might opt for the inefficient means of warfare. In these cases, two causal mechanisms prevent the peaceful resolution of conflicts: the deliberate creation of information asymmetries, and the effects of the commitment problem under the features of anarchy.

A core insight of rationalist ontology lies in the dictum that whenever two actors share the same level of information on a specific issue, they cannot agree to disagree in their respective assessments of the situation.[35] This insight ought to hold especially true when it comes to the use of force. All parties involved in a given conflict should thus be well aware *ex ante* which one of them has the most promising chance of emerging as the winner from a military struggle, which in turn should further increase the already existing incentives to strive for a non-violent resolution. "Conflicting estimates ... occur only if the agents have different and so necessarily private information."[36] Rational actors should thus reveal a common interest to share their secret information in order to avoid dangerous and costly miscalculations. In addition, creating a common level of information would further contribute to the realization of what is in any case the less cost-intensive and thus preferable outcome of a negotiated solution. Accordingly, explaining why war occurs between states led by rational leaders requires addressing what prevents them from sharing such information during the *ex ante* negotiations. Here, actors typically try their best to achieve their respective maximum demands, which in turn creates incentives to restrain or misrepresent information. This can lead rational actors to "exaggerate their true willingness or capability to fight, if by doing so they might deter future challenges or persuade the other side to make concessions."[37] By keeping information deliberately secret, or when actors make tactical use of communication in order to increase their bargaining position by instigating a bluff, they produce information asymmetries that can narrow the overall bargaining range to such an extent that a peaceful resolution becomes unattainable.[38]

The second causal mechanism that prevents the non-violent settlement of conflicts between rationally acting states is the commitment problem.[39] Here, Fearon's affiliation with Neorealist theory becomes clearly visible, as he borrows the holy grail of this paradigm to demonstrate why states cannot trust each other to uphold the deal, even though they share the same assessment of the bargaining range. The reasons for this are to be found in the constraining features of the anarchical structure.[40] As anarchy creates a self-help system by stimulating uncertainty and competition, mutual trust becomes a scarce resource. Consequently, actors have to worry about how long their counterparts are willing to keep their end of the bargain, especially as they also receive structural incentives to break the agreement.[41] In contrast to competition, neorealists consider cooperation a rather short-lived phenomenon, thus preventing the materialization of sound and sustained settlements.[42] In this perspective, compromises are regarded as deferred contestations, prone to re-erupt sooner or later, rather than as actual settlements of conflicts: "The strategic dilemma is that without some third party capable of guaranteeing the agreements, state A may not be able to commit itself to future foreign policy behavior that makes B prefer not to attack at some point."[43]

Requirements for an explanation of China's use of force

As the survey of Realism's inventory for explaining the causes of interstate warfare demonstrated, my case sample confronts Classical Realism, as well as Structural and Offensive Neorealism, with some insurmountable challenges. While these well-established explanatory models might pass the 'grandmother test,'[44] they obviously fail to cope with the dissenting empirical data when reducing the complexity of social processes to intuitively convincing but obviously oversimplified explanations.[45] Consequently, these theories are not capable of realizing my research objective. In contrast, Fearon's 'rationalist explanation for war' offers a more sophisticated analytical tool and therefore qualifies as my *alternative explanatory model*. Based on the insights gained in the previous sections, and by comparing Fearon's model (second image) with the three other theoretical approaches (first and third images), I posit that a capable theory needs to fulfill the following criteria in order to sufficiently explain the causation of particular wars.

First, the theory needs to open the 'black box'[46] by bridging the three levels of analysis in order to explain *specific foreign-policy decisions*. As even third-image advocates have to admit,

> the immediate causes of war are to be found in the first and second image. It is the specific acts by individuals and states that are the efficient causes of war, [even though] the international system provides the permissive cause of all interstate wars.[47]

Second, in contrast to realist approaches that regard warfare as a goal-directed strategy, Jack Levy and William Thompson emphasize that "understanding the causes of war requires an explanation of the *strategic interaction* of the two (or more) adversaries."[48] For sure, the final decision to go to war is made by an actor unilaterally. However, this decision is not made *in vacuo* but is extremely context-dependent, and thus heavily affected by the process of interaction leading up to it.[49] Consequently, a logically complete explanation for the occurrence of warfare is in need of a *processual understanding* of its causation. Adding to this, as wars do not simply erupt but usually require a catalyst, a capable explanatory model should also specify what kind of observable *trigger events* lead to the outbreak of military violence:

> In the absence of an appropriate catalyst ... events like wars and revolutions will not occur even if the appropriate underlying conditions are present. The only exception in the case of war are situations in which a state is intent on war and prepared to invent a pretext if one does not conveniently come along.[50]

Third, with regard to the four cases of China's use of military force, it seems as if material objectives such as occupying territory or weakening a rival's power potential did not play the crucial role postulated by Offensive Realisms. In order to make sense of these outlier cases, an inclusive explanatory model should also encompass *non-material incentives* as motives behind the use of military force. As yet, however, the independent explanatory power of such incentives (such as emotions, human drives, and considerations about social status) has largely been neglected in IR theory-building, mainly because of these factors' incompatibility with the dominant rational-choice assumption.[51] As Reinhard Wolf aptly observes, "in a traditional methodological framework the rational-choice assumptions functions as the *baseline*, while [non-material factors such as] emotions are merely used to explain any remaining variance."[52] However, the significance of these factors in guiding social behavior and for shaping decisions should be well known, as it evidently reveals itself in our individual everyday experience of social interaction. Likewise, as "[s]tates are not gigantic calculating machines [but] hierarchically organized groups of emotional people,"[53] the independent role and analytical relevancy of this non-material dimension in the formation of (foreign) policy should be as obvious as it is omnipresent.[54] In view of this, I argue that a capable explanatory model for explaining human-made foreign-policy decisions has to sacrifice the exclusiveness of the rational-choice assumption and take emotions and other non-material incentives into account. This does not mean, however, that (subjective) *emotio* now has to replace (objective) *ratio*. Instead, both concepts should be used as complementary tools in order to create ontologically more sophisticated assumptions and thus logically consistent rationalizations of actors' behavior.[55] As there simply is no such thing as a universal rationality, such an *integrated ontological approach* appears to be an especially promising alternative, from which a comprehensive and convincing explanation for China's use of force should depart.

A Cultural Theory of International Relations

Fortunately, I do not have to engage in theory-building on my own, as Ned Lebow has already outlined an innovative theoretical argument that comprehensively meets my criteria for a capable explanatory model. In contrast to other theories that delineate the international level as an autonomous domain, Lebow's approach is based on the insight that "international relations is at the apex of multiple levels of social aggregation, and is significantly influenced, if not shaped, by what happens on other levels."[56] By emphasizing the centrality of human agency on all of these levels, he notes that in order

> to understand foreign policy and international relations, we must understand the motives, goals and emotions of relevant actors. There is simply no such thing as a universal strategic logic or hierarchy of motives that we can take for granted and use to model behavior.[57]

Accordingly, Lebow's goal consists in constructing a theory of international relations that is based "on a more comprehensive understanding of human motives and their implications for political behavior."[58] In search of such a sophisticated understanding, he goes back to ancient Greek philosophy and conceptually borrows from the works of Plato, Aristotle, and Thucydides.[59] Following his Greek predecessors, Lebow posits that all human behavior can be fundamentally traced back to four motives: *appetite, spirit, fear,* and *reason*.[60]

Existing paradigms of IR are based on only two of these motives, namely *appetite* (Liberalism) and *fear* (Realism), combined with an instrumental understanding of *reason* (i.e. rational choice).[61] In contrast to that, modernity seems to have "forgotten the importance of the spirit and no longer sees politics driven by honor,"[62] even though the motive *spirit* has not lost any potency or relevancy.[63] Moreover, this shortcoming appears strikingly problematic, as each of the four motives – including *spirit* – also "generate[s] different logics concerning cooperation, conflict and risk-taking"[64] at every level of social aggregation, which, however, are neither identified nor adequately addressed by established theories due to their oversimplified assumptions. In order to overcome this deficit and to show the distinct characteristics and implications of his four basic motives for human behavior, Lebow outlines a typology of ideal-type behavior of actors dominated by one specific motive.

Table 2.2 Overview: motives and implications

Motive	Goal	Instrument/Mean	Principle	Status hierarchy
Spirit	Self-esteem	Obtaining honor and standing	Fairness	Clientelistic
Appetite	Welfare, physical wellbeing	Pursuing particular interests	Equality	Informal, oriented on relative economic success
Fear	Security/survival	Maximizing power/alliance formation	Threat	Possible, intra-alliance specific
Reason	Good life/ *eudaimonia*	Practical wisdom/ self-restraint	Justice	Possible, depending on the concrete principle of justice

Source: author.

Spirit

The journey to rediscover the motive *spirit* starts with the observation that people – individually and collectively – seek self-esteem through excelling in activities valued by one's peer group or society. Following ancient Greek philosophy, Lebow identifies the spirit, an efficacious human drive, as the principal cause of this desire, which is observable as a universal phenomenon across cultures and epochs.[65] The spirit is profoundly dependent on a social framework to function because the individual (or internal) dimension of esteem is created through the external awarding of *honor* and *status*.[66] Honor is understood as "a status ... that describes the outward recognition we gain from others in response to our excellence."[67] When an actor's performance is regarded as honorable by society, his or her deeds will be collectively awarded with honor, given that the actor is a member of the societal subgroup in which the competition for honor is allowed.[68]

However, the society's appreciation does not only come along with privileges for the honored actors. In spirit-based worlds, *noblesse oblige* and honor are thus also accompanied by social obligations and responsibilities for the privileged vis-à-vis the non-privileged members of a society, as the bestowal of honor concurrently establishes social inequalities: "Honor is inseparable from hierarchy. Hierarchy is a rank ordering of status, and in honor societies honor determines the nature of the statuses and who fills them."[69] In order to legitimate their respective *status rank* and the associated privileges it confers, high-status actors thus need to comply with their societal responsibilities and obligations:

> In return for honoring and serving those higher up the social ladder, those beneath them expect to be looked after in various ways. Protecting and providing for others is invariably one of the key responsibilities of those with high status.[70]

By fulfilling their assigned duties, actors are continuously esteemed by their society, which in turn allows them to satisfy their desire for self-esteem and to avoid internal *shame* or public *disgrace* resulting from non-compliance.[71] In doing so, these actors also contribute to maintaining the stability and functionality of their societal framework.[72]

The 'social contract' of spirit-dominated societies, however, is an inherently fragile structure, because standing is a highly relational concept. Moreover, the "value placed on honor in spirit-based worlds, and the intensity of competition for it, tempt actors to take short cuts to attain it."[73] The potential cleavages in spirit-dominated worlds are diverse. Their erosion can be *top-down*, when high-status actors fail to perform their social responsibilities and/or exploit the privileges associated with their status, or *bottom-up*, when the cohesion of spirit-based societies is challenged by actors being denied entry to the elite circle in which they can compete for honor. A third cleavage can emerge within the elite of spirit-dominated societies, especially between members that occupy similar status ranks, because "actors not infrequently disagree about whom deserves a particular status or office."[74]

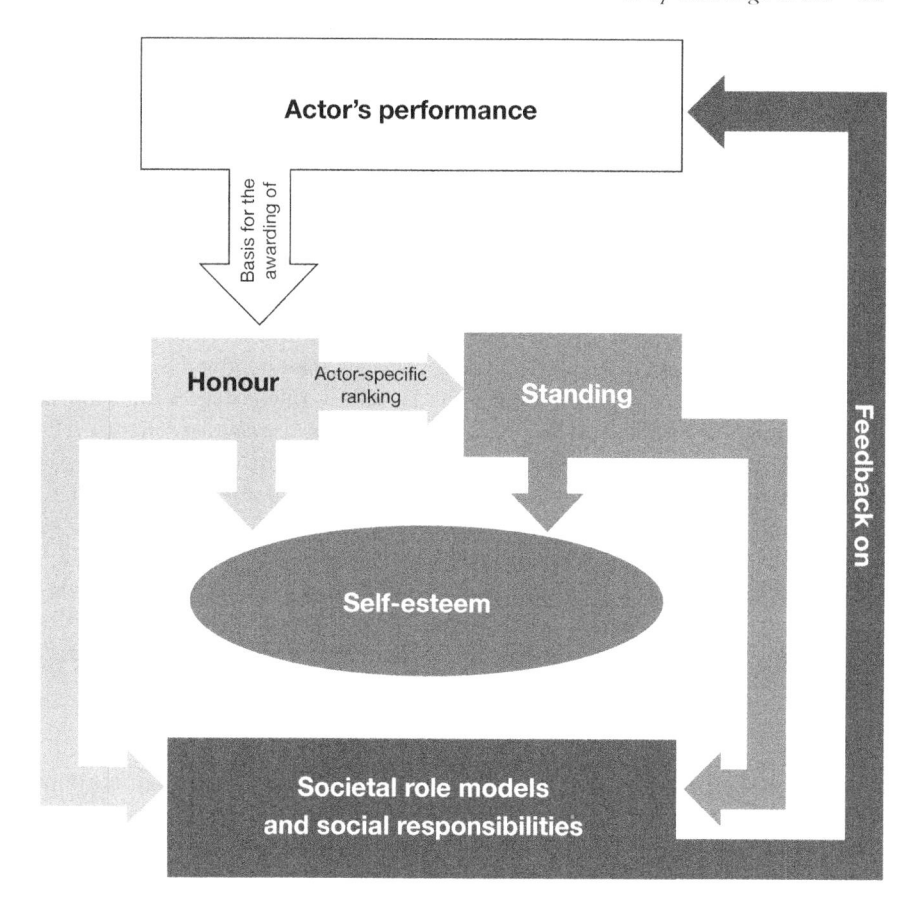

Figure 2.1 The 'social contract' of spirit-worlds

Spirit-based worlds are thus highly fragile and incorporate significant potential for conflict, as the spirit not only gives rise to stabilizing effects on society but also incorporates the latent potential for its destruction. In robust societies, these negative implications are moderated through self-restraint or are channeled outwards. However, if too many actors ignore the normative agreement underlying the society's order (*nomos*) without being punished, the ordering based on individual honor is devalued and loses legitimacy. Then, the competition for honor is transformed into a competition for status, which is more unconstrained and violent.[75] In such degenerated spirit-worlds, the increase in violence results from the overwhelming value that actors place on their individual status as their most precious possession. Accordingly, challenges to one's status are unacceptable when they come from equals, and even more so when they come from inferiors. Conflicts over competing status claims have a high tendency to escalate into violence. The choice of this means to decide a conflict reflects the emotional state an actor experiences when his or her status is offended, degraded, or even negated by others. Such slights evoke anger and the immediate desire to revenge the suffered humiliation because "challenges to an actor's status ... can only be appeased by punishing the offender and thereby 'putting him in his place'."[76] If actors fail to instantly punish offenses, they lose not only in their individual dimension of esteem but also in how they are esteemed by others, as such humiliations usually take place in the public sphere of society.[77] Degraded actors thus behave highly emotionally, often act prematurely, and show great willingness to take high risks. "When the spirit is dominant, when actors seek self-esteem through honor, standing or autonomy, they are often willing to risk, even sacrifice, themselves or their political units in pursuit of these goals."[78]

Even though members of *honor*-worlds frequently resort to force in order to decide competing status claims and to revenge offenses, the extent of these outbreaks of violence is kept decidedly limited and typically reflects rule-governed duels (*agon*). "These limitations, however, apply only to warfare between recognized members of the same society. War against outsiders, or against non-elite members of one's own society, often has a no-holds-barred quality."[79] In sum, spirit-dominated worlds show an inherently high potential for conflict and violence, which is caused by its members' extreme emotional sensitivity to matters of social status and their willingness to accept high risks. On the other hand, the same emotional setting also facilitates cooperation, which is based upon the obligations and responsibilities arising from the social contract, as well as on friendship and family commitments.[80]

Appetite

The motive *appetite* is the drive with which we are most familiar – and not only because appetite and its characteristics are broadly reflected by the liberal paradigm of IR theory.[81] "Appetite ... includes all primitive biological urges – hunger, thirst, sex and aversion to pain – and their more sophisticated expressions."[82] In contrast to spirit, appetite does not necessarily need a societal framework to function but, as Adam Smith found, is much easier to satisfy within societies, because the primary goal of actors motivated by appetite consists in increasing their material welfare.[83] In doing so, actors also prioritize their parochial (economic) interests over political and social preferences. Appetite-dominated societies rest upon the principle of formal equality and replace the traditional forms of status with welfare and material display. Social inequality is then the result of the specific distribution of wealth, which in turn translates into an informal status hierarchy.[84] Here, man forges his own destiny – but at the same time, every man is also for himself: as society does not grant any privileges to its members, no social responsibilities arise, and consequently "[t]here is no requirement to share resources with others who are less well off."[85]

As economic interests thus dominate relationships in appetite-worlds, they also influence the character of cooperation, conflict, and risk-taking. While converging interests function as the prerequisite for cooperation and also determine its duration and intensity, diverging interests result in conflict. Conflicts, however, are usually non-violent and rule-governed, because all actors "recognize their overriding interests in maintaining peaceful relations and the institutions, procedures and general level of trust that enabled peaceful relations."[86] With regard to risk behavior, actors in appetite-worlds follow the postulations of economics' prospect theory, and are thus risk-averse when making gains but more risk-accepting when it comes to preventing losses.[87]

Reason

Reason and its social manifestations represent an ideal-type in the truest sense of the word. Worlds dominated by reason reflect utopias, described by political philosophers as ideal development states of societies which are virtually impossible to achieve in practice. This is because the goal of reason consists in nothing less than the realization of the 'good life' (*Eudamonia*). This ambitious objective can only be achieved when reason is able to restrain the negative implications of spirit and appetite and educate their proper expressions.[88] As reason is the only drive with the capacity to generate normative judgments, its existence in social frameworks affects the emergence of sophisticated insights and practical wisdom (*phronesis*), which in turn facilitates the emergence of a social order based on the principle of justice.[89] In detail, actors dominated by reason gain the insight that order arises from their willingness to cooperate "even when it may be contrary to their immediate self-interests. All actors recognize that cooperation sustains the *nomos* that allows all of them to advance their interests more effectively than they could in its absence."[90] By inducing self-restraint among the members of a society and by educating them about the socially acceptable saturations of appetite and spirit, reason not only facilitates cooperation: worlds dominated by reason are also extensively free of conflict because existing disagreement would not threaten the legitimacy of the *nomos*, the fundamental agreement on norms and principles shared and accepted by all members of the society. This allows actors to solve disputes in an environment characterized by mutual trust and respect, which in turn enables the consensual resolution of conflicts. In this way, actors also contribute to the preservation and strengthening of the *nomos* as their society's basis, from which they all prosper.[91] The specific conceptualization of the *nomos* and the society's understanding of justice then define the concrete ordering principle and also determine the risk behavior of its members.[92]

Fear

Lebow's fourth motive, *fear*, is an emotion and thus requires social interaction to arise: "Fear is an affect, and a highly subjective one. It is based on idiosyncratic, and at times *irrational*, assessments of other's motives."[93] Worlds dominated by fear should be well known to students of IR, as the realist paradigm heavily draws upon the effects of this powerful emotion.[94]

According to Lebow, fear comes into play to the same extent that reason loses its restraining effects over spirit and appetite. When selfish actors begin to satisfy these drives outside socially accepted norms, their behavior erodes the society's underlying normative framework that governs the socially compatible pursuit of these drives.[95] If non-compliance remains unpunished, other actors will follow suit as they become entrapped in the problematic situation of a security dilemma, which in turn provides momentum for a spiral of growing insecurity that finally results in the complete disintegration of the *nomos*.[96] Fear then becomes the main driving force behind social behavior, as "[a]ctors make security their first concern and attempt to become strong enough to deter or defeat any possible combination of likely adversaries."[97] However, the desire to achieve the best individual security situation possible by maximizing military and economic capabilities fuels another dilemma, because security reveals itself as a zero-sum game. As a result, actors are doomed to compete over the scarce resource of security, making fear-dominated worlds highly prone to conflict, and in the absence of a shared *nomos*, "neither the ends nor the means of conflict are constrained by norms."[98]

The omnipresent security calculations in fear-dominated worlds profoundly affect the relations among its inhabitants: cooperation is based on shared threat perceptions, whereby the congruence of these perceptions decides the intensity and duration of the alliance.[99] However, alliance formation and the diplomacy of deterrence do not serve as panaceas for achieving security because these measures almost invariably provoke the outcomes they were intended to prevent.[100] Rather, the specific risk-aversion of actors motivated by fear reveals with moderating effect on the escalation of conflicts. Actors consider the use of force a much riskier and more cost-intensive strategy because warfare is no longer rule-governed and limited.[101] Fear-dominated worlds involve "wars that are often fought *à outrance* to destroy, or at least seriously weaken, opposing states and regimes."[102]

Ideal-types, real worlds, and the formation of foreign policy

Worlds dominated either by spirit, appetite, fear, or reason in such a degree of uniformity are never encountered in practice. Instead, these four worlds qualify as ideal-types, defined by Max Weber as "analytical accentuation[s] of aspects of one or more attributes of a phenomenon to create a mental construct."[103] When used as analytical templates to contrast the empirical manifestations of the phenomenon under investigation, ideal-types provide helpful insights into – and explanations for – an actor's behavior, its causes, and its implications.[104]

In real worlds, Lebow assumes, at least three of the four motives are present to varying degrees:

> Real worlds are lumpy in that their mix of motives differs from actor to actor and among the groupings they form. Multiple motives generally mix rather than blend, giving rise to a range *of behaviors that can often appear contradictory*.[105]

Such contradictory behavior among actors who are confronted with the same problem presents anomalies for mono-causal explanatory models, and particularly for those that are based on the rational-choice assumption. Lebow's theory, in contrast, is able to explain these 'outliers' by taking the specific effects of all four motives into account. This superior analytical capacity clearly demonstrates the added value of the Cultural Theory compared to existing IR theories.[106]

In empirical worlds, interactions among actors and societies, as well as the interplay between their motivations, produce situational and/or actor-specific hierarchies of motives. Depending on the specific configuration of these hierarchies, real worlds gradually lean towards the respective ideal-type of the dominant motive.[107] Inside political units, the accumulation of such hierarchies (i.e. the mix of motives at play among individual actors) also affects the formation of the unit's foreign policy.[108]

This brings us to the international level. Here, existing societal structures are not only extraordinarily thin and lumpy but also reveal the defining characteristics of a traditional warrior society. This society represents a special type of social order as it combines the elements and principles of spirit and appetite-worlds.[109] Characteristics of the latter are reflected by the principle of formal equality among its members and by the focus on material welfare as a secondary status-marker. But wealth alone does not promote a nation into the elite of the international society, as its high status ranks have traditionally been – and are still – occupied by the militarily most capable states: the great powers. This type of hierarchy clearly shows the relicts of a spirit-dominated warrior society in the international system.[110] Adding to this, great powerdom "is both a rank ordering of status and an office"[111] and thus gives rise to patterns of relations that closely resemble the ideal-type social contract of spirit-worlds: in return for their rank and the privileges it confers, high-ranking actors provide security and assume responsibility for the well-being of lower-status actors.

> Contrary to the assumptions of realism, there are strong incentives for powerful actors to conform to the rules of the system – to the extent that regional or international society is thick enough for them to develop. It allows actors to translate their power into influence in the most efficient and effective manner.[112]

However, the question remains as to how states, as the principal actors in international society, can be affected by the four motives without having a psyche or emotions. As the personal union of state and ruler that has characterized international relations in former epochs no longer applies, Lebow has to take the alternative route via the motives of socially interacting elites, in order to transfer his approach to contemporary international relations: in the era of nationalism, when individuals construct their personal identities by identifying with the distinctiveness of their nations, the pursuit of self-esteem is regularly substituted through identification with the accomplishments of one's collective.[113] This linkage appears particularly pronounced for actors that occupy governmental offices and political or military functions, as these elites identify themselves to the most significant extent via their affiliated nation.[114] Since they "project their psychological needs on to their political units, and feel better about themselves when those units win victories and perform well,"[115] the motives of these elites thus reveal themselves to have critical importance for the formation of the nation's foreign policy. In the same way, these elites also function as 'transmission belts' for inner-societal motives and emotions.

Operationalization

As all human behavior can be fundamentally reduced to the effects of spirit, appetite, reason, and fear, Lebow's theory principally offers four independent variables. However, only two of them can be held responsible for the outbreak of violence at all levels of social aggregation, including the international arena: spirit and fear. If

Lebow's argument is valid, the empirical analysis should thus evidently reveal the *independent causal effect* of either spirit or fear on the actions and decisions of *China's political and military elites*.[116] However, as Ned Lebow correctly emphasizes, "[t]o assert that political units are motivated by fear, interest, honor or any other motive, is not the same as demonstrating it. To do this, we must show that important decisions over time reflect these motives."[117] Accordingly, my analysis needs to demonstrate that the behavior of the Chinese elite, including the decision to resort to military force, approached the ideal-type of either a spirit-based or fear-based world over time. Thereto, the theory offers three analytical categories (cooperation, conflict, and risk behavior) with well-defined characteristics for each motive, allowing for a clear-cut correlation of observable behavior and corresponding motive.

Defining empirical tests

In order to validate Lebow's theory, the case studies should reveal the independent effects of the four motives on China's elites during the process leading up to the confrontation, during the decision-making itself, and during the actual use of military force. Even though the theory is not sufficiently specified to allow for deducing more fine-graded process hypotheses, the following general steps should be observable.

The starting point would be a balance of motives among China's political and military elites. With the occurrence of a trigger event, this balance is interrupted and a significant increase on behalf of either the motive spirit or fear materializes, which should be especially pronounced among China's key leaders. The concrete effects of this catalyst are dependent on how the Chinese elites subjectively perceive and frame the issue at stake. Accordingly, an objective deterioration of China's security situation might not necessarily be perceived as such, but may instead be framed primarily as an affront against Chinese interests or as a humiliation with regard to China's status. If the thesis that imbalances on the individual level also affect the balance of motives at higher levels is valid, then this crosscutting effect should become observable during the deliberations in the decision-making process. The actions and decisions of the People's Republic of China should then approach one of the ideal-types – either spirit or fear – regarding the three analytical categories of cooperation, conflict, and risk behavior. Even at this late stage in the process, divergence in opinion and even contradictory behavior among China's elites is expected to occur, as the leaders should be affected by the external stimulus to varying degrees and thus should adhere to a logic of 'subjective rationality.' An observation of that kind would strongly support Lebow's argument, as it would contradict the rationalists' dictum that rational actors sharing the same information cannot agree to disagree in their assessments of a specific issue.

Expectations: spirit

In the case that spirit is stipulated and becomes the dominant motive, China's actions should approach the *spirit's logic of appropriateness*. Cooperation should then be primarily motivated by the social responsibilities that resemble the social contract of

Table 2.3 Expectations: *spirit*

	Willingness for cooperation	Specifics	Potential for conflict	Specifics	Risk behavior
Logic of appropriateness	High	Based on friendship, family relations and social responsibilities Highly durable Major impediment: cooperation between actors with similar status-ranks	Very high	Resorts to force resemble duels, are limited and rule-governed Exception: warfare against outsiders	Very risk-taking, including self-sacrifice to prevent losses

Source: author.

spirit-based worlds. In order to preserve China's status, the elite should demonstrate great willingness to fulfill these obligations, even though this might run contra to China's parochial interests and is accompanied by high risks. Risk-taking should even increase if the elite perceives the conflict as a humiliation with regard to China's status.

If this is the case, the Chinese leadership should not only react in a highly emotional manner but should also show determination to avenge the suffered slight. Accordingly, a strong confirmation for the motive spirit would be a decision to resort to military force even though the elite simultaneously reaches the conclusion that the respective opponent does not pose a threat to China's security. Considerations about arising risks should only play a minor role, or should even be neglected, during the decision-making process, as actors motivated by spirit are "often willing to risk, even sacrifice, themselves or their political units in pursuit of [honor and standing]."[118] The phenomenology of the actual use of force would then serve as another indicator. When motivated by spirit, a limited and rule-governed outbreak of violence should be observable, given that the opponents are members of the same society and/or elite.[119] "Warfare ideally takes the form of highly stylized combat or contest (agon) between two warriors, closely governed by a series of rules, well-understood and respected by all participants, that encourage a fair fight."[120] Thereby, at best, material war objectives such as territory or strategic positioning should play no role.

Expectations: fear

In contrast, considerations about individual security and arising risks should dominate the discussions and actions of the Chinese elite when fear becomes the determining motive, because actors then make security their first concern. In fear-based worlds, social obligations and duties cease to function as the basis for

Table 2.4 Expectations: *fear*

	Willingness for cooperation	Specifics	Potential for conflict	Specifics	Risk behavior
Logic of consequences	Low	Based on shared threat-perceptions (balance of threat) Highly fluctuant Primarily as alliance formations	High	Warfare is no longer rule-governed or restraint in its extent; Oriented on material objectives Primary goal: survival	*Neutral* No distinctions between gains and losses; If survival is threatened: increased willingness to accept risks

Source: author.

cooperation. Instead, the willingness to cooperate is dependent on shared threat perceptions, and cooperation should thus materialize primarily in fluctuant military alliances. As fear comes into existence when the *nomos* is lost, neither the end nor the means of conflict is limited, which makes escalations of violence significantly more risky and costly. Consequently, actors cease to risk life and limb for others but become evidently more self-interested and follow their parochial (material) interests. China's leadership should thus act in a rather more risk-averse or neutral manner, and should not resort to the use of military force before a vital threat to China's security is perceived. If this is the case, then an increase in risk-taking may also be observable, in order to realize the primary goal of surviving.

Expectations: Fearon's rationalist explanation

As "[t]he plausibility of an explanation is enhanced to the extent that alternative explanations are considered and found to be less consistent with the data, or less supportable by available generalizations,"[121] I employ Fearon's 'rationalist explanation for war' as my alternative explanatory model. In Fearon's approach, the anarchical structure of the international system serves as the independent variable, which qualifies his two identified causal mechanisms as intervening variables. In order to furnish proof for the independent causal impact of Fearon's variables, either the perceived commitment problem or the intentional creation of information asymmetries by China or the respective opponent should evidently reveal itself as the central problem during the decision-making process, and should effectively prevent a non-violent resolution of the conflict under investigation.

It needs to be admitted at this point that as I am primarily concerned with analyzing and explaining the decisions and actions taken by the People's Republic of China, the respective opponents do not receive the same amount of analytical attention. Even so, I will provide sufficient insight into the dyadic dimension of the four conflicts under investigation. In doing so, I will be able to comprehensively

Table 2.5 Expectations: *rationalist model*

	Willingness for cooperation	Specifics	Potential for conflict	Specifics	Risk behavior
Logic of consequences	Low	Based on calculations about relative gains	Medium	Incentives for non-violent conflict resolutions exist; Impediments: commitment problem, private information	Averse or neutral

Source: author.

evaluate the explanatory capacity of James Fearon's rational-choice approach for each of the four cases under investigation.

'Measuring' motives: methodological challenges

In contrast to the uniformity of Lebow's ideal-types, the empirical complexity of real worlds complicates the selective differentiation between the motives at play. Adding to this, actors rarely provide direct insights into their specific motivation, which further complicates the task of explaining behavior by attributing it to the specific effects of a distinct motive.[122] Heikki Patomäki thus poses the reasonable question: "how do we know what the true or prevailing motives of actors are?"[123] As Lebow argues, "these problems should not deter us from making careful efforts to determine the hierarchy of motives behind foreign policy decisions, [but] make it essential that we supplement these efforts with [methodological] approaches."[124] The crux of the matter is that in order to show that leaders acted on the basis of specific motives, the analysis has to demonstrate that "important decisions *over time* reflect these motives."[125] At least three methods appear suitable for the required longitudinal investigation of case studies: the analysis of discourses and documents, process tracing, and congruence tests. All three methods offer several advantages and analytical strengths, but inherit certain deficits and problems regarding their implementation as well.

Analyzing discourses or documents

The analysis of documents or of discourses in society and/or between elites can provide insights into what specific motives are regarded as legitimate and which kind of hierarchy is established among them.[126] Moreover, analyzing discourses over time can also allow for observing changes in the motivations of specific actors. However, as William Wohlforth notes, analyzing discourses is only an expedient line of inquiry if the participating actors also state their respective motivation.[127] In the sphere of international relations and diplomacy, where "documents lie as much as diplomats,"[128] such plain depictions are rarely observable, as evidently demonstrated by the United States' attempt to justify the military intervention in Iraq before the

United Nations Security Council in 2003.[129] Actors often exploit socially accepted motives as pretexts in order to legitimate actions that can apparently be traced back to other motives. Consequently, even when actors outline their particular motivation for a specific action, such statements should not be taken at face value. Instead, there is a need to "read between the lines"[130] and critically question the stated motivation by contextualizing it within a broader analytical setting or by verifying the results of a discourse analysis with complementary methodological approaches.

Process tracing and congruence tests

The second, and probably more promising, research strategy is to reason backwards from observable behavior to theorized motives.[131] Thereto, process tracing and congruence tests qualify as methodological approaches. Process tracing is widely regarded as the strongest method for revealing the causal processes through which the independent variable produces causal effects.[132] Like the congruence method, process tracing rests upon within-case observations but requires that "these observations must be linked in particular ways to constitute an explanation of the case."[133] While process tracing can discover the *causal mechanism*[134] between the independent and dependent variables, the congruence method can only detect "similarities in the relative strength of hypothesized cause and observed effect"[135] and is thus a (weaker) method of causal interpretation. Although the strength of a congruence test can be enhanced by increasing the number of within-case observations, the detected co-variance between independent and dependent variable does not allow any indication of whether this relationship is causal or spurious.[136] Because of that, process tracing is regarded as the method of choice for analyzing causal interference. However, there is one impediment to employing process tracing as the single methodological approach for my project: the sophisticated requirements on the guiding theory. For rigorous process verification, process tracing ideally requires the deduction of a hypothesized process that covers *all* interim steps between the independent and dependent variable. Unfortunately, the Cultural Theory is not yet specified enough to offer these fine-graded process hypotheses. In this case, as Alexander George and Andrew Bennett note, "process verification can reach only provisional conclusions."[137]

Turning weaknesses into strengths: an integrated methodological approach

Instead of basing my case-study analyses on a single method of investigation, I employ three methods (process tracing, congruence tests, and discourse analysis) in an integrated methodological approach. In doing so, the deficits and shortcomings of each methods can be substituted by the strengths of the complementary approaches. This provides me with a sophisticated and strong analytical framework.

While Lebow's theory does not offer fine-graded process hypotheses, this does not mean that the model provides no expectations on the process at all: the Cultural Theory and Fearon's rationalist explanation for war indeed offer (roughly structured) hypothetical processes that can be tested by tracing them in my four case studies (see Figure 2.2).

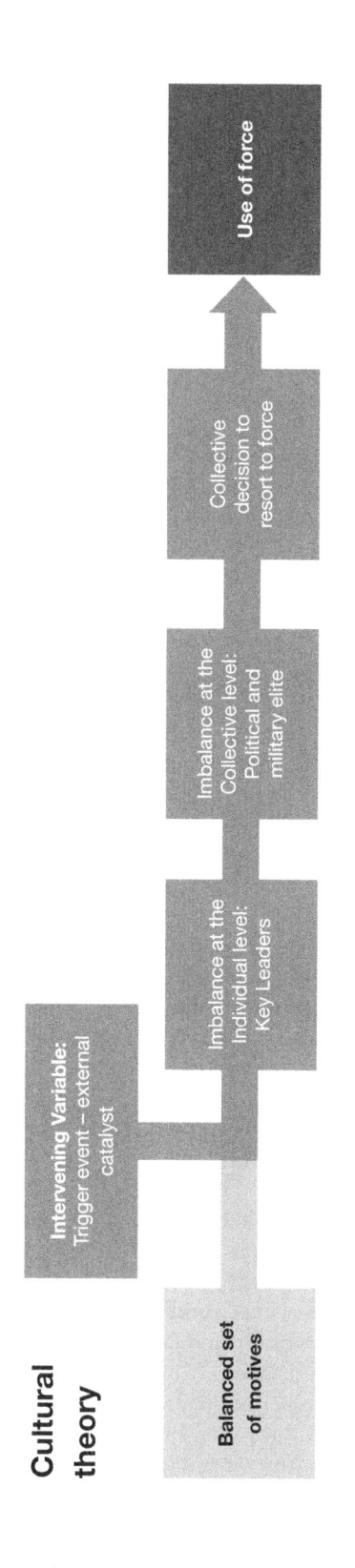

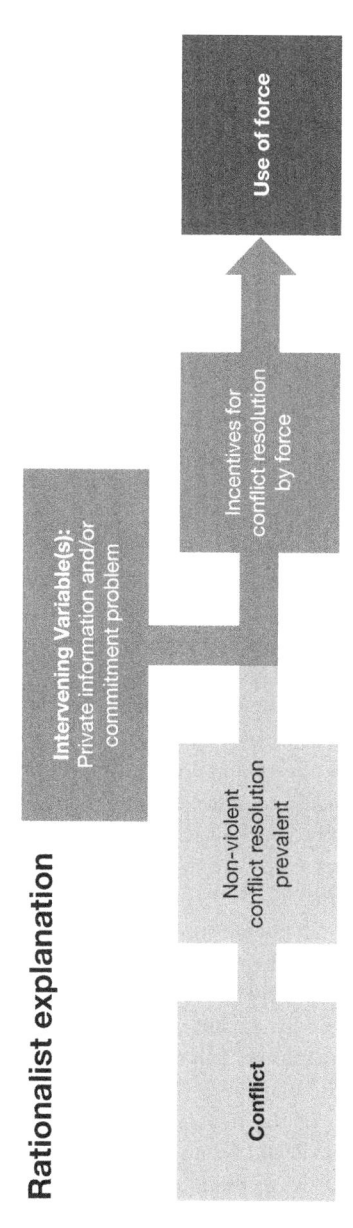

Figure 2.2 Overview: competing causal paths

To close the remaining gaps between the 'domino stones' and/or compensate for deficits in process data, I make use of within-case comparisons based on the congruence method in order to analyze whether the variables under investigation vary as theoretically expected. In addition, within-case observations can be applied to analyze the values of the three analytical categories (cooperation, conflict, and risk behavior) over time. Accordingly, if the cases are sufficiently data-rich to provide insights into the elites' deliberations, the examination will also be guided by the discourse analysis in order to make use of this valuable data.

As the partial analyses rest upon complementary methodological approaches, their respective findings can verify themselves reciprocally. Thereby, the study's integrated methodology unifies the specific advantages of each method, allowing utilization of the full range of accessible data (primary documentation, biographical accounts, secondary literature, and speeches and statements) while simultaneously providing the necessary analytical sensitivity to detect potential distortions and misguided conclusions. Most importantly, however, this integrated methodological approach allows the verification of the causal relationship between the independent and dependent variable to a significantly higher degree of certainty than could be provided by an analysis based on a single method.

The structure of the case-study analyses

In order to comprehensively cover the hypothetical processes as provided by the two competing explanatory models and to create the maximum amount of within-case observations for the three analytical categories (cooperation, conflict, and risk behavior), the case studies are separated into four analytical phases: (1) the formation of the conflict; (2) the decision to resort to military force; (3) the actual use of military force; and (4) the post-conflict phase.

The analysis of the conflict's formation traces the developments in the relationship between China and its respective opponent and thereby pursues three objectives. First, the analysis reveals which of Lebow's ideal-type worlds best resembles the empirical characteristics of the bilateral relationship under investigation. In a second step, the analysis identifies the central causes of friction in the relationship, provides insights into the nature of the bilateral conflict, and shows the parties' approaches in handling the conflict. Finally, by investigating how the conflict broke into the open, the study is able to identify which of the theoretically postulated intervening variables set off the escalation process. That concludes the first step of the process verification.

The investigation of the decision-making process should then provide further evidence for the verification of either Lebow's Cultural Theory or Fearon's rationalist explanation for war by confirming the respective process hypotheses. Accordingly, either one of Fearon's identified causal mechanisms or Lebow's imbalances on behalf of spirit or fear in the leadership's motivation should evidently reveal itself as the source for China's decision to resort to force. Furthermore, the analysis of the discourse reveals how the Chinese leadership framed the issue at stake. It should be noted that the analytical depth of this partial analysis is highly dependent on the availability of data. When data on the elite's discussions is not available, which is unfortunately the case for the decision-making leading up to the Sino-Soviet border clashes, my analysis will be able to only generate provisional results. But even then, the co-variance of the timing of the decision with the emergence of a trigger event allows for conclusions as to which of the competing theoretical models develops more explanatory power.

The third phase examines the phenomenology of China's resort to military force and thereby provides an assessment as to which of the two ideal-types of warfare was most closely approached. Adding to this, as war objectives may be amended during the course of the campaign, the analysis can also reveal further changes in the Chinese motivation during this phase.

Finally, the outcome dimension of China's resort to force is investigated. In a nutshell, the focus of the analysis lies on identifying the consequences of the use of force, i.e. whether it resulted in an improvement of China's security situation or in an increase of the PRC's international standing. In addition, the analysis examines the patterns of de-escalation from combat to non-combat.

Notes

1   For classics of IR discussing the causes of interstate war, see Brodie, Bernhard, *War and Politics* (London: Macmillan Publishers, 1973); Wright, Quincy, *A Study of War* (Chicago: Chicago University Press, 1965); Levy, Jack S., "The Causes of War: A Review of Theories and Evidence," in *Behavior, Society and Nuclear War*, ed. Tetlock, Philip E., et al. (New York: Oxford University Press, 1989); Blainey, Geoffrey, *The Causes of War* (New York: Free Press, 1988); Waltz, Kenneth N., *Man, State, and War: A Theoretical Analysis* (New York: Columbia University Press, 2001).
2   For excellent overviews on the various strands of theorizing the causes of war, see Levy, Jack S. and Thompson, William R., *The Causes of War* (Chichester: Wiley-Blackwell Publishing, 2010); Jäger, Thomas and Beckmann, Rasmus, *Handbuch Kriegstheorien* (Wiesbaden: VS Verlag für Sozialwissenschaften, 2011).
3   See Lebow, Richard N., *Why Nations Fight: Past and Future Motives for War* (Cambridge: Cambridge University Press, 2010), 23.
4   Posen, Barry R., "ESDP and the Structure of World Politics," *The International Spectator: Italian Journal of International Affairs* 39, no. 1 (2004): 15.
5   Grieco, Joseph M., "Realist International Theory and the Study of World Politics," in *New Thinking in International Relations Theory*, ed. Doyle, Michael and Ikenberry, G. John (Boulder: Westview Press, 1997), 163.
6   "Rationality is a core assumption of all existing theories of war. It provides the necessary link connecting systemic opportunities and constraints, formulations of the national interest and specific foreign policies": Lebow, *Why Nations Fight*, 44–45. On the logic of consequences/rational choice-assumption, see Snidal, Duncan, "Rational Choice and International Relations," in *Handbook of International Relations*, ed. Carls - naes, Walter, Risse, Thomas, and Simmons, Beth A. (London/Thousand Oaks/New Delhi: Sage Publications, 2006); Levy, Jack S., "Prospect Theory, Rational Choice, and International Relations," *International Studies Quarterly* 41, no. 1 (1997); Quackenbush, Stephen L., "The Rationality of Rational Choice Theory," *International Interactions* no. 30 (2004).
7   See Fearon, James D., "Rationalist Explanation for War," *International Organization* 49, no. 3 (1995): 380.

8 The categorization of the causes of war in these three levels of analysis was pioneered by Waltz, *Man, State, and War*, 12.
9 See Morgenthau, Hans J., *Politics among Nations: The Struggle for Power and Peace* (New York: Knopf, 1954), 25.
10 See ibid., 4.
11 Ibid., 5.
12 See Singer, J. David, "The Level-of-Analysis Problem in International Relations," *World Politics* 14, no. 1 (1961): 81; Guilhot, Nicolas, "Politics Between and Beyond Nations: Hans J. Morgenthau's Politics Among Nations," in *Classics of International Relations. Essays in Criticism and Appreciation*, ed. Bliddal, Henrik, Sylvest, Casper, and Wilson, Peter (London/New York: Routledge, 2013), 70.
13 See Lebow, *Why Nations Fight*, 24.
14 See Guilhot, "Politics Between and Beyond Nations," 73–74.
15 See Buzan, Barry, "The Timeless Wisdom of Realism," in *International Theory: Postivism and Beyond*, ed. Smith, Steve, Booth, Ken, and Zalewski, Marysia (Cambridge: Cambridge University Press, 1996), 59; Dunne, Timmothy, "Realism," in *The Globalization of World Politics: An Introduction to International Relations*, ed. Baylis, John and Smith, Steve (Oxford/New York: Oxford University Press, 1997), 110.
16 See Waltz, Kenneth N., *Theory of International Politics* (Reading: Addison-Wesley Publishing Company, 1979); Mearsheimer, John J., *The Tragedy of Great Power Politics* (New York/London: W.W. Norton & Company, 2001).
17 Waltz, Kenneth N., "The Origins of War in Neorealist Theory," *The Journal of Interdisciplinary History* 18, no. 4 (1988): 619. On the concept, origins, and implications of the security dilemma, see Herz, John, "Idealist Internationalism and the Security Dilemma," *World Politics* 2, no. 2 (1950): 157–80; Jervis, Robert, *Perception and Misperception in International Politics* (Princeton: Princeton University Press, 1976), 62–76; Glaser, Charles L., "The Security Dilemma Revisited," *World Politics* 50, no. 1 (1997).
18 Waltz, *Theory of International Politics*, 102.
19 See ibid., 67, 82, 97–99; Mearsheimer, *The Tragedy of Great Power Politics*, 334–35.
20 See Waltz, *Theory of International Politics*, 129–31.
21 See Lebow, *Why Nations Fight*, 27.
22 Waltz, *Theory of International Politics*, 113.
23 Waltz, Kenneth N., "The Origins of War in Neorealist Theory," 620.
24 See Schmidt, Brian C., "The Enduring Logic of the Three Images: Kenneth Waltz's Man, the State, and War," in *Classics of International Relations. Essays in Criticism and Appreciation*, ed. Bliddal, Henrik, Sylvest, Casper, and Wilson, Peter (London/New York: Routledge, 2013), 84.
25 See Waltz, *Theory of International Politics*, 126; Grieco, "Realist International Theory," 186–90; Snyder, Jack, *The Myth of Empire. Domestic Politics and International Ambition* (Ithaca/London: Cornell University Press, 1991), 6.
26 See Mearsheimer, *The Tragedy of Great Power Politics*, 29; "Power and Fear in Great Power Politics," in *One Hundred Year Commemoration of the Life of Hans Morgenthau (1904–2004)*, ed. Mazur, G.O. (Oxford: Oxford University Press, 2004), 184.
27 Toft, Peter, "John J. Mearsheimer: An Offensive Realist between Geopolitics and Power," *Journal of International Relations and Development* 8, no. 1 (2005): 385.
28 See Mearsheimer, *The Tragedy of Great Power Politics*, 37, 128–33; Taliaferro, Jeffrey W., "Security Seeking under Anarchy: Defensive Realism Revisited," *International Security* 25, no. 3 (2001): 128.
29 See Little, Richard, *The Balance of Power in International Relations: Metaphors, Myths and Models* (New York: Cambridge University Press, 2007), 225; Rosecrance, Richard N.,

"War and Peace," *World Politics* 55, no. 1 (2002): 139.
30 Mearsheimer, *The Tragedy of Great Power Politics*, 37.
31 In adherence to Waltz's pragmatic advice for counting the poles of the Asia-Pacific system, one might argue that the subsystem was characterized by bipolarity (United States and Soviet Union) until China emerged as an independent political center of gravity in the aftermath of the Sino-Soviet split.
32 Fearon, "Rationalist Explanation for War," 380.
33 See ibid., 380–83; Gartzke, Erik, "War Is an Error Term," *International Organization* 53, no. 3 (1999): 570.
34 See Fearon, "Rationalist Explanation for War," 388–90. Fearon notes that there may exist some rare cases of 'issue indivisibility' for which his third assumption does not apply: see ibid., 381–82.
35 See Niou, Emerson, Ordeshook, Peter, and Rose, Gregory, *The Balance of Power: Stability in the International System* (Cambridge: Cambridge University Press, 1989), 59; Harsanyi, John C., "Games with Incomplete Information Played by 'Bayesian' Players, Part III," *Management Science* no. 14 (1968): 487.
36 Fearon, "Rationalist Explanation for War," 392.
37 Ibid., p. 395. See further Filson, Darren and Werner, Suzanne, "A Bargaining Model of War and Peace: Anticipating the Onset, Duration, and Outcome of War," *American Journal of Political Science* 46, no. 4 (2002): 831–32; Wagner, R. Harrison, "Bargaining and War," *American Journal of Political Science* 44, no. 3 (2000): 472.
38 See Fearon, "Rationalist Explanation for War," 400.
39 The commitment problem refers to "situations in which mutually preferable bargains are unattainable because one or more states would have an incentive to renege on the terms": ibid., 381.
40 See ibid., 401; Powell, Robert, "War as a Commitment Problem," *International Organization* 60, no. 1 (2006): 170.
41 See Fearon, "Rationalist Explanation for War," 403; Powell, Robert, "The Inefficient Use of Power: Costly Conflict with Complete Information," *American Political Science Review* 98, no. 2 (2004): 237.
42 See Glaser, Charles L., "Realists as Optimists. Cooperation as Self-Help," *International Security* 19, no. 3 (1994/95): 50.
43 Fearon, "Rationalist Explanation for War," 405.
44 "None of the findings are counter-intuitive and none could be said to pass the 'grand-mother test', something that any lay person might not reasonably propose after a few minutes of reflection": Lebow, *Why Nations Fight*, 61.
45 See Rengger, Nicolas, "Remember the Aeneid? Why International Relations Theory Should Beware of Greek Gifts," *International Theory* 2, no. 3 (2010): 457–58.
46 See Schweller, Randall L., "The Progressiveness of NeoClassical Realism," in *Progress in International Relations Theory: Appraising the Field*, ed. Elman, Colin and Fendius Elman, Miriam (Cambridge: MIT Press, 2003), 316–17; Van Evera, Stephen, *Causes of War – Power and Roots of Conflict* (Ithaca, NY: Cornell University Press, 1999), 160–65; Walt, Stephen M., *The Origins of Alliances* (Ithaca/London: Cornell University Press, 1987), 17–50; Singer, "The Level-of-Analysis Problem in International Relations," 89–90.
47 Schmidt, "The Enduring Logic of the Three Images," 84 [emphasis added].
48 Levy and Thompson, *The Causes of War*, 19 [emphasis added].
49 See Rhodes, Edward, "Why Nations Fight: Spirit, Identity, and Imagined Community," *Security Studies* 21, no. 2 (2012): 352–53; Singer, "The Level-of-Analysis Problem in International Relations," 87.

50 Lebow, *Why Nations Fight*, 61.
51 See Bleiker, Roland and Hutchinson, Emma, "Fear No More: Emotions and World Politics," *Review of International Studies* no. 34 (2008): 116–19; Crawford, Neta C., "The Passion of World Politics: Proposition on Emotions and Emotional Relationships," *International Security* 24, no. 4 (2000): 117.
52 Wolf, Reinhard, "Der 'emotional turn' in den IB: Plädoyer für eine theoretische Überwindung methodischer Engführung," *Zeitschrift für Außen- und Sicherheitspolitik* 5, no. 4 (2012): 677 [own translation].
53 Hymans, Jacques E., "The Arrival of Psychological Constructivism," *International Theory* 2, no. 3 (2010): 462.
54 See Bleiker and Hutchinson, "Fear No More," 115.
55 See Wolf, "Der 'emotional turn' in den IB," 618–21.
56 Lebow, Richard N., *A Cultural Theory of International Relations* (Cambridge: Cambridge University Press, 2008), 1.
57 Lebow, Richard N., "Motives, Evidence, Identity: Engaging My Critics," *International Theory* 2, no. 3 (2010): 487.
58 Lebow, *A Cultural Theory*, 16.
59 See ibid., 41. See also the criticism by Rennger, "Remember the Aeneid?" 454–60; Patomäki, Heikki, "Back to Renaissance?" *International Relations* 23, no. 1 (2009): 144–59.
60 See Lebow, *A Cultural Theory*, 114; *Why Nations Fight*, 14; Onuf, Nicholas, "Motivation," *International Relations* 23, no. 1 (2009): 143; Suganami, Hidemi, "Man, Culture and the Theory of International Relations," *International Relations* 23, no. 1 (2009): 149. On the selection of these four motives and their relevancy to the field of international relations, see Lebow, Richard N., "Theory, Motives, and Falsification," *International Relations* 23, no. 1 (2009): 168; "Motives, Evidence, Identity," 486–87; Rennger, "Remember the Aeneid?" 457.
61 See Lebow, *A Cultural Theory*, 15–16, 60, 76, 509–12.
62 Welch, David A., "A Cultural Theory Meets Cultures of Theory," *International Theory* 2, no. 3 (2010): 448.
63 See Weber, Max, "The Profession and Vocation of Politics," in *Weber – Political Writings*, ed. Lassmann, Peter and Speirs, Ronald, Cambridge Texts in History of Political Thought (Cambridge: Cambridge University Press, 2003), 365.
64 Lebow, *A Cultural Theory*, 6.
65 See ibid., 61–65; Coker, Christopher, "A Matter of Honor: Ned Lebow, A Cultural Theory of International Relations," *International Relations* 23, no. 1 (2009): 161.
66 See Lebow, *A Cultural Theory*, 5, 61–63, 432; *Why Nations Fight*, 16.
67 Lebow, *A Cultural Theory*, 64.
68 See ibid., 62–68, 144–45.
69 Ibid., 64.
70 Ibid., 65.
71 See ibid., 63; Coker, "A Matter of Honor," 192.
72 "Societies have strong incentives to nurture and channel the spirit. It engenders self-control and sacrifice from which the community as whole prospers": Lebow, *A Cultural Theory*, 62.
73 Ibid., 66.
74 Ibid., 67. In the same way, equal or similar ranks in status also serve as the principal challenge for cooperation among actors in spirit-based worlds.
75 See Morrow, James D., "Eight Questions for a Cultural Theory of International Relations," *International Theory* 2, no. 3 (2010): 477; Lebow, *A Cultural Theory*, 67; Der

Derian, James, "Reading Lebow: A Funny Thing Happened on the Way to the Oracles," *International Theory* 2, no. 3 (2010): 483.

76 Lebow, *A Cultural Theory*, 65. Lebow's conception of "anger" is borrowed from Aristotle, understood here as "response to an *oligoria*, which can be translated as a slight, lessening or belittlement. Such a slight can issue from equals, but provokes even more anger when it comes from an actor who lacks the standing to challenge or insult us": ibid., 69.

77 See Coker, "A Matter of Honor," 162.

78 Lebow, *A Cultural Theory*, 19. "The active pursuit of honor and standing by individuals and states is often costly; vast sums of money have been spent in colonies, national airlines and space exploration, often with no expectations of material net gain. Foolhardy feats in battle, accepting war under unfavorable circumstances or building battle fleets that needlessly provoke a conflict with another major power indicate that honor and standing are not infrequently pursued at significant cost to security": ibid., 509.

79 Ibid., 71.

80 See ibid., 72; Suganami, "Man, Culture and the Theory of International Relations," 151.

81 See Lebow, *A Cultural Theory*, 15, 76. However, Lebow found that many "liberals nevertheless make the mistake of confusing their ideal-type description of an interest-based world with the real world, which is a mixed world in which interest is only one of multiple motives": *Why Nations Fight*, 80.

82 Lebow, *A Cultural Theory*, 431.

83 See Smith, Adam, *Der Wohlstand der Nationen – Eine Untersuchung seiner Natur und seiner Ursachen*, trans. Recktenwald, Horst Claus (München: Deutscher Taschenbuch Verlag, 2005), 10–15.

84 See Lebow, *A Cultural Theory*, 74–75.

85 Ibid., 76.

86 Ibid.; see further Morrow, "Eight Questions for a Cultural Theory of International Relations," 476.

87 See Lebow, *Why Nations Fight*, 168–69.

88 See *A Cultural Theory*, 79.

89 See ibid., 80–81, 512–14.

90 Ibid., 77.

91 See Suganami, "Man, Culture and the Theory of International Relations," 151; Lebow, *A Cultural Theory*, 77.

92 See *A Cultural Theory*, 77, 515.

93 Ibid., 119 [emphasis added].

94 See Mearsheimer, *The Tragedy of Great Power Politics*, 32, 35–36. In a nutshell, it is not the existence of anarchy per se but the emergence of fear in the international system that kicks off the causal logic of Neorealist theory.

95 See Lebow, *A Cultural Theory*, 82–88, 113–16, 559; Wohlforth, William C., "A Matter of Honor," *International Theory* 2, no. 3 (2010); Morrow, "Eight Questions for a Cultural Theory of International Relations," 475. "Disregard ... takes two forms: non-performance of duties (including self-restraint) by high-status actors, and disregard of these status and associated privileges by actors of lesser standing. The two forms of non-compliance are likely to be self-reinforcing and have the effect of weakening hierarchies and ... the orders they instantiate": Lebow, *Why Nations Fight*, 85.

96 See Lebow, Richard N., "Fear, Reason, and Honour: Outlines of a Theory of International Relations," *International Affairs* 82, no. 3 (2006): 447; *A Cultural Theory*, 27, 86,

92. The development of a security dilemma is indicated by the emergence of stereotypical enemy-images, mutual escalations, armament races, alliance formation, military forward deployments, and preemptive action.

97   *A Cultural Theory*, 90. Herein lies the main difference between Lebow's understanding of fear-based worlds and that of Neorealism: it is the breakdown of the *nomos* – not the existence of an anarchical structure – that causes fear among actors and creates the desire to seek security through accumulating power. Moreover, the first actors caught by fear are not the weak ones but the elite of a society, as they see their status and privileges most threatened by the erosion of the *nomos*. See ibid., 89–90; Wohlforth, "A Matter of Honor," 469.

98   Lebow, *A Cultural Theory*, 90.

99   See Suganami, "Man, Culture and the Theory of International Relations," 151.

100 See Lebow, *A Cultural Theory*, 91; *Why Nations Fight*, 87–88.

101 See *A Cultural Theory*, 91; *Why Nations Fight*, 87.

102 *A Cultural Theory*, 32.

103 Weber, Max, "'Objectivity' in Social Science and Social Policy," in *Max Weber: The Methodology of the Social Sciences*, ed. Finch, H.E. and Shils, E.A. (New York: Free Press, 1949), 90–95.

104 See Lebow, *A Cultural Theory*, 95.

105 Ibid., 27 [emphasis added].

106 See ibid., 517; *Why Nations Fight*, 91.

107 "Real worlds are mixes of all three motives, and in those I refer to as honor-based societies, honor is more important for the elite than appetite. The reverse is true for interest-based worlds. For either kind of society to exist in practice, reason must to some degree restrain and educate spirit and appetite alike": *A Cultural Theory*, 162.

108 See "Theory, Motives, and Falsification," 170.

109 See *A Cultural Theory*, 541.

110 See Wohlforth, "A Matter of Honor," 472; Rennger, "Remember the Aeneid?" 455; Lebow, "Motives, Evidence, Identity," 570.

111 *A Cultural Theory*, 66.

112 Ibid., 497.

113 "It is readily apparent ... that people join or support collective enterprises in the expectation of material and emotional reward. They can build self-esteem in the same way, through the accomplishments of nations with which they affiliate": ibid., 62.

114 See ibid., 17; Jervis, Robert, "Fighting for Standing or Standing to Fight?" *Security Studies* 21, no. 2 (2012): 343–44.

115 Lebow, *A Cultural Theory*, 509.

116 See Welch, "A Cultural Theory Meets Cultures of Theory," 447.

117 Lebow, *A Cultural Theory*, 159.

118 Ibid., 19.

119 "War against outsiders, or against non-elite members of one's own society, often has a no-holds-barred quality": ibid., 71.

120 Ibid., 150.

121 George, Alexander L. and Bennett, Andrew, *Case Studies and Theory Development in the Social Sciences* (Cambridge/London: MIT Press, 2005), 91.

122 "Individual policymakers' motives are hard to pin down: the players seldom explain them honestly, nor do they even always understand their own motives": Betts, Richard K., "Strong Arguments, Weak Evidence," *Security Studies* 21, no. 2 (2012): 346.

123 Patomäki, "Back to Renaissance?" 156.

124 Lebow, *A Cultural Theory*, 160.

125 Ibid., 159 [emphasis added].
126 See *Why Nations Fight*, 105. As Richard Betts aptly observes, "documents lie as much as diplomats, especially about motives": Betts, "Strong Arguments, Weak Evidence," 374.
127 See Wohlforth, "A Matter of Honor," 469–70.
128 Betts, "Strong Arguments, Weak Evidence," 374.
129 See Bierling, Stephan, *Geschichte des Irakkries. Der Sturz Saddams und Amerikas Alptraum im Mittleren Osten* (München: Verlag C.H. Beck, 2010), 86–112.
130 Lebow, "Motives, Evidence, Identity," 489.
131 See Betts, "Strong Arguments, Weak Evidence," 347.
132 See George and Bennett, *Case Studies and Theory Development*, 205–06; Van Evera, Stephen, *Guide to Methods for Students of Political Science* (Ithaca/London: Cornell University Press, 1997), 65.
133 George and Bennett, *Case Studies and Theory Development*, 207.
134 George and Bennett define "causal mechanisms" as "ultimately unobservable physical, social, or psychological processes through which agents with causal capacities operate, but only in specific contexts or conditions, to transfer energy, information, or matter to other entities": ibid., 137.
135 Ibid., 183.
136 Ibid., 180; Schimmelfennig, Frank, "Prozessanalyse," in *Methoden der Politikwissenschaft: neuere qualitative und quantitative Auswahlverfahren*, ed. Behnke, Joachim, Gschwend, Thomas, and Schindler, Delia (Baden-Baden: Nomos, 2006), 263–64.
137 George, Alexander L. and Bennett, Andrew, "Process Tracing in Case Study Research." Paper presented at the MacArthur Foundation Workshop on Case Study Methods, Harvard University, Cambridge, October 17–19, 1997, 11.

Bibliography

Betts, Richard K. "Strong Arguments, Weak Evidence." *Security Studies* 21, no. 2 (2012): 345–51.

Bierling, Stephan. *Geschichte des Irakkries. Der Sturz Saddams und Amerikas Alptraum im Mittleren Osten*. München: Verlag C.H. Beck, 2010.

Blainey, Geoffrey. *The Causes of War*. New York: Free Press, 1988.

Bleiker, Roland, and Hutchinson, Emma. "Fear No More: Emotions and World Politics." *Review of International Studies* no. 34 (2008): 115–34.

Brodie, Bernhard. *War and Politics*. London: Macmillan Publishers, 1973.

Buzan, Barry. "The Timeless Wisdom of Realism." In *Internationa2l Theory: Postivism and Beyond*, edited by Steve Smith, Ken Booth, and Marysia Zalewski, 47–65. Cambridge: Cambridge University Press, 1996.

Coker, Christopher. "A Matter of Honor: Ned Lebow, A Cultural Theory of International Relations." *International Relations* 23, no. 1 (2009): 161–65.

Crawford, Neta C. "The Passion of World Politics: Proposition on Emotions and Emotional Relationships." *International Security* 24, no. 4 (2000): 116–36.

Der Derian, James. "Reading Lebow: A Funny Thing Happened on the Way to the Oracles." *International Theory* 2, no. 3 (2010): 481–85.

Dunne, Timmothy. "Realism." In *The Globalization of World Politics: An Introduction to International Relations*, edited by John Baylis and Steve Smith, 109–24. Oxford/New York: Oxford University Press, 1997.

Fearon, James D. "Rationalist Explanation for War." *International Organization* 49, no. 3 (1995): 379–414.

Filson, Darren, and Werner, Suzanne. "A Bargaining Model of War and Peace: Anticipating the Onset, Duration, and Outcome of War." *American Journal of Political Science* 46, no. 4 (2002): 819–37.

Gartzke, Erik. "War is an Error Term." *International Organization* 53, no. 3 (1999): 567–87.

George, Alexander L., and Bennett, Andrew. "Process Tracing in Case Study Research." Paper presented at the MacArthur Foundation Workshop on Case Study Methods, Harvard University, Cambridge, October 17–19, 1997.

George, Alexander L., and Bennett, Andrew. *Case Studies and Theory Development in the Social Sciences*. Cambridge/London: MIT Press, 2005.

Glaser, Charles L. "Realists as Optimists: Cooperation as Self-Help." *International Security* 19, no. 3 (1994/95): 50–90.

Glaser, Charles L. "The Security Dilemma Revisited." *World Politics* 50, no. 1 (1997): 171–201.

Grieco, Joseph M. "Realist International Theory and the Study of World Politics." In *New Thinking in International Relations Theory*, edited by Michael Doyle and G. John Ikenberry, 163–201. Boulder, CO: Westview Press, 1997.

Guilhot, Nicolas. "Politics Between and Beyond Nations: Hans J. Morgenthau's *Politics Among Nations*." In *Classics of International Relations. Essays in Criticism and Appreciation*, edited by Henrik Bliddal, Casper Sylvest, and Peter Wilson, 69–79. London/New York: Routledge, 2013.

Harsanyi, John C. "Games with Incomplete Information Played by 'Bayesian' Players, Part III." *Management Science* no. 14 (1968): 486–502.

Herz, John. "Idealist Internationalism and the Security Dilemma." *World Politics* 2, no. 2 (1950): 171–202.

Hymans, Jacques E. "The Arrival of Psychological Constructivism." *International Theory* 2, no. 3 (2010): 461–67.

Jäger, Thomas, and Beckmann, Rasmus. *Handbuch Kriegstheorien*. Wiesbaden: VS Verlag für Sozialwissenschaften, 2011.

Jervis, Robert. *Perception and Misperception in International Politics*. Princeton, NJ: Princeton University Press, 1976.

Jervis, Robert. "Fighting for Standing or Standing to Fight?" *Security Studies* 21, no. 2 (2012): 336–44.

Lebow, Richard N. "Fear, Reason, and Honour: Outlines of a Theory of International Relations." *International Affairs* 82, no. 3 (2006): 431–48.

Lebow, Richard N. *A Cultural Theory of International Relations*. Cambridge: Cambridge University Press, 2008.

Lebow, Richard N. "Theory, Motives, and Falsification." *International Relations* 23, no. 1 (2009): 167–71.

Lebow, Richard N. "Motives, Evidence, Identity: Engaging My Critics." *International Theory* 2, no. 3 (2010): 486–94.

Lebow, Richard N. *Why Nations Fight: Past and Future Motives for War*. Cambridge: Cambridge University Press, 2010.

Levy, Jack S. "The Causes of War: A Review of Theories and Evidence." In *Behavior, Society and Nuclear War*, edited by Philip E. Tetlock, Jo L. Husbands, Robert Jervis, Paul C. Stern, and Charles Tilly, 209–333. New York: Oxford University Press, 1989.

Levy, Jack S. "Prospect Theory, Rational Choice, and International Relations." *International Studies Quarterly* 41, no. 1 (1997): 87–112.

Levy, Jack S., and Thompson, William R. *The Causes of War*. Chichester: Wiley-Blackwell Publishing, 2010.

Little, Richard. *The Balance of Power in International Relations: Metaphors, Myths and Models*. New York: Cambridge University Press, 2007.

Mearsheimer, John J. *The Tragedy of Great Power Politics*. New York/London: W.W. Norton & Company, 2001.

Mearsheimer, John J. "Power and Fear in Great Power Politics." In *One Hundred Year Commemoration of the Life of Hans Morgenthau (1904–2004)*, edited by G.O. Mazur, 71–88. Oxford: Oxford University Press, 2004.

Morgenthau, Hans J. *Politics among Nations: The Struggle for Power and Peace*. New York: Knopf, 1954.

Morrow, James D. "Eight Questions for a Cultural Theory of International Relations." *International Theory* 2, no. 3 (2010): 475–80.

Niou, Emerson, Ordeshook, Peter, and Rose, Gregory. *The Balance of Power: Stability in the International System*. Cambridge: Cambridge University Press, 1989.

Onuf, Nicholas. "Motivation." *International Relations* 23, no. 1 (2009): 143–48.

Patomäki, Heikki. "Back to Renaissance?" *International Relations* 23, no. 1 (2009): 155–59.

Posen, Barry R. "ESDP and the Structure of World Politics." *The International Spectator: Italian Journal of International Affairs* 39, no. 1 (2004): 5–17.

Powell, Robert. "The Inefficient Use of Power: Costly Conflict with Complete Information." *American Political Science Review* 98, no. 2 (2004): 231–41.

Powell, Robert. "War as a Commitment Problem." *International Organization* 60, no. 1 (2006): 169–203.

Quackenbush, Stephen L. "The Rationality of Rational Choice Theory." *International Interactions* no. 30 (2004): 87–107.

Rengger, Nicolas. "Remember the Aeneid? Why International Relations Theory Should Beware of Greek Gifts." *International Theory* 2, no. 3 (2010): 454–60.

Rhodes, Edward. "Why Nations Fight: Spirit, Identity, and Imagined Community." *Security Studies* 21, no. 2 (2012): 352–61.

Rosecrance, Richard N. "War and Peace." *World Politics* 55, no. 1 (2002): 137–66.

Schimmelfennig, Frank. "Prozessanalyse." In *Methoden der Politikwissenschaft: neuere qualitative und quantitative Auswahlverfahren*, edited by Joachim Behnke, Thomas Gschwend, and Delia Schindler, 263–71. Baden-Baden: Nomos, 2006.

Schmidt, Brian C. "The Enduring Logic of the Three Images: Kenneth Waltz's *Man, the State, and War*." In *Classics of International Relations: Essays in Criticism and Appreciation*, edited by Henrik Bliddal, Casper Sylvest, and Peter Wilson, 80–88. London/New York: Routledge, 2013.

Schweller, Randall L. "The Progressiveness of NeoClassical Realism." In *Progress in International Relations Theory: Appraising the Field*, edited by Colin Elman and Miriam Fendius Elman, 311–47. Cambridge: MIT Press, 2003.

Singer, J. David. "The Level-of-Analysis Problem in International Relations." *World Politics* 14, no. 1 (1961): 77–92.

Smith, Adam. *Der Wohlstand der Nationen – Eine Untersuchung seiner Natur und seiner Ursachen*. Translated by Horst Claus Recktenwald. München: Deutscher Taschenbuch Verlag, 2005.

Snidal, Duncan. "Rational Choice and International Relations." In *Handbook of International Relations*, edited by Walter Carlsnaes, Thomas Risse, and Beth A. Simmons, 73–94. London/Thousand Oaks/New Delhi: Sage Publications, 2006.

Snyder, Jack. *The Myth of Empire: Domestic Politics and International Ambition*. Ithaca/London: Cornell University Press, 1991.

Suganami, Hidemi. "Man, Culture and the Theory of International Relations." *International Relations* 23, no. 1 (2009): 149–54.

Taliaferro, Jeffrey W. "Security Seeking under Anarchy: Defensive Realism Revisited." *International Security* 25, no. 3 (2001): 128–61.

Toft, Peter. "John J. Mearsheimer: An Offensive Realist between Geopolitics and Power." *Journal of International Relations and Development* 8, no. 1 (2005): 381–408.

Van Evera, Stephen. *Guide to Methods for Students of Political Science*. Ithaca/London: Cornell University Press, 1997.

Van Evera, Stephen. *Causes of War – Power and Roots of Conflict*. Ithaca, NY: Cornell University Press, 1999.

Wagner, R. Harrison. "Bargaining and War." *American Journal of Political Science* 44, no. 3 (2000): 469–84.

Walt, Stephen M. *The Origins of Alliances*. Ithaca/London: Cornell University Press, 1987.

Waltz, Kenneth N. *Theory of International Politics*. Reading: Addison-Wesley Publishing Company, 1979.

Waltz, Kenneth N. "The Origins of War in Neorealist Theory." *The Journal of Interdisciplinary History* 18, no. 4 (1988): 615–28.

Waltz, Kenneth N. *Man, State, and War: A Theoretical Analysis*. New York: Columbia University Press, 2001.

Weber, Max. "'Objectivity' in Social Science and Social Policy." In *Max Weber: The Methodology of the Social Sciences*, edited by H.E. Finch and E.A. Shils, 76–112. New York: Free Press, 1949.

Weber, Max. "The Profession and Vocation of Politics." In *Weber – Political Writings*, edited by Peter Lassmann and Ronald Speirs. Cambridge Texts in History of Political Thought, 309–69. Cambridge: Cambridge University Press, 2003.

Welch, David A. "A Cultural Theory Meets Cultures of Theory." *International Theory* 2, no. 3 (2010): 446–53.

Wohlforth, William C. "A Matter of Honor." *International Theory* 2, no. 3 (2010): 468–74.

Wolf, Reinhard. "Der 'emotional turn' in den IB: Plädoyer für eine theoretische Überwindung methodischer Engführung." *Zeitschrift für Außen- und Sicherheitspolitik* 5, no. 4 (2012): 605–24.

Wright, Quincy. *A Study of War*. Chicago, IL: Chicago University Press, 1965.

3 China's Korean War, 1950–1953

On June 25, 1950, the Democratic People's Republic of Korea (DPRK) invaded the Republic of Korea (ROK). But what started as a fratricidal war immediately became internationalized as the United States and the United Nations (UN) rushed to the defense of South Korea. For China, the outbreak of the Korean War came at a more than inconvenient moment, as Beijing then desperately needed a phase of external stability and peace in order to heal the wounds of the Civil War and to solidify the CCP's claim to power.[1] Obviously, the last thing Beijing's leadership then wanted was to become entangled in a major war abroad. Only four months later, however, China launched a massive intervention in order to rescue the North Korean regime from falling prey to the U.S./UN forces. With regard to the desolate state of China's military capabilities at that time, the intervention can be aptly characterized as a spirited attempt without any certainty of success. Why did China commit itself to the Korean War under such unfortunate circumstances? What motivated Beijing to join the fight against a military superpower?

When following the established line of argument, these questions are easily answered: as Beijing's attempts to deter the United States from crossing the 38th parallel had failed and U.S./UN troops rapidly advanced northwards, the Chinese leadership could not be assured that Washington would not expand the war into China in order to reverse the failure it experienced in losing this country to Communism. Consequently, the intervention became imperative to safeguard China's sociopolitical and territorial security.[2] While this explanation is intuitively convincing, I attempt to prove the exact opposite in the following. I argue that the principal causes for the intervention are found in China's social obligations toward the Soviet Union and North Korea, and in Mao Zedong's personal quest for status. For Mao, the Korean War provided the first opportunity to regain China's lost status on the world stage by proving his nation's revolutionary commitment. The intervention was by no means structurally forced upon China, or had become a one-way road Beijing had to take in order to safeguard China's security. Rather, it was primarily the result of Mao's personal enthusiasm to deploy Chinese troops to Korea for the sake of China's international status and glory. I do not claim, however, that security considerations played no role at all. On the contrary, my analysis will show that the 'national security interest' was indeed a deliberately introduced and clear-cut pretext expected to bring the highly reluctant Chinese leadership into line and on the course toward intervention.

Outline of the chapter

This chapter is organized into five main parts. In the first section, I explicate the self-conception and historical mission of the 'New China,' and examine China's entry into the international socialist society and the obligations for the PRC arising therefrom. Following on that, I focus on the triangular relationship between Beijing, Moscow, and Pyongyang and highlight China's reluctant role in the prelude to the Korean War. In the second section, I analyze China's initial reactions to the outbreak of the Korean Crisis and the decision-making process that finally resulted in the Chinese intervention. In doing so, I demonstrate that it was foremost Mao's determination that set the course for China's military engagement abroad: already well before the Inchon landing, Mao had positioned the PLA for battle in Korea, although major parts of China's political and military leadership were then highly reluctant to join the fight against the United States. The third section provides a detailed assessment of the numerous and prohibitive risks the Chinese leadership – and especially Mao – were willing to take in order to realize the intervention. Following on that, China's conduct of warfare and Beijing's position during the cease-fire talks are investigated. The analysis will show that on both 'battlefields' of the Korean War, Chinese troops and negotiators fought for China's status and prestige rather than due to considerations about national security. In this section, I also discuss several arguments for the breakthrough in negotiations during the Panmunjom Round and argue that Stalin, who passed away in March 1953, can be regarded as the key 'victim' of the Korean War, as his death apparently paved the way for Beijing to successfully conclude the armistice and exit the war. Finally, in the concluding section, the findings of my partial analyses are presented and evaluated under the lenses of the two competing explanatory models in order to provide a conclusive answer to the above-stated questions.

Setting the scene

When the first Chinese units crossed the Yalu River on October 18, it was just one month since the PRC had celebrated its first anniversary. However, the principal reasons for China's intervention in Korea are to be found in a period that pre-dates the formal proclamation of the People's Republic. In the following section, I identify these causes by examining the development of the triangular relationship between Pyongyang, Moscow and Beijing during the pre-war period. My analysis unfolds in two parts: in the first, I outline revolutionary China's self-definition, its historical mission, and the formation of Sino-Soviet relations. In the second, I focus on the respective roles of China, the Soviet Union, and North Korea in the run-up to the Korean War.

China enters the socialist society

When the Communist victory in the Chinese Civil War loomed, the CCP's leaders realized that the demanding task of governing the war-shattered country would soon rest on their shoulders.[3] Accordingly, a post-war strategy for the Chinese state became an urgent necessity, including the designation of a foreign-policy line. In order to define China's position in world affairs, the CCP developed a unique interpretation of the contemporary international situation in the so-called 'theory of the intermediate zone.'[4] Although the model acknowledged the existence of a bipolar confrontation, it ascribed China the crucial position in the zone in-between the spheres of influence of the United States and the Soviet Union. As the principal contest of the Cold War would not take place between the two superpowers but rather in this intermediary zone, the CCP's leaders were convinced that China would play the central role in determining its outcome. At its core, the CCP's perspective rested on the conviction that China was not one of many peripheral sites, but the central battleground for the contest between socialism and capitalism–imperialism. However, this also implied that the Chinese revolution was likely to become the target of an imperialist intervention and was thus in need of external protection and support. During the final phase of the Civil War, Mao thus paid increasing attention to relations with the Soviet Union.[5] From an ideological point of view and in congruence with the theory of the intermediate zone, the Soviet Union was the CCP's natural ally. However, the Chinese Communists knew from experience that Stalin was not the most reliable partner: on several occasions, he had utilized Soviet support for the CCP as a bargaining chip *vis-à-vis* the Chinese Nationalist Party (GMD).[6] As Stalin's interest-based *realpolitik* had actively hindered the Chinese revolution, severe frictions between the CCP and Moscow had emerged and an atmosphere of latent distrust characterized the relationship between Mao and Stalin.[7] As a result, the alliance between Moscow and the New China did not necessarily develop out of shared ideological convictions and cannot be regarded as a self-evident consequence of the CCP's takeover in Beijing.

When the CCP's victory was imminent, Stalin finally started to back the winning horse.[8] Mao, on the other hand, felt the need to strengthen the CCP's relations with the Soviet Union in order to acquire desperately needed economic and security assistance. In doing so, Mao was willing not only to overlook Stalin's previous policy shifts but also to prove in advance the CCP's loyalty to Moscow through a series of carefully orchestrated statements and publications.[9] On June 30, 1949 this approach reached its climax with Mao's 'Leaning to One Side' speech, in which the Chairman declared China's intention to join the alliance "with the Soviet Union, with the People's Democracies and with the proletarian and broad masses of the people in all other countries, and form an international united front."[10] Mao's statement was the clearest affirmation of China's desire to enter the international socialist society under the lead of the Soviet Union. For Mao and the CCP leadership, this crucial step had become a logical necessity, because "the Soviet Union was ... the only great power that was willing to back the PRC."[11] In the crucial final phase of China's revolution, and with regard to the upcoming tasks of securing, rebuilding, and governing the New China, taking the Soviet Union's side had become imperative for the CCP in order to carry the revolution to the end.[12]

One aspect mentioned in Mao's statement is of crucial importance: he not only implicitly highlighted China's painful experiences with imperialist powers since the Opium Wars but also explicitly borrowed Sun Yat-sen's well-known dictum, 'unite with those nations that treat us as equals.' In essence, both aspects reveal themselves as two sides of the same coin, as China's colonial period was and is still characterized as the 'century of the unequal treaties.' It is hard to overestimate the impact of this epoch on China's national identity, as it resulted in a collective trauma and a deeply rooted anti-imperialist reflex in China's self-conception that continues to date, and thus definitely influenced the thinking of Mao and the CCP leadership:

> China's modern exchanges with the West were, to Mao and his comrades, most humiliating and painful. China had lost its historical glory as a result of Western incursion after the 1840 Opium War. [The] Western powers had never treated China equally in modern history.[13]

However, one of the imperialist powers that had significantly contributed to the Middle Kingdom's sinking into insignificance had been Czarist Russia. With regard to the Soviet Union as its successor, the Chinese leadership expected that history would not be repeated: the New China was not about to become a Soviet satellite, even though Beijing acknowledged the Soviet lead in the world revolutionary movement. The CCP leadership, and particularly Mao, were thus extremely sensitive about avoiding being treated by Stalin as 'little brothers.' As China now "had stood up,"[14] it would no longer tolerate any unequal or humiliating treatment.[15]

The leaders of the New China were thus willingly accepting their historical and cultural heritage: layers of Marxism–Leninism were obviously unable to replace the continuation of the Sino-centric worldview as a fundamental part of China's national identity. Also, the desire to restore China's rightful status as Asia's 'Middle Kingdom' was deeply rooted in the self-conception of the Chinese revolution: "the Communist most wanted to restore what they perceived as China's rightful place in the world. This article of faith rested on the conviction that China was unique, its countless people destined for world power status."[16] In order to fulfill this historic mission, the New China had to carry the revolution to the end, and in doing so China entered the international socialist society.[17]

Mao's speech definitely set the basic tone for the further course of the Sino-Soviet relationship. During the subsequent meeting between Liu Shaoqi and Stalin, the Soviet leader honored the CCP's strategic decision, apologized for having failed to assist the CCP in the Civil War, and promised to immediately recognize the PRC after its proclamation.[18] Liu's visit also resulted in another highly important outcome, in Stalin's offer to Beijing of its own sphere of responsibility: "while the Soviet Union would remain the center of the international proletarian revolution, the promotion of Eastern revolution would become primarily China's duty."[19] By acknowledging the CCP's leading role in Asia and by dedicating to the New China its own sphere of influence, Stalin fulfilled one of Mao's most long-standing desires. From the Chinese perspective, Stalin had thereby also confirmed that he would from now on treat China not only as equal, but as the Soviet Union's primary strategic partner.[20] This implied a major Soviet reevaluation of China's international status.

The bilateral alliance was formalized with the conclusion of the 'Sino-Soviet Treaty of Friendship, Alliance and Mutual Assistance' during Mao's following visit to Moscow. After the signing ceremony, Mao appeared visibly relieved: he had managed to gain Stalin's support for the Chinese revolution and had acquired the

Soviet security guarantees that would allow China to take a desperately needed "breathing spell of three to five years to restore its economy to the pre-war level and to stabilize the nation"[21] in order to restore "the sovereignty and interests that China had lost in 1945."[22] Although the outcome of Mao's visit was thus highly successful, various episodes demonstrate there was a rather uncomfortable mood to the meetings between the two giants of the socialist bloc. Stalin and Mao obviously could not overcome their troubled relationship of the past, as both showed latent distrust and used ambiguity.[23] Probably most importantly, both seemed to be highly sensitive regarding issues of respect and relative standing.[24] Even though a clear-cut ordering of ranks between Stalin and Mao was never laid out, the Soviet leader occasionally pulled rank on Mao.[25] For the Chairman, this indicated that the relationship between Stalin and himself still resembled more that of a teacher and student.[26] Against this background, it must have been highly satisfactory for Mao to enjoy standing ovations at Stalin's birthday celebration.[27] On this very special evening, the assembled socialist leaders from all over the world honored Mao for his revolutionary achievements and paid tribute for adding the weight of China to the socialist bloc – a "triumph that could be called the second October Revolution."[28] Inside the socialist society, it seemed as if the young Chinese state had already managed to successfully restore its rightful place as Asia's 'Red Middle Kingdom.'

While visiting Moscow, Mao made two wide-ranging foreign-policy decisions: Beijing started to provide military assistance to the Viet Minh and repatriated around 14,000 ethnic-Korean PLA soldiers to North Korea.[29] Six months later, these soldiers would form the vanguard of the North's invasion force.[30] When viewed against the background of the just agreed-upon Sino-Soviet burden-sharing on the promotion of world revolution, two conclusions can be drawn from this. First, Beijing took its regional obligations seriously and started to support the revolutionary movements in Asia. Second, it appears very likely that Kim Il-sung's invasion plans had been subject to the Mao–Stalin deliberations.

Kim Il-sung's military ambitions between Beijing and Moscow

In 1948, North Korea's leader, Kim Il-sung, found himself blessed with the military capabilities to realize his long-harbored ambition of unifying the divided peninsula under his banner: the Korean People's Army (KPA) could draw on vast amounts of military hardware that had been left behind after the Japanese and Soviet withdrawal.[31] But before he could go on and launch his invasion, Kim first needed Stalin's approval.[32] However, the Soviet leader was greatly reluctant to grant his permission, as he "feared any conflict that might provoke an American confrontation with the Soviet Union."[33] As Stalin categorically rejected Kim's appeals, the North Korean leader then turned to Mao for support.[34]

The Chinese Communists had benefited extensively from the support they had received from their Korean comrades in the past. During the Civil War, North Korea had functioned as a vital sanctuary and supply hub for the PLA. More than one hundred thousand ethnic Koreans had manned three of the finest PLA divisions, and Pyongyang had provided Mao's troops with more than 2,000 railway cars of military supplies.[35] Against this background, it was no surprise that Kim now expected China's solidarity in the unification of Korea, and deeply resented Beijing's refusal to grant assistance. While Mao's attitude might have been slightly more enthusiastic, he nonetheless shared Stalin's worries about the possibility of U.S. intervention in Korea.[36] Kim thus learned that both of his patrons were not in favor of his invasion. Instead, Mao and Stalin shared a common interest in preserving peace on the Korean Peninsula.[37] For both, the major threat to this interest came not from Kim but from the U.S.-sponsored ROK.[38] For Moscow and Beijing, it thus appeared essential to provide the DPRK with enough military power to deter the anticipated South Korean offensive while at the same time delicately balancing the North's offensive potential to prevent Kim from launching his own invasion.[39] By keeping North Korea's forces on a short leash and by coordinating their positions, Stalin and Mao were able to exercise control over Kim's belligerent intentions: both repeatedly warned Kim off undertaking offensive action in the "near future because the world conditions were unfavorable."[40]

The turning point in Stalin's thinking came in the spring of 1950, after Mao's visit and the successful conclusion of the Sino-Soviet alliance.[41] According to the memoirs of Nikita Khrushchev and of Mao's secretary Shu Zhi, Stalin had been particularly interested in Mao's opinion on the likelihood of U.S. intervention in a Korean civil war.[42] While Mao put forward the opinion that Washington might not interfere since the war would be an internal matter, he nonetheless emphasized that the Korean comrades needed to take the possibility of a limited intervention into account. Mao's judgment mirrored the PLA General Staff's contemporary assessment of U.S. capabilities and strategic intentions, resting particularly on the broad demobilization of U.S. troops, the public exclusion of Taiwan and Korea from the U.S. defense perimeter, and Washington's noninterference in China's civil war. With regard to the PLA's upcoming Taiwan campaign, at that point the PLA still calculated that a limited U.S. military intervention was a possible eventuality. Against this background, it seems highly unlikely that Mao gave Stalin an unconditional go-ahead on the Korean issue.[43]

Even so, Stalin's position on Kim's war plans fundamentally changed in the aftermath of Mao's visit, and in April 1950 the Soviet leader eventually gave the green light to the North's offensive.[44] However, he emphasized three crucial points: first, Kim should not expect more than covert support from the Soviet Union; second, that "China was now first among equals within the revolutionary movement in Asia"[45] – implying that Kim also needed Beijing's approval; third, and most importantly, the Soviet Union would not rescue Kim if his invasion failed. Stalin vividly highlighted that "[i]f you should get kicked in the teeth, I shall not lift a finger. You have to ask Mao for all the help."[46] Thereby, Stalin relieved the Soviet Union from the risks and accountabilities associated with Kim's military adventure while simultaneously maneuvering the Chinese – in accordance with Sino-Soviet burden-sharing – into the position of bearing these responsibilities.[47]

When Kim arrived in Beijing in mid-May 1950, the Chinese leadership was greatly surprised about the Soviet approval for Kim's war. As Stalin had neglected to inform Beijing of his change of mind, an astonished Zhou Enlai first had to call the Soviet Embassy and ask for clarification. At the moment that Kim's message was confirmed, Beijing's leverage reduced considerably, and "Mao had no choice but to support Moscow's new position."[48] After the meeting, an enthusiastic Kim explained to the Soviet ambassador that all relevant issues had been agreed upon by the Chinese side. "It is imaginable how complacent Kim was and how embarrassed Mao must have felt at this moment."[49] The Stalin–Kim collaboration confronted the Chinese leadership with a more-than-awkward *fait accompli*. Henceforth, Beijing was excluded from the operational planning of the North Korean invasion: neither Stalin nor Kim "did … in the slightest way reveal details of the war plans to Mao."[50] Tellingly, the Chinese leadership learned about the onset of the Korean War through media reports, as their comrades had felt no need to inform Beijing beforehand.

Interim conclusion: honor and obligations

Ideological reasons played only a subordinate role in China's decision to enter the international socialist society by leaning toward the side of the Soviet Union. Rather, the PRC's strategic orientation at the onset of the Cold War was influenced by a mélange of China's material needs and emotional desires: on the one hand, China was in desperate need of external assistance and protection, while on the other, the revolutionary self-conception of the New China and its historical mission were deeply linked by the quest to restore its formerly lost status as Asia's 'Middle Kingdom.' By entering the international socialist society, Beijing was able to realize both dimensions: the Soviet Union granted China assistance and security, while the society's members paid tribute to China's outstanding contributions for the common cause. Most importantly, the Soviet Union, as the society's lead nation, also honored China's revolutionary contributions by dedicating to the People's Republic its own sphere of responsibility and influence. In this way, China was promoted into the elite of the socialist international society. China's new status, however, also came along with new obligations. Furthermore, there existed another set of obligations between Beijing and Pyongyang, as the North Koreans had crucially contributed to the success of the Chinese revolution in the past. For Kim, it was thus reasonable to expect Mao's support for his military invasion – but Beijing then prioritized parochial interests over reciprocal solidarity. Nevertheless, after the onset of the Korean War, Mao was more eager to fulfill both China's internationalist obligations and those toward North Korea. As I will show in the next section, China's parochial interests then no longer played a determining role.

On the course to intervention

For the PRC, the Korean War could not have erupted at a more inconvenient point in time, as the crisis profoundly collided with China's post-Civil War agenda. Beijing faced at least three domestic challenges. First, even though the CCP had won the Civil War, its claim to power had yet to be solidified.[51] Second, this imperatively required rebuilding the national economy, as the overall situation had then become so critical that it was "even shaking the basis of people's state power in the cities."[52] Third, in order to realize both objectives, Beijing had to prioritize domestic reconstruction over military spending, and thus ordered the demobilization of 1.5 million troops in April 1950.[53] In order to realize all three tasks simultaneously, however, China was in desperate need of a phase of external stability.[54] In sum, Beijing was comprehensively preoccupied with domestic issues and had neither anticipated nor could afford to become militarily engaged abroad. When viewed from an interest-based perspective, and adding the fact that Moscow and Pyongyang had felt no need to inform Beijing about their joint military adventure in detail beforehand, China would have had every reason to follow Stalin's example and stay out of the Korean War.[55]

Mao once remarked that "'going to Korea was decided by one man and a half': by himself and Zhou Enlai."[56] Indeed, there is little to question this assessment. Shortly after the outbreak of the war, the two most senior Chinese leaders set in motion a process that eventually resulted in the Chinese intervention. In less than three weeks, the Mao–Zhou collaboration had accomplished three crucial requirements for a military intervention: the reorientation of China's military force posture, the organization of an actual intervention capability, and an astonishingly early commitment to the Soviet Union to deploy Chinese troops to Korea. All these steps were implemented well before the Inchon landing and the onset of formal decision-making. The pace and extent of China's strategic reorientation appear the more remarkable as, at that point in time, the North Korean forces were still advancing southward and the Chinese leadership was preoccupied with domestic issues. Even so, the Chairman had already set the course toward a Chinese intervention in Korea.

China's early commitment

In a meeting with the Soviet ambassador in Beijing on July 2, Zhou Enlai stated that "if the United States crossed the 38th parallel, Chinese troops would enter the war disguised as North Korean soldiers and that, for this purpose, China had already assembled three armies (120,000 troops) near Shenyang."[57] Besides its explosive content, this statement appears highly remarkable for two more reasons: the Chinese Premier made this commitment just one week after the outbreak of war. At that point, Beijing had neither received any information on the battlefield situation nor had assembled three armies in the Northeast, and there existed no political decision to do so.[58] As "the leadership did not convene decision-making meetings on new military deployments aimed at Korea until two weeks after the outbreak of the war,"[59] Zhou's early commitment was thus not backed by a formal decision. Rather, it seems as if the commitment had its roots in a shared conviction on the part of Zhou and Mao. This argument is supported by the observation that during the further course of China's handling of the Korean Crisis, Mao and Zhou not only repeatedly highlighted the imperative of being prepared to enter the war, but also never got tired of emphasizing the necessity to do so. As early as August 4, more than a month before the Inchon landing, Mao declared in the CCP Politburo: "We should not fail to assist the Koreans. We must lend them our hands, in the form of sending our military volunteers there."[60] Apparently, Mao had made his decision already at this early stage of the war, and the Chairman was thus determined to lead China into the Korean War. Now, it was up to Zhou Enlai to implement Mao's determination in the PRC's decision-making process.

NEBDA – assembling an intervention force

Zhou's role as facilitator is particularly well observable in the second step that eventually enabled the Chinese intervention: the reorientation of the PLA's force posture toward the Korean theater. With the final stages of the Civil War taking place in the South and Southwest, China's military capabilities in the Northeast were notably weak.[61] This changed around two weeks after the outbreak of the Korean War, when the Chinese leadership as a collective focused for the first time on the situation in Korea and its implications for the PRC.[62] At the beginning of the conference, it was Zhou who "conveyed to the participants Mao's analysis of the situation which emphasized that it was necessary to establish a 'North-east Border Defense Army', so that 'in case we needed to enter the war we would be prepared.'"[63] As this proposal was approved, the first collective decision of the Chinese leadership in response to the onset of the Korean War established the Northeast Border Defense Army (NEBDA). The CMC immediately transferred a total of four armies, three artillery divisions, and three air-defense corps to China's Northeast.[64] In doing so, Beijing substantially reoriented China's military focal point toward Korea.

Even though its designation as a 'border defense army' might suggest that NEBDA's primary mission was a defensive one, its establishment orders disclosed a twofold objective: "to safeguard the North-east region and assist North Korea if necessary."[65] 'Assisting North Korea' was thus an integral component of NEBDA's purpose from its establishment, and there is good reason to argue that this mission was not only the secondary objective of this force dispositive: as the organizational arrangements and the enormous logistical preparations indicate, Beijing created a genuine intervention capability with NEBDA.

Immediately after the orders had been issued, the Northeastern military regions began to store massive amounts of military material: the operative reserves for NEBDA consisted of food supplies for three months, fuel for six months, and 1,600 tons of ammunition. The PLA medical service set up field hospitals for more than 100,000 patients.[66] Moreover, China assembled the best combat units the PLA could muster. The first units assigned to NEBDA were battle-hardened PLA armies of the strategic reserve which, in contrast to other units, had undergone constant combat training and were thus prepared to join the fight at short notice. The number of troops also increased from 250,000 to 700,000 in late August.[67] These forces were reinforced with heavy weapons and "underwent intensive combat training with the U.S. Army as their postulated enemy."[68] With regard to this massive build-up of troops, and when taking the enormous logistical preparations into account, Chen Jian reaches the conclusion that these forces had "not only [been assembled] for battles on the Chinese–Korean border areas but also for possible military operations in Korea."[69] Apparently, Beijing anticipated large-scale engagements with the enemy, including a massive intervention, rather than skirmishes at the border. Remarkably, there is no reference in the available literature to NEBDA troops actually under-taking any measures to fortify the border region, which further reinforces the conclusion that this force dispositive was created under the premise that Chinese troops would undertake combat operations in Korea sooner or later.[70] For Mao, this prospect had then already materialized. On August 5, he ordered that the NEBDA units "should complete preparations ... and await an order to deploy into battle,"[71] possibly in early September. It needs to be emphasized once more that at this point in time, the Inchon landing had not taken place, nor did there exist any formal decision as to whether to commit troops to Korea or not. Still, the KPA was victoriously rushing southwards and was about to condense the U.S./UN forces in the Pusan Perimeter. Nonetheless, Mao had then already assembled a combat-ready intervention capability.

The tide changes: constructing an intervention with Chinese characteristics

On September 15, the U.S. X Corps landed at Inchon. It recaptured Seoul in only a few days, and opened up a second frontline at the rear of the KPA forces. The tide of the battle began to turn swiftly. For the Chinese leaders, these developments did not come as a genuine surprise, because the PLA General Staff had anticipated a possible U.S. amphibious operation at Inchon at least since August 1950, and had warned Pyongyang to prepare for this contingency.[72] As the PLA assessments had foreseen a priori, the successful landing at Inchon changed the "entire situation of the Korean War ... immediately in the enemy's favor."[73]

For Moscow, however, Inchon came as a real shock. Only days after the landing, Stalin wrote off his satellite Kim. Stalin "believed that the United Nations force's advance could in no way be checked unless the Soviet Union directly intervened. However, that was the last thing he wished to do."[74] But the Soviet leader did not want to lose his client either. Accordingly, he turned to China: only two days after the landing had taken place, Stalin asked Mao if China was ready to commit troops to Korea in order to rescue Kim.[75] However, although the Soviet leader went on to outline the urgency of a Chinese intervention by emphasizing that the enemy forces "would approach the Yalu River and pose a direct threat to Manchuria,"[76] he had to show patience, as Mao would not provide him with an answer for more than 14 days.

These two weeks of reprieve appear highly remarkable, as the Inchon landing and its subsequent implications would have presented China with substantial reason to intervene. The KPA's deteriorating situation also turned out to have profoundly negative effects for the People's Republic: as Stalin correctly emphasized, a threat to China's Northeast then started to materialize as the combat zone moved north.[77] In addition, the timeframe for an effective Chinese intervention was swiftly closing – or, according to U.S. military intelligence reports, had already closed.[78] Finally, one of the revolutionary movements in Asia, which China had taken over the responsibility of safeguarding, was now about to fall prey to the imperialist forces.[79] Beijing's leadership was definitely aware of the deteriorating situation in Korea and the subsequent imperative to intervene. Shortly after Inchon, Mao emphasized in a letter to Gao Gang that China "had no choice but to enter the conflict and that war preparations needed to be further accelerated."[80] However, even though the Inchon landing should have immediately triggered an intervention, China's forces would not cross the Yalu River for the time being.

Why did Mao wait two more weeks before introducing his conclusion on the necessity to intervene in the formal decision-making process? The question gains even more in significance as the majority of China's political and military leaders harbored serious reservations about a military engagement in Korea.[81] Even though Mao held an outstanding position inside the leadership, he could not dictate his conclusion as a decision but had to convince his colleagues in deliberations, which would take additional time.[82]

For sure, the delay may be explained by the fact that the Chinese troops were not yet fully prepared to enter a war. Since the establishment of NEBDA, the Chinese leadership had learned that the troops' state of preparedness constantly lagged behind the schedule that had been set.[83] However, the following observations profoundly counter this line of argument. First, an immediate Chinese intervention would have resulted in a much more promising overall battlefield situation for the Communist forces, as the KPA was not yet in the state of serious disintegration that was the case when China decided to enter the war in mid-October.[84] Second, although not all Chinese forces may have been fully prepared, the elite divisions that had been earmarked for the Taiwan campaign definitely commanded a level of combat-readiness that would have allowed them to effectively join the battle.[85] Their instant deployment would have immediately strengthened North Korea's defense and might also have stopped the U.S./UN forces farther south of the Yalu.[86] Third, exactly two weeks later, Mao did not hesitate to send his troops to battle "ahead of the original schedule"[87] and thus before all NEBDA units could complete their preparations. When the Chinese forces eventually entered Korea, their level of combat-readiness, state of weaponry, and morale had not been noticeably improved.

Besides the obvious imperative of these operative considerations to intervene at an early stage, it remains highly puzzling why Mao did not set the decision-making process in motion immediately after Inchon, especially as the Chinese assessments had concluded a priori that the landing would result in a breakdown of North Korea's defense capacities. In order to make sense of this problem, I argue that Mao may have intentionally waited out the crucial time-span of two weeks in order to obtain the conditions for what could be regarded as a just intervention in the internal affairs of another socialist country: such an intervention with 'Chinese characteristics' apparently required a *causa iusta* as an initial, as well as the *legitima auctoritas* to fight.

The just cause: waiting for the enemy to cross the 38th parallel

Although Inchon was a major blow to the KPA, the survival of North Korea was not yet comprehensively endangered, as the fighting was still limited to areas south of the 38th parallel. As Zhou had explicitly confirmed to the Soviet ambassador shortly after the outbreak of the Korean War, the enemy's crossing of the 38th parallel was the red line for a Chinese intervention.[88] This action would go well beyond the restoration of the status quo ante bellum and would threaten the existence of an Asian socialist regime, which China had taken the responsibility to safeguard.

At least since August 1950, the criticality of this line, as well as the implications of its crossing, had been made known to the enemy as well.[89] In a series of warnings to the United States via the Indian Embassy and in various statements and publications, Beijing unmistakably declared that China would intervene militarily if U.S. troops crossed the parallel.[90] These warnings were further underlined by China's military build-up along the Sino-North Korean border, for which no significant camouflaging attempts were made. Finally, after President Truman ordered U.S. troops to attack northward of the 38th parallel, Zhou Enlai issued China's final and most explicit warning on October 2: "If the U.S. troops [cross the parallel], we cannot sit by idly and remain indifferent. We will intervene."[91] Due to its unambiguous formulation, it seems almost impossible to misinterpret the content of this warning. The U.S. State Department, however, dismissed Zhou's statement as a bluff, stating that the Chinese Prime Minister was not the authorized spokesperson of the PRC.[92] When the first U.S. forces then crossed the demarcation on October 8, Mao issued the operative order for the intervention.[93] In Mao's eyes, the aforementioned implications of an U.S./UN crossing of the 38th parallel apparently culminated in a necessary condition for China's intervention. It seems important to note that the advance of ROK troops north of the parallel was accepted by Beijing, as the Chinese leadership regarded the Korean War primarily as an inner Korean affair.[94]

The right to intervene: Kim's personal request

The second condition that needed to be in place before a Chinese intervention could occur was – in accordance with international law and the more relevant Chinese principle of noninterference[95] – the legitimation to unilaterally intervene in the Korean War. "Since its founding in 1949, the PRC's foreign policy has been characterized ... by adherence to a rigid conception of state sovereignty and steadfast insistence on the principle of noninterference in other states' internal affairs."[96] The PRC's orthodoxy in matters of sovereignty and noninterference can only be understood with reference to China's traumatic historical experiences with foreign interference in the Middle Kingdom's internal affairs, which had resulted in the demise of China's power, status, and glory. This orthodoxy held true from the first day of the People's Republic, as the Communist regime claimed its legitimacy on the basis that Mao and his comrades had successfully stopped foreign interference. Against this background, it seems more than appropriate to argue that in order to honor this fundamental principle, Mao needed a permissive request by Pyongyang before Chinese troops could cross the Yalu.

Shortly after Inchon, such a request had already reached Beijing, as two high-ranking North Korean functionaries asked China to deploy troops to Korea.[97] However, the Chinese leadership was well aware that the two delegates belonged to the pro-Chinese faction inside the Korean Workers' Party (KWP) that opposed Kim's pro-Soviet course.[98] If Mao had accepted this request, he would have interfered in the internal affairs of the DPRK by strengthening the position of the pro-China faction. When balancing the value of the principle against the strategic advantages of an early Chinese entry in the Korean War, it seems as honoring the principle weighed more heavily for Mao. Accordingly, "[w]ithout Kim's invitation, Chinese leaders preferred not to go ahead."[99]

The decision: an intervention by invitation

Only after Kim's personal request for a Chinese intervention finally reached Beijing, on October 1, did Mao set the decision-making process in motion.[100] The next day, the Chairman opened a meeting of the enlarged CCP Politburo by declaring that

> the question now is not whether we should send troops to Korea or not, but how fast we can do this. ... Today, we will discuss two urgent questions – when should our troops enter Korea and who should be the commander.[101]

For him, the issue was already a done deal: China would send troops and they should be ready to enter Korea in less than two weeks.[102]

Even though the participants reached a fragile consensus in support of Mao's assessment, the meeting nonetheless revealed that a number of key leaders still harbored strong reservations on the wisdom of intervening: "the decision to fight was not without controversy, as the next few days would reveal."[103] For example, Marshal Lin Biao, one of China's most respected military leaders, consistently raised serious doubts about a Chinese involvement in Korea. His outspoken opposition and profound reservations culminated in a courageous statement before the CMC four days later: "I have no certainty of success [in fighting the highly modernized and nuclear-armed U.S. army]. The central leaders should consider this with great care."[104] With this statement, Lin was at least repeating the concerns of many other civilian and military leaders: the sobering prospect of having to fight a nuclear-armed superpower. Other prominent opponents to an intervention were Gao Gang and Marshal Nie Rongzhen, chief of the PLA's General Staff. While Gao emphasized the urgent need for a period of peace for China's economic and social recovery, Nie probably made the strongest point against a proactive engagement by arguing that "[i]t would be better not to fight this war as long as it was not absolutely necessary."[105]

The October 2 decision to deploy troops thus had merely provisional character, as it rested on a more than unsound basis of consent. Nevertheless, Mao informed Stalin of this outcome on the same day.[106] As the Chairman highlighted in his cable, Beijing was willing to fulfill the task the Soviet leaders had assigned to China: in order to safeguard a revolutionary movement in Asia, Mao was willingly accepting waging war against the United States.

Bringing the leadership into line: the "national security interest"

On October 4, Mao called in another leadership meeting, in which the Chairman asked his colleagues to state their opinions on the Politburo's decision of October 2. "Following Mao's call, most people attending the meeting expressed their reservations about the decision to enter the war"[107] by pointing out internal political and economic challenges, the PLA's material inferiority, and that Taiwan would pose the more imminent threat to China's security.[108] In the end, the collective opinion was brought forward that it would be "best to postpone the intervention for a few years so that China could properly prepare itself."[109] Mao, who listened carefully to these arguments, used his final remark to aim at the moral consciences and the revolutionary spirit of his colleagues: "What you have said sounds reasonable. But it would be shameful for us to stand by seeing our neighbors in perilous danger without offering any help."[110] If China decided to just stand idly by, "we [would] feel terrible inside, no matter what we may pretend."[111] Adding to this, China's reputation would be heavily damaged – not to think of the consequences if China were to be in need of help. If the Chinese leadership now shied from intervention because of its risks, "[i]nternationalism would be empty talk."[112]

Before the meeting resumed the next day, Mao invited Peng Dehuai to a private conversation. Although Mao had anticipated criticism, he apparently felt the need to convince a key person of the correctness of his course toward intervention. In Mao's eyes, this person was General Peng, who had an excellent reputation as commander in battle and military strategist. His judgment would carry weight.[113] Moreover, Peng had openly stated his reservations about an intervention, and was known for being straightforward and frank – if Mao could bring the general into line, the Politburo would surely follow.[114] As it turned out, Mao did not need a lot of persuasion: Peng swiftly arrived at the conclusion that the Chairman's decision was correct as it "combined the ideal of internationalism with considerations of patriotism, but was also crucial to the safety of China's Northeastern border."[115] In return, the Chairman honored the general's loyalty by offering him command over the Chinese forces in Korea, and "a relieved Mao asked Peng to express his opinion to the politburo."[116] As Mao had anticipated, Peng's change of mind generated the desired effect inside the Chinese leadership. To Mao's highlighting, the previous day, of China's socialist obligation to intervene, Peng now added the imperative of the national security interest:

> If [we] allow the enemy to occupy the entire Korean peninsula, the threat to our country is very great. In the past, when the Japanese invaded China, they used Korea as springboard. ... We cannot overlook this lesson of history. We must fight the enemy now.[117]

This statement turned the course of the discussion and a strong consensus in favor of the intervention emerged among the leaders.[118]

As the course of the deliberations shows, at first, the majority of the Chinese leaders, and even Peng, had not been – or, at least, had not fully been – convinced of the necessity to intervene. A military involvement in Korea was assessed as running contra to China's national interests, and 'proletarian solidarity,' as Andrew Scobell observes, was apparently no sufficient reason to dispose China toward intervention.[119] Only when Mao had added the highly esteemed voice of Peng Dehuai – and thereby brought the rationale for China's intervention down to the level of "the defense of the motherland"[120] – did the situation change in his favor. Peng's enlightenment, however, came literally overnight, and there is profound reason to argue that the general was not wholeheartedly convinced, as "Peng clearly had serious reservations about the [intervention] and agonized over his decision."[121] In view of that, the national security interest's introduction into the decision-making process by a high-ranking military expert can primarily be regarded as part of Mao's approach to overcome the opposition to the intervention that had formed inside the Chinese leadership.[122]

The decision stands firm

When the first U.S. units crossed the 38th parallel on October 8, Mao issued the order to send Chinese troops to Korea, and NEBDA became the Chinese People Volunteers (CPV). While the soldiers undertook the final preparations for entering Korea, the decision to intervene was suddenly challenged by two major developments. Externally, Beijing was confronted with Stalin's reneging on his promise of Soviet air cover for the CPV in Korea. As I will outline in more detail in the following section, this development resulted in an immediate full stop to the intervention and forced Mao to reconsider China's battle-plan. Internally, Chinese military leaders, and especially the CPV unit commanders, became increasingly concerned: the deteriorating situation of the North Korean troops, the swift and seemingly unstoppable advance of the U.S./UN forces, and the crystallizing lack of Soviet support had evidently cooled their fighting spirit. On October 17, these concerns materialized in a telegram in which the commanders proposed postponing the intervention.[123] In other words, just two days before the intervention was scheduled, Mao had to learn that the CPV's top-level officers ultimately questioned the wisdom and the necessity of intervention.

Both problematic developments resulted in two additional rounds of decision-making. But in contrast to the previous leadership meetings, the decisions were now exclusively made by Mao and executed by Zhou Enlai and Peng Dehuai. As all three actors were in favor of the intervention, the course for it remained unchanged, and emerging challenges and risks were being blanked out rather than seriously considered. Zhou had been a strong proponent of intervention from the outset. During the decision-making in the Politburo, he had fought the turf battles for Mao, giving the paramount leader the chance to remain on the sidelines and avoid criticism.[124] Peng, in contrast, can be regarded as the tragic figure in Mao's Korean War drama. The general had harbored serious doubts regarding the necessity to intervene, and continued to do so even after being appointed as CPV commander.[125] He later characterized himself as a soldier who did not know how to say 'no.'[126] Consequently, after having received the orders from his commander-in-chief, Peng performed his task as Mao's key military person in the Politburo and in the PLA. The Chairman apparently wanted the intervention regardless of costs and risks.[127] After learning that the Soviets had denied the vital air support for the CPV and that the morale of his commanders had broken down, he kept to his decision.[128] Mao dominated the Politburo discussions of October 11 and October 18, silenced critical voices, downgraded the negative developments, and ignored implicated risks.[129] Finally, he answered the CPV commanders' telegram by issuing the final orders for the intervention on October 18. Now, it was on Peng to lead his men into Korea, and when the troops crossed the Yalu River that night, the Chairman, "for the first time in many days … had a sound sleep."[130]

China's Korean War: assessing the risks

Mao's sound sleep appears particularly surprising when considering the enormous risks that emerged from China's intervention. For sure, waging a war is never free of risk, but the prospect of a direct face-off with the United States must have appeared as an extremely adventurous endeavor prima facie: with its deficient capabilities, the PRC seemed hardly capable of posing a serious challenge to the principal military superpower of that time.[131] China's intervention thus incorporated a high probability of military failure or even a crushing defeat.[132] The course of the Korean War proves this pessimistic assessment strikingly wrong. However, *ex post* results seldom reflect a priori judgments: in order to assess the latter, I focus on the run-up to the intervention and analyze how the Chinese leadership anticipated, evaluated, and handled emerging risks. I focus on three crucial factors for the success of the intervention (ground forces, air power, and operative planning), trace these indicators over the decision-making process, and demonstrate that the Chinese leadership was evidently aware of a number of substantial and even prohibitive risks, which further mounted shortly before the intervention. Even so, their accumulation did not affect Beijing's course toward a military engagement in Korea. In view of that, the conclusion suggests itself that China's leadership was acting in a highly risk-taking manner when entering the Korean War.

The state of combat-readiness of China's ground forces

As the PLA had emerged as a revolutionary peasant army under civil-war conditions and thus lacked an industrial base, the principal method of acquiring weaponry and supplies had consisted in capturing them from the enemy. With the end of the Civil War, however, these sources of supply had run dry. Consequently, Beijing approached the Soviet Union to equip its troops for the upcoming Taiwan campaign.[133] The outbreak of the Korean War and the mounting prospect of direct Chinese involvement then raised the importance of substantial Soviet supplies to cruciality: the largely unsuccessful campaigns against GMD-controlled islands of the previous year had already revealed to the Chinese leadership many of the poorly equipped PLA's shortcomings and problems.[134] Now, however, the PLA was about to face an even more powerful enemy.

Throughout the entire decision-making process, China's leaders thus signaled to Moscow the imperative to improve the CPV's combat capacity by equipping the intervention force with modern weaponry, sufficient ammunition, and supplies. From Beijing's perspective, the Soviet Union's military assistance constituted a basic requirement for China to enter the Korean War: as Mao unambiguously emphasized in a telegram to Stalin in October, without Soviet weaponry, the Chinese would not fight.[135] While Moscow assured Beijing it would meet the Chinese demands, Soviet military assistance materialized much more slowly than promised: when the CPV entered Korea in mid-October, the troops had not yet received the modern Soviet weaponry but were still mainly equipped with the same mix of arms they had used in the Civil War.[136] In terms of heavy weaponry and air support, the Chinese infantry was desperately outgunned by the enemy, and even the soldiers' personal gear was not suited for the looming winter season.[137] In sum, the CPV was poorly armed, badly equipped, and chronically undersupplied.

Beijing's leadership was clearly aware of the CPV's material inferiority a priori. Even so, Chinese propaganda claimed one distinct advantage for the Chinese troops that, according to Mao's own writings, could even be regarded as decisive: "Weapons are an important factor in war, but … it is people, not things, that are decisive."[138] Based on his personal experience as a commander in battle, Mao was convinced that soldiers with fighting spirit and high morale could overcome even materially superior enemies. Consequently, these thoughts also formed the baseline for the political mobilization of the Chinese soldiers earmarked for deployment to Korea.[139] While this mobilization campaign indeed proved quite effective among the already politically loyal officers and soldiers, at least three observations allow for the conclusion that China's leaders may not have been profoundly convinced of the superior quality and morale of their troops, and thus acted against their better judgment when sending the CPV to Korea.

First, there exists a conceptual problem in transferring the doctrine of 'Men over Weapons' to the Korean War situation. In Mao's writings, this doctrine is crucially linked to the characteristics of the 'People's War,' an asymmetric conflict that has no established frontlines and in which the revolutionary forces weaken the enemy in a war of attrition.[140] In such a situation, the most important factor for the revolutionaries' success is the broad support they enjoy among the civilian population (food, loyalty, shelter), which in turn provides the most effective motivation for the fighters.[141] In Korea, however, the situation differed markedly, as a full-scale war with clear frontlines had already erupted, the suffering civilian population could not provide the CPV with sufficient support, and the Chinese soldiers felt they were fighting far away from their homes.[142] Second, the Chinese leadership must have been aware of a critical mass of politically unreliable soldiers in the ranks of the CPV. A large amount of the intervention force consisted of former GMD troops who had joined the PLA for pragmatic rather than ideological reasons.[143] In October 1950, a survey of the CPV's political department revealed that around half of the soldiers did not show a positive attitude toward participating in the Korean War, while one quarter of them were even identified as politically very unreliable.[144] Beijing's leaders were thus clearly aware that around 50 percent of the CPV soldiers did not show the morale expected from politicized PLA soldiers. Third, as these figures revealed the state of morale before the intervention, China's leadership – estimating with up to 200,000 casualties during the first 12 months of fighting – could by no means be certain that the troops' morale would stabilize in the future.[145] On the contrary, by sending forces into battle with insufficient personal equipment, deficient weaponry, and unsteady supplies, China's leadership knowingly accepted a potential breakdown of the troops' morale during the early stages of the intervention.

Air power: Soviet air cover for the CPV

When compared to the state of the newly established People's Liberation Army Air Force (PLAAF), the many shortcomings of China's ground forces appear almost trivial. In numbers, China commanded an air-warfare capability that equaled that of a single World War II Essex-Class aircraft carrier with about 80–100 fighters.[146] With such a limited force, the PLAAF was already overextended with the defense of the mainland against GMD air raids, not to speak of conducting offensive operations abroad.[147] However, the enemy's armored and highly mobile force dispositive, as well as the geographical setting on the Korean Peninsula, called for close air–ground operations.[148] China's leadership was clearly aware of the PLAAF's numerous shortcomings and their severe implications, and Mao in particular expressed doubt as to whether the CPV would be able to annihilate an entire U.S. army during the critical onset of the intervention without having air cover and support.[149] Wile the PLAAF assured Beijing optimistically that the air force would be able to shoulder its burden in later stages of the war, this prospect did not solve the current shortcomings.[150] With regard to the aerial dimension of the upcoming intervention, China's military planners identified three pressing issues: the defense of Chinese territory, the defense of the CPV's supply lines and staging areas, and, most importantly, the provision of tactical air support for Chinese troops fighting in Korea.[151] As none of these tasks could be accomplished by the PLAAF, Beijing was thus fundamentally dependent on the Soviet Union for air power.

The provision of Soviet air cover for the CPV in Korea was a bedrock assumption against which China's military leaders outlined their plans. Facing an enemy that utilized its air superiority with devastating effect for the North Korean forces, the PLA strategists greatly worried about how their own troops would perform under these conditions.[152] In a detailed assessment in late August, they thus identified the imperative of acquiring strong Soviet air support as an utmost priority and necessary precondition for a successful Chinese intervention, and recommended "that Beijing make every effort to secure more Soviet air support and equipment before Chinese troops went into combat. If air support by the Soviets could not be guaranteed, they proposed that China delay sending troops into Korea."[153] Beijing had already requested Soviet air-force units in July to strengthen the defense of NEBDA, and Stalin had dispatched 124 MiG-15 fighters.[154] From Moscow's perspective, the primary task of the Soviet air detachment was not to engage in combat operations but to train PLAAF pilots for three months, then hand over the aircraft and leave the scene. As this schedule was way too tight for the inexperienced PLAAF pilots, both sides agreed to extend direct Soviet air assistance until spring 1951.[155] Consequently, "it was clear [from the beginning] in both Beijing and Moscow that China would depend on the Soviets for air support"[156] for at least a nine-month period and concerning all eventualities – including a Chinese intervention. With regard to the latter prospect, Stalin had promised on July 5 that the Soviet Union would "try to provide air cover for [Chinese] volunteer actions in North Korea in case the enemy crosses the 38th parallel."[157] For the Chinese leadership, this promise was thus a clearly agreed-upon fundament on which Beijing based its further handling of the Korean Crisis.[158]

When Stalin then requested an immediate Chinese intervention on October 1 and Mao "reminded the Soviet leader of his promise,"[159] Stalin first confirmed his part of the Sino-Soviet burden-sharing: the Chinese would fight on the ground under the cover of Soviet air-force units.[160] Only ten days later, however, Beijing learned that the Soviet air cover would be limited to areas along the Yalu River.[161] In other words, shortly before the onset of the intervention, the Chinese leadership learned that the CPV would have to enter Korea without any form of air cover or support.[162] This jeremiad forced Mao to fundamentally reconsider the intervention. On October 12, he ordered the postponement of all preparations.[163] In Mao's eyes, Stalin's denial of the promised air cover was a serious betrayal of confidence that forced him into a difficult position.[164] Now, it was on him to decide whether China should keep its already stated promise and rescue North Korea by taking a much greater risk, or to adjust the course according to the new circumstances, cancel the intervention, and follow Stalin's example of keeping out of 'Kim's affair.'

The answer to this crucial question was finally found during a highly emotional Politburo meeting on the next day. Again, it was the Chairman that set the course and brought the Chinese leadership back into line: Mao's dominating role fostered the consensus to adhere to the initial decision and go ahead with the intervention.[165] While the political leadership thus kept the course even without Soviet air cover, the CPV commanders worried extensively about the changed circumstances. As high-ranking and experienced officers, these men must have had a quite sobering evaluation of the many shortcomings, problems, and overall inferiority of their troops for a confrontation with an experienced enemy that commanded overwhelming firepower and undisputed air supremacy. Only two days before the Chinese troops were to cross the Yalu, their worries culminated in an astonishing telegram:

> [M]any comrades have expressed the opinion ... that [because] our troops have ... *no air support at this moment*, the enemy could concentrate large numbers of planes, artillery, and tanks to wage heavy attacks against us without any worries. ... If the enemy started an all-out offensive, *it would be less than possible for us to hold our ground*. The opinion of the majority is that as we have not been fully prepared ... *it would be better if we send off our troops not this winter* but next spring.[166]

As the cable highlights, the CPV commanders still assessed air support as a crucial requirement for the success of an intervention. Entering Korea without sufficient air cover entailed, in their opinion, the prohibitive risk of a crushing defeat. Under these circumstances, the officers' logical conclusion was to postpone the intervention until "there will be a guarantee for new equipment and particularly air force support."[167]

At that point, Beijing could be certain about only two facts: first, that the U.S. air supremacy over the Korean Peninsula had had devastating effects on the North Korean ground forces, and second, that the CPV was definitely entering Korea without any form of air cover for the time being. Consequently, the Chinese troops would be exposed to enemy air power to the same extent that the KPA was. As highlighted by the CPV commanders' telegram, this prospect incorporated a prohibitive risk that the officers were greatly unwilling to shoulder.

Implications for operative planning

Moscow's failure to honor its promise of air cover for the CPV and the slowly materializing supply of Soviet weaponry forced Beijing to reconsider the operative planning for the intervention at an extraordinarily late stage. Until then, the Chinese plans foresaw a joint deployment of Chinese ground and Soviet air units in order to deliver a 'sudden blow' to the U.S./UN forces.[168] This would allow the exhausted KPA to regroup behind the Chinese lines of defense and then rejoin the battle.[169] With the unified strength of the Communist forces seizing the offense, a decisive victory would be swiftly achievable. In short, China's initial battle-plan was to facilitate North Korea's military success with a limited military intervention.

Even after Inchon, the Chinese leadership still anticipated a short and decisive campaign, although it had then also become clear that the Chinese forces would have to bear the major part of the fighting.[170] Mao's October 2 telegram to Stalin provides a detailed summary of the type of war the Chinese leadership anticipated fighting in Korea: after an initial phase of deployment, the Chinese forces would quickly seize the initiative and annihilate a large number of U.S. troops.[171] High American casualties would send a message to Washington, which might be answered by the declaration of war on China, but would also force the United States to rethink its Korean adventure.[172]

First, however, it was Mao and Peng's responsibility to rethink China's military adventure in Korea after Stalin's denial of the promised air support. Moreover, the situation was also complicated by the deteriorating state of the North Korean forces. In early October, the KPA's lines of defense had collapsed.[173] From then on, the KPA was unable to mount organized resistance in order to halt the Allied advance.[174] These developments implied that when China entered the war at this stage, it was basically on its own, as Beijing could count on neither the Soviets nor the North Koreans for substantial assistance in combat: the CPV would now have to shoulder the entire burden of fighting.[175] The new situation demanded an operative reconsideration of the imminent intervention. Surprisingly, Mao and Peng based their adjustments largely on best-case assumptions that had already become obsolete or were at least outdated when the first Chinese units finally entered Korea. According to the modified strategy, Beijing envisaged a protracted war instead of a swift campaign.[176] Because of the lack of air power, offensive operations were canceled for a period of at least six months.[177] Instead, the Chinese troops were to establish defensive positions north of Pyongyang after stealthily entering Korea. According to Mao, the CPV's presence would deter the enemy from advancing further northward.[178] As the frontline would thus stabilize, the Chinese forces would not "have to engage in fighting but gain time to become well equipped and trained, and ... wait for the arrival of the Soviet air force."[179] After completing preparations, the first CPV offensive should avoid engagements with U.S. units and rather concentrate on the weaker ROK forces, "which our troops are quite capable to cope with."[180]

Mao and Peng based the modified strategy on the assumption that the CPV would have enough time to move into position before the enemy could take Pyongyang and Wonsan.[181] However, when the CPV eventually entered Korea, these cities had already fallen and the "Chinese leaders realized ... that the CPV would be forced to engage the enemy [much] earlier than they planned."[182] Just six days later, the stealth of the intrusion failed and Chinese troops experienced a baptism of fire at Onjung and Unsan. In sum, these developments show the ongoing validity of the military saying 'no plan survives the first contact.' This insight holds especially true for strategies so extensively based on best-case assumptions as the adjusted Chinese intervention plan, which consequently encompassed a high risk of military failure.

Interim conclusion: assessing the risks of China's Korean war

In almost perfect congruence, the three indicators show an evident increase in the amount of risk the Chinese leadership was willing to accept during the run-up to the intervention. At the onset of the decision-making, Beijing had gained a relatively clear picture about the inferior state of the PLA's capacities, and thus attempted to strengthen the CPV's combat potential by acquiring modern armaments and air cover from the Soviet Union. Both issues were at that point regarded by China's political and military leadership as necessary preconditions for successful military engagement in Korea. At this early stage, Beijing thus acted in quite a risk-averse manner: aware of its own material inferiority and the relatively weak morale of the CPV soldiers, the Chinese leadership seriously evaluated arising risks and made sincere attempts to diversify or contain them. Based on the relatively sober assessments about the state of China's military capabilities and assuming that the Soviet Union would provide the required weaponry and air cover, the leadership finally took the initial decision to intervene.

With the watershed of October 10, the preconditions for China's intervention drastically changed, and the Chinese leadership – to borrow MacArthur's words – now had to face an entirely new war. Mao's order to stop preparations for the intervention indicates that the emerging situation even forced the determined Chairman into a comprehensive reassessment of the pending intervention: without air cover and modern weaponry, a Chinese engagement in Korea now involved a decidedly higher amount of risk of military failure. Against these exceedingly unfavorable developments, however, the Chinese leadership – with Mao taking the lead – kept to the initial decision. At this point, the two prerequisites that had, at earlier stages, been regarded as absolutely necessary for the success of an intervention no longer played a decisive role. Beijing proceeded with the intervention by knowingly ignoring emerging risks instead of seriously considering them, as the modified operative strategy strikingly reveals. China's battle-plan had not the slightest chance of surviving the first encounter with the enemy as it was extensively based on best-case assumptions: in essence, Mao and Peng designed an intervention that could be aptly summarized as 'going to war without fighting, and hoping for the enemy to wait.'

When taking the whole range of negative developments and their implications into account, it seems more than appropriate to share the CPV commanders' conclusion as outlined in their telegram of October 17, 1950: without air cover and modern weaponry, the Chinese intervention incorporated incalculable risk. Under these circumstances, the commanders suggested not going ahead with the plan. The telegram is a remarkable piece of data as it provides a first-hand evaluation of the circumstances by experienced officers that, furthermore, can be regarded as politically reliable. If their assessment culminated in such a dissuasive conclusion, the inherent risks must have appeared prohibitive in their eyes. But against the sobering analysis of his commanders, Mao issued the final orders, and China entered the Korean War.

The CPV in Korea: fighting for China's glory

China's Korean War unfolded in two distinct phases: during the first, Beijing attempted to bring about the decision on the battlefield and the CPV fought five major offensives in a row. In the second, the war reached a stalemate and offensives were largely replaced by the struggle for an armistice agreement. In line with the findings of my other partial analyses, I demonstrate in what follows that China's conduct of warfare was primarily guided by political objectives rather than military considerations. The result was a conflict in objectives that characterized both phases of China's Korean War. During the offensive phase, China's military performance was unexpectedly successful as long as the operative planning rested mainly on the shoulders of CPV commander Peng Dehuai. However, when Mao started to overrule his field commanders by demanding increasingly ambitious offensives, severe military setbacks followed. The same pattern is observable during the second phase of the war. Even though all sides had then agreed on cease-fire talks, Mao was still eager to regain the initiative on the battlefield. Consequently, the first round of armistice negotiations failed. Only after Mao had abandoned this ambition did the first breakthroughs follow. Then, however, another political object – the POW-issue – emerged, and prolonged the Korean War for two more years – these being its bloodiest. Eventually, after the war had engulfed the lives of one million soldiers and up to three million civilians, the death of a single man apparently functioned as the crucial event that paved China the way to the successful conclusion of an armistice in 1953.

Phase I: the five Chinese offensives

Immediately after the intervention's onset, CPV commander Peng Dehuai found himself engaged in a two-front battle. In Korea, his troops faced well-equipped U.S./UN forces that threatened to reach the CPV's staging areas much faster than expected; on the home front, Peng was confronted with Mao's military ambitions. Just days after 300,000 Chinese troops had started to enter Korea, the Chairman ordered the CPV on the offensive.[183] For Peng, this meant that he had to send his troops into battle much earlier than envisaged even in the modified operative planning. Unwilling to do so, Peng reminded Mao of the necessity to set up a defensible bridgehead before launching a large-scale offensive.[184] But for Mao, the initial considerations had already become obsolete, as he was eager to deliver a blow to the advancing ROK divisions. With his personal battle-plan at hand, the Chairman expected nothing less than a complete victory from the CPV.[185] Mao, however, had developed his plan at the sand table and without taking the battlefield realities into account: in Beijing, he was easily able to surround and destroy entire enemy divisions by shuffling units on a map back and forth. In the field, the situation was quite different.

The prevalence of military considerations

The CPV's first offensive did not unfold as smoothly as the Chinese leaders had hoped, and also fell short of achieving Mao's ambitious goals. Nonetheless, it resulted in an advantageous outcome. For the first time since Inchon, the frontline stabilized as the CPV pushed back the enemy behind the Chongchun River, which provided the KPA with a desperately needed breathing spell.[186] The Chinese troops also fought considerably better than their leadership had expected. Even so, the CPV's evaluation in the aftermath of the offensive identified several disadvantages and shortcomings. One was the CPV's lack of mobility, which made each maneuver basically a race between American wheels and Chinese feet. The Chinese forces were simply too slow to successfully encircle and destroy large enemy units.[187] Another problem was the enemy's superior firepower: U.S./UN forces concentrated heavy weaponry and tactical air support with deadly efficiency to shatter the Chinese assault-waves.[188] Last, the deficient supply situation revealed itself as the most important problem, because it severely constrained the CPV's capacity to engage in sustained operations. Even at this early stage, the minimal requirements for the steadily growing number of troops could not be met, as the Chinese supply lines were reaching overstretch.[189] For Beijing, this list of disadvantages should not have come as a surprise, as all had been well known prior to the intervention.

After ten days of combat, Peng ordered that the offensive be ceased, as his troops were no longer in a fit condition to pursue the enemy. Mao, however, was highly displeased with this decision and ordered that the fighting continue.[190] Only after the CPV commander insisted that the circumstances did not allow for continuing the offensive did the Chairman finally agree to halt the pursuit, and the Chinese troops broke off the engagement.[191] For the Allied commanders, the end of the Chinese offensive came rather unexpectedly.[192] The disorganized retreat led them to conclude that the Chinese intervention was merely symbolic, numerically limited, and already exhausted.[193] Actually, however, the CPV had made every effort to create this impression – but as the prelude to a second offensive. Based on previous experience, Peng concluded that the farther the battlefield moved north, the more the CPV's disadvantages would be outweighed: there, the CPV enjoyed shorter supply lines and was able to numerically overwhelm the enemy, and the terrain favored the Chinese infantry.[194] Peng only needed the enemy to advance northward, and preferably do so in the incautious state of expecting a certain victory. For that reason, his troops masterfully feigned a withdrawal in order to lure General MacArthur's forces into a giant ambush.[195]

This bait did not fail to attract MacArthur's attention. Only days after the onset of his 'Home-by-Christmas' offensive, the CPV counterattacked in unexpected strength,[196] and the Allied offensive turned into the longest and "most infamous"[197] retreat in the history of the United States' armed forces. Driven back more than 180 kilometers, the Allied forces abandoned Pyongyang on December 6. One week later, the remnants of the U.S. Eighth Army again crossed the 38th parallel, but this time heading south. On December 25, when Chinese forward units reached the parallel, the status quo ante was restored.[198] The second offensive turned out to be a huge success for the CPV because it was the result of a well prepared and executed plan that was based on military assessments, battlefield realities, and tactical objectives.[199] Even so, China's victory came at an immense cost, as after this around 40 percent of the CPV troops were combat-ineffective, with tens of thousands killed or wounded.[200]

The predominance of political objectives

As the second campaign had significantly reduced the CPV's potential to conduct offensive operations, Peng thus requested to delay operations until the coming spring and proposed limiting the next offensive to areas north of the 38th parallel.[201] He was convinced that his troops were not yet prepared to overcome the enemy, which had fallen back to fortified positions.[202] Even so, Mao decided to launch the next offensive. This time, the CPV should cross the parallel, take Seoul, and advance further south.[203] For Mao, the previous successes had proven the apparent weakness of the enemy.[204] In his perspective, a total victory in Korea was in reach. Consequently, he ordered the CPV to again seize the offensive, even though Peng warned that the success of a follow-up campaign would be highly limited.[205] However, as Peng had to explain to his subordinates, the third offensive was necessary for "political reasons … and we are obliged to do so,"[206] even though he regarded it as an "unwise and untimely military operation."[207]

On New Year's Eve, CPV and KPA forces attacked southward of the 38th parallel.[208] Although the troops quickly took Seoul and some units even reached the 37th parallel, the momentum of the offensive was soon depleted.[209] As the battlefield results verified Peng's prior assessments, he ordered the offensive's cessation on January 8.[210] From a tactical perspective, this decision is absolutely comprehensible, as the desolate state of the Chinese troops did not allow for continuing the attack.[211] Up to January, the CPV had lost over 110,000 men, greatly reducing China's numerical advantage.[212] The supply problems amplified with every step the soldiers pushed south. Furthermore, a huge rear area had opened up that was highly vulnerable to amphibious assaults.[213] Under these circumstances, a more defensive tactic was imperative in order to safeguard the battlefield gains against expected Allied counteroffensives.[214]

On the political front, however, Peng's decision met strong disapproval, as the Soviets and North Koreans pressured him to continue the offensive.[215] Finally, Mao joined this chorus and ordered a follow-up offensive.[216] In Peng's eyes, Mao's demand was not only unachievable given the CPV's contemporary state, but also extremely dangerous: in contrast to Moscow, Pyongyang, and Beijing, Peng was convinced that the previous Chinese offensives had only had a very limited effect on the Allied combat capacity.[217] Even so, he implemented the order and his troops prepared for a fourth offensive, which had the designated – but, in Peng's assessment, unattainable – goal of driving the enemy completely off the Korean Peninsula.[218] At this point, the political interference in the CPV's operations had reached its peak, and the gap between political goals and tactical realities had become unbridgeable. The steady increase of political influence now resulted in the problematic situation in which not military considerations but political concerns dictated China's conduct of warfare in Korea.[219]

Only 17 days after Peng gave the order to halt the third offensive, an Allied counterattack took the Chinese forces by surprise.[220] As his troops were unable to hold their ground, Peng required permission to withdraw to more defensible positions. Highlighting the criticality of the situation, he even suggested Beijing's immediate acceptance of the UN cease-fire resolution.[221] Mao, however, had another idea about how to solve the situation, and ordered Peng to counter the Allied attack by antedating the CPV's fourth offensive. Instead of retreating, the Chinese troops should now head for the 36th parallel.[222] With regard to the CPV's apparent lack of preparedness, Mao lectured his commander: "It is ... not a great difficulty even if our forces have not been resupplied with munitions ... if we try our best."[223] It is more than obvious that Mao demanded achievement of the impossible when ordering the CPV to launch an offensive when not equipped with the absolute minimal requirement for the slightest chance of success – sufficient ammunition. At this point, it seems as if the Chairman had totally lost any sense of the battlefield realities, as he

> had stopped to fight for gains of terrain, tactical advantages, and the annihilation of the enemy's capacities. Now, he fought for prestige and the advance of his banner, regardless of the costs and if necessary, to the end of this world.[224]

Against the stubbornness of his commander-in-chief, the best "Peng could hope for ... was to minimize losses and satisfy Mao at the same time."[225] The Chinese offensive thus took place, but reflected merely a general withdrawal behind the 38th parallel.[226] After three months of combat, the Chinese troops were back in their initial position. However, given "the huge gap between the UN and CPV in terms of firepower, logistics, and maneuverability, as well as the gradual learning curve on part of the UN forces, the CPV was already in a more difficult situation."[227] Adding to this, Peng noted that "[t]he losses in this campaign were the highest suffered by our forces"[228] in the Korean War. The futile counteroffensive had resulted in a major defeat and had bled the CPV white.

In mid-February, Peng made a hurried visit to Beijing. Harboring increasing concerns about Mao's unrealistic expectations and constant political interference in his command, he felt the need to explicate the sobering battlefield situation.[229] However, Mao did not abandon his ambition for another offensive and ordered "Peng to gather all his forces along the 38th Parallel to counterattack U.S./UN forces before they could get a firm foothold."[230] This time, the CPV would receive the long-awaited Soviet weaponry that, in Mao's eyes, would bring the desired victory. Reequipped and substantially reinforced, the CPV launched its fifth offensive on April 22, 1951.[231] However, the attack was not nearly as successful as expected.[232] When the offensive ground to a halt north of Seoul, a clueless Peng had to inform Mao that his forces were not able to realize the pre-set objectives and proposed ceasing the attack.[233] As Mao rejected this proposal, the offensive continued until

May 21, when Peng, afraid of heavy losses, decided to withdraw the main force.[234] After 40 days of combat, the CPV had lost an estimate of 85,000 men without achieving noteworthy territorial gains.[235] During the following week, however, another 100,000 Chinese casualties followed, as an Allied counteroffensive hit the Chinese just hours before their scheduled withdrawal on May 23.[236] On June 2, the U.S./UN forces ceased their advance, as they had reached their designated objectives north of the 38th parallel, and a new frontline was established that would remain virtually unchanged for the last two years of the war.[237] The fifth offensive marked the CPV's worst defeat in the Korean War. During the chaotic retreat, whole divisions had been lost and the Chinese forces had been driven back to the same positions they had held in late 1950. Considering these results, Mao was forced to rethink his obviously overambitious objectives. He reached the conclusion that the goal of driving the U.S./UN forces out of Korea was apparently unattainable.[238] As Mao had to adapt the overall war objectives to the new circumstances, a modified battlefield strategy followed.

Phase II: cease-fire negotiations

In June 1951, Mao explained the principles he envisioned for continuing the war along a static frontline: in order to prepare for Allied offensives, the Chinese troops should fortify their current positions and conduct limited offensives against exposed enemy positions. The new strategy had two central aims: first, the enemy should be worn down in a war of attrition;[239] second, and most importantly, the switch to positional warfare should buy time to prepare for a new offensive, which Mao had scheduled for September 1951.[240] In order to realize the latter objective, Beijing also entered into cease-fire negotiations.[241] In general, China's position toward a negotiated settlement of the war mirrored the course of its battlefield performance: after the unexpected successes of the first and second offensives, Mao had not been interested in an armistice, as he was then convinced that his forces would be able to achieve a total victory.[242] This changed only after the disastrous fifth offensive. Consequently, Mao became willing to enter into negotiations.[243] Before doing so, however, he first had to consult his allies: in contrast to Kim Il-sung, whose consent was just a formal matter, Stalin's approval was critical. However, as the Soviet leader suggested "not to rush to the end of the war,"[244] Mao had to send Gao Gang and Kim Il-sung to Moscow in order to clarify the seriousness of the situation before Stalin finally gave consent and Beijing was able to proceed to the negotiating table.[245]

On July 10, the armistice negotiations started in Kaesong. Although the Communist delegation was officially headed by DPRK's Vice Premier Nam Il, the North Koreans – and their South Korean counterparts – played only a subsidiary role, as the actual talks took place between the Americans and the Chinese.[246] For the PRC, the negotiations were an important opportunity to underline China's new great-power status.[247] Accordingly, the Chinese delegation had been carefully prepared.[248] The first outcome of the negotiations, the adoption of an agenda, consisted of four points: (1) determination of the military demarcation line (MDL) and the demilitarized zone (DMZ), and the cessation of hostilities; (2) arrangements for cease-fire, armistice, and the supervising organization; (3) arrangements for prisoners of war (POW); (4) recommendations to the governments of both sides.[249] The consensual phase had already ended, however, by the time it came to determination of the MDL. While the Communist delegation proposed the 38th parallel, the Allied counterproposal insisted on a line that reflected the relative military capabilities and current exigencies and thus proposed the Pyongyang–Wonsan line.[250] As neither side showed any willingness to compromise, the negotiations reached deadlock.[251]

The failure of the first round of armistice negotiations was not only the result of disagreement on substantial issues. Mao still harbored the ambition for a new Chinese offensive.[252] Rather than seriously negotiating a compromise, Mao intended to present a new *fait accompli* on the battlefield, which should force a concession from the UN. However, the onset of the Allied summer offensive, resulting in over 30,000 CPV casualties, largely brought an end to his plans. After the CPV commanders convinced Mao that an offensive was unrealizable in mid-August 1951, a reconsideration of China's negotiation strategy followed.[253]

On October 25, 1951, the two sides met again in Panmunjom. Only four weeks later, consent was reached on the substantial issues that had been fiercely contested during the previous round.[254] With no more alternatives at hand, Mao was now seriously interested in negotiating an end to the war. On November 27, the two most critical issues were solved when both sides agreed to accept their currently held positions as the provisional MDL and to withdraw two kilometers to establish a DMZ.[255] In essence, this hard-won agreement would have effectively brought an end to the bloodshed, as none of the parties had any further incentives to change the status quo.[256] As the end of hostilities was virtually in reach, the time frame for concluding the final armistice under the validity of the above-mentioned conditions was set at 30 days.[257]

The POW issue – a matter of principle and pride

One month later, however, the conclusion of the armistice had receded into the distance. In early December, disagreement had emerged on an issue that could have been assumed to be taken for granted: the exchange of POW. While Beijing expected the United Nations to adhere to Article 118 of the Geneva Convention, which mandated the repatriation of all POW,[258] the UN delegation proposed an exchange based on the principal of 'voluntary repatriation,'[259] for at least two reasons. First, the Allied forces had detained around 130,000 POW, more than ten times the number the Communist forces were holding captive (fewer than 12,000 POW). An immediate release of this large number of soldiers would have greatly altered the military balance, to the disadvantage of the U.S./UN forces.[260] Second, Washington faced a moral problem in indiscriminately repatriating POW under Communist jurisdiction.[261]

For 18 months, disagreement on this issue deadlocked the negotiations, which swiftly degraded into an arena for fierce accusations and bitter competition between "human rights and legal rights, and between humanitarianism and Communist Party pride."[262] With regard to the latter, the Chinese had been especially devastated by the fact that only 5,100 of 20,000 Chinese POW expressed the wish to be sent back to the PRC; in comparison, the percentage of North Korean repatriates was much higher (53,900 of 93,530 POW).[263] For Beijing, this result came as a shock, and the implications were perceived as a serious setback for China's international prestige.[264] In order to avoid this loss in reputation, Mao ordered that "a hard line position on the POW issue" be taken.[265]

Behind the scenes, however, Zhou Enlai sounded out solutions: in May 1952, he explained to the Indian ambassador that a compromise could be reached if a total of 100,000 CPV and KPA prisoners were returned.[266] But when the updated UN figures of July showed that around 82,000 POW were willing to be repatriated – a number that came close to China's previous estimate of a maximum of 90,000 repatriates[267] – Mao was extremely unhappy to see only one third of the Chinese POW on the list. In September 1952, the Communist delegation amended its proposal and now demanded the complete repatriation of the Chinese POW, while leaving open the question of North Koreans' repatriation.[268] All this indicates that Beijing's main concerns with regard to the POW issue were primarily to be found in the anticipated negative implications for the PRC's standing.

The emergence of the POW issue as a bone of contention stalled the armistice negotiations until March 1953. Then, however, things suddenly moved very fast. On March 23, Mao accepted a UN proposal to exchange wounded and sick POW ('Operation Little Switch').[269] One week later, Zhou presented a new proposal, in which the DPRK and the PRC suggested "that both parties ... should undertake *to repatriate immediately* after the cessation of hostilities all prisoners of war in their custody *who insist upon repatriation* and to hand over the remaining prisoners of war to a neutral state."[270] In doing so, Beijing de facto agreed on the UN's 'no forced repatriation' principle. By giving in on that point, China's modified position paved the way for the conclusion of the armistice. Only a few days later, the Korean War Armistice Agreement was finalized, and the signing ceremony was scheduled for June 19.

China's last battle in the Korean War

During this phase of optimism and new impetus to strive for resolution of the conflict, a disturbing factor emerged, in the person of ROK President Rhee Syngman. Seeing his own ambitions dashed, Rhee sharply criticized the hard-won agreement and demanded the immediate withdrawal of all foreign forces from Korea. To make matters worse, Rhee not only declared that he was willing to fight toward the Yalu but also released 27,000 POW on June 18, in an obvious attempt to sabotage the conclusion of the armistice.[271] Washington immediately declared its noninvolvement and assured Beijing that similar incidents would not occur. Nevertheless, Mao decided to punish Rhee for the arrogance he had shown. Two days after the incident, he gave Peng permission to delay the signing of the armistice and ordered an offensive against ROK troops: the Chairman wanted to remind Rhee of what he had to expect if South Korea dared to fight toward the Yalu.[272]

The CPV's last offensive in the Korean War began on July 13 and ended six days later. For the area of operation, CPV acting commander Deng Hua had carefully selected a section of the frontline where the CPV faced mainly ROK defenders.[273]

Moreover, even though the plan foresaw that the offensive would be kept deliberately limited, Deng ordered four CPV armies to attack in order to guarantee that a massive blow would be dealt to Rhee's troops.[274] This objective was accomplished within less than 24 hours, when four ROK divisions were completely annihilated.[275] According to Chinese accounts, this last offensive resulted in up to 78,000 ROK casualties, at the price of 19,000 Chinese losses.[276] Also, the CPV had gained around 180 square kilometers of territory, but instead of fortifying their positions, the Chinese immediately withdrew.[277] Evidently, China's final offensive in the Korean War had the single objective of punishing Rhee Syng-man.[278]

With the CPV's last combat mission successfully accomplished, Marshal Peng signed the Korean War armistice on July 27, 1953. Three years to the day after U.S. forces had landed in Pusan, the Korean War turned cold. At 10 p.m. on the day the cease-fire came into effect, and only seconds after the last shot had been fired, the "fighting men of the opposing sides emerged from their defensive lines to exchange Chinese rice wine for American chocolate."[279]

The success of the Panmunjom negotiations: in search of explanations

It took three years of bloody warfare and two years of thorny negotiations to achieve the crucial breakthroughs at the conference table in April and May 1953 that eventually enabled the conclusion of an armistice. The Korean War ended in conditions that virtually reflected the status quo ante and which had already been achieved on the battlefield when the cease-fire negotiations started. In this section I will analyze the principal drivers for the success of the Panmunjom Round. Thereto, I will present, discuss, and evaluate three clusters of arguments that might explain why China was finally willing to compromise in mid-1953. These clusters consist of arguments related to military developments, China's domestic situation, and the demise of Joseph Stalin.

Military developments

The first cluster of factors that could have affected China's willingness to seek a genuine compromise might have resulted from military developments in Korea and beyond. With regard to the relevant time frame, three specific types of military developments can be identified: the development of the balance of forces in Korea, the effects of the U.S. aerial bombing campaigns, and intensified nuclear coercion on the part of the United States.

First, with regard to the military balance and the battlefield situation in Korea, there is no observable development in April and May 1953 that would have forced China to suddenly seek a compromise. Exactly at that point in time, the balance of forces had shifted in China's favor as the CPV reached the peak of its combat strength, with 1.34 million men deployed to Korea.[280] Moreover, the switch to positional warfare had also equalized Chinese disadvantages concerning logistics, weaponry, and mobility.[281] During the crucial period of April and May, the CPV's state of combat-readiness had also reached a new high as the troops were prepared to counter an expected Allied landing operation.[282] In view of this, it becomes understandable that Peng, when singing the armistice, even "felt a bit disappointed because we had just become so well organized for combat. We had not fully used our might to deliver bigger blows to the enemy."[283]

Second, the intensified U.S. aerial bombing campaigns, intended to pressure the PRC–DPRK coalition into concessions, had little influence on Mao's determination to keep a hard-line position as the bombings only affected North Korean territory, infrastructure, and population.[284] Chinese troops in Korea were less exposed to these bombardments because their fortified positions and bunkers provided sufficient shelter.[285]

Third, a number of U.S. government officials – with President Eisenhower and Secretary of State Dulles taking the lead – have linked the successful outcome of the Panmunjom negotiations with the intensified nuclear pressure on China in May 1953.[286] According to this perspective, China was forced to accept the UN proposal because Washington threatened to expand the war beyond Korea, including the use of nuclear weapons against China, if the conclusion of the armistice was further delayed.[287] A closer look reveals, however, that the supposed link between Washington's nuclear coercion and the outcome of the armistice negotiations is far from established, highly questionable, and can be regarded merely as another example of the many dangerous 'nuclear myths'[288] rather than a verified causal connection.[289] The U.S. nuclear arsenals and explicitly stated nuclear threats against the PRC had not deterred the Chinese leadership from intervening in Korea or from crossing the 38th parallel.[290] The reasons for this may be found in Mao's doctrine on nuclear warfare, which foresaw that China would actually win a nuclear engagement given the size of its population and its rural economy. As the Chinese leadership did not reassess their thoughts on nuclear weapons and warfare until late 1954, Beijing was obviously not to be discouraged from maintaining its course by the intensified U.S. nuclear coercion in mid-1953.[291] Also, the credibility of Washington's nuclear threat was highly questionable: while Truman had 'only' been determined to fight a prolonged conventional war for a favorable solution to the POW issue, Dulles' nuclear-coercion strategy now literally committed the United States to risking a nuclear Third World War for the sake of 16,000 Chinese POWs. As China had a viable military alliance with the Soviet Union, Washington thus risked a Soviet retaliatory strike when extending the war into China.[292] Probably most importantly, the two crucial Chinese concessions – Beijing's approval of 'Operation Little Switch' and Zhou's modified proposal of March 30 – evidently predate the onset of the U.S. coercion strategy and thus cannot be regarded as its results.[293] Taken together, these observations demonstrate that China's position during the Panmunjom negotiations was not affected by Washington's intensified nuclear coercion.

Domestic considerations

The second set of arguments highlights domestic considerations, and particularly the financial burden of China's engagement in Korea. According to this line of reasoning, the Chinese leadership reached the conclusion that the national economy would collapse if military expenditure was not drastically reduced.[294] Consequently, when the first Chinese five-year plan was announced in December 1952, the termination of the Korean War had already become an urgent necessity.[295]

Indeed, China's military engagement came at an astronomical price: between 1950 and 1953, an average of 50 percent of China's gross domestic product was flowing unproductively into the Korean War.[296] As the economy still had not recovered, domestic development and reconstruction thus had to be significantly curtailed. Also, every bullet, grenade, or missile fired by Chinese soldiers in Korea increased the PRC's financial liabilities to Moscow, as the overwhelming majority of the CPV's supplies were bought from the Soviet Union on credit, and Moscow expected China to pay back this debt, preferably in hard currency.[297]

While the desperate economic situation thus might have played a facilitating role in Beijing's decision to end the war with a negotiated settlement, it generates only marginal explanatory power when it comes to explaining the modified position on the POW issue. From a financial point of view, China had been already war-weary since November 1951, when the skyrocketing military expenditure had come to absorb 32 percent of the national budget.[298] For Beijing, the financial burden of the Korean War had thus been an acute problem virtually from the onset of the intervention. If Mao's primary interest had consisted in avoiding unnecessary costs, why had Beijing not accepted one of the many cease-fire initiatives or agreed earlier to the UN proposal of 'no forced repatriation'? Even though domestic calculations apparently played a role in moving China toward a negotiated termination of the war, they were obviously not the decisive factors that influenced Beijing's change of position in the spring of 1953.

Stalin's death

The third and most promising line of argument is related to an event that took place on March 5, 1953. On this day, Joseph Stalin passed away. As my analysis has shown, Stalin's green light to Kim was the decisive factor that had unleashed the Korean War. In addition, I have demonstrated that Stalin's transfer to China of the obligation to safeguard the Asian revolutionary movements was the crucial factor that led to Beijing's intervention. Continuing this line of thought, I argue in the following that Stalin's death was the crucial event that ended the Korean War, as it allowed China to accept the UN proposal on the POW issue.

A comparison of China's negotiation positions before and after March 1953 reveals significant variation. Before Stalin's death, Beijing's negotiation strategy had been a hard-line one, particularly with regard to the POW issue. On the one hand, this position resulted from the nature of the issue at stake, which had become a matter of pride and thus of principle. On the other, it had also been the result of Stalin's constant advice to Mao, and as Beijing consulted Moscow on virtually every important development and decision during the Korean War, Stalin's influence on Beijing was substantial, if not decisive.[299] Following Stalin's counsel, Mao had rejected the UN cease-fire proposal of January 1951 and had kept a firm position on the POW issue.[300] When India sponsored a resolution in November 1952 that later became the basis for the settlement of the POW question, it was immediately criticized by Moscow and rejected by Beijing. The last time Mao declared the UN demands to be unacceptable was in February 1953. And then, Stalin died.

Almost instantly, Beijing surprisingly made dramatic moves to push the negotiations toward success: on March 23, Beijing consented to the proposal for 'Operation Little Switch,' which had been pending for one month. A week later, China agreed to the 'no forced repatriation' principle, and on June 8 the settlement of the POW issue was accomplished. Two principal reasons can be found for the 180-degree turn in Beijing's position, and both depart from the proposition that Stalin's death was the immediate cause.

First, Moscow's agenda of interest abruptly changed with the demise of the paramount leader. For Stalin, the Korean War had provided an extraordinary opportunity to 'wear the Americans down by holding the Chinese in while keeping the Russians out.' What he had aimed for was a textbook example of what John Mearsheimer describes as a combined bait-and-bleed and bloodletting strategy, with the aim of gaining power at the expense of one actual rival – the United States – and one potential rival – the People's Republic of China – at the same time.[301] For Moscow, the PRC was like a dual-edged sword: while China "constituted a new Soviet security shield" in the region, "it would possibly become a threat to Soviet security and interests"[302] should it fully reemerge as Asia's 'Middle Kingdom' and a potent great power. For those reasons, Stalin kept the conflict boiling via his influence on Mao, but also carefully balanced the Soviet Union's military commitment to China and Moscow's diplomatic initiatives in the UN in order to prevent the Korean War from uncontrollably boiling over. After Stalin's death, the new Soviet leadership immediately shifted the agenda from subversive prevention of an end of the Korean War to its comprehensive termination. In doing so, the new leadership invited Zhou Enlai to Moscow for extensive discussions. The most important outcome of these consultations was presented on March 19, when the Soviet Council of Ministers decided to support the proposal for 'Operation Little Switch' and suggested that POWs should not be repatriated against their will.[303] Moscow's new position picked up the exact content of the Indian resolution of November 1952, which at the time had been harshly criticized by the Soviet Union. This change in position, as well as the subsequent acceptance of Eisenhower's 'Chance for Peace' initiative, revealed the onset of comprehensive Soviet policy realignment in the post-Stalin era, which was eventually to result in a period of détente.

Second, with Stalin's demise the patron–client relationship that had been established between the Soviet leader and Mao – and which also characterized Sino-Soviet relations – came to an end. When, in 1949, Stalin promoted China to *primi inter pares* of the Asian revolutionary movements and Moscow's most important strategic ally, this meant, at least in Stalin's perspective, that China was now the Soviet Union's junior partner. For Mao, however, the relationship should have been that of partners on equal footing. When entering the Korean War, the Chairman certainly attempted to establish this desired relationship of equality, as Moscow then desperately needed China to rescue the Soviet model state in Asia. For a short period, Mao then actually approached Stalin at eye level, because the CPV's unexpected successes enhanced Beijing's standing in Moscow.[304] But the longer the war endured, the greater became China's material dependency on the Soviet Union, and the smaller was Beijing's leeway in decision-making.[305] When the prospects for ending the war on the battlefield had diminished, Beijing found itself trapped in a dilemma: with the PRC unable to lift itself up by its own military bootstraps and highly dependent on the Soviet Union, Mao felt pressure to comply with Stalin's demands for continuing the war.[306] When Beijing finally decided to enter into cease-fire negotiations, China's status *vis-à-vis* the Soviet Union once again resembled that of a client to its patron. As neither Mao nor Kim had any experience with international armistice negotiations and thus had to turn to Stalin for advice, it was easy for the Soviet leader to influence the negotiations in his favor.[307]

The patron–client relationship was eventually dissolved with Stalin's death, which in turn greatly eased China's Korean War dilemma because, once again, the new leadership in Moscow was in need of a commitment from China – this time, to end the war. When Zhou Enlai visited Moscow, the Chinese Premier not only met the new Soviet leaders at eye level but also presented the bill for China's intervention and withdrawal from Korea: Moscow agreed to provide China with more than 160 major industrial and science projects, which would later become the fundament for China's industrial development and unprecedented economic rise.[308] This massive concession would definitely not have been achievable if Zhou had approached the new Soviet leaders only as solicitant. Stalin's death thus had profound effects on Beijing's redefinition of its status *vis-à-vis* the Soviet Union, and consequently, this redefinition resulted in increased Chinese self-confidence at the negotiations in Panmunjom. Relieved from Stalin's shadow, Mao was then willing to make the necessary concessions that paved the way for the conclusion of the armistice. In this line of argument, Stalin can be regarded as the most important 'victim' of the Korean War, as his death enabled the other relevant actors to finally bring an end to the hostilities.

Interim conclusion: Mao's Korean War

The analysis of the CPV's five offensives strikingly disclosed that tactical considerations, military necessities, and battlefield realities played only a marginal role in China's conduct of warfare in Korea. From the onset of the intervention, the Chairman fought his campaigns in obvious disregard of the CPV commanders' advice and at any cost and risk. Accordingly, Mao's war objectives obviously did not consist in safeguarding China's national security. Mao fought this war for prestige, status, and the advance of his banner. When he first ordered the CPV to take the offense, the troops had not even set up a defensible bridgehead. Had the offensive resulted in a military debacle, China's northeastern flank would have been vulnerably exposed. One might ask whether China's intervention would have been likewise successful if Peng Dehuai had not acted in this moderating manner with regard to Mao's increasingly ambitious military objectives.

As was revealed by the second part of the analysis in particular, the prestige dimension of Mao's Korean War had two sides: on the one hand, Mao's personal status and his standing *vis-à-vis* Stalin, and on the other, China's standing in the world. As long as the CPV fought one offensive after another, Mao was able to stand away from Stalin's shadow. But, as the investigation of China's strategy during the armistice negotiations revealed, Mao then once more became Stalin's pupil. In addition, the analysis of China's position toward the POW issue demonstrated that Mao was primarily concerned with China's standing inside the socialist society. It was only after Stalin had died – in turn promoting Mao to the most senior socialist leader – that China's position underwent a dramatic shift and the Korean War armistice was successfully concluded. However, before the agreement could be signed, the CPV had to fight a final battle to punish Rhee Syng-man for the disrespect he had shown for China's status. This final episode alone provides evidence that Mao's Korean War was not fought for the sake of China's national security.

Conclusion: China's intervention in the Korean War

In the following section, I briefly summarize my central findings, before approaching the task of validating the two competing theoretical models' capacities to explain the reasons behind China's intervention in the Korean War.

First, my investigation of China's immediate reaction to the outbreak of the Korean Crisis demonstrates that Mao Zedong and Zhou Enlai set the course for intervention long before a formal decision was made or the Inchon landing had taken place. In line with the findings of my analysis on the pre-war phase, this strong determination indicates that the two most senior Chinese leaders were eager to fulfill the social obligations that had been transferred to Beijing by the Soviet Union.

Second, my analysis has shown that Mao Zedong deliberately introduced the rationale of the 'national security interest' into the Chinese decision-making process via his key military person, Marshal Peng Dehuai. Only after Peng, a distinguished and respected military expert, argued in favor of the intervention, outlining the necessity to intervene for the defense of the motherland, was consent reached among the Chinese leaders. However, there is good reason to argue that even Peng was not wholeheartedly convinced of the necessity and wisdom of intervention.

Third, the Inchon landing had no immediate effect on the Chinese decision to intervene. Even though a threat to China's security then began to materialize due to the swift advance of U.S./UN forces northward, Mao waited for two more weeks before he eventually introduced his personal decision into the formal decision-making process. This observation underlines that security considerations or strategic implications apparently played no role in the decision to intervene militarily in the Korean War. Only after the two identified prerequisites for a Chinese intervention in a socialist sister state were met did Mao call in the Chinese leadership to announce the decision he had already made regarding the necessity to intervene for the sake of socialist internationalism.

Fourth, the analysis of Beijing's risk behavior shows that China's risk-taking increased as the intervention grew closer. When the Chinese intervention finally took place, the incorporated risks were apparently prohibitive, as was evidently revealed in the CPV unit commanders' outspoken unwillingness to intervene under the then accrued circumstances. The Chairman, however, was nonetheless eagerly willing to bear these enormous risks in order to realize the intervention.

Fifth, the findings of the partial analyses solidly indicate that the emotional setting on the individual level played a significant – if not decisive – role in shaping the course for China's intervention. As outlined above, Mao showed his strong determination before any security-related trigger event had happened. Furthermore, the analysis also demonstrated that the individual level – and in particular the emotional dimension of relations between Mao and Stalin – had a significant effect on the definition of China's status *vis-à-vis* the Soviet Union and on China's conduct of negotiations during the armistice talks.

When these findings are taken into account, James Fearon's rationalist explanation is fighting a losing battle, as neither all of its underlying premises nor the two postulated causal mechanisms apply to the case at hand, even though the material issue under contestation, i.e. the Korean Peninsula, was perfectly divisible, as demonstrated to this day. As the successful conclusion of the armistice agreement shows, the commitment problem did not emerge either. However, as both China and the United States decided to act in highly risk-taking manners, Fearon's assumption on risk-averse or risk-neutral actors does not hold true. The United States acted in this way when disregarding Zhou Enlai's warnings, and China took high risks by intervening in the Korean War despite its low military capabilities in relation to its enemy, and with no certainty of success. In sum, as the two proposed causal mechanisms did not function as problems that impeded a non-violent solution to the conflict, Fearon's rationalist model is unable to generate explanatory power for the case at hand.

In contrast, Ned Lebow's Cultural Theory of International Relations captures almost perfectly the dynamics and processes of the Chinese intervention from the pre-war phase to the conclusion of the armistice: China's twofold intentions for entering the socialist society reflect the two motives *spirit* and *appetite*. Almost ideal-typically, the international socialist society reveals the characteristics of a spirit-based world. The Soviet Union as the lead nation honored Beijing by promoting China into the elite circle of this society, while its members publicly paid tribute to the People's Republic for its revolutionary achievements for the common cause, i.e. the society's underlying *nomos*. With regard to the historical mission of the New China, the resulting elevation of the PRC's international status must have been heart-balm for the self-esteem of Mao and his fellow CCP comrades. Adding to this, the continuing personal discrepancies between Stalin and Mao confirm Lebow's assumption that cooperation in spirit-based worlds is most difficult among actors that claim equal status rank. Such honors as the PRC received inside the socialist international society are usually accompanied by societal obligations and responsibilities, and, as Lebow reminds us, in order to preserve their status and the associated privileges, actors have to fulfill these obligations. My analysis shows that Mao was obviously eagerly willing to fulfill China's socialist obligations in order to preserve and further raise the PRC's standing inside the socialist society, as well as to realize his personal status demands *vis-à-vis* Stalin. The smoking gun for the spirit as Mao's dominant motive is his own statement before the Chinese leadership on October 4, 1950: "What you have said sounds reasonable. But it would be *shameful* for us to stand by seeing our neighbors in perilous danger without offering any help."[309] If China were to decide to stand idly by, "we [would] *feel terrible inside*, no matter what we may pretend."[310]

China's intervention in the Korean War unfolded in almost perfect accordance with the hypothetical process as outlined by Ned Lebow: imbalances at the individual level of China's key leaders (Mao and Zhou) gave rise to imbalances at the collective level (Chinese leadership), which eventually enabled them to arrive at the decision to resort to force. Thereby, the onset of the Korean War functioned as the principal catalyst for Mao and Zhou. The results of all partial analyses strongly confirm that Mao Zedong's – and thus China's – decision to intervene was not motivated by security considerations (*fear*) but rather by the *spirit*: the transfer of social obligations to China thereby reveals itself as the *underlying cause* for China's intervention in the Korean War, whereby Mao's spirit-induced willingness to fulfill these obligations in order to saturate the quest for (his personal and) China's status functioned as the *immediate cause*. In short, rather than for reasons of national security, China fought the Korean War in order to preserve and gain status.

Notes

1 See Shen, Zhihua, *Mao, Stalin and the Korean War. Trilateral Communist Relations in the 1950s* (London/New York: Routledge, 2012), 155; Nie, Rongzhen, "Beijing's Decision to Intervene," in *Mao's Generals Remember Korea*, ed. Bin, Yu, Millet, Allan R., and Li, Xiaobing (Lawrence: University Press of Kentucky, 2001), 39.
2 See Whiting, Allen S., *China Crosses the Yalu – The Decision to Enter the Korean War* (New York: Macmillan Publishers, 1960).
3 See Shen, *Mao, Stalin and the Korean War*, 66.
4 The theory was more than just an ideological construction, as it "reflected CCP leaders' fundamental perceptions of China's position in the post-war world" and can thus be regarded as highly important guideline along which the new Chinese foreign policy was formulated and executed: Chen, Jian, *China's Road to the Korean War – The Making of the Sino-American Confrontation* (New York: Columbia University Press, 1994), 20.
5 See Shen, *Mao, Stalin and the Korean War*, 67.
6 See Gurtov, Melvin and Hwang, Byong-Moo, *China under Threat: The Politics of Strategy and Diplomacy* (Baltimore/London: The Johns Hopkins University Press, 1980), 44–45.
7 See Goncharev, Sergei N., Lewis, John W., and Xue, Litai, *Uncertain Partners – Stalin, Mao, and the Korean War* (Stanford: Stanford University Press, 1993), 28.
8 See Shen, *Mao, Stalin and the Korean War*, 66–67.
9 See Goncharev, Lewis, and Xue, *Uncertain Partners*, 33, 66.
10 Mao, Zedong, *On the People's Democratic Dictatorship* (June 30, 1949).
11 Chen, *China's Road to the Korean War*, 23.
12 See Shen, *Mao, Stalin and the Korean War*, 69.
13 Chen, *China's Road to the Korean War*, 42.
14 Mao, Zedong, *The Chinese People Have Stood Up!*, Opening Address at the First Plenary Session of the Chinese People's Political Consultative Conference (September 21, 1949).
15 See Goncharev, Lewis, and Xue, *Uncertain Partners*, 85.
16 Ibid., 47. "For Mao and his comrades, the final goal of their revolution was more than the total transformation of the old Chinese society they saw as corrupt and unjust; they would pursue at the same time changing China's weak [international] status … China's standing up among the nations of the world, according to Mao's logic, would be realized through China's promotion of Asian and world revolutions, thus bringing

about the rejuvenation of China's central position in the international community": Chen, *China's Road to the Korean War*, 22.
17 See Goncharev, Lewis, and Xue, *Uncertain Partners*, 51.
18 See Shen, *Mao, Stalin and the Korean War*, 80–81.
19 Chen, *China's Road to the Korean War*, 74; see further Goncharev, Lewis, and Xue, *Uncertain Partners*, 65; Shen, *Mao, Stalin and the Korean War*, 81.
20 See Goncharev, Lewis, and Xue, *Uncertain Partners*, 64, 71–73.
21 Niu, Jun, "The Transformation of Chinese Foreign Policy and Its Impact on East Asia: International Patterns in the 1950s," in *Empire and After: Essays in Comparative Imperial and Decolonization Studies*, ed. Uyama, Tomohiko (Sapporo: Hokkaido University Press, 2012), 85.
22 Shen, *Mao, Stalin and the Korean War*, 105.
23 For a detailed account of the meetings see Chang, Jung and Halliday, John, *Mao – The Unknown Story* (New York: Anchor Books, 2006), 340–49.
24 See Chen, Jian, *Mao's China and the Cold War* (London, Chapel Hill: The University of North Carolina Press, 2001), 53.
25 "Years later, Mao was still nursing a deep sense of grievance over how he was treated by Stalin": Shen, *Mao, Stalin and the Korean War*, 94.
26 See Chen, *Mao's China*, 53; Di, He, "The Most Respected Enemy: Mao Zedong's Perceptions of the United States," *The China Quarterly* no. 137 (1994): 146.
27 Chang and Halliday, *Mao*, 345; Yang, Kuisong, *The Sino-Soviet Alliance and Nationalism: A Contradiction*, Parallel History Project on NATO and the Warsaw Pact: The Cold War History of Sino-Soviet Relations, ETH Zürich (June 2005), 5.
28 Chang and Halliday, *Mao*, 345.
29 See Li, Xiaobing, *A History of the Modern Chinese Army* (Lexington, KY: The University Press of Kentucky, 2007), 81.
30 See Goncharev, Lewis, and Xue, *Uncertain Partners*, 141.
31 See Ohn, Chang-Il, "The Causes of the Korean War, 1950–1953," *International Journal of Korean Studies* 14, no. 2 (2010): 24.
32 See Weathersby, Kathrin, "Soviet Aims in Korea and the Origins of the Korean War, 1945–1950: New Evidence from Russian Archives," *Cold War International History Project, Working Paper No. 8* (Washington, D.C., 1993), 28.
33 Goncharev, Lewis, and Xue, *Uncertain Partners*, 139.
34 See Shen, Zhihua, "Alliance of 'Tooth and Lips' or Marriage of Convenience? The Origins and Development of the Sino-North Korean Alliance, 1946–1958," in *Working Paper Series, U.S. Korea Institute, School of Advanced International Studies SAIS* (Washington, D.C., 2008), 6.
35 See Lee, Chae-Jin, *China and Korea: Dynamic Relations* (Standford, CA: Hoover Press, 1996), 21; Shen, *Mao, Stalin and the Korean War*, 127.
36 See Shen, *Mao, Stalin and the Korean War*, 6–7.
37 See Goncharev, Lewis, and Xue, *Uncertain Partners*, 140.
38 Shen, "Alliance of 'Tooth and Lips'," 6. The United States, too, feared that Seoul might launch an attack and thus kept South Korea short of heavy weapons.
39 See Shen, *Mao, Stalin and the Korean War*, 110.
40 Matray, James I., "Dean Acheson's Press Club Speech Reexamined," *The Journal of Conflict Studies* 22, no. 1 (2002).
41 See Shen, *Mao, Stalin and the Korean War*, 106.
42 Shi Zhe's account of the Mao–Stalin meeting is cited in Chen, *China's Road to the Korean War*, 88.
43 See Goncharev, Lewis, and Xue, *Uncertain Partners*, 140; Hao, Yufan and Zhai, Zhihai,

"China's Decision to Enter the Korean War: History Revisited," *The China Quarterly* no. 121 (1990): 109.
44 See Ohn, "The Causes of the Korean War," 34; Weathersby, "Soviet Aims in Korea," 28.
45 Goncharev, Lewis, and Xue, *Uncertain Partners*, 144.
46 Appleman, Roe E., *Disaster in Korea: The Chinese Confront MacArthur* (College Station, TX: A&M University Press, 1989), 50.
47 See Elleman, Bruce A., *Modern Chinese Warfare, 1795–1989* (New York: Routledge, 2001), 237.
48 Shen, "Alliance of 'Tooth and Lips'," 8.
49 Ibid.
50 Shen, *Mao, Stalin and the Korean War*, 131.
51 See Chen, *China's Road to the Korean War*, 10.
52 Shen, *Mao, Stalin and the Korean War*, 156.
53 See Li, *A History of the Modern Chinese Army*, 87; Chae, Han Sook et al., *The Korean War – Volume II* (Lincoln, NE: University of Nebraska Press, 2001), 26.
54 See Nie, "Beijing's Decision to Intervene," 39.
55 See Shen, *Mao, Stalin and the Korean War*, 136.
56 See Chang and Halliday, *Mao*, 365.
57 Lee, *China and Korea*, 13.
58 See Shen, *Mao, Stalin and the Korean War*, 137.
59 Chen, *China's Road to the Korean War*, 134.
60 Cited in ibid.
61 See Shen, *Mao, Stalin and the Korean War*, 131; Goncharev, Lewis, and Xue, *Uncertain Partners*, 152–53.
62 See Shen, *Mao, Stalin and the Korean War*, 140.
63 Chen, *China's Road to the Korean War*, 136.
64 See Chae et al., *The Korean War*, 23.
65 Ibid., 29.
66 See Chen, *China's Road to the Korean War*, 138.
67 See Shen, *Mao, Stalin and the Korean War*, 141; Sartori, Anne E., *Deterrence by Diplomacy* (Princeton/Oxford: Princeton University Press, 2005), 22.
68 Goncharev, Lewis, and Xue, *Uncertain Partners*, 162.
69 Chen, *China's Road to the Korean War*, 139.
70 See Du, Ping, "Political Mobilization and Control," in *Mao's Generals Remember Korea*, ed. Bin, Yu, Millet, Allan R., and Li, Xiaobing (Lawrence: University Press of Kansas, 2001), 66.
71 Cited in Shen, *Mao, Stalin and the Korean War*, 141.
72 See Zhang, Guang Shu, *Deterrence and Strategic Culture: Chinese–American Confrontations, 1949–1958* (Ithaca/London: Cornell University Press, 1992), 91–93; Tan, Kwoh J., "The Korean War June–October 1950: Inchon and Stalin in the 'Trigger vs. Justification' Debate," *Cold War International History Project, Working Paper No. 105* (Singapore, 2006), 21.
73 Chen, *China's Road to the Korean War*, 148.
74 Hao and Zhai, "China's Decision to Enter the Korean War," 109.
75 See Shen, *Mao, Stalin and the Korean War*, 144; Zhang, *Deterrence and Strategic Culture*, 95.
76 Di, "The Most Respected Enemy," 149.
77 See Tan, "The Korean War June–October 1950: Inchon and Stalin in the 'Trigger vs. Justification' Debate," 22.
78 See Elleman, *Modern Chinese Warfare*, 240–44; Friedrich, Jörg, *Yalu – an den Ufern des dritten Weltkriegs* (Berlin: Propyläen Verlag, 2007), 288.

79 See Chen, *China's Road to the Korean War*, 159.
80 Ibid., 160.
81 See Shen, *Mao, Stalin and the Korean War*, 156.
82 See Chen, *China's Road to the Korean War*, 28, 155.
83 See Goncharev, Lewis, and Xue, *Uncertain Partners*, 171.
84 See Elleman, *Modern Chinese Warfare*, 243–44.
85 See Goncharev, Lewis, and Xue, *Uncertain Partners*, 39–40, 69, 79, 148–49.
86 Even after the U.S. troops crossed the 38th parallel, the KPA was still able to mount organized resistance for one more week and considerably slowed down the advance of the enemy.
87 Cited in Chen, *China's Road to the Korean War*, 173.
88 See Shen, *Mao, Stalin and the Korean War*, 137.
89 See Sartori, *Deterrence by Diplomacy*, 22.
90 See Nie, "Beijing's Decision to Intervene," 41; Sartori, *Deterrence by Diplomacy*, 23–24; Panikkar, Kavalam M., *In Two Chinas – Memories of a Diplomat* (London: George Allen Unwin, 1955), 108.
91 Cited in Goncharev, Lewis, and Xue, *Uncertain Partners*, 179.
92 See Hao and Zhai, "China's Decision to Enter the Korean War," 103; Whiting, *China Crosses the Yalu*, 96, 110.
93 See Elleman, *Modern Chinese Warfare*, 243.
94 See Panikkar, *In Two Chinas*, 110. At that point, ROK forces had already crossed the parallel and were fighting on North Korean territory.
95 See Cohen, Arthur, "China and Intervention: Theory and Practice," *University of Pennsylvania Law Review* 121, no. 3 (1973): 474–75.
96 Davis, Jonathan E., "From Ideology to Pragmatism: China's Position on Humanitarian Intervention in the Post-Cold War Era," *Vanderbuilt Journal of International Law* 44, no. 2 (2011): 224.
97 See Chen, *China's Road to the Korean War*, 162.
98 See Chen, "Limits of the 'Lips and Teeth' Alliance: An Historical Review of Chinese–North Korean Relations," *Asia Program Special Report* 115 (2003): 5.
99 Chen, *China's Road to the Korean War*, 156.
100 See Ibid.
101 Cited in Myers, Robert J., *Korea in the Cross Currents. A Century of Struggle and the Crisis of Reunification* (New York: Palgrave, 2001), 89.
102 See Tan, "The Korean War June–October 1950: Inchon and Stalin in the 'Trigger vs. Justification' Debate," 23–24.
103 Goncharev, Lewis, and Xue, *Uncertain Partners*, 176.
104 Cited in ibid., 167.
105 Li, *A History of the Modern Chinese Army*, 83.
106 See Chen, *China's Road to the Korean War*, 175. The cable contains no reference to a security-related consideration as reason for the Chinese intervention.
107 Ibid., 182.
108 See Hao and Zhai, "China's Decision to Enter the Korean War," 105.
109 Scobell, Andrew, *China's Use of Military Force – Beyond the Great Wall and the Long March* (Cambridge: Cambridge University Press, 2003), 83.
110 Cited in Sheng, Michael, "The Psychology of the Korean War: The Role of Ideology and Perception in China's Entry into the War," *The Journal of Conflict Studies* 22, no. 1 (2002).
111 Cited in Li, *A History of the Modern Chinese Army*, 84.
112 Cited in Hao and Zhai, "China's Decision to Enter the Korean War," 106.

113 See Shen, *Mao, Stalin and the Korean War*, 157.
114 See Scobell, *China's Use of Military Force*, 84–86; Hunt, Michael H., "Beijing and the Korean Crisis, June 1950–June 1951," *Political Science Quarterly* 107, no. 3 (1992): 462.
115 Chen, *China's Road to the Korean War*, 183. "Peng's deliberations highlight what seems to have been a considerable dilemma for many senior officers: Their political loyalty was torn between a sense of 'Chineseness' on one hand and a sense of global class-consciousness on the other": Scobell, *China's Use of Military Force*, 85.
116 Chen, *China's Road to the Korean War*, 183.
117 Cited in Scobell, Andrew, "Soldiers, Statesmen, Strategic Culture, and China's 1950 Intervention in Korea," *Journal of Contemporary China* 8, no. 22 (1999): 488. See further Peng, Dehuai, *Memoirs of a Chinese Marshal. A Cultural Revolution 'Confession' by Marshal Peng Dehuai (1989–1974)* (Beijing: Foreign Language Press, 1984), 474.
118 See Hao and Zhai, "China's Decision to Enter the Korean War," 107–08; Scobell, "Soldiers, Statesmen, Strategic Culture," 482.
119 See Scobell, *China's Use of Military Force*, 86.
120 Ibid.
121 Ibid., 83.
122 See Chen, *China's Road to the Korean War*, 184–85; Scobell, *China's Use of Military Force*, 86.
123 See Chen, *China's Road to the Korean War*, 207.
124 See Shen, *Mao, Stalin and the Korean War*, 154.
125 See Zhang, Guang Shu, "Command, Control, and the PLA's Offensive Campaigns in the Korean War, 1950–1951," in *Chinese Warfighting: The PLA Experience since 1949*, ed. Ryan, Marc A., Finkelstein, David M., and McDevitt, Michael A. (Armonk/London: East Gate Books, 2003), 95; Chen, *China's Road to the Korean War*, 195.
126 See Scobell, "Soldiers, Statesmen, Strategic Culture," 488.
127 See Chen, *China's Road to the Korean War*, 202.
128 See Hao and Zhai, "China's Decision to Enter the Korean War," 111; Zhang, Guang Shu, *Mao's Military Romanticism: China and the Korean War, 1950–1953* (Lawrence, KS: University Press of Kansas, 1995), 85.
129 See Scobell, *China's Use of Military Force*, 91; Chen, *China's Road to the Korean War*, 201–02; Tan, "The Korean War June–October 1950: Inchon and Stalin in the 'Trigger vs. Justification' Debate," 31.
130 Chen, *China's Road to the Korean War*, 209.
131 See Li, *A History of the Modern Chinese Army*, 80.
132 See Zhang, "Command, Control, and the PLA's Offensive Campaigns," 112.
133 See Goncharev, Lewis, and Xue, *Uncertain Partners*, 58.
134 See Di, He, "The Last Campaign to Unify China: The CCP's Unrealized Plan to Liberate Taiwan, 1949–1950," in *Chinese Warfighting – The PLA Experience since 1949*, ed. Ryan, Marc A., Finkelstein, David M., and McDevitt, Michael A. (Armonk/London: East Gate Books, 2003), 78.
135 See Chen, *China's Road to the Korean War*, 176; Shen, *Mao, Stalin and the Korean War*, 161.
136 See Peters, Richard and Li, Xiaobing, *Voices from the Korean War. Personal Stories of American, Korean, and Chinese Soldiers* (Lexington, KY: The University of Kentucky Press, 2004), 24.
137 See Elleman, *Modern Chinese Warfare*, 247; Peters and Li, *Voices from the Korean War*, 24, 123–24.
138 Mao, Zedong, *On Protracted War* (May 1938), paragraph 48.
139 See Li, *A History of the Modern Chinese Army*, 91–92.

140 See Burles, Mark and Shulsky, Abraham N., *Patterns of China's Use of Force, Evidence from History and Doctrinal Writings* (Santa Monica: RAND, 2000), 23; Garver, John W., *Foreign Relations of the People's Republic of China* (Eaglewood Cliffs: Prentice Hall, 1993), 257.
141 See Peters and Li, *Voices from the Korean War*, 23.
142 See Zhang, *Mao's Military Romanticism*, 90; Goncharev, Lewis, and Xue, *Uncertain Partners*, 173.
143 See Li, *A History of the Modern Chinese Army*, 90.
144 See Du, "Political Mobilization and Control," 66–67; Chen, *China's Road to the Korean War*, 145.
145 See Hao and Zhai, "China's Decision to Enter the Korean War," 112; Bin, Yu, "What China Learned from Its 'Forgotten War' in Korea," in *Chinese Warfighting: The PLA Experience since 1949*, ed. Ryan, Marc A, Finkelstein, David M, and McDevitt, Michael A. (Armonk/London: East Gate Books, 2003), 125.
146 See Zhang, Xiaoming, "China and the Air War in Korea, 1950–1953," *The Journal of Military History* 62, no. 2 (1998): 339.
147 See Zhang, Xiaoming, *Red Wings over the Yalu. China, the Soviet Union, and the Air War in Korea* (College Station, TX: Texas A&M University Publishers, 2003), 6, 45.
148 See Peters and Li, *Voices from the Korean War*, 18.
149 See Li, Xiaobing, Wang, Xi, and Chen, Jian, "Mao's Dispatch of Chinese Troops to Korea: Forty-Six Telgrams July–October 1950," *Chinese Historians* no. 5 (1992): 68.
150 See Zhang, "China and the Air War in Korea, 1950–1953," 339.
151 See Chen, *China's Road to the Korean War*, 201–03.
152 See Werrell, Kenneth P., "Across the Yalu: Rules of Engagement and the Communist Air Sanctuary during the Korean War," *Journal of Military History* 72, no. 2 (2008): 461.
153 Zhang, *Red Wings over the Yalu*, 63.
154 See Chen, *Mao's China*, 55.
155 See Zhang, *Red Wings over the Yalu*, 60.
156 Ibid.
157 Chen, Jian, "China's Road to the Korean War," *Cold War International History Project Bulletin* no. 6–7 (1995/96): 43.
158 See Zhang, *Red Wings over the Yalu*, 65.
159 Goncharev, Lewis, and Xue, *Uncertain Partners*, 177.
160 See McCarthy, Michael J., "Uncertain Enemies: Soviet Pilots in the Korean War," *Air Power History* 44, no. 1 (1997): 110; Zhang, *Mao's Military Romanticism*, 82–83.
161 See Scobell, *China's Use of Military Force*, 82; Chen, *China's Road to the Korean War*, 200.
162 See Zhang, *Red Wings over the Yalu*, 70; Chen, *China's Road to the Korean War*, 201; O'Neill, Mark, "Soviet Involvement in the Korean War: A New View from the Soviet-era Archives," *Magazine of History* 14, no. 3 (2000): 21.
163 See Hao and Zhai, "China's Decision to Enter the Korean War," 110.
164 See Chen, *China's Road to the Korean War*, 200–01; Hunt, "Beijing and the Korean Crisis," 462–63.
165 Scobell, *China's Use of Military Force*, 91; Chen, *Mao's China*, 58.
166 Cited in Chen, *China's Road to the Korean War*, 207 [emphasis added].
167 Zhang, *Red Wings over the Yalu*, 76.
168 See Chen, *China's Road to the Korean War*, 150.
169 See Shen, *Mao, Stalin and the Korean War*, 47–48.
170 See Chen, *China's Road to the Korean War*, 158–59.
171 See Hunt, "Beijing and the Korean Crisis," 462. A translation of the telegram can be found in Chen, *China's Road to the Korean War*, 175–77.

172 See Chang and Halliday, *Mao*, 365.
173 See Peters and Li, *Voices from the Korean War*, 19; Zhang, "Command, Control, and the PLA's Offensive Campaigns," 97.
174 See Chen, Jian, "The Sino-Soviet Alliance and China's Entry in the Korean War," *Cold War International History Project, Working Paper No. 1* (Washington, D.C., 1992), 30.
175 See Elleman, *Modern Chinese Warfare*, 251.
176 See Zhang, *Red Wings over the Yalu*, 74.
177 See Zhang, *Deterrence and Strategic Culture*, 99.
178 See Zhang, *Red Wings over the Yalu*, 74; Zhang, *Deterrence and Strategic Culture*, 99.
179 Zhang, *Red Wings over the Yalu*, 74.
180 Cited in Chen, *China's Road to the Korean War*, 202.
181 See Hunt, "Beijing and the Korean Crisis," 463.
182 Zhang, *Red Wings over the Yalu*, 76.
183 See Zhang, "Command, Control, and the PLA's Offensive Campaigns," 98.
184 See *Mao's Military Romanticism*, 99–100.
185 See "Command, Control, and the PLA's Offensive Campaigns," 100.
186 See Li, *A History of the Modern Chinese Army*, 96; Lee, *China and Korea*, 25.
187 See Zhang, "Command, Control, and the PLA's Offensive Campaigns," 102.
188 During the first offensive the CPV suffered an estimate of 10,000 casualties: see Li, *A History of the Modern Chinese Army*, 95; Zhang, *Mao's Military Romanticism*, 106.
189 See Bin, Yu, "What China Learned from Its 'Forgotten War' in Korea," in *Chinese Warfighting: The PLA Experience since 1949*, ed. Ryan, Marc A., Finkelstein, David M., and McDevitt, Michael A. (Armonk/London: East Gate Books, 2003), 132.
190 See Zhang, *Mao's Military Romanticism*, 105–06.
191 See Stewart, Richard W., *American Military History Volume II: The United States Army in the Global Era, 1917–2008* (Washington, D.C.: Center for Military History, United States Army, 2010), 235.
192 Elleman, *Modern Chinese Warfare*, 247.
193 See Bin, "What China Learned from Its 'Forgotten War'," 128; Stewart, *American Military History*, 235. At this point, U.S. assessments calculated about 30,000 Chinese combatants.
194 See Peng, Dehuai, "My Story of the Korean War," in *Mao's Generals Remember Korea*, ed. Bin, Yu, Millet, Allan R., and Li, Xiaobing (Lawrence, KS: University Press of Kansas, 2001), 33.
195 See Bin, "What China Learned from Its 'Forgotten War'," 128.
196 See Peng, *Memoirs*, 476; Elleman, *Modern Chinese Warfare*, 249; Stewart, *American Military History*, 235–36.
197 Pollack, Jonathan, "The Korean War and Sino-American Relations," in *Sino-American Relations, 1945–1955: A Joint Reassessment of A Critical Decade*, ed. Harding, Harry and Min, Yuan (Wilmington, DE: Scholarly Resources, 1989), 224.
198 See Peng, *Memoirs*, 477; Zhu, Pingchao, *Americans and Chinese at the Korean War Cease-Fire Negotiations, 1950–1953* (Lanpeter: The Edwin Mellen Press, 2001), 25; Zhang, *Mao's Military Romanticism*, 118.
199 See Bin, "What China Learned from Its 'Forgotten War'," 130.
200 See Li, *A History of the Modern Chinese Army*, 99; Elleman, *Modern Chinese Warfare*, 246.
201 See Shen, Zhihua and Yafeng, Xia, "Mao Zedong's Erroneous Decisions During the Korean War: China's Rejection of the UN Cease-fire Resolution in Early 1961," *Asian Perspectives* no. 35 (2011): 195; Lee, *China and Korea*, 30.
202 See Bin, "What China Learned from Its 'Forgotten War'," 131.

203 "Stalin and Mao had reached a tacit agreement whether the CPV should cross to the south of the thirty-eighth parallel. The Soviet government had already expressed and attitude of 'striking while the iron is hot.' Under such circumstances, it was impossible for Mao to support Peng's request to temporarily suspend the offensive": Shen and Yafeng, "Mao Zedong's Erroneous Decisions," 195.
204 See Bin, "What China Learned from Its 'Forgotten War'," 131; Zhu, *Americans and Chinese at the Korean War*, 31.
205 See Peng, *Memoirs*, 478.
206 Cited in Zhang, *Mao's Military Romanticism*, 125.
207 Lee, *China and Korea*, 31.
208 See Stewart, *American Military History*, 238.
209 See Zhu, *Americans and Chinese at the Korean War*, 32.
210 See Zhang, "Command, Control, and the PLA's Offensive Campaigns," 104.
211 See Peng, *Memoirs*, 478.
212 See Peng, "My Story of the Korean War," 34.
213 See Zhang, "Command, Control, and the PLA's Offensive Campaigns," 104.
214 See Bin, "What China Learned from Its 'Forgotten War'," 133.
215 See Zhang, "Command, Control, and the PLA's Offensive Campaigns," 105; Shen, *Mao, Stalin and the Korean War*, 195–96; Friedrich, *Yalu*, 366.
216 See Bin, "What China Learned from Its 'Forgotten War'," 132.
217 See Peng, "My Story of the Korean War," 34.
218 See Shen and Yafeng, "Mao Zedong's Erroneous Decisions," 198.
219 Bin, "What China Learned from Its 'Forgotten War'," 132.
220 See Zhang, "Command, Control, and the PLA's Offensive Campaigns," 105.
221 See Elleman, *Modern Chinese Warfare*, 249; Lee, *China and Korea*, 32–33; Shen and Yafeng, "Mao Zedong's Erroneous Decisions," 188.
222 See Friedrich, *Yalu*, 372.
223 Cited in Zhang, "Command, Control, and the PLA's Offensive Campaigns," 106.
224 Friedrich, *Yalu*, 372 [own translation, emphasis added].
225 Zhang, "Command, Control, and the PLA's Offensive Campaigns," 109.
226 See Elleman, *Modern Chinese Warfare*, 249; Stewart, *American Military History*, 241; Lee, *China and Korea*, 34.
227 Bin, "What China Learned from Its 'Forgotten War'," 133.
228 Peng, *Memoirs*, 481.
229 See Zhang, "Command, Control, and the PLA's Offensive Campaigns," 108; Peng, *Memoirs*, 479–80.
230 Zhang, "Command, Control, and the PLA's Offensive Campaigns," 108.
231 By April 1951, the CPV had increased to a total of 950,000 men, including 750,000 combat troops: see Peng, "My Story of the Korean War," 36; Li, *A History of the Modern Chinese Army*, 93.
232 See Zhang, "Command, Control, and the PLA's Offensive Campaigns," 109.
233 See ibid., 110.
234 See Zhang, *Mao's Military Romanticism*, 152.
235 See Li, *A History of the Modern Chinese Army*, 101; Zhu, *Americans and Chinese at the Korean War*, 46.
236 See Elleman, *Modern Chinese Warfare*, 250; Friedrich, *Yalu*, 390.
237 See Friedrich, *Yalu*, 390; Shen and Yafeng, "Mao Zedong's Erroneous Decisions," 202.
238 Li, *A History of the Modern Chinese Army*, 102.
239 See Zhang, *Mao's Military Romanticism*, 154–57.
240 See Shen and Yafeng, "Mao Zedong's Erroneous Decisions," 202.

241 See Friedrich, *Yalu*, 392; Zhu, *Americans and Chinese at the Korean War*, 61; Joy, Turner C., *Negotiating while Fighting. The Diary of Admiral C. Turner Joy at the Korean Armistice Conference* (Stanford: Hoover Insitution Press, 1978), 10.
242 See Lee, *China and Korea*, 29–31; Shen and Yafeng, "Mao Zedong's Erroneous Decisions," 198.
243 See Zhu, *Americans and Chinese at the Korean War*, 4, 36, 175.
244 Cited in Shen and Yafeng, "Mao Zedong's Erroneous Decisions," 203.
245 See Zhu, *Americans and Chinese at the Korean War*, 49.
246 See Lee, *China and Korea*, 41–43.
247 See Zhu, *Americans and Chinese at the Korean War*, 63. With the onset of the talks, Mao appeared much more self-confident and also acted more independently from the Kremlin than before.
248 See Chai, Chengwen, "The Korean Truce Negotiations," in *Mao's Generals Remember Korea*, ed. Bin, Yu, Millet, Allan R., and Li, Xiaobing (Lawrence: University Press of Kansas, 2001), 186–88.
249 See Stueck, William W., *The Korean War: An International History* (Princeton: Princeton University Press, 1995), 225.
250 See Chai, "The Korean Truce Negotiations," 192–94.
251 See Zhu, *Americans and Chinese at the Korean War*, 72–73.
252 See Friedrich, *Yalu*, 394.
253 See Lee, *China and Korea*; Friedrich, *Yalu*, 416; Zhang, *Mao's Military Romanticism*, 158–60.
254 See Friedrich, *Yalu*, 418.
255 See Chai, "The Korean Truce Negotiations," 204; Joy, *Negotiating while Fighting*, 4; Lee, *China and Korea*, 44–45.
256 See Zhu, *Americans and Chinese at the Korean War*, 79.
257 See Joy, *Negotiating while Fighting*, 5.
258 See Lee, *China and Korea*, 46–47.
259 The UN delegation later modified the principle to "no forced repatriation": see Joy, *Negotiating while Fighting*, 8.
260 See Zhu, *Americans and Chinese at the Korean War*, 99–100.
261 See Zhang, *Mao's Military Romanticism*, 211–12. In particular, the UN command had been aware that captured ROK troops had been forced to fight in the North Korean forces and that a remarkably high number of Chinese POWs – especially former GMD soldiers, who made up 70 percent of the Chinese POWs – expressed the wish not to be sent back to the PRC.
262 Zhu, *Americans and Chinese at the Korean War*, 97.
263 See Joy, *Negotiating while Fighting*, 8; Lee, *China and Korea*, 47–48. Not surprisingly, virtually all of the 12,000 Allied POWs expressed the wish to be repatriated to their home countries.
264 See Joy, *Negotiating while Fighting*, 120; Friedrich, *Yalu*, 429; Zhu, *Americans and Chinese at the Korean War*, 109.
265 Cited in Lee, *China and Korea*, 48.
266 See Friedrich, *Yalu*, 422–24.
267 See Zhu, *Americans and Chinese at the Korean War*, 117.
268 See Foot, Rosemary, "Nuclear Coercion and the Ending of the Conflict," *International Security* 13, no. 3 (1998/89): 96.
269 See Zhu, *Americans and Chinese at the Korean War*, 147–48.
270 Cited in Central Intelligence Agency, *Intelligence Report: Asian Communist Employment of Negotiations as Political Tactic*, November 1966, 26.

271 See Chai, "The Korean Truce Negotiations," 229; Zhu, *Americans and Chinese at the Korean War*, 154–55; Zhang, *Mao's Military Romanticism*, 242; Friedrich, *Yalu*, 464–67.
272 See Chai, "The Korean Truce Negotiations," 229; Lee, *China and Korea*, 55.
273 See Zhang, *Mao's Military Romanticism*, 242.
274 See Chai, "The Korean Truce Negotiations," 230.
275 See Friedrich, *Yalu*, 446.
276 See Zhang, *Mao's Military Romanticism*, 243.
277 See Friedrich, *Yalu*, 467; Chai, "The Korean Truce Negotiations," 230.
278 See Friedrich, *Yalu*, 466.
279 Zhu, *Americans and Chinese at the Korean War*, 167.
280 See Zhang, *Mao's Military Romanticism*, 57.
281 See Lee, *China and Korea*, 45.
282 See Friedrich, *Yalu*, 456; Zhu, *Americans and Chinese at the Korean War*, 145–46.
283 Peng, "My Story of the Korean War," 37.
284 See Friedman, Edward, "Nuclear Blackmail and the End of the Korean War," *Modern China* 1, no. 1 (1975): 84; Friedrich, *Yalu*, 432–40.
285 See Zhang, *Mao's Military Romanticism*, 173–74.
286 See Eisenhower, Dwight D., *The White House Years: Mandate for Change, 1953–1956 (Vol. 1)* (Garden City: Doubleday & Company, 1963), 179–80; Brodie, Bernhard, *War and Politics* (London: Macmillan Publishers, 1973),105; Dingman, Roger, "Atomic Diplomacy During the Korean War," *International Security* 13, no. 3 (1988/89): 50.
287 See Foot, "Nuclear Coercion," 97–99; Adams, Sherman, *First-Hand Report: The Inside Story of the Eisenhower Administration* (New York: Harper & Brothers, 1961), 48; Friedman, "Nuclear Blackmail": 79.
288 By whispering this myth down the lane, it may have gained acceptance in certain circles, but certainly not empirical plausibility: see Dingman, "Atomic Diplomacy During the Korean War," 50.
289 See Friedman, "Nuclear Blackmail," 81.
290 See Goncharev, Lewis, and Xue, *Uncertain Partners*, 164–66; Friedman, "Nuclear Blackmail," 80–81.
291 See Foot, "Nuclear Coercion," 105–06.
292 See Zhang, *Mao's Military Romanticism*, 233–34; Goncharev, Lewis, and Xue, *Uncertain Partners*, 166.
293 See Foot, "Nuclear Coercion," 102–03.
294 See Friedrich, *Yalu*, 472.
295 See Zhu, *Americans and Chinese at the Korean War*, 89.
296 See ibid., 104.
297 See Shen, *Mao, Stalin and the Korean War*, 185; Zhu, *Americans and Chinese at the Korean War*, 135; Friedman, "Nuclear Blackmail," 86.
298 See Zhu, *Americans and Chinese at the Korean War*, 89.
299 See Shen, *Mao, Stalin and the Korean War*, 184, 201.
300 See Zhu, *Americans and Chinese at the Korean War*, 34, 86; Shen and Yafeng, "Mao Zedong's Erroneous Decisions," 203.
301 See Mearsheimer, John J., *The Tragedy of Great Power Politics* (New York/London: W.W. Norton & Company, 2001), 153–55.
302 Shen, *Mao, Stalin and the Korean War*, 118.
303 See Lee, *China and Korea*, 51–52.
304 See McCarthy, "Uncertain Enemies," 35.
305 See Zhu, *Americans and Chinese at the Korean War*, 135.
306 See ibid., 51.

307 See Shen, *Mao, Stalin and the Korean War*, 203.
308 See Friedrich, *Yalu*, 459.
309 Cited in Sheng, "The Psychology of the Korean War: The Role of Ideology and Perception in China's Entry into the War" [emphasis added].
310 Cited in Li, *A History of the Modern Chinese Army*, 84 [emphasis added].

Bibliography

Adams, Sherman. *First-Hand Report: The Inside Story of the Eisenhower Administration*. New York: Harper & Brothers, 1961.

Appleman, Roe E. *Disaster in Korea: The Chinese Confront MacArthur*. College Station: A&M University Press, 1989.

Bin, Yu. "What China Learned from Its 'Forgotten War' in Korea." In *Chinese Warfighting: The PLA Experience since 1949*, edited by Marc A. Ryan, David M. Finkelstein, and Michael A. McDevitt, 123–42. Armonk/London: East Gate Books, 2003.

Brodie, Bernhard. *War and Politics*. London: Macmillan Publishers, 1973.

Burles, Mark, and Shulsky, Abraham N. *Patterns of China's Use of Force, Evidence from History and Doctrinal Writings*. Santa Monica: RAND, 2000.

Central Intelligence Agency. *Intelligence Report: Asian Communist Employment of Negotiations as Political Tactic* (November 1966). Accessed at www.cia.gov/library/readingroom/document/intelligence-report-asian-communist-employment-negotiations-political-tactic-november-1966 (October 24, 2016).

Chae, Han Sook, Chung, Suk Kyun, Son, Moon Sik, McClanahan, Kay, and Kim, Cong Ku. *The Korean War – Volume II*. Lincoln, NE: University of Nebraska Press, 2001.

Chai, Chengwen. "The Korean Truce Negotiations." In *Mao's Generals Remember Korea*, edited by Yu Bin, Allan R. Millet, and Xiaobing Li, 184–232. Lawrence, KS: University Press of Kansas, 2001.

Chang, Jung, and Halliday, John. *Mao – The Unknown Story*. New York: Anchor Books, 2006.

Chen, Jian. "The Sino-Soviet Alliance and China's Entry in the Korean War." *Cold War International History Project, Working Paper No. 1*. Washington, D.C., 1992.

Chen, Jian. *China's Road to the Korean War – The Making of the Sino-American Confrontation*. New York: Columbia University Press, 1994.

Chen, Jian. "China's Road to the Korean War." *Cold War International History Project Bulletin* no. 6–7 (1995/96): 41–53.

Chen, Jian. *Mao's China and the Cold War*. London, Chapel Hill, NC: The University of North Carolina Press, 2001.

Chen, Jian. "Limits of the 'Lips and Teeth' Alliance: An Historical Review of Chinese-North Korean Relations." *Asia Program Special Report* 115 (2003): 4–10.

Cohen, Arthur. "China and Intervention: Theory and Practice." *University of Pennsylvania Law Review* 121, no. 3 (1973): 471–505.

Davis, Jonathan E. "From Ideology to Pragmatism: China's Position on Humanitarian Intervention in the Post-Cold War Era." *Vanderbuilt Journal of International Law* 44, no. 2 (2011): 217–83.

Di, He. "The Most Respected Enemy: Mao Zedong's Perceptions of the United States." *The China Quarterly* no. 137 (1994): 144–58.

Di, He. "The Last Campaign to Unify China: The CCP's Unrealized Plan to Liberate Taiwan, 1949–1950." In *Chinese Warfighting – The PLA Experience since 1949*, edited by Marc A. Ryan, David M. Finkelstein, and Michael A. McDevitt, 73–90. Armonk/London: East Gate Books, 2003.

Dingman, Roger. "Atomic Diplomacy during the Korean War." *International Security* 13, no. 3 (1988/89): 50–91.

Du, Ping. "Political Mobilization and Control." In *Mao's Generals Remember Korea*, edited by Yu Bin, Allan R. Millet, and Xiaobing Li, 61–105. Lawrence, KS: University Press of Kansas, 2001.

Eisenhower, Dwight D. *The White House Years: Mandate for Change, 1953–1956 (Vol. 1)*. Garden City: Doubleday & Company, 1963.

Elleman, Bruce A. *Modern Chinese Warfare, 1795–1989*. Routledge: New York, 2001.

Foot, Rosemary. "Nuclear Coercion and the Ending of the Conflict." *International Security* 13, no. 3 (1998/89): 92–112.

Friedman, Edward. "Nuclear Blackmail and the End of the Korean War." *Modern China* 1, no. 1 (1975): 75–91.

Friedrich, Jörg. *Yalu – an den Ufern des dritten Weltkriegs*. Berlin: Propyläen Verlag, 2007.

Garver, John W. *Foreign Relations of the People's Republic of China*. Eaglewood Cliffs, NJ: Prentice Hall, 1993.

Goncharev, Sergei N., Lewis, John W., and Xue, Litai. *Uncertain Partners – Stalin, Mao, and the Korean War*. Stanford, CA: Stanford University Press, 1993.

Gurtov, Melvin, and Hwang, Byong-Moo. *China under Threat. The Politics of Strategy and Diplomacy*. Baltimore, London: The Johns Hopkins University Press, 1980.

Hao, Yufan, and Zhai, Zhihai. "China's Decision to Enter the Korean War: History Revisited." *The China Quarterly* no. 121 (1990): 94–115.

Hunt, Michael H. "Beijing and the Korean Crisis, June 1950–June 1951." *Political Science Quarterly* 107, no. 3 (1992): 453–78.

Joy, Turner C. *Negotiating while Fighting. The Diary of Admiral C. Turner Joy at the Korean Armistice Conference*. Stanford, CA: Hoover Insitution Press, 1978.

Lee, Chae-Jin. *China and Korea: Dynamic Relations*. Standford, CA: Hoover Press, 1996.

Li, Xiaobing. *A History of the Modern Chinese Army*. Lexington, KY: The University Press of Kentucky, 2007.

Li, Xiaobing, Wang, Xi, and Chen, Jian. "Mao's Dispatch of Chinese Troops to Korea: Forty-Six Telgrams July–October 1950." *Chinese Historians* no. 5 (1992): 63–86.

Mao, Zedong, *The Chinese People Have Stood Up!*, Opening Address at the First Plenary Session of the Chinese People's Political Consultative Conference (September 21, 1949). Accessed at www.marxists.org/reference/archive/mao/selected-works/volume-5/mswv5_01.htm (August 5, 2016).

Mao, Zedong. *On Protracted War* (May 1938). Accessed at www.marxists.org/reference/archive/mao/selected-works/volume-2/mswv2_09.htm (August 5, 2016).

Mao, Zedong. *On the People's Democratic Dictatorship* (June 30, 1949). Accessed at www.marxists.org/reference/archive/mao/selected-works/volume-4/mswv4_65.htm (August 5, 2016).

Matray, James I. "Dean Acheson's Press Club Speech Reexamined." *The Journal of Conflict Studies* 22, no. 1 (2002). Accessed at https://journals.lib.unb.ca/index.php/jcs/article/view/ 366/578 (August 5, 2016).

McCarthy, Michael J. "Uncertain Enemies: Soviet Pilots in the Korean War." *Air Power History* 44, no. 1 (1997): 32–45.

Mearsheimer, John J. *The Tragedy of Great Power Politics*. New York/London: W. W. Norton & Company, 2001.

Myers, Robert J. *Korea in the Cross Currents. A Century of Struggle and the Crisis of Reunification*. New York: Palgrave, 2001.

Nie, Rongzhen. "Beijing's Decision to Intervene." In *Mao's Generals Remember Korea*, edited by Yu Bin, Allan R. Millet, and Xiaobing Li, 38–60. Lawrence, KY: University Press of Kentucky, 2001.

Niu, Jun. "The Transformation of Chinese Foreign Policy and Its Impact on East Asia: International Patterns in the 1950s." In *Empire and After: Essays in Comparative Imperial and Decolonization Studies*, edited by Tomohiko Uyama, 81–89. Sapporo: Hokkaido University Press, 2012.

O'Neill, Mark "Soviet Involvement in the Korean War: A New View from the Soviet-era Archives." *Magazine of History* 14, no. 3 (2000): 20–24.

Ohn, Chang-Il. "The Causes of the Korean War, 1950–1953." *International Journal of Korean Studies* 14, no. 2 (2010): 19–44.

Panikkar, Kavalam M. *In Two Chinas – Memories of a Diplomat*. London: George Allen Unwin, 1955.

Peng, Dehuai. *Memoirs of a Chinese Marshal. A Cultural Revolution "Confession" by Marshal Peng Dehuai (1989–1974)*. Beijing: Foreign Language Press, 1984.

Peng, Dehuai. "My Story of the Korean War." In *Mao's Generals Remember the Korean War*, edited by Yu Bin, Allan R. Millet, and Xiaobing Li, 30–37. Lawrence, KS: University Press of Kansas, 2001.

Peters, Richard, and Li, Xiaobing. *Voices from the Korean War: Personal Stories of American, Korean, and Chinese Soldiers*. Lexington, KY: The University of Kentucky Press, 2004.

Pollack, Jonathan. "The Korean War and Sino-American Relations." In *Sino-American Relations, 1945–1955: A Joint Reassessment of a Critical Decade*, edited by Harry Harding and Yuan Min, 217–35. Wilmington: Scholarly Resources, 1989.

Sartori, Anne E. *Deterrence by Diplomacy*. Princeton/Oxford: Princeton University Press, 2005.

Scobell, Andrew. "Soldiers, Statesmen, Strategic Culture, and China's 1950 Intervention in Korea." *Journal of Contemporary China* 8, no. 22 (1999): 477–97.

Scobell, Andrew. *China's Use of Military Force – Beyond the Great Wall and the Long March*. Cambridge: Cambridge University Press, 2003.

Shen, Zhihua. "Alliance of 'Tooth and Lips' or Marriage of Convenience? The Origins and Development of the Sino-North Korean Alliance, 1946–1958." In *Working Paper Series U.S. Korea Institute, School of Advanced International Studies SAIS*. Washington, D.C., 2008.

Shen, Zhihua. *Mao, Stalin and the Korean War. Trilateral Communist Relations in the 1950s*. London/New York: Routledge, 2012.

Shen, Zhihua, and Yafeng, Xia. "Mao Zedong's Erroneous Decisions During the Korean War: China's Rejection of the UN Cease-fire Resolution in Early 1961." *Asian Perspectives* no. 35 (2011): 187–209.

Sheng, Michael. "The Psychology of the Korean War: The Role of Ideology and Perception in China's Entry into the War." *The Journal of Conflict Studies* 22, no. 1 (2002). Accessed at https://journals.lib.unb.ca/index.php/JCS/article/view/367/581 (August 5, 2016).

Stewart, Richard W. *American Military History Volume II: The United States Army in the Global Era, 1917–2008*. Washington, D.C.: Center for Military History, United States Army, 2010.

Stueck, William W. *The Korean War: An International History*. Princeton, NJ: Princeton University Press, 1995.

Tan, Kwoh J. "The Korean War June–October 1950: Inchon and Stalin in the 'Trigger vs. Justification' Debate." *Cold War International History Project, Working Paper No. 105*. Singapore, 2006.

Weathersby, Kathrin. "Soviet Aims in Korea and the Origins of the Korean War, 1945–1950: New Evidence from Russian Archives." *Cold War International History Project, Working Paper No. 8*. Washington, D.C., 1993.

Werrell, Kenneth P. "Across the Yalu: Rules of Engagement and the Communist Air Sanctuary during the Korean War." *Journal of Military History* 72, no. 2 (2008): 451–75.

Whiting, Allen S. *China Crosses the Yalu – The Decision to Enter the Korean War.* New York: Macmillan Publishers, 1960.

Yang, Kuisong. *The Sino-Soviet Alliance and Nationalism: A Contradiction.* Parallel History Project on NATO and the Warsaw Pact: The Cold War History of Sino-Soviet Relations, ETH Zürich. June 2005.

Zhang, Guang Shu. *Deterrence and Strategic Culture: Chinese–American Confrontations, 1949–1958.* Ithaca/London: Cornell University Press, 1992.

Zhang, Guang Shu. *Mao's Military Romanticism: China and the Korean War, 1950–1953.* Lawrence, KS: University Press of Kansas, 1995.

Zhang, Guang Shu. "Command, Control, and the PLA's Offensive Campaigns in the Korean War, 1950–1951." In *Chinese Warfighting: The PLA Experience since 1949*, edited by Marc A. Ryan, David M. Finkelstein, and Michael A. McDevitt, 91–122. Armonk/London: East Gate Books, 2003.

Zhang, Xiaoming. "China and the Air War in Korea, 1950–1953." *The Journal of Military History* 62, no. 2 (1998): 335–79.

Zhang, Xiaoming. *Red Wings over the Yalu: China, the Soviet Union, and the Air War in Korea.* College Station, TX: Texas A&M University Publishers, 2003.

Zhu, Pingchao. *Americans and Chinese at the Korean War Cease-Fire Negotiations, 1950–1953.* Lanpeter: The Edwin Mellen Press, 2001.

4 The Sino-Indian War of 1962

At the height of the Cuban Missile Crisis, while the world's attention was absorbed by the nerve-racking standoff between the two superpowers in the Caribbean, a hot war erupted on the other side of the globe. On October 20, 1962, China launched a full-scale attack over the disputed Sino-Indian boundary. Less than a decade after both countries had agreed on the 'Five Principles of Peaceful Coexistence,' Chinese and Indian soldiers exchanged deadly fire in the icy heights of the Himalayas. The Sino-Indian War lasted a total of five weeks but saw less than 14 days of actual combat. The result was a humiliating defeat of India's unprepared, outnumbered, and poorly commanded armed forces.

In this chapter, I seek to answer the question of how a long-standing issue such as the border dispute could strain the bilateral relationship to such an extent that the two former friends clashed in open war. To do so, I will show that the causes for the outbreak of the Sino-Indian War are primarily to be found in the two states' colliding approaches towards a resolution of the boundary problem: while Beijing was genuinely interested in a mutually acceptable solution through negotiations, India's 'fixed and final' approach impeded any compromise. When the dispute then turned into a militarized conflict, Beijing still tried its best to contain the crisis from escalating and actively sought a non-violent solution. Nonetheless, when India's shown disrespect for China's interest, status, and military might had reached an extent that Beijing deemed intolerable, the Chinese leadership decided it was necessary to teach New Delhi a 'painful lesson' as to why China should be taken seriously. China's campaign against India had two principal objectives: on the one hand, the Chinese leadership intended to punish the Indian government for the impertinence it had shown; on the other, Beijing simultaneously aimed at bringing Nehru back to the negotiation table. In short, fighting the Sino-Indian War of 1962 had, in Beijing's perspective, become necessary to negotiate peace.

Outline of the chapter

The remainder of this case study is organized as follows. Before approaching the analysis of the formation of the Sino-Indian conflict, I present a brief outline of the border problem as the underlying cleavage. I then trace the deterioration in Sino-Indian relations from friendship to enmity and the simultaneous emergence of the boundary issue from a subcutaneous cleavage to the determining source of conflict.

The analysis is divided into four phases, each covering a distinct step in the development of the bilateral relationship, and shows the two actors' conflicting approaches toward the boundary issue and the corresponding escalation of the border dispute. In the next section, I examine China's political decision-making and operative planning. The analysis of both processes ascertains the two above-mentioned goals as the principal objectives of China's use of force, and highlights the emotionalized atmosphere in which the Chinese leadership decided on the war's objective and course. After that I analyze China's risk behavior. Thereto, I provide an overview of the characteristics and challenges of warfare at high altitudes and compare the two belligerents' military portfolios for this special type of military combat. The fourth section examines the course of China's use of force from the onset of the war up to Beijing's unilateral cease-fire and withdrawal, and shows how Beijing implemented its twofold war objective on the ground. By summarizing my central findings in the concluding section, I provide an answer to the general research question of this book and assess the explanatory power of the two competing theoretical models for the case under investigation.

The making of a conflict

When India gained its independence and the People's Republic emerged from the ruins of the Chinese Civil War, the young nations inherited a problematic legacy: a largely unstipulated, approximately 4,000-kilometer-long border that can be divided into three segments. The western sector runs from Kashmir over Aksai Chin/Ladakh to Nepal's western border; the central sector between Nepal and Bhutan; and the eastern sector from Bhutan's eastern border in the west to the boundary triangle of China, India, and Myanmar.[1] At its core, the Sino-Indian border dispute consisted of competing claims over territories that had been cut off by colonial boundary-drawing: in the east, the McMahon Line, unilaterally delineated by British India in 1914, constituted the de facto border but had left Chinese-claimed Arunachal Pradesh under Indian jurisdiction; in the west, India in turn claimed ownership over the desolate highlands of Aksai Chin, which, however, had been under China's control for decades and were thus regarded by Beijing as Chinese territory. As British India had not made any serious attempts to demarcate the boundary in the western sector, it had been up to China to unilaterally stipulate its course.[2] From the onset of their relationship, India and China were thus confronted with the problem of an unsettled border that had been unilaterally stipulated by China in the west and by India's affirmation of the McMahon Line in the east. As a result, competing claims about sovereignty over Aksai Chin (39,000 square kilometers) in the west and Arunachal Pradesh (82,000 square kilometers) in the east existed as a potential cleavage between New Delhi and Beijing.

Remarkably, it took more than a decade for this problem to become an actual source of conflict, and another two years for the border dispute to finally escalate into open war. This bears the conclusion that causes of the Sino-Indian War are not to be found in a spontaneous escalation of a militarized boundary dispute. Even though the border was the issue under contestation, the actual *casus belli* is rather to be found in the two actors' conflicting strategies toward the settlement of the border problem.

In the subsequent sections, I trace the evolution of the Sino-Indian conflict and demonstrate that, while China was willing to negotiate a mutually acceptable solution, India's approach increasingly impeded any compromise.

Phase I: a special relationship

Hindi Chini bhai bhai: Indians and Chinese are brothers. This slogan might best describe the cordial relationship between China and India during the 1950s.[3] With the exception of their different political systems, the two countries had much in common: having once been political and cultural centers of gravity, both had had to endure the demise of their former power and glory during the period of Western colonialism. Then, however, both had cast off the colonial yoke and now faced the same domestic challenges of economic and social development. Consequently, it was "reasonable to assume that neither country in their common predicament could afford to be antagonistic toward the other."[4] On the contrary, with the re-emergence of India and China, a new spirit of optimism and solidarity soon developed between Beijing and New Delhi. India was the first non-socialist country to formally recognize the People's Republic, and when China fought on the side of the 'progressive forces' in the Korean War it was New Delhi that served as tireless mediator, honest broker, informal communication channel, and occasionally even as Beijing's advocate. India also took the lead in the attempt to transfer the Chinese seat in the UN Security Council to Beijing, which would have significantly elevated the standing of the People's Republic. In return, Beijing honored India's support by departing from the clear-cut 'Leaning to One Side' policy in October 1952 in declaring that countries with differing social systems and ways of life could coexist peacefully. Two years later, the two governments formalized this idea in the 'Five Principles of Peaceful Coexistence'/*Panch Sheel* as the basis for a special relationship.[5] Following this, China and India even started to elaborate first ideas for an Asian collective security system.[6] This overall positive record allows for the conclusion that the brotherly relationship between India and China not only greatly benefited both countries, but also revealed the inherent potential for shaping the course of Asia's future[7] – under the premise, however, that *Hindi Chini bhai bhai* remained valid.

First clouds over the Sino-Indian honeymoon

During this honeymoon period, Beijing and New Delhi moved closer, not only with regard to their relationship but also concerning their common boundary. In the west, one outcome of the First Kashmir War (1947–9) decided that New Delhi and Beijing had to share a border in the Ladakh/Aksai Chin region. Beijing in turn completed the drawing of the frontier with the incorporation of Tibet under China's jurisdiction in May 1951.

Tibet was an issue of sensitivity for both India and China. For New Delhi, the Tibetan plateau had traditionally functioned as a strategic buffer to the north.[8] Also, India had long-standing ties with the Tibetan population because geographical features favored India's access to the highlands. Politically, New Delhi had supported the Tibetan government, and when it became obvious in 1950 that the PLA was about to march into Tibet, India assisted the Tibetan struggle for autonomy in word and deed.[9] For Beijing, the imperative of the New China's historical mission demanded that Beijing's sovereignty over territories lost during the Century of Shame had to be reasserted in order to eradicate China's mistreatment by imperialist forces.[10] Tibet was one of these lost territories. Its status had become somewhat undefined after the onset of the Chinese Civil War; however, according to Beijing's interpretation, Tibet had always been an integral part of China and therefore the reestablishment of Beijing's rule was a logical consequence of the founding of the PRC.

When the PLA eventually 'liberated' Tibet in October 1950, New Delhi unexpectedly decided not to oppose but rather to substantially support the annexation by backing the People's Republic internationally.[11] Moreover, India also convinced the Dalai Lama to stay and search for accommodation with China, which allowed Beijing to formalize the annexation in the 'Seventeen-Point Agreement' of May 1951 granting Tibet the status of an autonomous region.[12] India's support thus significantly facilitated the consolidation of China's control over Tibet. Furthermore, it also set the basic tone for the honeymoon period in Sino-Indian relations that followed, which culminated in the conclusion of the *Agreement between the Republic of India and the People's Republic of China on Trade and Intercourse between the Tibet Region of China and India* in April 1954. Thereby, India "formally recognized China's ownership of Tibet as part of an effort to reach a broader understanding with China."[13] With India's affirmation of Beijing's sovereignty over Tibet – "the biggest concession to China in modern Asian history"[14] – consent had been reached over what could have been regarded as the most sensitive issue in the bilateral relationship to that date. However, while the agreement solved one problem, another one started to emerge increasingly pronounced: with Tibet's reintegration into China, the virgin birth of the Sino-Indian frontier was completed, leaving New Delhi and Beijing with the task of its concrete stipulation. Thereby, the first dark clouds began to shadow the Sino-Indian honeymoon.

The eastern sector: the controversy over the 'illegal' McMahon Line

Immediately after gaining independence, New Delhi had declared "that its boundary with China, as delineated by India, has been fixed,"[15] and in November 1950, "India's Prime Minister Nehru affirmed that the frontier from Bhutan eastward had been clearly defined by the McMahon line."[16] In what followed, India continued to regard the McMahon Line as the well-established demarcation in the eastern sector of the border. As this line had left Arunachal Pradesh on India's side, New Delhi also regarded this area, then under the administration of India's North Eastern Frontier Agency (NEFA), as Indian territory.[17]

This collided with Beijing's interpretation, because the "Chinese (both Kuomintang and Communist) ha[d] maintained that the negotiating of the McMahon Line was a British trick, and ha[d] prefixed the word 'illegal' to any mention of the McMahon Line or the boundary it presented."[18] Consequently, Beijing responded to India's affirmation of the McMahon Line by insisting that the boundary had not yet been mutually stipulated, as China had neither recognized its legitimacy nor formally abandoned its claim on Arunachal Pradesh.[19] For the time being, however, Beijing suggested maintaining the status quo in the eastern sector. The principal reason why China was fundamentally unwilling to accept the McMahon Line as a de jure demarcation – although Beijing acknowledged it as a de facto boundary – is to be found in the fact that its formal recognition would have heavily undermined Beijing's position on the status of Tibet. According to Beijing's interpretation, the stipulation of the McMahon Line by the Simla Convention of 1914 was an unlawful act because Tibet had not been authorized to sign the convention, and especially as the Chinese delegation had already rejected the document and left Simla.[20] If the People's Republic now accepted the outcome of the convention, i.e. the legality of the McMahon Line, this would mean that Tibet had acted as an independent country in 1914, which would have "marked the PRC's actions in Tibet since 1950 as aggression or even imperialism."[21]

In essence, China's position on the boundary in the eastern sector was that the borderline had not been mutually stipulated and was thus subject to bilateral negotiations.[22] Despite this, Beijing agreed to accept the McMahon Line not only as a provisional boundary for the time being but also as the basis for the final settlement.[23] In other words, for the sake of a mutually stipulated boundary, China was willing to abandon its claim on Arunachal Pradesh.

The western sector: India's last-minute claim

The western sector did not emerge as the second pillar of contestation for a notably long time. "Neither government had raised the Aksai Chin boundary issue in a meeting to negotiate a 1954 trade agreement involving Tibet or in Zhou's talks with Nehru in 1956"[24] and, as Allen Whiting observed, "no Indian activity had sought to establish rule in this barren area."[25]

When entering the Tibetan highlands in 1950, the PLA had been confronted with the problem that no major road suitable for large troop movements led into the region.[26] In order to strengthen China's control over Tibet, Beijing thus decided in 1956 to upgrade a traditional caravan trail. The road was completed in October the next year.[27] This link between Xinjiang and Tibet was of strategic importance for China, as the road "provided the only means of modern transport … to facilitate troop movements between politically dissident and otherwise remote regions."[28] When the news about China's development of Aksai Chin caught New Delhi's attention in mid-1958, the Indian government dispatched patrols to ascertain the exact location of the new road. The results confirmed New Delhi's initial suspicions: around 180 kilometers of the road crossed through territory that India regarded – but until then had not officially claimed – as Indian.[29] On Chinese maps, however, the road was all within Chinese territory.

Not before October 1958, New Delhi unexpectedly informed Beijing about an Indian claim over 39,000 square kilometers in Aksai Chin.[30] Reaffirming this demand in a letter to Zhou Enlai in December, the Indian government stated that there could be "no question of these large parts of India being anything but India."[31] According to Melvin Gurtov and Byong-Moo Hwang, this "was the first time in recorded history that India had claimed ownership of Aksai Chin."[32] In his reply,

Zhou rejected the Indian demand but emphasized China's general position that the boundary had not been formally delineated yet, and reaffirmed the suggestion that both sides should maintain the status quo in both sectors of the border until a settlement was negotiated.

Phase II: friendship in crisis

At the end of 1958, "Chinese and Indian leaders began to realize that they were far apart in their understanding of the border between the two countries even though they did not deal with the issue in a contentious manner."[33] Until then, the boundary disagreement had taken place merely on paper and in secrecy. But the "violent incidents which took place along the India-China border in 1959 brought the conflict between these two countries into the open."[34] From then on, the problematic situation of dissenting border interpretations, competing territorial demands, and conflicting approaches toward a resolution revealed itself on the ground, and thus with far more serious consequences. Thereby, the cleavage turned into a full-fledged dispute, carried out in public, and soon became a serious source of conflict between India and China.

The Tibetan revolt and the breakdown of Sino-Indian friendship

Only half a year after its completion, China's new road saw its first use by the PLA, as reinforcements were ordered into Tibet to suppress a full-scale revolt.[35] Since China's 'liberation' of Tibet, tensions had mounted to such an extent that a single rumor was apparently enough to light the fuse for an uprising in Lhasa on March 10; in less than one week it had exploded into a region-wide rebellion. For China, the onset of the Tibet Crisis contained some controllable dangers, but was also a valuable opportunity. Now, Beijing had the pretext to implement its long-delayed reforms, which significantly curtailed Tibetan autonomy.[36] On May 20, the PLA marched into Lhasa, and one week later Beijing regained control over the situation and dissolved the Tibetan government.

Besides the Tibetan population, China's drastic handling of the crisis resulted in another victim: the cordial relationship between India and China. Like a magnifying glass, the events in Tibet "brought to the surface all the potential problems that had long existed between Beijing and New Delhi."[37] To the Chinese leadership, it had become obvious that India had played a major role in instigating the uprising. In addition, Beijing was well aware of ongoing covert operations by the United States, Great Britain, and the GMD in Tibet since the latter half of the 1950s that were, according to the Chinese perception, tacitly supported by New Delhi. In the eyes of the Chinese leadership, India had not only provided a safe haven for the Tibetan rebels, but also was actively involved in anti-China operations.[38] This perception was nurtured in numerous leadership meetings for several weeks after the Lhasa uprising but was still kept private. Only after thousands of Tibetan refugees flooded into India and Beijing's reputation came under pressure from world opinion did the Chinese leadership see the need to sacrifice a pawn in order to justify its suppression of the Tibetan unrest. This pawn was Prime Minister Jawaharlal Nehru. In late April

1959, Mao decided to publicize China's accusation against India, and Nehru became the main target of a "big campaign of criticism."[39] Mao emphasized that the campaign's central objectives were

> to help the Indian people learn the truth, to justify [China's stand] in the international struggle around the Tibetan rebellion, to crush the rebellion and promote democratic reforms in Tibet, [but also] to *preserve Chinese-Indian friendship* and compel Nehru to abide by the five principles of peaceful coexistence toward China.[40]

The inherent contradiction in objectives, i.e. launching polemics against Nehru in order to preserve Sino-Indian friendship, indicates that the Chinese leadership greatly underestimated the effects of such a campaign in a democratic-pluralist society like India. Consequently, when the article 'The Revolution in Tibet and Nehru's Philosophy' was published on May 6, the bilateral conflict flared into the open: in the subsequent slander campaign of mutual criticism and accusations, the subcutaneous cleavages that had been largely ignored for the sake of maintaining the cordial relationship surfaced.[41]

If India's support for China on the Tibet issue in 1950–1 had set the basic tone for Sino-Indian friendship, the final note in the brotherly relationship was obviously China's handling of the Tibetan rebellion and Beijing's scapegoating of Nehru, at the end of the decade. These developments, however, catapulted the simmering border dispute into the open; it then gained momentum as "leaked details of the various border disputes, including information on the Aksai Chin road, fed the flames of controversy"[42] inside India.

The militarization of the border

When the PLA moved into Tibet, the lack of a clearly demarcated boundary revealed itself for the first time as an acute and serious problem. In order to fight the insurgency effectively and to clear the rebels' strongholds in the border region, Beijing had to seal the border, and thus ordered the PLA into areas that were claimed by both China and India.[43] As India and China were now deploying armed forces to control what both countries regarded as their territory, it was just a matter of time before the first collision took place. India's actions, however, aggravated this already problematic situation even further so that the occurrence of a clash became inevitable. While Chinese patrols kept operations carefully limited to what Beijing had regarded since the 1950s as the de facto boundary in the east, Indian forces reportedly crossed into Chinese-claimed territory.[44] As was bound to happen, Indian and Chinese border guards exchanged deadly fire in a series of incidents in August and October 1959, resulting in the first Indian casualties.[45] All the clashes took place north of – "or at best at"[46] – the McMahon Line, and thus arguably more on the Chinese than on the Indian side of the traditional boundary.

It is not possible to identify which side can be held responsible for this intensification of violence, as Beijing and New Delhi immediately stated their respective versions of the incidents in which each side claimed that the other had fired first.[47]

But what differed even more than the competing accounts were the conclusions the two governments drew from these incidents, and their policies in the aftermath: while New Delhi transferred to the Indian army the responsibility for securing the Ladakh border and reinforced its forces in the region, Beijing "took the initiative to seek means to relax the tension and resolve the border disputes through dialogue."[48] In doing so, China implemented the following steps. First, Mao himself significantly curtailed Chinese border-guard commanders' leeway in decision-making.[49] In order to prevent further bloodshed, from then on the use of force was only allowed with Beijing's explicit permission. Second, Mao reached the conclusion that the first step to successfully deescalate the situation was to unwind the tense standoff between Indian and Chinese troops at the border. Accordingly, he proposed an immediate mutual withdrawal of 20 kilometers, and even ordered the Chinese forces to implement this measure unilaterally if New Delhi did not agree to withdraw.[50] Third, after their unilateral withdrawal, Chinese forces were ordered to stop patrolling, undertaking exercises, or gathering food in the 20-kilometer forward zone.[51] No Chinese presence in this area should provoke further clashes.

As a result of China's unilateral disengagement of forces, "tensions declined for twenty-three months."[52] Beijing undertook these precautionary measures under the assumption that a peaceful resolution of the dispute was not only the most desirable option but also an achievable one. This assumption rested on a strong and genuine Chinese conviction in Nehru's sincere desire to negotiate a settlement. As Mao explained to Khrushchev in October 1959,

> the border conflict ... is only a marginal issue, not a clash between two governments. Nehru himself is not aware of what happened ... When Nehru learned that their patrols had crossed the McMahon Line, he issued instructions for them to withdraw. We also worked towards peaceful resolution of the issue.[53]

In November 1959, the Chinese proposals for deescalating measures reached Prime Minister Nehru, together with an offer for bilateral consultations on the boundary problem.[54] Nehru's response neither fully rejected nor accepted the Chinese proposal. In essence, he reaffirmed India's demand, and Beijing's outright acceptance of it was, Nehru implied, a prerequisite for any form of consultations.[55] Even so, Nehru finally agreed to meet Zhou for talks.

Negotiations: Zhou Enlai in New Delhi

In late April 1960, the PRC's premier visited New Delhi to discuss the boundary problem with the Indian leadership. Even though Zhou's visit may be interpreted merely as a gesture "to display China's magnanimity toward the world,"[56] as Lorenz Lüthi noted, it nonetheless appears very likely that Beijing was sincerely interested in achieving a negotiated solution. Taylor Fravel has demonstrated that whenever the PRC found itself internationally isolated and internally vulnerable, Beijing showed an evident increase in willingness to settle border disputes through negotiations and compromise.[57]

Both conditions were obviously met during the relevant period. Domestically, China was facing grave social and economical problems as results of the Great Leap Forward (1958–61).[58] Mao's radical social-development experiment was about to fail drastically, as was already becoming obvious in mid-1959.[59] The largest famine in world history, and a series of natural disasters, hit China in the following two years, which can be aptly described as the bleakest in the history of the People's Republic: in the wake of the Great Leap Forward, "China descended into hell."[60] Externally, China's position was not much better. Relations with the Soviet Union had cooled drastically, and the Sino-Soviet split was looming sharply.[61] In the wake of the Taiwan Strait Crisis of 1958, the GMD – backed by Washington – now credibly threatened to invade the mainland.[62] The United States was about to establish a military presence in Laos and South Vietnam, and the Sino-Indian border had emerged as a new trouble-spot. The People's Republic thus faced pressure from the east and uncertain dangers from the south, and had been basically abandoned by its ally to the north.

With regard to the relevant time frame, both conditions for Fravel's argument were obviously 'over-fulfilled.' Adding to this, the empirical record of China's behavior toward unsettled borders at that time strongly supports Fravel's thesis: shortly before Zhou left for New Delhi, China concluded border agreements with Burma and Nepal. During the next three years, and thus in the immediate wake of the Sino-Indian War, China also demarcated its borders with Mongolia, North Korea, Pakistan, and Afghanistan.[63] In each of these instances, Beijing respected the status quo as the basis for the settlement (in the case of Burma, this meant a Chinese acceptance of the McMahon Line) and sought mutually acceptable agreements through compromise, which also included considerable territorial concessions. Against this background, there is good reason to conclude that China had a strong and sincere interest in accomplishing a settlement with India, too.

When Zhou arrived in New Delhi, his baggage included a package deal to solve the border dispute: China would accept India's control over the eastern sector if India, quid pro quo, abstained from its demand on Aksai Chin.[64] "From the Chinese point of view, the offer of an east-west swap was eminently fair and took into considerations the interests of both countries."[65] Each side would legalize its claim over territory it already administered, whereas the competing claims would have been eliminated as a source of conflict. Furthermore, as China asserted, at a minimum, the same amount of arguments and quality of evidence for the legitimacy of Beijing's claim over Aksai Chin as India brought forward for its demands in the east, the swap could have indeed functioned as a sound basis for a settlement.[66]

Nehru, however, immediately rejected Zhou's proposal and "insisted that China abandon its claim in the east *and* withdraw from Aksai Chin in the west."[67] It thus became obvious to the Chinese delegation that Nehru was unwilling to deviate from India's maximum demands. Even so, as indicated by the Chinese follow-up proposals on troop disengagement and a code of conduct for patrolling the disputed areas, Zhou Enlai was still inclined to break the impasse and reach at least a minimum agreement to prevent further clashes.[68] However, when Nehru and Zhou worked out the Joint Communiqué on the last day of his visit, Zhou came to realize "that his host wanted a communiqué that described the talks as a failure."[69] Consequently, the final document contained neither a reference to the Principles of Peaceful Coexistence nor included a declaration of mutual respect for the status quo at the border. Later that day, the two Prime Ministers explained the outcomes of the bilateral consultations to the press. While Zhou used the occasion to reaffirm the Chinese proposals, Nehru blamed his Chinese counterparts for the failure of the talks. Arguably, this was the most serious humiliation the Chinese Premier had to experience during his visit,[70] as it was conducted right before the eyes of the assembled international press. Zhou, who had "strenuously tried to move the discussions toward an agreement,"[71] thus left India highly embarrassed: "He was to say bitterly of his Indian counterpart, 'I have never met a more arrogant man than Nehru.'"[72]

Phase III: frustration – India's forward policy

In the aftermath of Zhou's visit, the Indian government reached the conclusion that further negotiations with China would not bring about the desired result. Consequently, a change in strategy became necessary.[73] Since China had stopped patrolling the forward areas in 1959, an empty space had opened up between the Indian and Chinese border positions. For New Delhi, this presented the opportunity to change the status quo on the border in India's favor with a twofold *fait accompli*. First, India formalized its maximum demand in the western sector.[74] From then on, New Delhi "asserted [that there was] no such thing as 'disputed territory': any and all territory claimed by India was ipso facto Indian and there could be no disputation about it, still less negotiation."[75] Second, New Delhi ordered its armed forces to bring these territories under control inch-by-inch "by placing continuous pressure and forward movement on Chinese forces along the disputed border."[76]

The forward policy: India's calculus and intentions

At its core, this 'forward policy' reflected an Indian intrusion into territory that was under China's de facto control. In other words, when implementing this highly confrontational approach, India was challenging China's territorial integrity, especially as the forward policy was executed by Indian armed forces that were ordered to expel the Chinese "by dominating Chinese positions and thus *forcing* their withdrawal."[77] However, the historical record of international relations unambiguously indicates that whenever the territorial integrity of a sovereign nation is violated by armed forces of another country, the most likely result is that the invaded state will resort to the use of force to stop and expel the intruder. Against this background, it appears appropriate to briefly clarify the forward policy's underlying calculus and New Delhi's associated expectations.

From the Indian point of view, the forward policy was a carefully elaborated, non-violent, and seemingly risk-averse strategy for "gaining territorial advantage over the opponent with the aid of only limited military resources and [by] avoiding direct confrontations."[78] The origins of this approach date back to the late 1950s, when the Indian defense community gained the insight that an Indian presence in Aksai Chin would impede further Chinese advances, strengthen India's diplomatic leverage *vis-à-vis* Beijing, and ultimately force China to withdraw its forces from the disputed area.[79] When the approach taken by New Delhi to persuade China of the righteousness of India's claims failed, these deliberations were turned from mental considerations into India's adjusted strategy on the ground. In order to assess the likely consequences and associated risks, the Indian government was able to draw on two appraisals of the forward policy that, however, reached fundamentally divergent conclusions: India's civil Intelligence Bureau found that "the Chinese would not react to our establishing of new posts and that they were not likely to use force against any of our posts even if they were in a position to do so"[80] but, in contrast, the Directorate of Military Intelligence's assessment "clearly indicated that the Chinese would resist by force any attempt to take back the territory held by them."[81] However, the Directorate's warning that the forward policy was bound to evoke a forceful Chinese reaction fell on deaf ears in New Delhi for at least two reasons: first, opposition to the forward policy ran out of supporters over the course of the decision-making process, as the number of critical voices decreased considerably as a result of selective personnel changes;[82] second, India's top-level political and military elites turned out to be strong proponents of the forward policy, with the lead taken by General B. M. Kaul, Chief of the Indian Army General Staff; Defense Minister Krishna Menon; and Prime Minister Nehru.[83] The formation of this influential coalition in support of the forward policy fostered the establishment of the Intelligence Bureau's extremely problematic assessment as an "unchallengeable political orthodoxy"[84] behind India's adjusted strategy:

> There was a virtual consensus among Indian leaders that China would not respond with military force to Indian advances, and that if it did, any military response would be extremely limited. A Chinese resort to large-scale military force was deemed impossible.[85]

In New Delhi's perspective, the restrained character of the strategy guaranteed that "China would not act in keeping with the spirit of the game and would not 'overreact' by mounting a large-scale military operation."[86] Based solely on this more-than-questionable premise, the Indian forward policy negligently blanked out the evidently prohibitive risk of uncontrollable escalation, which had been unmistakably highlighted by India's Directorate of Military Intelligence. India's new strategy was thus not only "unwise and even dangerous,"[87] but also prone to collide with the territorial integrity of the People's Republic of China. As one Indian scholar found, the forward policy can be regarded as a "typical case of allowing domestic political considerations to override those of national security"[88] as it posed, as Neville Maxwell put it, "a military challenge to a militarily far superior neighbour."[89]

The implementation of the forward policy started around April 1961.[90] During the initial phase, Indian forces prepared the infrastructure necessary for the following push into Chinese-claimed territory, regularly dispatched patrols into the forward area that had opened up after the Chinese withdrawal of 1959, and set up a series of new fortified positions.[91] The immediate result was several encounters with Chinese troops, whereby the Chinese reportedly maintained restraint even when fired upon and taking casualties.[92] These 'victories' further nurtured the conviction in New Delhi that "the Chinese would not be assertive and that [the] forward policy ... was the correct course for India."[93] The actual implementation of the strategy then took place when Indian forces systematically infiltrated Aksai Chin.[94] The push forward materialized slowly but steadily. At the end of 1961, India had established a total of 43 new outposts on the Chinese-claimed side of the traditional boundary in Aksai Chin, as well as several new sentry posts in the eastern sector, and had gained control over 500 square kilometers of territory without having received a strong reaction to this. In accordance with their orders, Chinese forces withdrew when encountering a newly erected Indian outpost.[95] Obviously reassured by these initial successes, New Delhi decided to further accelerate the forward policy. In December 1961, the Indian Army General Staff issued directives that permitted forward patrolling in the western sector "as far as possible from our present position towards the international border as recognized by us."[96] Beginning in February 1962, Indian troops thus pushed more assertively into Aksai Chin and controlled more than 6,500 of the total of 39,000 square kilometers of disputed territory up to August 1962.[97] According to a report to the Indian Parliament, at that point India had established three times as many outposts as China and had significantly intensified patrolling activities.[98] In addition, to sustain the growing number of outposts, India's air force had considerably increased the number of sorties to airdrop supplies over disputed territory and thus was systematically violating Chinese-claimed airspace.[99]

China's response: armed coexistence

The onset and intensification of India's forward policy confronted the Chinese leadership with the problem of Indian forces vigorously pushing back China's presence in the strategically important Aksai Chin region. For Beijing, this development proved two long-held suspicions true: first, it clearly demonstrated that India was not interested in a settlement of the dispute by compromise; second, it revealed India's expansionist ambitions and willingness to unilaterally change the status quo by 'nibbling off' Chinese-claimed territory.[100] However, even though Beijing was clearly aware of the developments on the ground and their potential implications, the Chinese leadership did not react precipitately but rather exercised considerable restraint. Still, Beijing's primary interest consisted in a negotiated settlement of the conflict, and therefore the crisis had to be contained from further escalation.[101]

Shortly after reports from the Tibet Military Region had revealed the onset of India's forward policy, the CMC met to discuss potential reactions. To illustrate the accrued situation and its implications, Mao used a metaphor from *Xiangqi* (traditional Chinese chess):

> [India's] continually pushing forward is like crossing the Han-Chu boundary [the centerline of the board]. What should we do? We can also set out a few pawns, on our side of the river. If they don't cross over, that's great. It they do cross, we'll eat them up [a metaphor for taking the opponents' chess pieces].

However, the Chairman cautioned that "we cannot blindly eat them [because a lack of] forbearance in small matters upsets great plans."[102] In line with Mao's assessment, China's response to India's confrontational policy unfolded in a decidedly defensive-oriented and reactive fashion. Moreover, the Chairman now took personal charge of the 'struggle with India.'[103]

First, besides a series of angry diplomatic protests, Beijing consistently reaffirmed its commitment to a consensual solution of the territorial dispute.[104] However, the numerous appeals for a negotiated settlement were basically met by New Delhi with "the demand for a total Chinese withdrawal from all territory claimed by India."[105] Second, when it became clear that diplomatic efforts would fail, the Chinese forces were ordered to cease withdrawal and resume patrols within the forward zone on China's side of the actual line of control.[106] With Indian troops pushing forward and encircling Chinese positions, once again Chinese and Indian forces faced each other 'nose-to-nose' in the kind of dangerous and tense standoff that Mao had sought to avoid in late 1959. This time, however, a further withdrawal would have only generated further incentives for India to push even more swiftly forward. Based upon these considerations Mao outlined a defensively oriented strategy for countering the Indian forward policy in his 20-character directive of July 1962: "Never make a concession, but try your best to avert bleeding; form a jagged, interlocking pattern to secure the border; and prepare for a long-time armed co-existence."[107] In the eyes of the Chinese leadership, 'armed coexistence' was apparently the best option available in order to preserve the fragile status quo at the border by stopping further Indian advances without having to resort to force, while keeping open the door to a non-violent resolution. In practice, armed coexistence meant that when India's forces set up an outpost to encircle a Chinese position, the Chinese in turn should establish even more outposts to counter-encircle the Indian positions. In that way, Chinese and Indian positions would form an interlocked pattern that would finally stabilize the situation. "But the Chinese forces were also to seek to avoid bloodshed. They were absolutely not to fire without orders from above."[108] Third, based on Mao's directive, the PLA General Staff drafted rules of engagement that had to be strictly obeyed. The essence of these rules, as well as the underlying Chinese intention, was as follows: Chinese troops should show a presence, but also should keep their distance from Indian forces; should always leave enough room to react on sudden developments; and should withdraw when the Indian force posture permitted withdrawal in order to avoid the outbreak of violence.[109]

In sum, China's response aimed at signaling to New Delhi that the forward policy rested on a false assumption. Beijing would not indefinitely tolerate the forceful expulsion of its presence in a territory legitimately claimed by China. As even India's official history of the Sino-Indian War has to admit, the strategy of armed coexistence "clearly showed that the basic assumption behind the Forward Policy decision was no longer valid, and a serious reappraisal of the new situation should have been undertaken."[110] On the other hand, the threefold response and, especially, Beijing's restraining rules of engagement indicate that China still had not abandoned its hope for a non-violent resolution of the territorial dispute. To keep this option on the table, Beijing ordered its troops to "avoid at all costs actions that would cause a further worsening of the border situation."[111]

Armed coexistence meets forward policy in the Himalayas

Beijing's attempt to counter India's forward policy produced mixed results. In the western sector, the interlocked pattern of Chinese and Indian positions proved capable of preventing further Indian advances. However, this prompted New Delhi to shift the focus of the forward policy to the eastern sector.[112] On the ground, China's 'armed coexistence' thus failed to stop the forward policy and deter India's forces from advancing: as a quite undeterred high-ranking Indian officer summarized his impression of the situation, "[w]e thought it was a sort of a game. They would stick up a post and we would stick up a post and we did not think it would come to much more."[113] This 'game,' however, was prone to turn bloodily serious.

When Indian forces established a new outpost to cut off a Chinese position, the Chinese standard procedure was to encircle the Indian post with superior forces.[114] With regard to this tense standoff, the Indian General Staff's directive of July 1962 was arguably the worst measure that could have been taken, as the order "gave discretion to all post commanders to fire on the Chinese if their posts were ever threatened."[115] In other words, the commanders on the spot, usually in the ranks of inexperienced junior officers, received the competence to open fire at will. Unsurprisingly, the post commanders made frequent use of this new leverage, as they often found themselves surrounded and thus threatened by overwhelming Chinese forces. The result was a noticeable increase of violence and casualties at the border.[116] In contrast, Beijing was still restricting the use of force to contain the conflict from further escalation. Only after the clashes intensified as Indian troops frequently opened fire were the PLA's rules of engagement adapted to the new circumstances. But even then, the use of force was still restricted to self-defense situations.[117]

URGENT WARNINGS AND STRONG SIGNALS: BEIJING'S FINAL ATTEMPTS AT CRISIS MANAGEMENT

In mid-1962, Beijing found itself confronted with an ever more aggressively conducted forward policy. Due to New Delhi's 'fire at will' order, the level of violence along the entire boundary had drastically increased, claiming a steadily growing number of Chinese casualties. For the Chinese troops, the situation was worsening constantly. Reports from the border area indicated that Chinese forces could no longer block the Indian advances without proactively engaging in combat.[118] But even under these deteriorating circumstances, Beijing exercised remarkable restraint. Instead of contributing its share to the spiral of violence, Beijing maintained its defensively oriented crisis-management strategy of armed coexistence.

Even so, in summer 1962, "the minatory tone and content of Beijing's diplomatic protests about the forward policy steadily mounted [and China's] threats of counter-force became more open."[119] By signaling quite plainly the seriousness of the situation and the potential consequences of India's misguided approach, Beijing apparently hoped to dissuade New Delhi from continuing its aggressive policy, without having to resort to force. China's numerous warnings in diplomatic notes, governmental statements, and quasi-official publications thus became more pronounced and explicit.[120] In July, for example, the *People's Daily* emphasized that India's authorities would be making a big mistake by taking China's restraint as an indication of weakness, and warned New Delhi that if "the Indian Government refuses to withdraw immediately its troops which have already penetrated into Chinese territory ... India will be fully held responsible for all the consequences arising therefrom."[121] Moreover, the seriousness of China's warnings was underlined by using the formulation "the Chinese government will not stand idly by" – New Delhi should have been quite familiar with this phraseology and its associated implications, as in autumn 1950 China had used the very similar wording to warn the United States, via the Indian Ambassador, not to cross the 38th Parallel:

> The Chinese Government has repeatedly stated that China is not willing to fight with India. ... It has all along exercised the greatest forbearance and self-restraint [but it] *can by no means sit idly while its frontier guards are being encircled and annihilated by aggressors.*[122]

Beijing also substantiated the gravity of these warnings with concurrent military activities in preparation for combat operations. Without undertaking any measures of concealment, Beijing deployed reinforcements and heavy weaponry to Tibet. Along the entire Sino-Indian boundary, Chinese soldiers constructed defense works, expanded the tactical infrastructure, and set up ammunition and supply depots in the immediate vicinity of their positions.[123] All this was plainly visible to the Indian soldiers, who in turn reported the intensified Chinese activities to New Delhi. As China's military activities clearly indicated, Beijing's crisis-management repertoire now included mounting potential for a large-scale use of force. On June 10, China demonstrated this prospect on the ground for the first time, when 300 PLA soldiers surrounded an Indian outpost in the Galwan Valley. Even though the Chinese soldiers did not attack, they effectively cut off ground supplies to the post in order to force its withdrawal. "This attempt was a major PLA countermove to halt the Indian forward movement" by challenging the forward policy's underlying premise and to "apply pressure that would bring Nehru to the conference table."[124] Nonetheless, Beijing not only kept the door open for negotiations, but again took the initiative. During the Geneva Conference in late July, a meeting between PRC Foreign Minister Chen Yi and India's Defense Minister Krishna Menon resulted in a glimmer of hope that New Delhi was willing to re-enter into talks.[125] Beijing immediately decreased its diplomatic and public pressure in order to pave Nehru's way to the negotiating table. The Indian Prime Minister, facing severe domestic pressure for being too soft on China, soon dismissed the Menon–Chen meeting as irrelevant and reverted to India's initial position. As the prospects for negotiations collapsed in late August, China returned to its policy of providing ever sharper warnings.

Short of resorting to large-scale military force, China had then already climbed every step on the ladder of escalation: Chinese troops had ceased their withdrawal before Indian advances and set up blocking positions to interdict further Indian intrusion. Before the eyes of the Indian soldiers, the PLA had strengthened its force posture and had made great efforts to improve its tactical infrastructure. In addition to a series of diplomatic notes and firm warnings, the PLA had not only exchanged live fire with Indian troops but also conducted an outright, but non-violent, assault on an Indian position. None of these measures dissuaded India from continuing its forward policy or led it to "abandon its illusion of Chinese weakness."[126] As Allen Whiting observes, the Indian conviction that China would not fight was so dominant that "no amount of warning, diplomatic or political, seemed to shake it."[127]

DHOLA: INDIA'S LARGE-SCALE USE OF FORCE OUTSIDE INDIAN-CLAIMED TERRITORY

In early September, around 60 PLA soldiers executed the Chinese standard procedure of surrounding an Indian position north of Dhola in the Thag La area.[128] This outpost had been set up in June 1962 even though "the area was marked on Indian Army maps ... as Chinese territory."[129] The Indian post commander was apparently too inexperienced to handle the situation: threatened by the presence of Chinese troops he reported that 400 to 600 PLA soldiers had encircled his unit in order to swiftly receive reinforcements.[130] The consequences of this report, however, were enormous: even though the outpost was located several miles north of the McMahon Line and thus outside of any Indian claim ever stated, New Delhi dispatched about 400 troops to relieve the post and expel the Chinese troops from the entire Thag La area.[131] On September 14, while the Indian reinforcements were on the march, the post commander's error was corrected. Furthermore, Beijing issued a stern warning to India to refrain any military activities at Dhola, but also proposed a mutual withdrawal of 20 kilometers and the re-opening of talks, without any preconditions.[132] In response, India sent a twofold reply: on paper, New Delhi agreed to reopen negotiations on October 15; on the ground, the Indian government "still went forward with its plan to evict the Chinese, since the Indian Army had already dispatched a strong reaction force and it felt assured of success."[133]

From a tactical point of view, India's attempt to expel the Chinese from Thag La was sheer madness: the PLA units on top of the ridge far outnumbered the Indian detachment, held superior positions, and were supported by a large amount of heavy weaponry.[134] New Delhi should have been clearly aware of China's military superiority in the area, as "the PLA dug in on the Thag La ridge slope in full view of Indian observation."[135] From the political point of view, the same conclusion can be drawn: India's military action not only knowingly violated China's territorial integrity but also undermined the inherent calculus of its own forward policy. With regard to the former, New Delhi was clearly aware that Thag La lay north of the McMahon Line. As an Indian source acknowledges, even though China had never formally accepted the McMahon Line as a boundary, the Dhola area "was not strictly territory that 'we should have been convinced was ours'".[136] Regarding the latter, the incursion of an Indian brigade into Chinese territory revealed a significant change in the 'rules of the game.' Thus far, the forward policy had unfolded only on disputed territory, and such large-scale encounters had not previously taken place. Now, however, India had not only deployed a considerable number of combat troops to undisputed territory, but also intended to use force in order to expel the Chinese from the area: even though "the Dhola post was virtually defenseless from both a political and a military standpoint"[137] and despite India having nowhere near the necessary means to bring a defended Thag La Ridge under control, New Delhi nonetheless knowingly escalated the situation.

In Beijing, all this nurtured the impression that the Nehru administration was now running amok. Despite China's stern warnings and evident military superiority, the Indian forces continued their advance. Finally, on the night of September 20, Indian and Chinese forces clashed at the Namka Chu River.[138] While India suffered only a minor number of wounded troops, the encounter resulted in 22 Chinese soldiers reportedly killed or wounded.[139] As the Sino-Indian standoff escalated into bloodshed, so did the tone and content of Beijing's warnings: one day after the clash, China issued its most serious warning, stating that the "situation in the [Dhola] area is extremely dangerous and flames of war may break out here."[140] But even this warning fell on deaf ears: the Indian detachment was not withdrawn but was ordered to repel the PLA, and another clash followed, with five Chinese soldiers killed in battle.[141] In addition to this, at the end of the month, Indian forces proactively made use of their newly available mortar capability. According to Indian reports, the mortar fire led to "fourteen corpses and some 'walking wounded' being carried away by the Chinese."[142] Confronted with this deteriorating situation, on October 3 Beijing sent to New Delhi the last in a long series of Chinese appeals to stop the bloodshed and seek a peaceful solution through negotiations.

Interim conclusion: from cleavage to conflict

At the end of 1958, disagreement over the course of the bilateral boundary had emerged as a cleavage between New Delhi and Beijing. Besides the fact that China and India had agreed to disagree on the concrete delineation of their common border, their respective ways of handling the issue had already revealed two colliding strategies: Beijing stood firm on the position that the border had not yet been stipulated, but was nonetheless willing to accept the status quo as the basis for a compromise. New Delhi's position, on the other hand, appeared rather contradictory. In the eastern sector, India accepted its British inheritance of the McMahon Line and thus affirmed the boundary as being "fixed and final."[143] In the western sector, India's last-minute claim reflected the most far-reaching demand ever considered, but never proposed to China, by British India, and thus departed from the argument of historical precedence.[144] As even an Indian expert emphasized, there was "no basis in treaty, usage, or geography"[145] for the Indian claim over Aksai Chin. Probably the most problematic part of India's 'fixed and final' approach, however, was the hardening of the Indian position on the maximum demand, with which New Delhi self-curtailed its domestic leeway.[146]

When "the friendship and cooperation that had so benefited Beijing and New Delhi throughout the 1950s [finally] collapsed"[147] in the wake of the Tibetan revolt, the subcutaneously simmering boundary dispute broke into the open. From then on, the issue emerged as a serious conflict between India and China. For Beijing, this conflict was severe but not intractable: China not only employed several measures unilaterally in order to ease the tension after the first clashes had taken place, but was also genuinely interested in a resolution by compromise. Zhou's proposal of April

1960 could indeed have functioned as the basis for a sound settlement.[148] Even so, a compromise was out of reach because India was fundamentally unwilling to depart from its maximum demands, but instead started to implement them on the ground. The forward policy can thus be regarded as the logical continuation of India's 'fixed and final' approach, which in the end "foreclosed the sole means of resolving the dispute peacefully."[149] But on the ground, India's approach resulted in far more serious consequences, as the forward policy deliberately and unnecessarily escalated the conflict. India's nibbling-off of Chinese-controlled territory with military means was only the first observable change in the 'rules of the game.' The second change followed in July 1962 with New Delhi's 'fire at will' order, which clearly escalated the level of violence at the border. In both instances, Beijing exercised remarkable restraint, even though India's aggressively conducted policy surely frustrated the Chinese leadership. Beijing still harbored the hope that a peaceful resolution of the dispute could be accomplished, and thus sought to defuse the arising crisis with its policy of 'armed coexistence.'

In sum, both sides basically kept to their initial approaches: New Delhi's strategy focused on confrontationally realizing India's maximum demand through military means, whereas China tried its best to contain the conflict from escalating and actively pursued a negotiated settlement. But when New Delhi decided to change the 'rules of the game' for the third time with a moribund attempt to seize the Thag La area, the Indian government not only undermined the self-set calculus underlying the forward policy but also steered full-speed toward a military confrontation with China. The substantial intensification of Beijing's warnings and the gradual escalation of China's military signals and deterrence measures were apparently not enough to dissuade India from the course toward collision: as I will show in the following, China's patience with New Delhi was then exhausted.

Offended: Beijing's decision for war with India

After India rejected Beijing's final proposal on October 6, Mao Zedong, Zhou Enlai, and Defense Minister Lin Biao met to discuss further steps.[150] Despite China's warnings and diplomatic initiatives, Indian forces continued to advance. The recent Indian military activities at Dhola had resulted in severe Chinese causalities. Moreover, reconnaissance reports indicated that an attack on the Chinese positions at Thag La Ridge was to be expected around October 10.[151] The situation thus rapidly sharpened.

In Mao's assessment, these developments furnished the proof that armed coexistence had comprehensively failed. For him, it had become obvious that "Nehru really wants to use force. This isn't strange. He has always wanted to seize Aksai Chin and Thagla Ridge. He thinks he can get everything he desires."[152] At this point, India's offensive adventures had exhausted the Chairman's patience: by challenging China's sovereignty at Dhola, Nehru had crossed the Rubicon. Consequently, Mao was willing to answer appropriately:

> We fought a war with old Chiang. We fought a war with Japan, and with America. With none of these did we fear. And in each case we won. Now

the Indians want to fight a war with us. ... We cannot give ground. ... Since Nehru sticks his head out and insists on us fighting him, for us not to fight with him would not be friendly enough. Courtesy emphasizes reciprocity.[153]

Lin and Zhou agreed with Mao's conclusion. Zhou highlighted that Nehru's confrontational policy and India's demonstrated reluctance to work constructively toward a non-violent solution would at this point leave no alternative but to respond to India's provocations by resorting to force.[154] As consent among the three key leaders was reached, the decision to go to war with India was principally made. Even so, Mao decided to leave the concrete arrangement to deliberations in larger meetings.

In contrast to the discussions over China's intervention in Korea, this time a strong consensus emerged among the Chinese leaders: even though they shared the assessment "that the Indians posed no immediate military threat" to China,[155] their statements broadly echoed Mao's and Zhou's opinions on the urgent necessity to put India in its place.[156] During an enlarged CCP Politburo meeting on October 18, Mao summarized the Chinese calculus: "India is deliberately provoking armed conflicts. ... It is definitely going too far. ... A colloquial saying goes 'conflict creates communication.' If we counterattack, then the border will become stable, and the boundary problem can be peacefully resolved."[157]

For the Chairman, however, the decision to go to war against India had not been an easy one: with regard to the exceptional friendship that had characterized Sino-Indian relations in the past, Mao acknowledged that a "war between China and India is truly a most unfortunate event."[158] Reportedly, Mao had studied the history of the bilateral relationship when Sino-Indian tension intensified, and had been struck by the record of friendly and beneficial interactions between the two countries over the preceding centuries. Besides, Mao surely remembered the brotherly relationship of the recent past, and India's cooperation with the young People's Republic in times of crisis.[159] Weighing the legacy of the past against the most recent experiences with Nehru's India, Mao emphasized that the war against China's former friend should follow two general principles: "First, the PLA had to secure victory and 'knock Nehru to the negotiating table.' Second, Chinese forces had to be restrained and principled [in order to avoid unnecessary excesses of violence]."[160] China's 'knock' to Nehru, however, should be "fierce and painful," as Mao declared in his authorization order to the PLA General Staff on October 6, 1962.[161]

China's operative consideration

Shortly after the decision was taken, the CMC and the PLA General Staff began its implementation by reinforcing China's military posture in Tibet and drafting the battle plan. With regard to the latter, Mao's principles categorized China's war objective: forcing the Indian government to return to the negotiating table by delivering a crushing, painful defeat to the Indian armed forces in the border sectors. Consequently, this objective predefined China's operative considerations.

First, although Chinese assessments "judged Indian forces inferior to the Chinese in combat and war-fighting capability,"[162] the General Staff concentrated additional, combat-tested divisions in the area of operation. According to PLA Chief Strategist Marshal Liu Bocheng,

> the crux of success in the coming war ... was 'concentration of local superiority to achieve a swift war and a swift decision.' ... The PLA must absolutely fight well [as victory] was a matter directly connected to the prestige of the Chinese army and nation.[163]

To ensure that the PLA would not only fight well but also would be able to achieve a decisive victory, the General Staff mustered the most experienced PLA divisions available, equipped them with adequate weaponry suited for combat at high altitudes, and ensured sufficient supplies were stored.[164] Moreover, the Chinese military planners emphasized that the PLA could not allow itself any arrogance in terms of underestimating the enemy. Consequently, they concentrated a larger force than had otherwise been necessary in order to be prepared for all eventualities and to guarantee the desired 'fierce and painful' blow.[165]

Second, by determining the course of action for the 'counterattack in self-defense,' the planners took into account the primary objective of forcing the Nehru administration to the negotiating table. In order to demonstrate this intent, the campaign should unfold in three steps: China would open the hostilities with a high-intensity combat phase in order to achieve a swift and decisive victory on the battlefield. After that, the PRC would unilaterally declare a cease-fire. Depending on India's response, hostilities could end or be continued in an extended offensive. Finally, Chinese forces would withdraw to their initial position after Beijing offered negotiation proceedings.[166] In sum, the campaign was designed not to occupy the disputed territory by force, but to "compel India to accept the fact that negotiating with China was the only way to achieve a complete settlement of the territorial issue."[167]

Third, in order to foster this insight in New Delhi and to punish India for the disrespect and arrogance it had shown toward China, a 'fierce and painful' lesson was regarded as essential to bring Nehru's ambitions back to earth. This calculus is reflected in the decision regarding which border sector the PLA's main assault should unfold in. Due to the geographical setting, the west favored neither the Chinese nor the Indians; however, China's forces there were significantly stronger than their Indian counterparts.[168] Even so, the Chinese planners decided to situate the focus of the upcoming attack in the eastern sector. India had already deployed some of its elite units here, and both the topographical setting and the existing infrastructure would allow New Delhi to swiftly reinforce the frontline.[169] China's strategists were not only well aware of the Indian advantages in the east, but deliberately calculated for them: in order to inflict the desired crushing defeat on India, "a 'big battle' was required. A powerful Chinese offensive that met only thin Indian forces would not fulfill that political objective."[170] Consequently, it was ordered that the PLA's main assault would take place in the east, coordinated with a minor offensive in the western sector of the border.

India's lost opportunity for a final course correction

On October 10, India started an offensive to chase off the Chinese from Thag La. Around 100 Indian soldiers encircled the PLA position and opened fire.[171] Obviously, the Indians expected that the Chinese would withdraw without mounting resistance, as had been the case in earlier encounters. Only days earlier, the Indian General J. S. Dhillon stated that "experience in Ladakh ha[s] shown that a few rounds fired at the Chinese would cause them to run away."[172] This time, however, the Chinese soldiers did not run away, but instead counterattacked in unexpected strength. Against 100 Indian troops, China threw about 1,000 soldiers into battle.[173] With this drastic show of force, Beijing intended to convey to New Delhi the unmistakable message that the underlying assumption for India's forward policy had become fundamentally obsolete: China would no longer refrain from the use of large-scale military force.[174]

For a brief moment, it seemed as if New Delhi had grasped the seriousness of China's broad hint. But only two days later, Nehru issued a directive to "launch an all-out attack against Chinese frontier guards on the border."[175] Publicly, the Prime Minister declared that India's armed forces were still under orders to free Indian territory from Chinese occupation.[176] By failing to alter its course after the major encounter of October 10, New Delhi probably dismissed its final opportunity to avoid the outbreak of war at the Sino-Indian border.

In Beijing, Nehru's statement and India's continuing attempts to seize Thag La Ridge were perceived as an expanded offensive against China.[177] Searching for the Indian rationale, it became apparent to the Chinese leadership that New Delhi was obviously convinced that China was simply bluffing and believed it "barks but does not bite."[178] Even though China had already demonstrated its military might, in addition to a long list of serious warnings,[179] India was apparently still refusing to take the People's Republic seriously. Arguably, this last occasion of evidenced disrespect for China's power, status, and interests was the straw that broke the camel's back.[180] When Mao was briefed on these findings on October 16, the Chairman reached the conclusion that, under these circumstances, it had become an absolute necessity to teach New Delhi a drastic lesson about why China should be taken seriously: "It seems like this is indeed that sort of a situation. In this case, we cannot but fight a war. Well, since Nehru says we only 'bark but don't bite', we absolutely must fight. We have no other choice."[181]

Over the following two days, the CMC and the enlarged Politburo formally approved the initial decision of October 6, and the Tibet Military Region received orders "to muster and concentrate its forces for a quick and decisive battle against the Indian Army, seeking first to encircle the invading Indian troops and then to wipe them out."[182] The starting date for China's 'counterattack in self-defense' was set as October 20, 1962.

Assessing the risks of China's lesson[183]

With regard to the military balance between India and the People's Republic, the conclusion suggests that China's offensive incorporated a rather controllable level of risk. On paper, the numbers unquestionably favored China. In 1962, the PLA had a total strength of about three million soldiers, around 160,000 of whom were stationed in Tibet. In contrast to that, India could only muster a total of about 350,000 men, dispersed over the whole country.[184] As New Delhi had constantly neglected the possibility of a large-scale military confrontation with China, only about 25,000–30,000 soldiers were deployed near the border, with no noteworthy reinforcements nearby. Against India's quite limited defensive potential, China's battle-hardened divisions should have been able to achieve an easy victory, especially as the advantageous element of surprise was on China's side. *Ex post facto*, the course and outcome of the Sino-Indian War proves this assessment right.

But was China's leadership also *ex ante* certain about its decisive military superiority? Unfortunately, the available literature provides only very limited insights into the decision-making process and the risk calculation of China's military and civilian leaders. In order to cope with this lack of data, in the following I present an indirect approach toward a risk assessment. The starting point of my argument is Mao Zedong's reminder of October 18, two days before the onset of China's offensive, "not to underestimate India's military force."[185] Moreover, even though Chinese assessments accurately judged the Indian army's combat capacity as inferior, the PLA leadership nonetheless stressed that the unit commanders should not take the forthcoming battles too lightly.[186] What was the intention behind these reminders? As I have already outlined above, there is good reason to argue that these warnings were issued in order to guarantee the desired 'fierce and painful blow' to India. However, it also seems likely that, even though the PLA reconnaissance had provided accurate information on the strength and position of India's troops, the Chinese leadership were aware their calculations could not account for all possibilities. Consequently, with the material dimension of the forthcoming war abundantly clear, I argue that if there existed any uncertainty for the Chinese leadership with regard to the upcoming campaign, it was to be found in the crucial question of how the PLA would perform in high-altitude combat.

Fighting in the Himalayas: challenges and capabilities in high-altitude combat

The designated area of operation was no ordinary battlefield. The Chinese offensive was about to unfold atop the 'roof of the world,' with much of the fighting taking place in altitudes up to three and a half times higher than the Alps and in temperatures as low as minus 50 degrees Celsius. Conducting combat operations under these circumstances means that the already life-threatening engagements are taking place in a hostile-to-life environment: "At altitude, the first enemy is the environment. The second enemy is the human foe."[187]

The primary challenge for military operations in terrain over 3,000 meters are the effects of altitude itself. As atmospheric pressure drops sharply at about 2,500 meters, the percentage of oxygen in tidal air decreases exponentially. Weather phenomena also manifest in a more extreme way. Both effects compromise the operative capacity of armed forces, as simultaneously men, material, and animals are affected in their ability to conduct sustained operations. Even when properly acclimatized, dwelling time at high altitudes is still limited, as the human body is not designed to exist at these altitudes. A second set of challenges is posed by the distinct characteristics of the terrain itself. Mountainous areas are marked not only by their inhospitality but also by their specific impassability. Steep slopes, rock faces, and deep gorges limit the mobility of troops and swiftly exhaust men and material. Movement at high altitude is dictated by the setting of the terrain – interestingly, this holds true even for aerial units.[188] The only military formations capable of mastering these challenges are light infantry and artillery forces; however, these are operatively limited by the available supply capabilities and dependent on their own carriage capacities, firepower, and range of mobility.

With regard to these challenges, two risk potentials accompanied China's war against India. First, the offensive was to take place in late October, and the winter season was already looming.[189] Consequently, "extensive combat ... would have to be completed before the December storms engulfed the Himalayan heights with fierce winds and deep snow."[190] As the onset of the winter season is hard to predict exactly, Beijing thus risked the incapacitation of its offensive before the campaign's objectives had been achieved. Second, the Chinese troops were disadvantaged by the fact that mountainous terrain naturally favors defense. When concentrated at tactical key positions, defending forces can effectively interdict any enemy advances.[191] By taking the offense, China thus had to bear the greater risk. Even so, the PLA planners were informed that India's troops had been stationed in static positions, which in turn allowed the PLA to extract advantages from its mobility by concentrating forces at focal spots. The result was that in each battle, the PLA outnumbered the Indian defenders, even though China and India had roughly equal forces to hand during the initial phase of the war: in the east, 10,000 PLA troops stood against 16,000 Indian defenders, while the western sector was defended by 6,000 Indian soldiers against 6,300 Chinese.[192] In sum, while the incalculable weather revealed itself to be relatively risky for the success of China's campaign, the risk involved in taking the offense appeared rather acceptable.

Key capabilities for combat at high altitude

Warfare at high altitudes is without doubt an exceptionally demanding form of military combat. Accordingly, this battlefield calls for distinct core capabilities in order to withstand both the environmental conditions and the enemy's forces: experienced soldiers, prudent leadership, and continuous supplies.

First, high altitude, harsh weather, and inaccessible terrain demand for experienced soldiers. Although acclimatization serves as a fundamental requirement for the ability to operate in high altitudes, "[a]n acclimated soldier is still not an experienced mountaineer."[193] All armed forces with a specific mountaineer branch agree on that point, and as the example of Italia's *Alpini* shows, a training period of ten years or more is not too long to produce a truly capable mountain warrior. The second crucial factor in high-altitude warfare is the particularly critical role of leadership.[194] At the operative level, commanders need to have a sense of the challenges and characteristics of mountain warfare, as well as their soldiers' proficiencies. In addition, as "nothing is fast in high-altitude combat,"[195] profound planning and preparation are imperative to the success of combat operations. At the tactical level, the battlefield calls for strong leadership by junior officers, as it places far greater responsibility and self-sufficient decision-making on their shoulders than their comrades in the lowlands must carry. Third, if sufficient supplies function as the basic requirement for sustaining operations in all theaters of war, the guaranteed flow of supplies to troops at high altitudes is absolutely mandatory. In contrast to the lowlands, mountains are characterized by a scarcity of food, water, and even wood to use for cooking or heat. Frontline troops require supplies of not only these elementary resources but also need replacements, weaponry, materials and ammunition to engage in sustained operations.[196] Therefore, the logistical element of mountain warfare is a highly challenging task, contains decisive implications for operative effectiveness, and is the most important capability for conducting combat at high altitudes.

The combatants' military portfolios for high-altitude combat

A comparison of the two belligerents' military capabilities and actual performance in the field against the three identified core capabilities for warfare in high altitudes allows assessment of which side was better prepared for this special form of combat, what in turn allows to approximate the risk-behavior of the Chinese leadership.

With regard to the level of experience among the soldiers, it was the Tibetan trouble-spot that presented China with a decisive advantage, as the latent instability in the region had made it necessary to permanently station large PLA contingents.[197] Beijing could thus draw on a potential of 160,000 soldiers, acclimatized to 4,500-meter altitude and experienced in combat in mountainous terrain.[198] The Chinese troops were also well prepared and equipped for this type of warfare.[199] India's forces, on the other hand, although acclimatized and used to the terrain, were not only greatly outnumbered but also "in a poor state, especially in their readiness for alpine warfare. Their firepower, supply system, training, and readiness for mountain operations were all quite lacking."[200] With regard to these striking deficits, James Calvin concluded that "[t]o pit troops in such circumstances against an enemy superior in every detail of military strength would be absurd."[201]

This brings us to the second key capability of prudent leadership: despite their numerous shortcomings, India's armed forces were "told to go into combat by civilian authorities,"[202] which clearly reveals a striking deficit in leadership with regard to both civilian leaders and military commanders. As outlined above, it was the Nehru administration's momentous miscalculation underlying the forward policy that had steered India toward a confrontation with China on a battlefield for which the Indian army was not prepared.[203] At the operative level of command, India's military leadership also fundamentally lacked the ability to correctly judge China's military capacity, which led to constant — and occasionally even arrogant — underestimations.[204] At the tactical level, India's field commanders proved unable to use the advantages that mountainous terrain provides for the defending party. Instead of concentrating forces on focal points, Indian troops engaged in a widely dispersed positional defense.[205] China's political and military leadership, in contrast, had a strong personal sense of the challenges and hardships of combat at high altitudes, as every Chinese leader that had participated in the Long March had gained first-hand experience in moving and fighting on mountainous terrain.[206] At the tactical level, the PLA not only profited from the combat experience of Korean War veterans, who at this time filled the ranks of officers and non-commissioned officers, but could also draw on well-educated and tactically skilled junior officers due to Peng Dehuai's military reforms.[207] As a result, PLA commanders from squad to division level were capable of mastering their leadership tasks in the Himalayas. As the course of the war revealed, the Chinese commanders competently maneuvered troops over difficult terrain, made extensive use of tactical advantages, and avoided being disadvantaged by topography or inflexibility. In sharp contrast to the latent political interference in military decision-making during the Korean War, field officers now enjoyed significantly more freedom of command.[208] Taken together, this meant the PLA troops were well organized and prepared, led by experienced and competent commanders, and enjoyed the advantage of a civilian leadership that understood the rigors of combat at high altitude.

Finally, with regard to logistics, the area of operation seemed to favor India. China's supply lines ran over 2,000 kilometers from Xinjiang to Tibet and depended on roads.[209] India's lines of supply were not only much shorter but could also rely on the railroad. However, the most crucial distance for logistics in mountain warfare is that which lies between the road-heads and the frontline. This last link in the chain of supply functions as a bottleneck: the shorter the distance, the more supplies can be provided, which in turn increases the number of deployable combat troops.[210] While the Indian army was able to swiftly transport large quantities of supplies using the railroad, their roads ended 20 kilometers before the border, nullifying this advantageous means of transportation. The distance between China's road-heads and frontline positions was significantly shorter.[211] Moreover, as China's military planners had started preparations for a possible Sino-Indian confrontation as early as 1959, the logistical infrastructure had already been improved and the PLA could draw on large stockpiles of supplies in the expected area of operation.[212] The opposite holds true for India's supply situation: as New Delhi's leadership had constantly neglected the possibility of military confrontation with China, no such contingency planning was at hand. Consequently, Indian troops were chronically short of supplies, which significantly reduced their combat capacity during the war.[213]

Interim conclusion: assessing the risks of China's Himalayan campaign

There is no doubt that the PLA had a decisive edge over the Indian army when it came to warfare in high altitudes. As my analysis has demonstrated, the PLA's superiority in all relevant areas was so striking that the possibility of it not being known to China's political and military leadership appears highly unlikely. Consequently, there is good reason to conclude that Beijing was vividly aware of the military balance between India and China: before the onset of the offensive, the "PLA intelligence made it apparent that the military balance in the front regions … weighed heavily in China's favor."[214] Apparently, China's military intelligence reached the same obvious conclusion as my analysis: although waging warfare is never free of risk, China's military offensive in the Himalayas incorporated a low level of foreseeable risk due to India's overall military inferiority. Compared to the enormous risks China was willing to shoulder when intervening in Korea, the punitive campaign against India was a rather safe operation. The only factor that Beijing could not calculate with some certainty was the onset of the winter season in the Himalayas, which could have abruptly brought an end to the campaign and forced China to withdraw. This might explain why the Chinese leadership emphasized the necessity of achieving a decisive victory in a short campaign. It thus seems reasonable to conclude that on the whole, the Chinese leadership assessed the associated risks as acceptable.

Fighting a war to negotiate the peace: the PLA in the Himalayas

As envisaged in the General Staff's planning, China's campaign against India unfolded in three distinct phases. In the first week, the PLA delivered the desired punitive blow to the Indian forces on the Chinese side of the traditional boundary. With this objective accomplished, the next phase consisted of three weeks of virtual cease-fire in order to set the basis for negotiations. However, when India rejected the Chinese proposal, an extended offensive followed as a humiliating demonstration of China's military might. After scoring a crushing victory, Beijing then ceased the offense and withdrew its forces instead of realizing China's territorial claims.

China's initial offensive

In the morning hours of October 20, 1962, China's 'counterattack in self-defense' unfolded simultaneously in both sectors of the border. The PLA's offensive – now unleashed of political restraints and conducted in full force – pulverized the Indian defenses.[215] In the east, India's pride, the elite 7th Brigade, was completely destroyed in less than 48 hours. By October 22, Chinese troops had already advanced to the McMahon Line at Walong.[216] The next day, the PLA seized the strategically important Tawang. As China's operative objectives in the eastern sector were accomplished, the PLA ceased the offensive. In the west, Chinese troops halted on October 27.[217] In only one week, PLA troops had "eliminated parts of the four Indian battalions that made up the 114th Brigade, and recovered 1,900 square kilometers of Chinese territory."[218] Most importantly, however, the offensive had completely expelled Indian troops from the disputed territory claimed by China.

Even though the Indian units had been forced into a disorganized withdrawal, thus making additional territorial gains for China easily possible, the PLA refrained from further pursuit.[219] The PLA had successfully managed to inflict the desired 'fierce and painful' blow to India, as the desperate retreat of India's armed forces, the considerable loss of formerly Indian-controlled territory, and the substantial number of Indian casualties demonstrated. As the first goal of China's campaign had thus been accomplished, Beijing now focused on realizing the second objective: resuming negotiations with New Delhi.[220]

On October 24, a letter reached Prime Minister Nehru in which Zhou Enlai, in polite, diplomatic language, clarified that "China does not want a single inch of

132   *The Sino-Indian War*

India's territory"[221] before outlining measures to deescalate the current situation, to end the combat, and to strive for a peaceful resolution of the boundary dispute through negotiations. As the basis for such a settlement, China proposed the same conditions it had repeatedly offered to India since 1959. Consequently, there was no apparent reason to question the sincerity of Beijing's new offer. In addition, their most recent experiences with China's military power should have presented good reasons for the Indian government to accept the Chinese proposal at this point: as the preceding days had demonstrated, the PLA did not need to go to great lengths to annihilate some of India's best troops, force the remaining Indian units into a desperate retreat, and completely expel India's military presence from the disputed area.[222] Moreover, India had no acclimatized reinforcements at hand with which to strengthen the Himalayan frontline.[223] Finally, the fact that the PLA had ceased the offense was due to Beijing's good will and continued interest to settle the conflict through bilateral negotiations.[224] If Nehru had drawn the requisite conclusions at this point and reoriented India's China policy, the next phase of the Sino-Indian War very probably could have been avoided.[225]

Three weeks of quiet on the Himalayan front

New Delhi, however, "prodded to war by the Indian press and encouraged by [American, British, and Soviet] support,"[226] rejected the Chinese proposal out of hand. Even so, no Chinese reaction on the battlefield followed. Moreover, even as it became clear that Indian forces were concentrating for a counterattack in the northeast, Beijing maintained its implicitly proposed cease-fire for three full weeks. Why did China introduce this lull in battle, which allowed India to regroup and build up its battered troops? Allen Whiting argues that the three weeks of quiet on the Himalayan frontline were deliberately initiated by Beijing to allow the Indian leadership to pragmatically assess the recent developments, to draw some obvious conclusions, and to alter India's confrontational approach toward China.[227] There is good reason to agree with Whiting's argument. First, it seems likely that Beijing had anticipated an immediate and emotional rejection of the Chinese proposal, but also hoped that with some reprieve, the factuality of the situation would bring India's leaders to their senses and thereby back to the negotiating table.[228] In order to allow for a sober reconsideration of the situation, China had to stop mounting military pressure and prove credibly that it harbored no further offensive intentions. Second, the lull in battle was consistent with China's operative planning. According to John Garver, "[c]urrently available Chinese sources do not indicate another decision for war after the October 6 and 16 decisions."[229] Consequently, it appears very probable that China stuck to the initial planning without altering operative or political objectives. As outlined above, this meant that the Chinese offensive was to halt in order to enable a solution of the border conflict through consultations. Third, only after Beijing received India's inclusive and final rejection in word and deed on November 14, 1962, did China's unilateral cease-fire end. In word, the Indian reply reached Beijing in a letter from Nehru, in which he declared in forthright language India's definite rejection of the Chinese proposal.[230] In deed, the rejection was accompanied by an Indian counteroffensive on November 14, 1962. On that day, the

Indian Parliament legitimated the use of force in order to "drive out the invaders of the sacred soil of India, however long and hard the struggle may be."[231] Subsequently, Indian forces launched a fiercely conducted attack in the eastern sector.[232]

In sum, the three observations above strongly support Whiting's conclusion. Only after India's military response to China's diplomatic initiative finalized New Delhi's verbal rejection did Beijing reach the conclusion that Nehru was averse to talking and more eager to fight. As courtesy emphasizes reciprocity, to borrow the Chairman's words, the Chinese forces were prepared to accommodate the Indian Prime Minister's request for battle.

The humiliation of India's armed forces

The three weeks of virtual cease-fire allowed New Delhi to regroup and strengthen its battered forces under the advantageous condition of a quiet frontline: following the declaration of a state of national emergency on October 26, around 50,000 additional troops were thrown to the frontline.[233] As India's Home Minister Shastri publicly declared on November 12, India was "now strong enough to repulse the Chinese attackers and was building its military might to drive the invaders from Indian soil."[234] On the Chinese side of the border, the PLA General Staff had ordered two more divisions into Tibet in response. The military balance before the third and final phase of the Sino-Indian War had thus changed as follows: in the east, around 22,000 Indian troops stood against 25,000 PLA soldiers, while in the west, India had increased its troops to 15,000 men in order to compensate the heavy losses of the first engagements.[235] While many Chinese soldiers were acclimatized and familiar with the terrain, only a few Indian troops were in a state of preparedness to successfully engage in high-altitude combat as they were deployed ad hoc to the Himalayan front. Consequently, even though the Indian reinforcements increased the number of Indian troops, their deployment did not result in a significant increase of India's combat capacity *vis-à-vis* the PLA. Given India's latent shortcomings for combat at high altitudes as identified in the preceding analysis, manning the frontline with more soldiers thus could not compensate the Indian army's striking lack of preparedness for this very special type of warfare. As a result, India's futile counter-offensive of November 14 did not even come close to developing enough momentum to turn the tide of the battle on a single spot.[236] Now, however, it was on China's forces to deliver an answer to India's ongoing defiance "by launching a massive, preplanned offensive"[237] on November 16.

The offensive's principal goal, as outlined by the CMC plan of operations, consisted in destroying a substantial number of Indian forces.[238] Only hours after the offensive's onset, the PLA had already captured Walong and thereby annihilated more than 1,200 Indian defenders.[239] Already at this early stage of the offensive, General Kaul's frantic report to New Delhi drastically revealed the seriousness of the emerging situation, as well as India's epic underestimation of China's military power:

> [I]t seems beyond the capability of our armed forces to stem the tide of the superior Chinese forces which has and will continue to concentrate against us to our disadvantages. This is not a counsel of fear, but facing stark realities.[240]

Two days later, the three remaining Indian brigades in the eastern sector were largely wiped out and the PLA had "recovered a great deal of Chinese territory south of the McMahon Line."[241] In the west, organized Indian resistance collapsed on November 20.

Only four days after the onset of the second offensive, the PLA achieved a total victory over India's armed forces. Chinese troops had not only eliminated the entire Indian defense in the disputed areas, but this time did "not halt until Chinese soldiers locked out from the Himalayan foothill to the broad valley of the Brahmaputra River."[242] For India, the defeat was absolute, as the course of battle could not have turned out much worse: in the eastern sector, the PLA now stood only 30 kilometers north of Tezpur and seriously threatened the Brahmaputra Valley. The only available Indian defense consisted of no more than a single battalion.[243] In the west, China had gained control over the whole Aksai Chin area, while New Delhi simply had no more troops to command, because organized resistance had collapsed with the disintegration of India's last brigade on November 20.[244] In sum, the Indian government could basically do nothing by itself to reverse the war's outcome. "Under these circumstances," in Feng Chen and Larry Wortzel's apt assessment, "China had full capacity to realize the boundary it claimed."[245] But once again, Beijing exercised restraint.

China's unilateral cease-fire and withdrawal

On the eve of India's crushing defeat, Zhou Enlai informed the Indian *chargé d'affaires* in Beijing that Chinese forces would unilaterally implement a cease-fire along the entire frontline.[246] On November 21, 1962, the government of the People's Republic reaffirmed this intent and also announced that Chinese forces would begin a unilateral withdrawal on December 1. Explaining the rationale behind these measures, the statement again strongly reaffirmed Beijing's genuine intention to settle the Sino-Indian boundary conflict by non-violent means:

> These measures taken by the Chinese Government on its own initiative demonstrate its great sincerity for stopping the border conflict and settling the Sino-Indian boundary question peacefully. It should be pointed out, in particular, that after withdrawing, the Chinese frontier guards will be far behind their positions prior to September 8, 1962.[247]

As the extent of China's withdrawal and the wording of the statement indicate, Beijing had not intended to gain control over disputed territory by the use of force. Broken down into numbers, China's cease-fire conditions resulted in a de facto partition of the disputed area, whereby India received the 82,000 square kilometers of Arunachal Pradesh while China kept the 39,000 square kilometers of Aksai Chin. "Rather than the 'victor keeping the spoils', Peking kept only what was strategically vital: the area surrounding her critical military road in Aksai Chin."[248] Nonetheless, Beijing warned India in unmistakable terms to refrain from undertaking offensive action against Chinese troops or crossing the line of actual control to recover the positions held by India prior to the war. Should any of these eventualities occur, "[t]he Chinese Government solemnly declares that ... China reserves the right to strike back in self-defense, and the Indian Government will be completely held responsible for the grave consequences arising therefrom."[249]

As had been the case during the earlier phases of the Sino-Indian conflict, it was China that once again took the first steps to deescalate the situation and strive for its peaceful solution: at the stroke of midnight on November 21, Chinese troops ceased fire on all frontlines.[250] With India's defeat being absolute, and with pressure coming from the United States, New Delhi "had little choice but to acquiesce."[251] Once again, the Himalayan frontlines fell quiet. On December 1, the Chinese forces started their planned withdrawal and took positions 20 kilometers behind the line of actual control as determined in November 1959, the traditional Sino-Indian boundary. China thereby concluded the PLA's Himalaya campaign as envisaged in the initial planning, and the Sino-Indian War came to an end.

The outcome: a "most unfortunate war"

When striking the balance for China's military campaign against India, at least one of Beijing's objectives was comprehensively achieved. As intended, the crushing defeat of India's armed forces put India 'in its place.' On the other hand, with India's humiliation on the battlefield, a compromise on the border dispute receded into the distance. The defeat of the Indian army in 1962 resulted in a collective trauma of victimization in India's society. This painful experience affects the relationship between Beijing and New Delhi to this day and thereby prevents a resolution of the territorial dispute.[252]

As Mao had predicted, the war between China and India was "truly the most unfortunate event" for the future course of a bilateral relationship, which had incorporated the potential to cooperatively shape Asia's future. In 2011, China's then Vice Premier, Li Keqiang, apparently drew on this vision when declaring that the relationship would be the most important bilateral partnership of the century.[253] But the border conflict still reveals itself as a principal source of tensions between China and India.

Conclusion: warfare between friends

Before assessing the two competing theoretical models' capacity to explain the outbreak of the Sino-Indian War, I briefly summarize the central findings of the preceding analysis.

First, China resorted to military force even though the Chinese leadership had reached the conclusion that India did not pose a military threat to China's security. Moreover, the Sino-Indian War erupted during a period in which China was experiencing severe domestic crises as well as a deteriorating external security situation because of the onset of the Sino-Soviet split, the intensification of U.S. military activities in Southeast Asia, and the increased threat of a potential invasion of the mainland by the GMD. According to Taylor Fravel, under such unfavorable conditions the PRC typically showed notable restraint and an increased willingness to compromise in its territorial disputes.[254] This finding holds true for the period I investigated in this case study, as Beijing at this time reached a number of border settlements with neighbors, with the Sino-Indian territorial conflict as the single exception.

Second, the potential for a non-violent resolution of the Sino-Indian territorial conflicts did essentially exist, as shown by the Chinese proposal for a swap of competing claims and the delineation of the boundary based on the existing status quo. In addition, my analysis has demonstrated that China was genuinely interested in a negotiated and mutually acceptable solution throughout the entire process leading up to the escalation, and also went to great effort to keep open the door to a non-violent resolution. In line with this interest, the analysis of China's decision-making process revealed that Beijing's resort to force aimed at establishing the preconditions for such a settlement by forcing New Delhi to abandon its forward policy and by fostering the insight that a negotiated resolution was the only way to solve the territorial conflict effectively.

Third, the analysis shows that the principal cause for the outbreak of the Sino-Indian War is to be found not in the existence of competing territorial claims, but in the conflicting approaches employed by the two parties to the dispute. While Beijing showed willingness and effort to seek a mutually acceptable solution through negotiations, and thereto was willing to abandon its claim over Arunachal Pradesh, the Indian 'fixed and final' approach and its logical continuation in the forward policy basically impeded any compromise, as New Delhi was reluctant to depart from its maximum demand. Moreover, New Delhi started to act in a highly risk-taking manner when implementing the forward policy: the Indian government had been informed about the potential risk of a Chinese military action in response to this strategy but had decided to dismiss this risk, turning a blind eye to the assessment put forward by India's Military Intelligence.

Fourth, the analysis of Beijing's operative planning and the actual use of force demonstrated that China's military campaign in the Himalayas incorporated a decidedly punitive element. In line with my findings on the formation of the conflict, the central object of this punitive lesson was apparently the Indian administration, and not India as a collective. It seems that personality played a significant role in shaping the course of the bilateral relationship for the worse – in particular, Nehru's perceived arrogant attitude toward the Chinese leadership.

Fifth, the identification of the Dhola incident as the immediate trigger for China's resort to force, as well as the examination of the deliberations inside the Chinese leadership, highlight that emotions played a significant role in arriving at the decision to resort to force against India. Although Beijing was already becoming increasingly frustrated by India's highly provocative forward policy, the decision to resort to military force was not taken before New Delhi's evidenced disrespect for China had reached a peak with its perception that China was simply bluffing and would finally bow before India's military pressure. This, however, deeply offended China's pride:

> China had 'stood up,' as Mao said when proclaiming ... the People's Republic in October 1949. It would no longer be bullied by foreign powers. The PLA had fought the United States in Korea and performed credibly, at least in the

judgment of the Chinese leaders. Yet here was India acting as though the PLA would turn tail and run rather than fight to defend Chinese territory and honor.[255]

In the eyes of China's leaders, the Sino-Indian territorial conflict had then become a clear-cut competition for status, and they were willing to defend China's rank *vis-à-vis* India by teaching New Delhi a 'painful lesson' on the Himalayan battlefield.[256]

When taking these findings into account, Fearon's rationalist model is challenged by the problem that neither all of its underlying assumptions, nor the two postulated causal mechanisms, apply to the case under investigation. With regard to the first assumption, the material issue as a bone of contestation was evidently divisible: as Dawa Norbu found, the territorial conflict as such could have been "easily settled,"[257] and this even without reference to the problematic Simla Convention. Besides, Beijing and New Delhi were both clearly in the picture about the balance of forces and China's military superiority even before the conflict eventually escalated. Finally, as New Delhi decided to implement a high-risk strategy, none of Fearon's three basic assumptions of rational conflict management are met in the case at hand. For that reason, my analysis is unable to furnish any proof that either the commitment problem or the existence of information asymmetries prevented a negotiated settlement of the dispute. Instead, all partial analyses strongly support my central argument that the actual conflict in the Sino-Indian territorial dispute is to be found in the collision of two fundamentally incompatible strategies toward its solution. The resulting deadlock of 1962 was thus "more on emotional rather than territorial grounds."[258]

As the immediate causes for China's resort to force are thus found in the non-material dimension, Lebow's explanatory model, the Cultural Theory of International Relations, is capable of providing a more comprehensive and convincing explanation. During the honeymoon phase in Sino-Indian relations, both actors subordinated particular interests for the sake of their bilateral friendship, which in turn resulted in extensive cooperation. Thereby, the special relationship between Beijing and New Delhi approached the ideal-type of a *spirit-world*. Patterns of conflict then enter the Sino-Indian micro-society, where Beijing perceived a violation of its underlying *nomos* (i.e. the Five Principles of Peaceful Coexistence) with the Nehru administration's involvement in the Tibetan revolt and was forced to react in order to preserve China's international standing. While friendship then ceased to function as the defining element of the bilateral relationship, China's motivation still revealed a *balanced set* of *spirit* and *reason*, as demonstrated by Beijing's cooperative approach toward the territorial dispute. Even after the onset of the forward policy, China demonstrated remarkable forbearance toward India. Eventually, spirit became the dominant motive, first among China's key leaders and then among the elite, when India's provocations climaxed with the Dhola incident, which triggered a foremost emotionally induced decision to put the Nehru administration in its place due to the disrespect it had shown China. The analysis of China's conduct of war comprehensively corresponds with this line of reasoning: even though China could have easily deployed more troops in the initial offensive, the balanced numbers of forces on the Himalayan frontline allowed a duel to come to pass that Beijing then willingly accepted. The findings of all my partial analyses strongly indicate the dominance of the spirit as the central motive for China's resort to force against India in October 1962. The only exception here is the investigation of Beijing's risk behavior. This indicator could not provide insights into China's motivation, because the analysis cannot show the high risk-taking behavior associated with the ideal-type when there are simply no risks to take.

Summing up, while Fearon's explanatory model could not generate any explanatory capacity for the case at hand, my findings comprehensively confirm the hypothesized process as deduced from the Cultural Theory. While the border dispute existed as a cleavage from the onset, it first needed the breakdown of the Sino-Indian friendship as the *antecedent condition* in order to turn the border into an issue of contestation. The actual conflict – as shown above – resided within the two actors' fundamentally colliding strategies toward a solution of the territorial issue. However, the *immediate cause* for Beijing's resort to military force is to be found in the escalation of the bilateral status dimension of the Sino-Indian conflict.

Notes

1. For a summary on the history of the Sino-Indian border, see Calvin, James B., "The China–India Border War (1962)" (Quantico, VA: Marine Corps Command and Staff College, 1984), 4–12; Gupta, Karunakar, *The Hidden History of the Sino-Indian Frontier* (Calcutta: Minerva Associates, 1974).
2. See Calvin, "The China–India Border War (1962)," 8.
3. "India had been China's first non-Communist friend after 1949. Chinese–Indian relations were warmer and closer than China had with any other power, including Russia": Salisbury, Harrison E., *War between Russia and China* (New York: W.W. Norton & Company, 1969), 48.
4. Rowland, John, *A History of Sino-Indian Relations: Hostile Co-Existence* (Princeton, NJ: D. Van Nostrand, 1967), 81.
5. The Five Principles are "mutual respect for each other's territorial integrity and sovereignty, mutual non-aggression, mutual non-interference in each other's internal affairs, equality and mutual benefit, and peaceful coexistence": Dave, Shri A.K., "The Real Story of China's War on India, 1962," *Occasional Paper No. 1, Centre for Armed Forces Historical Research* (New Delhi: United Service Insitution of India, 2006), 2–3.
6. See Basu, A.R., "India's China Policy in Historical Perspective," *Contemporary Southeast Asia* 13, no. 1 (1991): 103.
7. See Abitbol, Aldo D., "Causes of the 1962 Sino-Indian War: A System Level Approach," *Josef Korbel Journal of Advanced International Studies* no. 1 (2009): 75; Maxwell, Neville, "Forty Years of Folly: What Caused the Sino-Indian Border War and Why the Dispute is Unresolved," *Critical Asian Studies* 35, no. 1 (2003): 99.
8. See Norbu, Dawa, "Tibet in Sino-Indian Relations. The Centrality of Marginality," *Asian Survey* 37, no. 1 (1997): 1078–79.
9. See Garver, John W., "China's Decision for War with India in 1962," in *New Directions in the Study of China's Foreign Policy*, ed. Johnston, Alastair and Ross, Robert S. (Stanford, CA: Stanford University Press, 2006), 91.
10. See Chen, Jian, "The Tibetan Rebellion of 1959 and China's Changing Relations with India and the Soviet Union," *Journal of Cold War Studies* 8, no. 3 (2006): 57–58.
11. See Garver, "China's Decision for War with India," 92.

12 See Rowland, *Sino-Indian Relations*, 66–67.
13 Garver, "China's Decision for War with India," 92.
14 Norbu, "Tibet in Sino-Indian Relations," 1080.
15 Feng, Cheng and Wortzel, Larry M., "PLA Operational Principles and Limited War: The Sino-Indian War of 1962," in *Chinese Warfighting – The PLA Experience since 1949*, ed. Ryan, Marc A., Finkelstein, David M., and McDevitt, Michael A. (Armonk/London: East Gate Books, 2003), 174.
16 Gurtov, Melvin and Hwang, Byong-Moo, *China under Threat: The Politics of Strategy and Diplomacy* (Baltimore, London: The Johns Hopkins University Press, 1980), 115.
17 See Feng and Wortzel, "The Sino-Indian War," 176.
18 Calvin, "The China-India Border War (1962)," 10–11.
19 See Gurtov and Hwang, *China under Threat*, 115.
20 See "Report of the Officials of the Governments of India and the People's Republic of China on the Boundary Question"; Sinha, Nirmal C., "The Simla Convention 1914: A Chinese Puzzle," *Bulletin of Tibetology*, no. 1 (1977): 35–38.
21 Lüthi, Lorenz, "Sino-Indian Relations, 1954–1962," *Eurasia Border Review* 3 (2012): 114.
22 See Van der Mey, Leo, "The India–China Conflict: Explaining the Outbreak of War in 1962," *Diplomacy & Statecraft* 5, no. 2 (1994): 187–88.
23 See Garver, "China's Decision for War with India," 104; Dave, "The Real Story of China's War on India, 1962," 5–6.
24 Gurtov and Hwang, *China under Threat*, 116.
25 Whiting, Allen S., *The Chinese Calculus of Deterrence: India and Indochina* (Ann Arbor, MI: The University of Michigan Press, 2001), 9.
26 See Chen, "The Tibetan Rebellion," 59.
27 See Feng and Wortzel, "The Sino-Indian War," 180.
28 Whiting, *The Chinese Calculus on Deterrence*, 8.
29 See Abitbol, "Causes of the 1962 Sino-Indian War," 77–79; Elleman, Bruce A., *Modern Chinese Warfare, 1795–1989* (New York: Routledge, 2001), 260.
30 See Whiting, *The Chinese Calculus on Deterrence*, 9. The Indian demand "reflect[ed] the furthest claim ever considered by the British (and never proposed to China)": Maxwell, Neville, "Settlements and Disputes – China's Approach to Territorial Issues," *Economic and Political Weekly* 41, no. 36 (2006): 3877.
31 Cited in Gurtov and Hwang, *China under Threat*, 116.
32 Ibid.
33 Ibid., 115.
34 Van der Mey, "The India–China Conflict," 186.
35 See Abitbol, "Causes of the 1962 Sino-Indian War," 76.
36 See Chen, "The Tibetan Rebellion," 72–75; Li, Xiaobing, *A History of the Modern Chinese Army* (Lexington, KY: The University Press of Kentucky, 2007), 199.
37 Chen, "The Tibetan Rebellion," 84.
38 See Garver, "China's Decision for War with India," 92–93; Chen, "The Tibetan Rebellion," pp. 84–86; Whiting, *The Chinese Calculus on Deterrence*, 12–19.
39 Chen, "The Tibetan Rebellion," 88.
40 Ibid., 87–88 [emphasis added].
41 See Van der Mey, "The India–China Conflict," 186.
42 Whiting, *The Chinese Calculus on Deterrence*, 10.
43 See Chen, "The Tibetan Rebellion," 86–89; Norbu, "Tibet in Sino-Indian Relations," 1085; Deepak, B.R., *A Century of Peace and Conflict: China and India, 1904–2004* (New Delhi: Manak Publications, 2005), 216.

140 *The Sino-Indian War*

44 See Lüthi, "Sino-Indian Relations," 106–07; Maxwell, "Forty Years of Folly," 101.
45 See Wortzel, Larry M., "Concentrating Forces and Audacious Action: PLA Lessons from the Sino-Indian War," in *The Lessons of History: The Chinese People's Liberation Army at 75*, ed. Burkitt, Laurie, Scobell, Andrew, and Wortzel, Larry M. (Carlisle: Strategic Studies Institute: U.S. Army War College, 2003), 331; Addis, J.M., "The India–China Border Question [The "Addis Paper"]" (Cambridge: Centre for International Affairs, 1963), 69–70.
46 Calvin, "The China–India Border War (1962)," 14.
47 See Feng and Wortzel, "The Sino-Indian War," 177; Garver, "China's Decision for War with India," 105.
48 Feng and Wortzel, "The Sino-Indian War," 177.
49 See "Discussion between N.S. Khrushchev and Mao Zedong" (October 3, 1959), 4.
50 See Feng and Wortzel, "The Sino-Indian War," 177.
51 See Dave, "The Real Story of China's War on India, 1962," 8; Whiting, *The Chinese Calculus on Deterrence*, 45.
52 Garver, "China's Decision for War with India," 106.
53 "Discussion between N.S. Khrushchev and Mao Zedong" (October 3, 1959), 5.
54 See Dave, "The Real Story of China's War on India, 1962," 8.
55 "Nehru ruled out the idea of withdrawing from the McMahon line, but proposed instead that each side refrain from sending patrols forward. For Aksai Chin, Nehru proposed that each side withdrew behind the line claimed by the other; this would have necessitated no drawback by the Indians in the west, but would have deprived China of its two Aksai Chin roads": Calvin, "The China–India Border War (1962)," 15.
56 Lüthi, "Sino-Indian Relations," 113.
57 See Fravel, Taylor M., *Strong Border, Secure Nation: Cooperation and Conflict in China's Territorial Disputes* (Princeton, NJ: Princeton University Press, 2008).
58 See Gernet, Jacques, *Die chinesische Welt. Die Geschichte Chinas von den Anfängen bis zur Jetztzeit* (Frankfurt am Main: Suhrkamp, 1997), 555–56.
59 See Whiting, *The Chinese Calculus on Deterrence*, 20–21; Gurtov and Hwang, *China under Threat*, 99, 108.
60 Dikötter, Frank, *Mao's Great Famine. The History of China's Most Devastating Catastrophe, 1958–62* (London: Bloomsburry, 2010), x.
61 See Whiting, *The Chinese Calculus on Deterrence*, 20–21.
62 Gurtov and Hwang, *China under Threat*, 127–28.
63 See Maxwell, "Settlements and Disputes," 3874–75; Lüthi, "Sino-Indian Relations," 117.
64 See Gurtov and Hwang, *China under Threat*, 118.
65 Garver, "China's Decision for War with India," 104.
66 See Lüthi, "Sino-Indian Relations," 115.
67 Garver, "China's Decision for War with India," 104 [emphasis added].
68 See Lüthi, "Sino-Indian Relations," 115.
69 Ibid.
70 See Van der Mey, "The India-China Conflict," 193.
71 Lüthi, "Sino-Indian Relations," 114.
72 Van der Mey, "The India-China Conflict," 194.
73 See Maxwell, Neville, *India's China War* (Bombay: Jaico Publishing House, 1970), 173–84; Van der Mey, "The India–China Conflict," 191.
74 For the eastern sector, the Indian demand had already been formalized in 1950.
75 Maxwell, "Forty Years of Folly," 103.
76 Feng and Wortzel, "The Sino-Indian War," 178.

77 Maxwell, Neville and Noorani, A.G., "India's Forward Policy," *The China Quarterly* no. 45 (1971): 158 [emphasis added].
78 Van der Mey, "The India–China Conflict," 191.
79 See Gurtov and Hwang, *China under Threat*, 119.
80 Maxwell and Noorani, "India's Forward Policy," 157. The "Father of Intelligence" in modern India and head of the Intelligence Bureau, B.N. Mullik, is quoted as saying: "[O]nce we claimed a territory to be our won we were free to go and open our posts there, no matter whether the Chinese disputed our claims and raised protests": cited in Maxwell, "Forty Years of Folly," 103.
81 Maxwell and Noorani, "India's Forward Policy," 157.
82 See Maxwell, "Forty Years of Folly," 103.
83 See Garver, "China's Decision for War with India," 109; Maxwell and Noorani, "India's Forward Policy," 157; Maxwell, *India's China War*, 170, 224.
84 Garver, "China's Decision for War with India," 109.
85 Ibid.
86 Van der Mey, "The India–China Conflict," 191. According to Neville Maxwell, the forward policy "was irrational, because its fundamental premise was that no matter how many posts and patrols India sent into Chinese-claimed and occupied territory the Chinese would not physically interfere with them – provided only that the Indians did not attack any Chinese positions": *India's China War*, 175.
87 Lüthi, "Sino-Indian Relations," 116.
88 Noorani, A.G., "India's Forward Policy. A Review Article," *The China Quarterly* no. 43 (1970): 136.
89 Maxwell, *India's China War*, 179. "In spite of the clear Indian recognition of China's military superiority in the frontier regions, Indian leaders reached the conclusion that China's superiority was irrelevant. If India demonstrated firm intent, China would back down": Garver, "China's Decision for War with India," 109.
90 Due to conflicting accounts in the available literature, it is hard to determine an exact date for the start of the forward policy.
91 See Wortzel, "Concentrating Forces and Audacious Action," 335; Maxwell, "Forty Years of Folly," 106.
92 See Calvin, "The China–India Border War (1962)," 16–17; Feng and Wortzel, "The Sino-Indian War," 181.
93 Calvin, "The China–India Border War (1962)," 16.
94 There is some difficulty in determining the onset of the second phase, as the transition from the initial phase to the systematic implementation of the policy seems more fluid than clear-cut.
95 See Garver, "China's Decision for War with India," 106.
96 Gurtov and Hwang, *China under Threat*, 119–20.
97 See Whiting, *The Chinese Calculus on Deterrence*, 77.
98 See Gurtov and Hwang, *China under Threat*, 119–20.
99 "If supplies could be dropped, so could troops. Previous PLA calculations based on the tortuous land routes now were challenged by New Delhi's growing ability to support operations in the high Himalayan plateau": Whiting, *The Chinese Calculus on Deterrence*, 56.
100 See Gurtov and Hwang, *China under Threat*, 121; Maxwell, "Forty Years of Folly," 104–06.
101 See Garver, "China's Decision for War with India," 108.
102 Cited in ibid., 107.
103 See Maxwell, "Forty Years of Folly," 106; Garver, "China's Decision for War with India," 107.

104 See Feng and Wortzel, "The Sino-Indian War," 180; Whiting, *The Chinese Calculus on Deterrence*, 51.
105 Maxwell, "Forty Years of Folly," 106.
106 However, "Mao stressed to PLA Chief of Staff Marshal Luo Ruiqing that the firing of the Chinese 'first shot' must be personally approved by himself": Garver, "China's Decision for War with India," 107.
107 Feng and Wortzel, "The Sino-Indian War," 180.
108 Garver, "China's Decision for War with India," 108.
109 See Feng and Wortzel, "The Sino-Indian War," 180–81.
110 Sinha, B. and Athale, A. A., *History of the Conflict with China, 1962* (New Delhi: Ministry of Defense, 1992), xx.
111 Garver, "China's Decision for War with India," 108.
112 In the east, "Indian forces [advanced] across the McMahon Line on those places where New Delhi thought it necessary to correct Sir Henry's cartographical shortcomings": Maxwell, "Forty Years of Folly," 107.
113 Van der Mey, "The India–China Conflict," 191.
114 See Calvin, "The China–India Border War (1962)," 19.
115 Garver, "China's Decision for War with India," 109.
116 See Calvin, "The China–India Border War (1962)," 20; Maxwell, "Forty Years of Folly," 106–07.
117 "When PLA forces encountered Indian forces, they first fired warning shots if they believed that Indian troops were guilty of intentional provocations. Finally, they returned fire or attacked in self-defense if fighting broke out": Feng and Wortzel, "The Sino-Indian War," 181.
118 See Maxwell, "Forty Years of Folly," 107.
119 Ibid., 106.
120 See Whiting, *The Chinese Calculus on Deterrence*, 50.
121 Cited in Gurtov and Hwang, *China under Threat*, 121.
122 Cited in Whiting, *The Chinese Calculus on Deterrence*, 83 [emphasis added].
123 See ibid., 93.
124 Gurtov and Hwang, *China under Threat*, 121.
125 See Maxwell, "Forty Years of Folly," 107.
126 Garver, "China's Decision for War with India," 100.
127 Whiting, *The Chinese Calculus on Deterrence*, 168.
128 See Dave, "The Real Story of China's War on India, 1962," 15–20; Whiting, *The Chinese Calculus on Deterrence*, 96–98, 155.
129 Feng and Wortzel, "The Sino-Indian War," 181.
130 See Calvin, "The China-India Border War (1962)," 21.
131 See Whiting, *The Chinese Calculus on Deterrence*, 99; Garver, "China's Decision for War with India," 113–14.
132 See Whiting, Allen S., "China's Use of Force, 1950–96, and Taiwan," *International Security* 26, no. 2 (2001): 112; Feng and Wortzel, "The Sino-Indian War," 182.
133 Ibid.
134 See Maxwell, "Forty Years of Folly," 109.
135 Whiting, *The Chinese Calculus on Deterrence*, 99. Adding to this, the Indian Air Force regularly conducted reconnaissance flights over the Chinese positions.
136 Noorani, "India's Forward Policy," 138.
137 Whiting, *The Chinese Calculus on Deterrence*, 97.
138 See Dave, "The Real Story of China's War on India, 1962," 22; Garver, "China's Decision for War with India," 114.

139 Gurtov and Hwang, *China under Threat*, 123.
140 Whiting, *The Chinese Calculus on Deterrence*, 102.
141 See Garver, "China's Decision for War with India," 114.
142 Whiting, *The Chinese Calculus on Deterrence*, 106.
143 See Maxwell, "Forty Years of Folly," 100–02.
144 See Maxwell, "Settlements and Disputes," 3877.
145 Gupta, *The Hidden History of the Sino-Indian Frontier*, 52.
146 See the counterfactual argument developed by Maxwell, "Forty Years of Folly," 102.
147 Chen, "The Tibetan Rebellion," 89.
148 See Van der Mey, "The India–China Conflict," 190.
149 Maxwell, "Forty Years of Folly," 102.
150 See Gurtov and Hwang, *China under Threat*, 122. The rejection of the Chinese proposal and India's military actions at Dhola led Beijing to conclude that India "had finally categorically shut the door to negotiations": Maxwell, "Settlements and Disputes," 3877.
151 Cited in Garver, "China's Decision for War with India," 115.
152 Cited in Maxwell, "Forty Years of Folly," 108.
153 See Garver, "China's Decision for War with India," 115.
154 Ibid.
155 Maxwell, "Forty Years of Folly," 109.
156 Cited in Garver, "China's Decision for War with India," 116–17.
157 Cited in Fravel, Taylor M., "Power Shifts and Escalations: Explaining China's Use of Force in Territorial Disputes," *International Security* 32, no. 3 (2007/2008): 70–71.
158 See Garver, "China's Decision for War with India," 116.
159 See Salisbury, *War between Russia and China*, 48.
160 See Garver, "China's Decision for War with India," 116.
161 Ibid., 117.
162 Ibid., 118.
163 Cited in ibid., 119.
164 See Maxwell, "Forty Years of Folly," 110.
165 See Garver, "China's Decision for War with India," 118.
166 See Whiting, *The Chinese Calculus on Deterrence*, 158–66.
167 Garver, "China's Decision for War with India," 119.
168 See Dave, "The Real Story of China's War on India, 1962," 27.
169 See Gurtov and Hwang, *China under Threat*, 146.
170 Garver, "China's Decision for War with India," 119. See further Feng and Wortzel, "The Sino-Indian War," 182; Wortzel, "Concentrating Forces and Audacious Action," 339.
171 See Elleman, *Modern Chinese Warfare*, 261.
172 Cited in Dinesh, Lal, *Indo-Tibet-China Conflict* (New Delhi: Kalpaz Publication, 2008), 178.
173 See Garver, "China's Decision for War with India," 119.
174 Whiting, *The Chinese Calculus on Deterrence*, 114; Noorani, "India's Forward Policy," 140.
175 Feng and Wortzel, "The Sino-Indian War," 182.
176 See Gurtov and Hwang, *China under Threat*, 123.
177 See Elleman, *Modern Chinese Warfare*, 261.
178 Garver, "China's Decision for War with India," 120. General Kaul, Commander of the Indian Army and thus probably the most influential military adviser to the Indian Prime Minister, later revealed that the Chinese assessments of Nehru's opinion about China's weakness were very accurate: see Gurtov and Hwang, *China under Threat*, 120.

144 *The Sino-Indian War*

179   The October 14, 1962 editorial of the *People's Daily* contained China's final warning to India: see Orton, Anna, *India's Borderland Disputes: China, Pakistan, Bangladesh, and Nepal* (New Delhi: Epitome Books, 2010), 50.
180   "At this juncture … China seems to have reached a decision that the provocations were no longer tolerable, especially given New Delhi's arrogance and imperviousness to Chinese diplomatic protests": Feng and Wortzel, "The Sino-Indian War," 182.
181   Cited in Garver, "China's Decision for War with India," 120.
182   Feng and Wortzel, "The Sino-Indian War," 182.
183   Besides the quoted literature, this section is based on several conversations with Lieutenant Colonel Jan Kars, Heeresbergführer of the Bundeswehr and senior analyst at George C. Marshall European Center for Security Studies, Garmisch-Partenkirchen (Germany).
184   See Calvin, "The China–India Border War (1962)," 17–18.
185   Garver, "China's Decision for War with India," 122.
186   See ibid., 118–19.
187   Grau, Lester W. and Vasquez, Hernan, "Ground Combat in High Altitude," *Military Review* 82, no. 2 (2002): 23.
188   See ibid., 28.
189   "The best time for military operations in the Himalayas was July–September. By October, the weather was already becoming cold, and heavy snowfalls were possible. The Tibet military district reported that once such snowfalls began, the PLA would encounter 'great difficulties' in moving supplies and reinforcements across the high passes to frontline Chinese forces. Major PLA action would have to come soon or be deferred to mid 1963": Garver, "China's Decision for War with India," 121.
190   Whiting, *The Chinese Calculus on Deterrence*, 98.
191   See Malik, Mohammed M., "Mountain Warfare: The Need for Specialized Training," in *Mountain Warfare and other Lofty Problems: Foreign Perspectives on High Altitude Combat*, ed. Grau, Lester W. and Bartles, Charles K. (Fort Leavenworth, KS: Foreign Military Studies Office, 2011), 16.
192   See Wortzel, "Concentrating Forces and Audacious Action," 339–40.
193   Grau and Vasquez, "Ground Combat in High Altitude," 24.
194   See Malik, "Mountain Warfare," 15.
195   Grau and Vasquez, "Ground Combat in High Altitude," 24.
196   See ibid., 28.
197   See Feng and Wortzel, "The Sino-Indian War," 176.
198   See Calvin, "The China–India Border War (1962)," 17.
199   See Feng and Wortzel, "The Sino-Indian War," 194; Calvin, "The China–India Border War (1962)," 18.
200   Calvin, "The China–India Border War (1962)," 19.
201   Ibid.
202   Feng and Wortzel, "The Sino-Indian War," 173.
203   See Garver, "China's Decision for War with India," 39; Li, *A History of the Modern Chinese Army*, 201.
204   See Elleman, *Modern Chinese Warfare*, 260–61.
205   Feng and Wortzel, "The Sino-Indian War," 186.
206   See Barnouin, Barbara and Yu, Bin, *Zhou Enlai – A Political Life* (Hong Kong: The Chinese University Press, 2006), 61.
207   See Li, *A History of the Modern Chinese Army*, 204.
208   See Feng and Wortzel, "The Sino-Indian War," 190–91.
209   In 1962, a famine struck Tibet and the food situation became desperate. Accordingly,

all provisions for the PLA had to be transported into Tibet: see Gurtov and Hwang, *China under Threat*, 122.
210   See Grau and Vasquez, "Ground Combat in High Altitude," 24.
211   See Feng and Wortzel, "The Sino-Indian War," 180, 93.
212   See ibid., 180.
213   See Li, *A History of the Modern Chinese Army*, 201.
214   Garver, "China's Decision for War with India," 121.
215   See Feng and Wortzel, "The Sino-Indian War," 182.
216   See Maxwell, "Forty Years of Folly," 111; Berding, Andreas, "Der indisch-chinesische Grenzkrieg," *Militärgeschichte: Zeitschrift für historische Bildung* no. 4 (2011): 16.
217   See Garver, "China's Decision for War with India," 122; Berding, "Der indisch-chinesische Grenzkrieg," 16–17.
218   Feng and Wortzel, "The Sino-Indian War," 186.
219   See Whiting, *The Chinese Calculus on Deterrence*, 120; Gurtov and Hwang, *China under Threat*, 141.
220   See Feng and Wortzel, "The Sino-Indian War," 186.
221   "Statement of the Chinese Government, 24 October 1962." In *White Paper VIII – Notes, Memoranda and Letters Exchanged and Agreements Signed between the Governments of India and China (October 1962–January 1963)*, Ministry of External Affairs, Government of India.
222   "The realities of the military balance, that is, the PLA's clear superiority over Indian forces in the frontier region, should also haven been clear": Garver, "China's Decision for War with India," 122.
223   See Feng and Wortzel, "The Sino-Indian War," 186.
224   See Gurtov and Hwang, *China under Threat*, 141.
225   See Garver, "China's Decision for War with India," 122.
226   Wortzel, "Concentrating Forces and Audacious Action," 341.
227   See Whiting, *The Chinese Calculus on Deterrence*, 125.
228   After receiving the Indian rejection on October 27, Zhou Enlai even sent a second letter on November 4, 1962, outlining at length the Chinese standpoint on the border dispute.
229   Garver, "China's Decision for War with India," 122.
230   See "Letter from the Prime Minister of India to Premier Chou En-lai (November 14, 1962)." In *White Paper VIII – Notes, Memoranda and Letters Exchanged and Agreements Signed between the Governments of India and China (October 1962–January 1963)*, Ministry of External Affairs, Government of India.
231   Cited in Jetly, Nancy, *India–China Relations, 1947–1977: A Study of Parliament's Role in the Making of Foreign Policy* (Atlantic Highlands: Humanities Press, 1979), 187.
232   See Elleman, *Modern Chinese Warfare*, 262.
233   See Wortzel, "Concentrating Forces and Audacious Action," 341.
234   Cited in Whiting, *The Chinese Calculus on Deterrence*, 144.
235   See Feng and Wortzel, "The Sino-Indian War," 186–87.
236   See Calvin, "The China-India Border War (1962)," 25.
237   Garver, "China's Decision for War with India," 123.
238   See Feng and Wortzel, "The Sino-Indian War," 186–87.
239   See Elleman, *Modern Chinese Warfare*, 264.
240   Cited in Maxwell, *India's China War*, 394.
241   Feng and Wortzel, "The Sino-Indian War," 187.
242   Garver, "China's Decision for War with India," 123.
243   See Feng and Wortzel, "The Sino-Indian War," 187.

244 See Whiting, *The Chinese Calculus on Deterrence*, 146; Calvin, "The China–India Border War (1962)," 28.
245 See Feng and Wortzel, "The Sino-Indian War," 187.
246 See Li, *A History of the Modern Chinese Army*, 202; Feng and Wortzel, "The Sino-Indian War," 187.
247 "Statement given by the Chinese Government, 21 November 1962." In *White Paper VIII – Notes, Memoranda and Letters Exchanged and Agreements Signed between the Governments of India and China (October 1962–January 1963)*, Ministry of External Affairs, Government of India.
248 Calvin, "The China–India Border War (1962)," 29.
249 "Statement given by the Chinese Government, 21 November 1962."
250 Calvin, "The China–India Border War (1962)," 29.
251 Gurtov and Hwang, *China under Threat*, 142; Whiting, *The Chinese Calculus on Deterrence*, 150.
252 See Maxwell, "Forty Years of Folly," 100.
253 See "US, China Woo India for Control over Asia-Pacific," *Times of India*, June 7, 2012.
254 See Fravel, "Power Shifts and Escalations."
255 Garver, "China's Decision for War with India," 109–10.
256 See Liegl, Markus B., "Status, Prestige, and Emotions: The Social Dimension of the Sino-Indian Territorial Dispute." Paper presented at the Annual Convention of the International Studies Association, New Orleans, February 18–21, 2015.
257 Norbu, "Tibet in Sino-Indian Relations," 1087.
258 Ibid., 1088.

Bibliography

Abitbol, Aldo D. "Causes of the 1962 Sino-Indian War: A System Level Approach." *Josef Korbel Journal of Advanced International Studies* no. 1 (Summer 2009): 74–88.

Addis, J.M. "The India–China Border Question [The "Addis Paper"]." Cambridge: Centre for International Affairs, 1963.

Barnouin, Barbara, and Yu, Bin. *Zhou Enlai – A Political Life*. Hong Kong: The Chinese University Press, 2006.

Basu, A.R. "India's China Policy in Historical Perspective." *Contemporary Southeast Asia* 13, no. 1 (June 1991): 103–15.

Berding, Andreas. "Der indisch-chinesische Grenzkrieg." *Militärgeschichte: Zeitschrift für historische Bildung* no. 4 (2011): 14–17.

Calvin, James B. "The China–India Border War (1962)." Quantico, VA: Marine Corps Command and Staff College, 1984.

Chen, Jian. "The Tibetan Rebellion of 1959 and China's Changing Relations with India and the Soviet Union." *Journal of Cold War Studies* 8, no. 3 (2006): 54–101.

Dave, Shri A.K. "The Real Story of China's War on India, 1962." *Occasional Paper No. 1, Centre for Armed Forces Historical Research*. New Delhi: United Service Insitution of India, 2006.

Deepak, B.R. *A Century of Peace and Conflict: China and India, 1904–2004*. New Delhi: Manak Publications, 2005.

Dikötter, Frank. *Mao's Great Famine. The History of China's Most Devastating Catastrophe, 1958–62*. London: Bloomsbury, 2010.

Dinesh, Lal. *Indo-Tibet-China Conflict*. New Delhi: Kalpaz Publication, 2008.

"Discussion between N.S. Khrushchev and Mao Zedong" (October 2, 1959). Accessed at Wilson Center Digital Archive, http://digitalarchive.wilsoncenter.org/document/ 112088.pdf?v=401979fac3f7d5e1d51d0bcd3a80f4c5 (August 2, 2016).

Elleman, Bruce A. *Modern Chinese Warfare, 1795–1989*. Routledge: New York, 2001.

Feng, Cheng and Wortzel, Larry M. "PLA Operational Principles and Limited War: The Sino-Indian War of 1962." In *Chinese Warfighting – The PLA Experience since 1949*, edited by Marc A. Ryan, David M. Finkelstein and Michael A. McDevitt, 173–97. Armonk/London: East Gate Books, 2003.

Fravel, Taylor M. "Power Shifts and Escalations: Explaining China's Use of Force in Territorial Disputes." *International Security* 32, no. 3 (2007/2008): 44–83.

Fravel, Taylor M. *Strong Border, Secure Nation: Cooperation and Conflict in China's Territorial Disputes*. Princeton, NJ: Princeton University Press, 2008.

Garver, John W. "China's Decision for War with India in 1962." In *New Directions in the Study of China's Foreign Policy*, edited by Alastair Johnston and Robert S. Ross, 86–130. Stanford, CA: Stanford University Press, 2006.

Gernet, Jacques. *Die chinesische Welt. Die Geschichte Chinas von den Anfängen bis zur Jetztzeit*. Frankfurt am Main: Suhrkamp, 1997.

Grau, Lester W. and Vasquez, Hernan. "Ground Combat in High Altitude." *Military Review* 82, no. 2 (2002): 22–31.

Gupta, Karunakar. *The Hidden History of the Sino-Indian Frontier*. Calcutta: Minerva Associates, 1974.

Gurtov, Melvin and Hwang, Byong-Moo. *China under Threat. The Politics of Strategy and Diplomacy*. Baltimore, London: The Johns Hopkins University Press, 1980.

"Letter from the Prime Minister of India to Premier Chou En-lai (November 14, 1962)." In *White Paper VIII – Notes, Memoranda and Letters Exchanged and Agreements Signed between the Governments of India and China (October 1962–January 1963)*, Ministry of External Affairs, Government of India. Accessed at www.claudearpi.net/maintenance/uploaded_pics/White_Paper_08.pdf (August 2, 2016).

Jetly, Nancy. *India–China Relations, 1947–1977: A Study of Parliament's Role in the Making of Foreign Policy*. Atlantic Highlands: Humanities Press, 1979.

Li, Xiaobing. *A History of the Modern Chinese Army*. Lexington, KY: The University Press of Kentucky, 2007.

Liegl, Markus B. "Status, Prestige, and Emotions: The Social Dimension of the Sino-Indian Territorial Dispute." Paper presented at the Annual Convention of the International Studies Association, New Orleans, February 18–21, 2015.

Lüthi, Lorenz. "Sino-Indian Relations, 1954–1962." *Eurasia Border Review* 3 (Spring 2012): 95–120.

Malik, Mohammed M. "Mountain Warfare: The Need for Specialized Training." In *Mountain Warfare and other Lofty Problems: Foreign Perspectives on High Altitude Combat*, edited by Lester W. Grau and Charles K. Bartles, 15–29. Fort Leavenworth, KS: Foreign Military Studies Office, 2011.

Maxwell, Neville. *India's China War*. Bombay: Jaico Publishing House, 1970.

Maxwell, Neville. "Forty Years of Folly: What Caused the Sino-Indian Border War and Why the Dispute Is Unresolved." *Critical Asian Studies* 35, no. 1 (2003): 99–112.

Maxwell, Neville. "Settlements and Disputes – China's Approach to Territorial Issues." *Economic and Political Weekly* 41, no. 36 (2006): 3873–81.

Maxwell, Neville and Noorani, A.G. "India's Forward Policy." *The China Quarterly* no. 45 (1971): 157–63.

Noorani, A.G. "India's Forward Policy. A Review Article." *The China Quarterly* no. 43 (1970): 136–41.

Norbu, Dawa. "Tibet in Sino-Indian Relations. The Centrality of Marginality." *Asian Survey* 37, no. 1 (1997): 1078–95.

Orton, Anna. *India's Borderland Disputes: China, Pakistan, Bangladesh, and Nepal*. New Delhi: Epitome Books, 2010.

"Report of the Officials of the Governments of India and the People's Republic of China on the Boundary Question" ["Chinese Report," Part I]. Accessed at www.claudearpi.net/maintenance/uploaded_pics/ORC_01-32_Part1.pdf (August 2, 2016).

Rowland, John. *A History of Sino-Indian Relations: Hostile Co-Existence*. Princeton, NJ: D. Van Nostrand, 1967.

Salisbury, Harrison E. *War between Russia and China*. New York: W.W. Norton & Company, 1969.

Sinha, Nirmal C. "The Simla Convention 1914: A Chinese Puzzle." *Bulletin of Tibetology* no. 1 (1977): 35–39.

Sinha, P.B. and Athale, A.A. *History of the Conflict with China, 1962*. New Delhi: Ministry of Defense, 1992.

"Statement Given by the Chinese Government, 21 November 1962." In *White Paper VIII – Notes, Memoranda and Letters Exchanged and Agreements Signed between the Governments of India and China (October 1962–January 1963)*, Ministry of External Affairs, Government of India. Accessed at www.claudearpi.net/maintenance/uploaded_pics/White_Paper_08.pdf (August 2, 2016).

"Statement of the Chinese Government, 24 October 1962." In *White Paper VIII – Notes, Memoranda and Letters Exchanged and Agreements Signed between the Governments of India and China (October 1962–January 1963)*, Ministry of External Affairs, Government of India. Accessed at www.claudearpi.net/maintenance/uploaded_pics/White_Paper_08.pdf (August 2, 2016).

"US, China Woo India for Control over Asia-Pacific." *Times of India*, June 7, 2012.

Van der Mey, Leo. "The India–China Conflict: Explaining the Outbreak of War in 1962." *Diplomacy & Statecraft* 5, no. 2 (1994): 183–99.

Whiting, Allen S. "China's Use of Force, 1950–96, and Taiwan." *International Security* 26, no. 2 (Fall 2001): 103–31.

Whiting, Allen S. *The Chinese Calculus of Deterrence: India and Indochina*. Ann Arbor, MI: The University of Michigan Press, 2001.

Wortzel, Larry M. "Concentrating Forces and Audacious Action: PLA Lessons from the Sino-Indian War." In *The Lessons of History: The Chinese People's Liberation Army at 75*, edited by Laurie Burkitt, Andrew Scobell and Larry M. Wortzel, 327–52. Carlisle: Strategic Studies Institute: U.S. Army War College, 2003.

5 The Sino-Soviet border clashes of 1969

In March 1969, the world learned about the existence of an island in the Sino-Soviet boundary river Ussuri, as this tiny and worthless piece of land was "treated to the spectacle of the two giant, 'peace-loving, Socialist champions of the oppressed' shooting it out over ... a frozen river at the far reaches of their territories."[1] On March 2 and March 15, firefights between Chinese and Soviet troops erupted on the island, known as Damansky in Russia and as Zhenbao in China.[2] These clashes brought the PRC and the Soviet Union to the brink of full-scale war, with the inherent potential to even cross the nuclear threshold. With regard to these highly dramatic implications, I fundamentally challenge Neville Maxwell's conclusion that "[t]he question who fired the first shot has minimal historical significance."[3] On the contrary, I argue that identifying which side can be held responsible for the outbreak of violence in March 1969 is the first step necessary in order to demonstrate the political significance of the Sino-Soviet border clashes and reveal the motivation behind China's decision to fire this crucial first shot.

Outline of the chapter

This case study unfolds as follows: the first section is devoted to clarifying the deliberate and proactive character of China's use of force at Zhenbao Island by examining in detail the two clashes of March 1969. This allows me to justify the inclusion of this case in the case sample of this book. Following that, I analyze the patterns of Sino-Soviet conflict management in the aftermath of the clashes. In the third section, I address the question why, after thousands of incidents and provocations had taken place, the Sino-Soviet border confrontation finally burst into flames in March 1969. I argue that it was not the existence of a boundary conflict per se that served as the necessary cause for the March clashes; rather, the crucial trigger is to be found in the formulation of Moscow's Brezhnev Doctrine. In the fourth section, I evaluate China's risk behavior. As Thomas Robinson has found, "Mao took a major chance in ordering the Damansky/Zhenbao action. He directly attacked a nuclear superpower, without any international support, at a time of internal chaos when the military was turned inward."[4] I partially share this conclusion, but my analysis – unfolding in two parts – demonstrates that on the tactical level, Beijing acted in quite a risk-averse way and introduced several measures to control arising risks. In contrast to that, Robinson's assessment definitely holds true for the strategic level, on which the prohibitive risk of an escalation to a full-scale Sino-Soviet war obviously existed; this, however, was largely blanked out in the Chinese calculations. Finally, after discussing the outcomes of the Sino-Soviet border crisis, I recapitulate the results of my partial analyses in the concluding section in order to identify the changes in China's set of motives before, during, and in the aftermath of the Sino-Soviet border clashes of 1969.

Who started the fight?

Shortly after the first clash had taken place on March 2, Beijing and Moscow set out their respective versions of the outbreak of hostilities at Zhenbao. While the Soviet Union claimed that its border guards had been ambushed by an overwhelming and well-prepared Chinese force of 200–300 soldiers, China declared that one of its patrols had come under attack and Chinese soldiers returned fire in self-defense. However, while both sides said the enemy had taken advantage of the valuable moment of surprise, both also stated that they were nonetheless able to regain control over the disputed islands in the end.[5] These two competing accounts, and their selective reception in the aftermath of the clashes, led to the emergence of many myths about the events of March 1969. In the West, as Neville Maxwell observed, "as usual, the weight of credence swung against China."[6]

Bloodshed at Zhenbao: the Chinese aggression

While the sources currently available still do not allow for a clear-cut identification of one side as the aggressor without some doubt remaining, there is nonetheless solid evidence in support of Moscow's version of a Chinese attack. First, Soviet troops suffered considerably high casualties, particularly with regard to the proportion of killed and wounded soldiers. According to Soviet testimonies, the losses numbered a total of 31 KIA and 14 WIA, while the Chinese side claimed 20 men KIA and 34 WIA. The unusual ratio of wounded to killed Soviet troops indicates that the Chinese attack was not expected by the Soviet border guards.[7] Second, both sides acknowledged that while the Chinese forces consisted mainly of infantry, several military vehicles, among them at least two BTR-60 armored personnel carriers (APC), accompanied the Soviet patrol.[8] These vehicles are typically armed with a rapid-fire cannon and a machine gun. If the Soviets had started the fight, it seems likely that they would have initially deployed this superior weaponry with devastating effect against the Chinese infantry. Under these circumstances, the overall amount of Soviet casualties would probably have been much lower. It seems, however, that the APCs' armament was mainly used to cover the withdrawal of the remaining Soviet troops.[9] Third, at the end of the first encounter, the Chinese remained – at least temporarily – in possession of the battlefield.[10] This fact is brutally illustrated by a Soviet autopsy report on the casualties of March 2. According to this report, the Chinese killed a total of 19 Soviet servicemen after the actual fighting had ceased. These soldiers were apparently wounded during the battle and then left to the Chinese, who brought them cruelly to death with bayonets, point-blank shots, and rifle buttstocks.[11] This once again indicates that the Soviets were obviously caught unprepared by a Chinese close-range-fire assault; then retreated for cover, but were unable to hold their position against an overwhelming force; and finally had to withdraw, without being able to save wounded comrades. Fourth, the Soviet leadership was not only caught by surprise when informed about the incident, but was also shocked by its potential ramifications for Soviet security: according to the memoirs of Arkady Shevchenko, the highest-ranking Soviet official to defect to the West during the Cold War,

> [t]he events on Damansky had the effect of an electric shock in Moscow. The Politburo was terrified that the Chinese might make a large-scale intrusion into Soviet territory. ... A nightmare vision of invasion by millions of Chinese made the Soviet leaders almost frantic.[12]

These distinct and tense impressions on the part of the inner circle would not have appeared as plainly in Shevchenko's memoirs if the Soviet leadership had intentionally escalated the conflict. At that time, Moscow's ideologists continued to rule out the likelihood of a military confrontation between China and the Soviet Union, although serious ideological and political differences had already emerged: "As to the possibility of war or military conflict inside the socialist camp, such ideas were not discussed because of their absolute impossibility and even absurdity."[13] Moreover, the Soviet Union was not interested in any further deterioration of relations with China, as Moscow was then preoccupied with managing a new epoch of Cold War relations with the United States and with asserting control over its Eastern European clients. Opening up a new and potentially uncontrollable hotspot at the Sino-Soviet border thus appeared greatly counterproductive. In sum, the evidence discussed above allows for the conclusion that the Chinese side can be held responsible for the outbreak of hostilities between the Soviet Union and the People's Republic of China at Zhenbao Island in March 1969.

An escalation by accident?

As the incident took place during the chaotic peak of China's Cultural Revolution, there is some reason to argue that the clash might have been the result of an initiative by a local Chinese border-guard unit acting without superior authorization.[14] According to one account, Soviet soldiers had inflicted a number of humiliations on Chinese civilians and the border guards themselves prior to the event, but the guards had orders to avoid provoking the Soviets, act defensively, and avoid direct encounters.[15] It thus seems possible that a local unit could have instigated the clash autonomously, motivated by frustration and anger and in search of revenge – emotions that might be reflected by the brutal methods the Chinese used to kill the wounded Soviet soldiers.[16] Beijing then might not have issued a statement to explain the concrete circumstances because it would have risked appearing as if it was not in control of its armed forces, thereby presenting to the outside world a picture of a China totally in chaos. However, two profound arguments counter this thesis. Why should the local Chinese border guards depart autonomously from the well-established practice of non-violent encounters with their Soviet counterparts, thereby exposing themselves and their comrades at other parts of the border to incalculable risks in future encounters with aware and aggressive Soviet patrols?[17] Also, the border guards risked severe punishment for acting without orders. In this phase of the Cultural Revolution, PLA commanders were known for enforcing discipline and allegiance with drastic measures, and the "CMC and the Politburo (and thus, presumably, Mao himself) were said to retain careful, direct, and detailed control over border matters."[18] For the border guards at Zhenbao, both strands of consequences resulting from unauthorized action must have been foreseeable and both would have led to great deterioration in their personal situations, potentially threatening their lives. Furthermore, the number of Chinese soldiers deployed and the heavy weaponry and specific military equipment used in the ambush bears the conclusion that the operation was carefully planned and commanded by higher authorities. According to Soviet documents, the ambush was conducted by an estimate of 200 to 300 heavily armed and specially trained PLA soldiers that had been brought to the island on the night of March 2, while the regular border guards played only the secondary role of luring the Soviets into the trap.[19] The quantity and quality of employed men and weaponry, as well as the sophisticated planning of the ambush, do not support the argument of a single unit acting spontaneously on its own: the pooling of several Chinese units from different military branches, among them soldiers from elite units; their logistical support; and the sophisticated armament used required a level of competence that clearly exceeded that of a local border-force commander.[20] In view of this, it seems more than reasonable to share Lyle Goldstein's conclusion "that the Sino-Soviet clashes did not simply 'erupt' ... but rather came as the result of a premeditated act of state violence."[21]

The second clash: March 15, 1969

Two weeks after the first incident, another clash between Chinese and Soviet forces occurred. Once again, it remains unclear which side initiated this second round of fighting, as both opponents claimed that their patrol was attacked. This time, however, it seems as if the Chinese account encompasses greater plausibility, because "the Soviet side went to no great pains to hide the fact that Russian forces had taken the initiative on this occasion."[22] According to the Chinese version of events, the Soviets had previously increased their patrol activities, and even had deployed a small detachment on the island before March 15. As the Chinese did not react to these provocations, they were followed by an extensive attack on the Chinese routine patrol and a show of force by Soviet aircraft: "more than one hundred Soviet troops and six tanks counterattacked. Heavy artillery ... shelled both shores. More than forty Chinese soldiers were killed. The Soviets lost eight men and one T-62 tank."[23] The small number of Soviet casualties, as well as the deployment of the then brand-new and top-secret T-62 main battle tank, allows for the conclusion that the Soviets initiated the offensive in apparent retaliation for the Chinese ambush of March 2. By annihilating the Chinese units with an overwhelming blow, the Soviets apparently intended not only to take revenge, but also to send a strong message of their superior military might in order to discourage further Chinese counter-attacks, as well as to demonstrate and underline Moscow's authority in the ongoing Sino-Soviet struggle for ideological and political leadership in the international socialist movement.[24]

However, as the subsequent nine hours of high-intensity combat showed, the Chinese forces were not intimidated, and now threw more than 2,000 men into the battle.[25] During the 12-day period between the two clashes, both sides had amassed troops and weaponry. On March 15, China enjoyed a slight numerical advantage, while the Soviets employed an overwhelming amount of heavy weaponry (around 50 APCs and tanks) and were thus easily able to shatter the Chinese counterattack. However, the Soviet commander apparently made the tactical mistake of regrouping his forces after each attack instead of employing them in a concentrated manner, which allowed the Chinese to bring in reinforcements and mount considerable resistance. Eventually, after three Soviet assaults had largely failed, an intensive artillery barrage 'pulverized' the Chinese positions. At the end of the battle, the PRC had lost an estimate of up to 800 troops (KIA and WIA). In contrast, the Soviet forces suffered only around 60 casualties. Although neither party had gained control of the island, both sides claimed victory.[26]

The Chinese forces had successfully managed to withstand this storm of Soviet firepower. In adherence with Mao's military principles, a pre-chosen battlefield presented them with the decisive advantages that allowed for the accomplishment of China's primary military objective: as Beijing had been aware of the Soviet build-up before the March 15 clash and thus expected military action in retaliation, the Chinese leadership "could only hope to soften the blow [and] discourage the Soviets from retaking the island permanently."[27] However, China's military performance did in fact fail to achieve its more general objective of dissuading Moscow from resorting to military action at other spots along the shared border.

Patterns of Sino-Soviet crisis management

In the aftermath of the two incidents, tension between China and the Soviet Union began to flare up as Soviet forces initiated a series of skirmishes along the Amur River and the border to Xingjian. On several occasions, these clashes involved a substantial number of Soviet troops, as Moscow intended to prove its readiness for escalation by ambushing and decimating – sometimes even annihilating – Chinese military units at various carefully chosen spots along the entire frontier.[28] Now, the Soviet Union intended to teach Beijing the highly symbolic and bitter lesson that China's security depended on Moscow's forbearance.[29]

This series of 'bloody noses' had been preceded by Soviet diplomatic initiatives that had aimed at deescalating tensions and at bringing Beijing back to the negotiating table.[30] Only days after March 15, Moscow thus had tried to re-establish top-level contact with China.[31] Mao, however, had not made a single move towards the Soviets: even though he had reached the conclusion that the "northeast, the north and the northwest should be prepared [because China is] now confronted with a formidable enemy,"[32] the Chairman was still convinced that the Soviet leadership would shy from the risks of climbing higher on the ladder of escalation. "For Mao Zedong, the whole thing was over."[33] Consequently, the "Chinese statements erected a wall against leadership contacts and chided the Soviets for their display of alarm and anxiety."[34] Drastically underestimating the seriousness of the situation, Beijing maintained its provocative course of offensively showing strength.

However, the Soviet series of 'bloody noses' – peaking in July and August 1969 – led Mao to reconsider this adventurous calculus: Moscow's unexpected steadfastness and Brezhnev's now proven willingness to escalate the crisis had left noticeable cracks in Mao's basic conviction that the Soviet Union would not risk an open war with China. As Beijing found itself confronted with a new quality of Soviet military pressure, this possibility gained more and more credibility. Adding to this, more than only rumors about the Soviet leadership discussing the option of punishing China with a preemptive nuclear strike then reached Beijing.[35]

> Mao was shocked by the intensity of the Soviet response both in terms of a near-term war scare and the fast-paced military buildup on the Chinese border that followed. Mao had not expected such a concerted response so soon, especially when it occurred far from European Russia, where the main Soviet forces and logistics bases were.[36]

The fear of war started to grasp Beijing, and the Chinese leadership showed greater anxiety about Soviet retaliation than had been the case at the onset of the crisis.[37] As Yang Kuisong observes, all this "was beyond Mao's worst expectations that the situation should have deteriorated to such an extent."[38]

At the end of August, Beijing was no longer able to assert even minimal control over the escalation of the crisis. Consequently, the majority of Chinese leaders, among them Mao Zedong and Zhou Enlai, felt the urgent need to defuse the situation – but to do so in a face-saving manner: although Mao was now willing to engage in serious talks with the Soviets, he wanted to avoid the impression that a scared China was bowing before the Soviet Union.[39] For that reason, the next Soviet initiative, by Soviet Prime Minister Kosygin at the occasion of Ho Chi Minh's funeral, was again discourteously rebuffed, only for Kosygin to be summoned to Beijing a few days later. The Chinese 'protocol' for the first Sino-Soviet high-level meeting in four and a half years by no means reflected the status of the Soviet official, as the Chinese arranged for the talks to take place in an airport lounge.[40] Ignoring this disrespectful treatment and the obvious paranoia that seemed to have grasped the Chinese leadership, Kosygin reached the consensus with Zhou Enlai that the boundary dispute should be settled by peaceful negotiations and until then, the two parties should maintain the status quo.[41] Kosygin's visit to Beijing and the agreed-upon Sino-Soviet code of conduct on the border dispute's handling managed to largely defuse the immediate crisis. After September 11, no further firefights at the Sino-Soviet border were reported.[42] The 'unshakable friendship' between China and the Soviet Union, however, had been irreversibly destroyed.

The formation of the conflict

Having answered the questions as to what happened in March 1969 at the Ussuri River, who can be held responsible for the outbreak of hostilities, and how full escalation of the crisis was eventually avoided, I can now approach clarification of the most interesting question for the work at hand: what motivated the Chinese leadership to resort to military force against the Soviet Union? As I show in the subsequent section, it was obviously not the border demarcation problem per se that served as the principal reason for this decision. Rather, my analysis identifies two cumulative strands of causes that led up to the Chinese ambush of March 2, 1969: at the international level, the overall deterioration of the Sino-Soviet relationship, culminating in Moscow's Brezhnev Doctrine, and at the domestic level, the anti-Soviet programmatic of China's Cultural Revolution.

The border issue: a mirror for Sino-Soviet relations

At first glance, the issue under contestation appears to be a classical militarized border dispute, caused by competing interpretations regarding the demarcation of the borderline. In order to serve as the primary cause for the outbreak of hostilities, however, the demarcation issue needs to reveal observable variation prior to the event. This is obviously not the case, because competing territorial claims had by no means been a new contentious issue between China and the Soviet Union.[43] Quite the contrary, bilateral boundary disputes can be dated back to the period of Imperial China and Czarist Russia, and had "occupied the forefront of Sino-Russian attention [for] several hundred years."[44] With regard to the relations between the two socialist successor states, discussions on the border problem had even predated the formal establishment of Sino-Soviet relations in 1949, and had also been a significant issue of disagreement during the negotiations for the Sino-Soviet Treaty of Friendship and Mutual Assistance in 1950.[45] Even so, for nearly a decade, border relations between the PRC and the USSR were amicable and occupied only a minor role. None of the parties made serious attempts to change the status quo unilaterally, as demonstrated by the conclusion of numerous bilateral treaties and agreements concerning the border management during that period.[46] During the decade that followed, however, Beijing's previously cooperative attitude underwent a considerable change, becoming a more confrontational and aggressive stance. It was not until then that the border began to emerge as a serious cleavage between Beijing and Moscow.[47] Consequently, the crucial causes for the rising tensions on the border and for the final escalation apparently cannot be found at the border itself, as the demarcation issue reveals itself as an underlying constant that existed well before the onset of Sino-Soviet relations.[48]

What clearly varied, however, were three factors: first, the different levels of attention the Chinese leadership paid to the border dispute; second, the variation in importance of the border as a source of conflict in China's foreign policy agenda; and third, the changing patterns of Chinese behavior at the border itself. As I argue in the following, these changes mirror and thus seem evidently linked to specific developments on the dyadic and/or domestic level that, in turn, affected Beijing's overall conduct of foreign policy towards the Soviet Union, including the decision to resort to military force.

In order to identify these 'trigger events,' a promising line of inquiry is to start with the known (i.e. China's changing behavior on the border) and then search for correlations within contemporary developments in Sino-Soviet relations and in

China's domestic politics. In the following section, three phases of Chinese behavior at the Sino-Soviet border and the corresponding trigger events are presented and discussed. My findings support the argument that the border issue was a symptom rather than the cause of rising tensions between the PRC and the USSR, but both sides "found the issue extremely useful as an instrument in their ideological and power-political rivalry."[49] As long as the relationship between Beijing and Moscow proceeded harmoniously, so did the situation at the border. When the relationship eventually deteriorated towards the end of the 1950s, so did the situation at the border.[50] Based on this insight, my central argument for explaining China's proactive use of force in March 1969 reads as follows. Dissatisfied with Moscow's policies of the post-Stalin era and 'betrayed' more than once by the Kremlin's lack of socialist solidarity, China emancipated itself comprehensively from the Soviet Union. As this challenged the Soviet Union's ideological authority and claim for leadership in the international socialist movement, the Sino-Soviet ideological split also became a political rivalry. Against this background, Moscow's proclamation of the Brezhnev Doctrine was perceived by Beijing as an arrogant and unacceptable attempt to bully China back into subordination and countervail its drive for independence. Consequently, Mao decided that the time had come to teach Moscow a lesson by spoiling Soviet blood on the ice of the Ussuri River.

Phase I: no use of force at all (1959–66)

After ten years of silence at the border, the first Chinese-initiated incidents started to occur in 1959, and increased steadily during the 1960s. In 1962, the previously sporadic incidents culminated in obviously orchestrated provocations along the whole boundary line. According to Soviet sources, unarmed Chinese military personnel and civilians then systematically violated the border in the attempt to absorb Soviet territory.[51] During this phase, the Chinese incursions followed a general pattern: groups of Chinese crossed the border and stayed on Soviet-claimed territory until their expulsion by Soviet border guards, without mounting strong resistance. Confrontations remained at the verbal level and none of the parties resorted to unnecessary violence.[52] Apparently, the Chinese had orders to refrain from using force during these encounters.

The Sino-Soviet split: from crop to harvest

If the seed of the Sino-Soviet split had already been sown in the process of China's intervention in the Korean War with Moscow's 'betrayal' on the issue of air cover, the seedling grew further as it was watered by Stalin's successor, Khrushchev, and the Soviet policies of the 1950s. Finally, the plant broke the ground with another Soviet 'betrayal' of China during the Sino-Indian border dispute.[53] In contrast to China, which had honored its socialist obligations by going as far as to risk fighting a long and costly war against the United States in Korea, Khrushchev's Soviet Union not only refused to pledge allegiance to China when the People's Republic was in need of assistance but even openly backed China's opponent, India. This ignited Mao's anger.[54] In 1950, Mao had had no choice "but to swallow the fruit of the Soviet betrayal"[55] because China had been fundamentally dependent on Soviet assistance in virtually all areas, from industry to foreign policy. This time, however, Mao's anger manifested verbally as well as materially: the People's Republic that had 'stood up' under his lead in 1949 would now emancipate itself ideologically and politically from the Soviet Union. And one of many spots on which the advent of the Sino-Soviet split became visible was the border. Hence, only after the bilateral relationship had suffered its first serious setback in 1959 did the border receive increasing attention in Beijing as

> Mao [then] changed the territorial border issue from a latent disagreement about claims on maps to claims on the ground. It was one thing to accept Soviet diktat when the overall relationship was beneficial to China but another thing to accept it when the relationship was, in Mao's view, worthless.[56]

The Khrushchev years

Ideologically, the period in which China sought to independently interpret the correct way to achieve Communism had already started in 1958 with the 'Great Leap Forward,' which had earned Beijing harsh criticism from Moscow. Politically, the split emerged prominently in 1960, when the Soviet Union, in reaction to China's new ambitions for ideological autonomy, cut off its assistance, revoked existing treaties on cooperation, recalled all Soviet advisory personnel from China, and denied the PRC the nuclear capability it had promised.[57] Intensified verbal criticism, starting at the anonymous party-to-party level but then escalating to a sprawling exchange of accusations between Mao Zedong and Nikita Khrushchev, characterized the next phase of Sino-Soviet relations.[58] This escalation on the personal level was not accidental, as once again personalities played a significant role in shaping Sino-Soviet affairs: after Stalin's death in 1953, Mao was not only the most senior leader in the socialist camp, but also the only one that had proven his courage to openly challenge the lead nation of the capitalist bloc. Consequently, the Chairman regarded himself as an outstanding authority on ideological and political matters. Inside China, this undisputed self-image found its expression in an extensive cult of personality that followed Stalin's example in many regards.[59] The Kremlin's new policy line of de-Stalinization, including the condemnation of personality cults, thus without doubt affronted Mao, especially as it was Khrushchev – only one of Stalin's former henchmen – who now dared to lay hands on the Chairman's and, even worse, on China's prestige.[60] "To Khrushchev, it was simply unthinkable to consider China an equal. He was unwilling to reach any kind of compromise on the matter."[61]

However, Khrushchev not only criticized Mao's leadership style, but the new Soviet policy also challenged the wisdom of one of Mao's most fundamental dogmas. The Chairman had laid out in length that a war between the socialist and the capitalist world was inevitable, thus leaving no room for an intermediary position, which made his 'Leaning to One Side' policy an absolute necessity.[62] Khrushchev's strategy of 'peaceful coexistence' argued for taking the middle ground, in a period when Mao was convinced that 'the east wind is prevailing over the west wind' – but instead of challenging the capitalists on all fronts, the Soviet Union now approached the United States. In Mao's perspective, and based on his long-held ideological and political convictions, the Soviet Union – having already betrayed China several times in the past – was at this point betraying socialism as a whole, by setting the international socialist movement on the wrong path. In essence, the Soviet policies endangered the success of world revolution.[63] This presented Mao with the opportunity to establish the PRC as the center of the international revolutionary movement.[64] Moscow's handling of the Cuba Crisis then served as the final proof for Mao's suspicions: the class enemy had forced Khrushchev to cave in. In Mao's eyes, this constituted a disgraceful reverse for the socialist movement. With the Soviet leader's open 'capitulationism' on this occasion, the cards were on the table, and in March 1963 the PRC openly challenged Moscow's claim to leadership in the international socialist movement.[65] This step virtually set the final accord in relations between the Chinese and Soviet Communist Parties, as now both referred directly to one another as adversaries.[66]

In the wake of these events, China started to question the legitimacy of the Sino-Soviet boundary by arguing that its course had been the result of 'unequal treaties' between China and Czarist Russia.[67] In Beijing's perspective, the border was thus an obvious subject for revision. The denomination of the underlying legal framework as 'unequal' added a dimension to the dispute on which Beijing was fundamentally unwilling to compromise, as the wording fueled China's historical trauma springing from its humiliating treatment by foreign powers during the Century of Shame. As Sarah Paine has observed,

> the boundary became the physical incarnation of China's failure to fend off the predations of European civilization, while for the Russians, their expanded boundary enshrined their country's great power status. Thus, the border became a potent but antipodal symbol for both countries – for one, it represented failure, for the other, success.[68]

In Beijing's perspective, the Soviet leaders had then already revealed their true faces as New Czars, which added the historical roots of the dispute to the issue – and thereby a tremendous portion of spice.

Border consultations

China's opportunity for a revision of the boundary came during the secret Sino-Soviet consultations in 1964, which apparently had been initiated by the Soviet side.[69] Lasting for more than six months, the talks produced ambivalent results. Due to Soviet concessions, the two sides managed to reach substantial agreement on three points:

> First, both acknowledged the necessity and desirability of a new, comprehensive border treaty. … Second, both concurred that ancient rights, old treaties, and associated historical practices should stay in effect until a new treaty was

negotiated. ... Finally, both sides agreed that the *degree of adjustment* necessary *was relatively small*, mainly affecting riverine islands.[70]

The main point of disagreement, however, emerged when it came to the procedural dimension, and thus to matters of principle. Apparently, the Chinese insisted that the Soviets acknowledge the 'unequal character' of the existing legal framework prior to negotiating and concluding a new treaty.[71] From a legal perspective, the implementation of this procedure would have meant that the Soviet claims would have been annulled before a new framework even existed. Moscow, unwilling to perform this 'kowtow' empty-handed, suggested performing both acts simultaneously. If the two parties had been seriously interested in a settlement, the Soviet proposal should have been acceptable, because the Chinese would still have extracted a Soviet admission of the old treaty's 'unequal' character while Moscow would have ensured the legal certainty of its territorial claims.[72] The Chinese side, however – reluctant to compromise on principles and to move away from its maximum demand concerning the procedure – stalled the consultations, which were eventually canceled, although substantial progress had already been made and a comprehensive settlement of the border issue was in reach.

Brezhnev: Cold War in the socialist world

With Khrushchev's ousting and the takeover by Leonid Brezhnev in late 1964, Moscow's China policy shifted from ideologized polemics to a more pragmatic approach. Subsequently, Mao sent Zhou Enlai to Moscow in order to sound out the new Soviet leadership's attitude towards Beijing. Zhou's report, however, confirmed Mao's suspicion of prevailing "Khrushchevism without Khrushchev"[73] in the Kremlin. Consequently, China's position *vis-à-vis* the USSR remained unchanged.

Brezhnev's approach to the unpleasant task of managing relations with the restive PRC consisted basically in 'hoping for the best while preparing for the worst': with regard to the former, Brezhnev kept the line of his predecessor throughout the next five years. He repeatedly proposed renewed bilateral border consultations in order to reach a negotiated settlement.[74] Regarding the latter, Moscow undertook a noticeable 'pivot to Asia' in order to increase its strategic positioning *vis-à-vis* China. Under Brezhnev, the Soviet military posture in the Russian Far East was comprehensively strengthened and now also included nuclear-tipped missiles.[75] In addition, Moscow sought to enlarge its political footprint by intensifying relations with Asian states, particularly with China's neighbors India, North Korea, Mongolia, and North Vietnam. This Soviet initiative, apparently intended to encircle the PRC, subsequently widened the Sino-Soviet split into a regional political rivalry and competition for influence.

While India had recently endured a crushing defeat by China and thus unsurprisingly favored the Soviet Union, North Korea had concluded mutual defense treaties with both disputants. Accordingly, Kim Il-sung was confronted with the decision whether to side with the Kremlin – which had enabled his personal rule and his country's existence, and still provided vital assistance for Pyongyang – or to back Mao's China, to which North Korea owed its sheer survival in times of desperate crisis. Eventually, Kim decided in favor of the Soviet Union, and this was received with immense discontent in Beijing: tensions began to mount between Kim and Mao, and China reopened an already resolved but highly symbolic boundary issue in an apparent attempt to punish Kim for his lack of loyalty to China.[76] In Mongolia's capital, Ulan Bator, the same decision had to be taken. Mongolia became independent in 1924 and the PRC accepted this status in 1950, since which time Mao had steadily attempted to improve the bilateral relationship. As Mongolia had formerly been part of China, Beijing regarded it as undoubtedly belonging to the PRC's sphere of influence, and thus provided it monetary and technical assistance. With the emergence of the Sino-Soviet split, China and the Soviet Union started to compete for Ulan Bator's loyalty. In addition to China's ongoing material support, Beijing attempted to strengthen bilateral ties by signing a Treaty of Mutual Assistance and Friendship in 1960, and even made wide-ranging concessions regarding Ulan Bator's territorial claims in 1962. Despite these initiatives, Mongolia eventually opted to take the Kremlin's side. This changeover unquestionably affronted Beijing, and after the conclusion of the Soviet–Mongolian defense treaty in 1966, China began to refer to Mongolia as a Soviet colony.[77]

Despite these setbacks, Beijing kept its line of socialist solidarity, particularly with regard to North Vietnam. As the United States' involvement in the Second Indochina War steadily increased during the 1960s, China provided large quantities of economic and military assistance to Hanoi. Mao even deployed PLA troops to secure Ho Chi Minh's rear areas and defend North Vietnamese cities and territory against U.S. air attacks.[78] Yet, China's most important contribution for Hanoi was the looming threat of a massive Chinese military intervention, which served as a valuable deterrent against a U.S. ground invasion. Although the Sino-Soviet split was in full swing, Beijing even allowed Moscow to transit assistance for Vietnam through China, but emphatically declined the proposal to transfer Soviet troops or to open an air corridor for Soviet aircraft: while China was willing to fulfill its responsibilities and obligations, its cooperation with the Soviet Union in doing so was limited to only the most necessary extent.[79] As Hanoi was dependent on ongoing support from both socialist camps, the Kremlin could not force Ho Chi Minh to openly choose sides in the Sino-Soviet dispute. Against this background, Moscow decided to increase the Soviet factor in order to win over the North Vietnamese in the long run, and thus began to compete with China on the issue of assisting Hanoi.[80] Beijing failed to convince Hanoi to abandon Soviet support, anticipating that a dependent Vietnam would inevitably be absorbed into Moscow's orbit of influence. Consequently, China's suspicion and mistrust grew, although Ho Chi Minh avoided taking sides up to his death in 1969. Beijing remained committed to the support of its ally until the fall of Saigon. Hanoi, however, soon forgot China's loyalty, and thus became next in the row of pupils which Beijing would summon to the classroom for some drastic lessons.

In sum, although Brezhnev's hedging approach was – in Moscow's perspective – a defensive strategy in response to China's unpredictability, it left Beijing with the perception that the 'New Czars' were in expansionist mode in Asia, perched in China's neighborhood with the distinct intention to encircle and isolate Beijing, and were about to return to Soviet control what Stalin had promised to China as its own sphere of influence.[81] Against this background, Mao emphasized that China would never again be the Soviet Union's 'younger brother' – this time, China was prepared to compete, and the Chairman accepted Moscow's challenge for rivalry. Consequently, he finalized the Sino-Soviet break in 1966, when China refused to participate in the Communist Party of the Soviet Union (CPSU) Twenty-third Party Congress, and the split between the two parties became official.[82]

Phase II: fight if necessary, but avoid shooting (1966–8)

Beginning in late 1966, the Chinese intrusions into Soviet territory took on a new quality, as Mao's composite groups were now ordered to "assert China's claims more forcefully but [still] without shooting."[83] In practice, this meant that larger groups of Chinese 'civilians' (sometimes numbering more than 1,000 persons) started to challenge the Soviet boundary and its border guards' authority at several focal points in a more confrontational manner. Furthermore, the Chinese intrusion parties now occasionally used sticks in corroboration of their verbal arguments.[84] This low-level use of violence had been permitted by Beijing "when normal patrol routes were blocked by Soviet border guards."[85] Even though the level of violence thus increased, the overall character of China's confrontational policy remained clearly nonmilitary, as the PLA soldiers involved were unarmed and disguised their profession.

During this period, Beijing also considered the use of military force as a policy option for the first time. In late 1967, a series of incidents revealed a new level of Soviet assertiveness: confronted with an increasing number of Chinese provocations and larger, well-organized incursion parties, the Soviet border guards were ordered to enforce the boundary line more vigorously.[86] On January 5, 1967, this new policy resulted in the first loss of life at the border, when five Chinese were run over by a Soviet military vehicle at Qiliqin Island.[87] Apparently in reaction to this event, the CMC decided to prepare for a military response at Qiliqin: an ambush was planned that was expected to follow the same pattern as the one that eventually took place one year later at Zhenbao.[88] While the option of using military force had thus been on the table since early 1968, the Chinese plan was not executed before March 2, 1969 and the Sino-Soviet border still remained relatively quiet.[89]

China's Cultural Revolution

Far from accidentally, the advent of this second phase coincided with the start of the "Great Proletarian Cultural Revolution" in the summer of 1966. Unprecedented in human history, the Cultural Revolution mobilized China's population in a single gigantic political campaign to eliminate all elements of 'liberal bourgeoisie' and to free the 'thoughts and actions' of China's youth in order to carry the Chinese revolution to a successful end.[90] Mao announced the campaign on May 16, just weeks after the political split between China and the Soviet Union had been formalized. The Cultural Revolution completed China's emancipation from the Soviet Union, as the campaign constituted an explicit Maoist anti-model to the

Soviet ideological line, comprehensively finalizing the ideological split: as such, it "reduced what was left of Sino-Soviet relations to ashes."[91]

China's youth, organized as Red Guards, immediately followed Mao's appeal and flooded the country in search of revisionist elements in society, administration, and party. At the end of the year, the campaign had gained the dynamic of an avalanche and encroached on the PLA, the working class, the party, and even the political leadership. At that time, control over the Cultural Revolution had largely been lost, as the movement had become a process of its own – with devastating consequences for the Chinese society, which was quickly caught up in the chaotic conditions of a civil war.[92] For Mao, however, the Cultural Revolution presented a unique opportunity to strengthen his personal claim to power by unleashing the masses to destroy 'revisionism' (i.e. opposition to Maoism) and pro-Soviet factions inside the party and society. As a result, Soviet 'revisionism' and the Soviet Union became central targets for the revolutionary movement.[93] Moreover, this was amplified even further by Mao's intensive utilization of the Soviet Union as a "convenient lightning rod"[94] for China's numerous domestic problems resulting from the Cultural Revolution. As Soviet criticism of Mao's course was countered by Chinese anti-revisionist propaganda, a circular dynamic of mutual accusations emerged, and Mao's anti-Soviet programmatic played a considerable role in fueling the thrust of the Cultural Revolution. Due to the already heated atmosphere, this dynamic incited the masses: inside China, Soviet citizens and diplomats were violently harassed in the streets. In 1967, Red Guards besieged the Soviet Embassy in Beijing and forced "many of its members to run a brutal gauntlet as they fled to the airport."[95] Beijing's law-enforcement authorities did not intervene, either unwilling or unable to do so. Internationally, the Cultural Revolution's anti-Soviet programmatic – and thus China's comprehensive emancipation from the Soviet Union – became visible in the substantial number of Chinese expatriates demonstrating in front of Soviet embassies in capitals around the globe.

Not surprisingly, the border swiftly emerged as a hotspot for the Cultural Revolution's agglomerated anti-Soviet programmatic. As the ideological rivalry was carried to the border, the Chinese incursions became distinctively politicized and more confrontational.[96] Chinese-initiated incursions following the same patterns also started to occur along the Sino-Mongolian boundary as well as on the Sino-North Korean border, obviously intended to chasten the two turncoats for their defection to the Kremlin. All this highlighted the onset of a new chapter in the Sino-Soviet split, which had evolved into full-fledged regional political competition. Despite the heated atmosphere, however, incidents at the Sino-Soviet border still occurred in a minimally violent fashion, as both sides refrained from the use of military capacities.[97]

Soviet invasion of Czechoslovakia: the Brezhnev Doctrine

The end of this second phase was obviously set by Moscow's intervention in Czechoslovakia (CSSR) in August, and by the subsequent declaration of the Brezhnev Doctrine in November 1968. According to the doctrine of 'limited sovereignty,' the Soviet Union reserved the right to intervene in any communist country in which socialism was endangered, because "[w]hen forces that are hostile to socialism try to turn the development of some socialist country towards capitalism, it becomes not only a problem of the country concerned, but a common problem and concern of all socialist countries."[98] In plain terms, Moscow not only declared itself to possess interpretational sovereignty over the definition of true socialism, but also denied other socialist countries – including the PRC – the rights of full sovereignty and territorial integrity. From that point in time, any socialist country whose way of interpreting and realizing socialism incurred Moscow's disapproval had to take a Soviet military intervention into account.[99] In Beijing's view, the People's Republic definitely took top ranking on Moscow's list of potential follow-up implementations of the Brezhnev Doctrine, as the Sino-Soviet rivalry, China's ideological and political emancipation from the Soviet Union, and Beijing's continuing criticism of the Kremlin's policies had rendered China a more than suitable candidate: "China's clear policy differences with the Soviets gave [the] pronouncement [of the Brezhnev Doctrine] the tone of a threat."[100] Consequently, this proclamation instantaneously transformed the Soviet Union into China's primary enemy, and the Chinese leadership "became acutely sensitive to the possibility of Soviet intervention in China and directly linked Soviet recklessness in Czechoslovakia to the Soviet threat to China's border areas."[101]

On the Sino-Soviet border, the enemy and its threat had already materialized. Following Brezhnev's takeover, the Soviet military presence in the regions bordering China had been steadily increased. In particular, the Red Army had significantly strengthened its potential for conducting offensive operations.[102] Moscow had also improved its strategic position *vis-à-vis* Beijing with the conclusion of the Soviet–Mongolian Mutual Assistance Treaty in 1966, which not only allowed the Kremlin to permanently station strong forces, including medium-range ballistic missiles, on Mongolian territory, but also brought "important Chinese population and industrial centers within easy Soviet striking distance."[103] All this nurtured the perception in Beijing that the Soviet–Mongolian alliance was unambiguously aiming at China and that "Khrushchev's successors had moved beyond political polemics, beyond what Mao referred to as 'war on paper', to a real and substantial buildup that could lead to war with bullets."[104]

The Brezhnev Doctrine thus completed the Soviet Union's looming threat to China in word and deed. However, while China's Defense Minister Lin Biao "allegedly warned the CCP Politburo and the Military Affairs Commission that China would be attacked by the Soviet Union,"[105] other Politburo members, including the Chairman himself, doubted Moscow's readiness to wage a war against the People's Republic.[106] The Soviet military build-up and the proclamation of the Brezhnev Doctrine did not frighten Mao. Quite the contrary, the "Soviet invasion of Czechoslovakia … strengthened Mao's determination not to retreat, not to be intimidated. … China would not be cowed by Soviet military power."[107]

Beijing's verbal reaction to the invasion of Czechoslovakia and the declaration of the Brezhnev Doctrine was remarkable, even in the contemporary phase of intense ideological criticism and polemics, as it "was one of unqualified condemnation."[108] Apparently, Moscow had underestimated the emotional 'flashback' that the declaration of the Brezhnev Doctrine caused in China: "The concept of limited sovereignty embodied in the Brezhnev doctrine was *repugnant* to the Chinese, and revived memories of the semicolonial status that had been forced upon China in the 19th century by the Western powers, including Tsarist Russia."[109] Tellingly, China's denomination of the Soviet Union changed from 'revisionist superpower' to 'social-imperialist superpower,' and the Chinese statements condemning the invasion of August 1968 referred at length to historical cases of

> fascist politics, great power chauvinism, national egoism, and social-imperialism [and] equated the invasion with Hitler in the 1930s, and with the American intervention in Vietnam. ... The commonwealth espoused by the Soviet Union was compared to Japan's "Greater East Asia Co-Prosperity Sphere," Hitler's "New Order" in Europe, and America's "Free World Community."[110]

These reactions obviously sprang from China's highly traumatic historical experiences with Western imperialism and especially with Russian imperialism, which China had had to endure even after the humiliating Century of Shame had come to an end. Against this background, China's revolution and the formation of the People's Republic had been accompanied by one fundamental promise: never again should China fall prey to foreign intervention and acts of imperialism. In light of this, the Chinese government issued a stern warning to Moscow in September 1968, stating that 700 million Chinese "are not to be bullied."[111] In Mao's eyes, Brezhnev could interfere in Czechoslovakia's internal affairs and bully the Czech people, but the Chairman was determined neither to allow the 'New Czar' to bully the Chinese people nor to permit the Soviet 'social imperialists' to lay hands on China. "Since China had 'stood up' there could be no course for the Chinese leadership other than resistance."[112] Consequently, besides its verbal condemnation of Moscow's perceived efforts of intimidation, Beijing prepared an appropriate, twofold answer of Chinese steadfastness. In response to the material threat of the Soviet military build-up in the Far East, Mao showed his willingness to play tit-for-tat: he ordered additional PLA units to reinforce China's border defense and, in October, China detonated its first hydrogen bomb.[113] However, with regard to the Brezhnev Doctrine, which in fact degraded the PRC to the status of a vassal state by Moscow's grace, Mao obviously concluded that the time had come to draw a red line. He ordered his troops to teach Moscow "a bitter lesson" about its arrogance and disrespect.[114]

Phase III: proactive use of military force (1969)

In the aftermath of the Soviet intervention in Czechoslovakia and Moscow's declaration of the Brezhnev Doctrine, Mao apparently decided to adopt an unambiguous military policy *vis-à-vis* the Soviet Union at the border.[115] Increasing Chinese military activity, especially in the area around Zhenbao, revealed the characteristics of this new approach: now, fully armed Chinese border guards were carrying out the intrusions under orders to forcefully stand their ground rather than avoiding contact with their Soviet counterparts. In the case of contact, they were now ordered to respond tit-for-tat to the Soviets' actions.[116] Although these orders left room for misunderstandings and accidental escalations, targeted shooting was still avoided and on most occasions, both parties kept to the long-established informal code of conduct for such encounters.[117] At Zhenbao, however, the level of violence steadily increased throughout December, January, and February as the Soviet border guards forcefully intercepted Chinese incursion parties.[118] In response to an incident of February 7 in which Soviet border guards fired the noteworthy number of 150 'warning shots,' the Chinese soldiers issued the last in a series of warnings and the stage for the Chinese ambush of March 2 was set.[119]

Setting the trap

According to Thomas Robinson and Yang Kuisong, who present the only two available – but still quite limited and partially conflicting – accounts of China's decision-making process, the planning for the ambush started in early January 1969 at the latest.[120] On February 19, the CMC and the Foreign Ministry approved the plan separately.[121] Orders were then passed to the executing Military District, and troops and commanders were selected from the three field armies of Shenyang Military Region and assembled for special training and preparation. As Robinson observes, the

> Central Military Commission, with Mao's personal approval, sent a second order to the Heilongjiang Military District to "fight tit-for-tat, don't move until the enemy moves, use reason but take every advantage, keep restraint, don't show weakness, but neither take the initiative nor look for trouble." At the same time, this order stressed that the border troops should prepare themselves thoroughly to undertake a "self-defense" battle in the service of the larger political struggle.[122]

Most remarkably, a direct line of communication was established in order to guarantee that the chain of command streamed uninterrupted from the CMC and the PLA General Staff down to the field headquarters at Gongsi, and even reached the two forward positions at the Ussuri River, from where the ambush was finally executed. Apparently, Mao and other Chinese leaders were not only aware of the situation at Zhenbao at all times, but also asserted direct command and control over the military action.[123] The preparations were concluded in late February, and Chinese forces subsequently executed the well-planned ambush only a few days later.

Alternative explanation: regaining control over the Cultural Revolution

At the domestic level, the timing of China's proactive use of military force also correlated with the run-up to the 9th CCP Congress, which was the first party summit to have taken place since 1956. At the height of the Cultural Revolution, and with intense factionalism spreading through the party, the successful conclusion of this event undoubtedly had significant implications for the stability of the CCP, and even more for the legitimacy of Mao's claim for leadership.[124] In view of that, Yang Kuisong has argued that "the military clashes were primarily the result of Mao

Zedong's domestic mobilization strategies connected to his worries about the development of the 'Cultural Revolution'."[125] According to this line of reasoning, Mao intentionally escalated the Sino-Soviet border dispute in order to unite the party and the Chinese people through the creation of an immediate external threat.[126] Due to the anti-Soviet programmatic of the Cultural Revolution, the most suitable enemy at hand to blame for China's domestic turmoil was the Soviet Union.

Yang's thesis is able to explain several observations. First, after the March incidents, the Chinese propaganda ignited a new campaign. The "news of the battles, dramatically retold, produced an outpouring of popular excitement over PLA heroism, intensified anti-Soviet antagonisms, and made it appear that Lin Biao's [i.e. Mao's chosen heir] troops were literally saving the Chinese people."[127] Accordingly, a new wave of anti-Soviet demonstrations swept through China. Second, although Mao was at that time fully convinced that the Soviet Union would not risk a large-scale exchange of hostilities with China, the propaganda nonetheless mobilized the Chinese population to expect a major war. At the same time, however, Zhou Enlai was apparently ordered to explain to the party why Mao was beating the war drums.[128] Third, Beijing had set a tight schedule for the preparation and execution of the ambush. In February, General Chen Xilian, commander of Shenyang Military Region and thus responsible for the implementation of the ambush, "apparently complain[ed] that it would take him two to three months to make preparations at Damansky/Zhenbao."[129] Beijing obviously insisted that the attack had to take place as soon as possible, and even advanced the schedule. With the ambush being executed in early March, the phase of active fighting at Zhenbao, including the expected Soviet military retaliation, was completed before the CCP congress took place in April. Fourth, with the Chinese propaganda clearly identifying the attitude of 'social imperialism' behind the violation of Chinese territory and the killing of Chinese soldiers, the pro-Soviet faction inside the CCP that had formed around Liu Shaoqi was silenced from the onset of the congress. Consequently, Mao did not have to fear any unpleasant surprises from this faction.[130]

While this data generates plausibility for Yang's thesis, Mao's calculations on the unifying effect of external pressure on party and population do not qualify as the primary trigger for China's ambush. As outlined above, Chinese leaders had considered military action against Soviet troops on the border as early as late 1967, in a period when the Cultural Revolution's turmoil was superseding even the level of chaos of 1968. While the Chinese leadership thus had – with virtually constant domestic conditions – this option at hand, the plan was not executed for the period of one full year, and unquestionably only after evident variation at the international/dyadic level in summer and autumn 1968 could be observed. In addition, Liu Shaoqi – 'China's Khrushchev,' and Mao's most important rival – had been formally removed as Mao's successor during the 12th Plenum of the CCP in October 1968. Following this he had disappeared from public life, and was thus unable to challenge the Chairman's authority.[131] With Liu's ousting, Mao had administered a severe blow to the CCP's pro-Soviet faction. Thereby, one of the most important goals of the Cultural Revolution had been accomplished, and Mao's legitimacy and authority had been significantly strengthened, almost six months before the ambush at Zhenbao was conducted.[132]

Interim conclusion: classifying triggers and conditions

In the previous section, I correlated the evolution of Beijing's conduct at the border with the corresponding developments at the domestic level and the Sino-Soviet dyadic level. My findings evidently show that the Chinese behavior at the border mirrored the overall deterioration of Sino-Soviet relations. The border issue did not reveal itself as a cleavage until the late 1950s and early 1960s, when the Sino-Soviet split had openly emerged. The subsequent phases of China's behavior at the border reflect in almost perfect congruence the further deterioration of Sino-Soviet relations, beginning as an ideological dispute, then turning into a political rivalry and competition for influence, and finally ending in open antagonism. China's ideological and political emancipation from the Soviet Union during the post-Stalin era confronted the Kremlin with a Chinese counter-model that challenged Moscow's claim to leadership in the socialist movement. These developments established the baseline of conflict in Sino-Soviet relations during the period of 1964–8.[133] The boundary issue played only a minor role as one of many points on which the bilateral rivalry materialized.[134]

As demonstrated by the course of the bilateral border consultations in 1964, for China the boundary problem was deeply rooted in its historical experiences with imperialism, and thus had obviously become a matter of principle on which Beijing was fundamentally unwilling to compromise. These historical experiences eventually re-entered the picture with the Kremlin's declaration of the Brezhnev Doctrine. This event apparently functioned as the straw that broke the camel's back, as the Chinese border policy subsequently entered a militarized phase and eventually resulted in the proactive use of force with the Chinese ambush at Zhenbao Island. Consequently, the Soviet invasion of Czechoslovakia and the proclamation of the Brezhnev Doctrine qualify as the immediate triggers for the Chinese-initiated escalation of March 1969, as both developments were perceived by Beijing as open challenges to China's sovereignty and its newly achieved ideological and political independence, and – most importantly – were framed as a crude attempt to intimidate China into submission.

With regard to this finding, Lyle Goldstein put forward the question: "how could a relatively minor event in Central Europe possibly become the basis for Chinese foreign policy?"[135] Goldstein seems to greatly underestimate China's traumatic historical experiences (apparently just as the Soviet leaders did when confronting Beijing with the doctrine). When approached from this perspective, the Brezhnev Doctrine and its implications were clearly unacceptable for Mao and the Chinese leaders, and thus sparked off the military reaction at Zhenbao. Yang's 'foreign domestic policy' thesis may have played an enabling, but obviously minor, role in the decision to use military force in order to teach the Soviets a bloody lesson.[136] As my analysis has shown, rather than the domestic power struggle, it was China's Cultural Revolution and Brezhnev's hedging approach that significantly influenced how the Chinese leadership, and especially Mao, framed the Sino-Soviet rivalry and its implications, and thus qualify as the necessary antecedent conditions for Mao's final decision.[137]

Assessing the risks: a well-calculated Chinese 'lesson'?

In the following section, I examine China's risk behavior in the run-up to and the aftermath of the clashes. As outlined above, the military escalation of March 2 resulted in a highly tense situation, in which "the possibility of a full-scale war between the USSR and China appeared increasingly likely."[138] Had the Chinese leadership considered this outcome in their a priori calculations? Or had this seemingly prohibitive risk simply been dismissed? In order to comprehensively answer this question, the following evaluation differentiates between the tactical (i.e. the Chinese action at the border and Beijing's considerations with regard to the March clashes) and the strategic levels for China and the Soviet Union.

Risk assessment I: the tactical level

Starting the analysis of China's risk behavior at the tactical level provides a limited but highly informative perspective on how the Chinese leadership assessed the implications and incorporated risks of the planned ambush. As outlined above, comparison of the three phases of China's confrontational attitude at the Sino-Soviet border shows at first glance an evident increase in Beijing's willingness to engage in risk-taking behavior at the turn of 1968/1969, as Chinese troops were then ordered to abandon the non-shooting principle by executing an ambush on Soviet border guards. This proactive escalation of the dispute to the level of lethal and organized force self-evidently incorporates the risk of a follow-up escalation to all-out war, and Beijing was apparently willing to bear this substantial, even prohibitive, risk. However, Mao calculated that this risk was rather small, as he intended to keep the extent and degree of hostilities at the border deliberately limited.

Limited provocation: China's risk control

The Chinese ambush of March 2, and – to a lesser extent – China's reaction to the subsequent Soviet retaliatory attack of March 15, reveal several self-imposed restraints concerning the area and timing of operations, as well as with regard to the scale of hostilities. On both occasions, Chinese forces obviously fought the battles guided by Mao's intention to control the risks that arose, and thus employed "tacit rules of engagement that reflected the determination"[139] to keep the outbreak of violence limited in order to minimize the risk of further escalation.

First, with regard to the area of operation, China's military action was limited to the immediate borderline and focused only on a single spot on it: Zhenbao Island. Although the initial planning had incorporated Qiliqin Island and a simultaneous Chinese military action at a second site would potentially have been viable in order to increase the blow to the USSR, this option was not implemented. By restricting the outbreak of hostilities to a single location, Beijing apparently wanted to prevent the impression that a larger Chinese military offensive was taking place. Consequently, on March 2, fire from Chinese heavy weapons was deliberately limited to affect only areas on the (Chinese-claimed) island and the ice of the river. Targeting the Soviet bank of the Ussuri was avoided, which allowed Soviet troops to move and engage from their shore without being fired upon.[140]

Second, the same calculation apparently limited the timeframe for the operations. After the ambush and the ensuing fight, fire from the Chinese shore was ceased. No further aggressive action was undertaken by the Chinese troops until the expected Soviet counterattack followed.[141] After this second engagement, the same Chinese restraint was observable, despite ongoing artillery barrages and machine-gun fire from the Soviet side.[142] At this point, Beijing saw no need for a follow-up offensive at Zhenbao or at other spots along the border, because for Mao the whole thing was already over.[143]

Third, in contrast to the Soviet Union, the Chinese refrained from deploying large amounts of heavy weaponry during both encounters. Remarkably, not a single PLA tank or APC took part in the battles, thus reducing the Chinese force disposition at Zhenbao to infantry supported by mortars and a small number of artillery.[144] With this composition of static and offensively quite limited forces, it seems as if Beijing wanted to prevent giving the impression that Chinese troops were amassed to conduct more far-reaching operations that would have threatened Soviet territory.

These three measures to restrain China's use and scope of force in March 1969 are unanimously reported in the relevant literature on the battles at Zhenbao. Accordingly, the conclusion suggests itself that these restraints were deliberately imposed, intended to limit the extent of hostilities and their implications concerning the potential for an escalation of the crisis and to minimize the risks involved in China's military action.

The choice for Zhenbao: a tactical perspective

Moreover, there is also good reason to argue that Beijing carefully selected Zhenbao Island as the location for a limited military operation. The specific setting at Zhenbao, as well as the island's location, allowed for a further minimization of risks.[145] In order to avoid a full-scale escalation of the Sino-Soviet conflict, the ambush was planned to occur on a "Chinese-sided island in a desolate, isolated area"[146] which simultaneously provided the Chinese troops with particular tactical advantages that made a Chinese military victory likely and also guaranteed that the PLA would not suffer a crushing defeat.

First, with regard to the legal dimension, the Soviet claim over the island was not as evidently established as was the case for other islands in the border rivers.[147] Zhenbao is located around 100 meters from the Chinese bank of the Ussuri, while the distance to the Soviet side is more than 400 meters. According to the Chinese interpretation of the boundary line that was oriented along the deepest part of the river, Zhenbao lay definitely more on the Chinese than on the Soviet side of the thalweg.[148]

Second, the island had no strategic or economic significance for China or the Soviet Union, as it was flooded for the most part of the year, making permanent settlement impossible. The material value at stake was therefore highly limited, which would – in the Chinese perspective – reduce the risk of a follow-up escalation.[149]

Third, from a tactical point of view, the location of the island and the specific setting on the Chinese bank provided the PLA with several advantages. Zhenbao was around 50 kilometers away from the next Soviet city and therefore, military action would not result in an immediate threat to the Soviet civilian population. In addition, the island was situated closer to a Chinese outpost than to a Soviet one, giving the Chinese an advantage in distance. Also, the two Soviet border posts in the area had no direct line of sight to the island, which allowed the Chinese to prepare the ambush covertly.[150] Furthermore, the high terrain on the Chinese shore enabled PLA troops to overlook the battlefield and to place their small number of heavy weapons in a superior position. Holding this dominating position also resulted in the most important tactical advantage, as forces attacking from the Russian bank would have had to occupy the high ground on the Chinese side before being able to take and hold the island.[151] Consequently, if the Soviets were willing to re-take the island after the ambush, the Red Army would have had to fight on Chinese soil: the tactical situation at Zhenbao thus presented the Soviets with the problem of having to decide whether to abandon an indefensible position or, by fighting on Chinese territory, risk the initiation of an all-out war with the PRC and open up a large and vulnerable frontline along the frozen boundary rivers.

In sum, "[t]he Chinese almost certainly selected the island as the site for prospective armed clashes"[152] because of the above presented properties that virtually guaranteed a Chinese military victory, reduced the risks of full escalation to an apparently acceptable level, and presented the Soviets with a significant tactical problem and its potential strategic implications. Zhenbao Island allowed the Chinese to minimize their overall amount of risk while simultaneously shifting the burden of deciding whether or not to engage in risk-taking onto the Soviets.

Risk assessment II: the strategic level

In contrast to the rather manageable amount of risk at the tactical level, China's military operation can be clearly depicted as a high-risk adventure when taking into account the implications at the strategic level. This is not only because China attacked and killed troops of a nuclear-armed superpower – still without possessing a credible nuclear-deterrence capacity – but also because a series of indicators reveal severe Chinese disadvantages *vis-à-vis* the Soviet Union.[153]

Force posture

First, the overall force disposition at the Sino-Soviet border favored the Soviet Union, although China enjoyed a numerical advantage: about 380,000 to 480,000 Chinese troops stood against 324,000 to 384,000 Soviet troops.[154] However, simple comparison of numbers rarely allows for sophisticated assessment of the concrete military capacities, as formations of the same quantity can reveal remarkable differences in quality and actual combat-effectiveness. Indicators for the latter include factors such as the troops' level of combat-readiness (training and morale), tactics, state and type of weaponry, mobility, and air support. In all these categories, the Soviet Union enjoyed overwhelming superiority.

The Red Army had a decisive edge in the quantity and quality of modern weaponry.[155] Compared to the PLA, the Soviet Union fielded superior numbers of up-to-date aircraft, tanks, artillery, and APCs, which enabled Moscow to launch highly mobile operations that could "deliver a fearful blow against the Chinese."[156] Large military arsenals, stockpiled for an all-out confrontation with NATO, allowed the Soviet Union the potential to re-equip its troops with state-of-the-art weaponry twice: the guaranteed flow of modern weapons and sufficient ammunition to a possible Sino-Soviet frontline was thus nearly limitless. In contrast, the Chinese heavy weaponry was inferior not only in quantity but also in quality. As a result of the deterioration of Sino-Soviet relations, in 1960 China had been cut off from Soviet military assistance, and thus from its only access to modern weaponry. China's own armament industry, ruined by the Cultural Revolution, lacked the capacity to manufacture modern weapons in the following years, and was consequently not on a par with the Soviet military-production capacity.[157]

A similar conclusion can be drawn when comparing the opponents' non-material factors for combat-effectiveness. During the skirmishes at the Sino-Soviet border, the Soviet forces demonstrated that their advanced tactics allowed them to overwhelm even numerically superior enemy forces. The incident of August 13 drastically underlined this observation. Supported by tanks and APCs, just 300 Soviet troops annihilated a whole Chinese brigade.[158] Moreover, as the Red Army's operational scenarios consisted in fighting NATO's armored forces in the European theatre, its units were sufficiently trained in combined operations and Soviet commanders were experienced in coordinating units from different military branches. Against the relatively static Chinese forces, the Soviet mobile-warfare tactics would have proven lethally efficient.[159] In contrast to that, the PLA's state of combat-readiness had drastically decreased due to the chaos of the Cultural Revolution, in which China's armed forces suffered "the most serious damage since the founding of the PRC."[160] At the command level, factional rivalries had left the headquarters paralyzed. During the high phase of the Cultural Revolution, from 1967 to 1969, around 80,000 PLA officers had fallen victim to political purges. As a result, the command structure and the internal cohesion of China's armed forces had been largely lost. As Andrew Scobell has observed, the excesses and the turmoil caused by the Cultural Revolution posed a significant threat "to the unity and very existence of the PLA."[161] During this phase, military training and education had largely stopped. Even after Mao's 1967 order to the PLA to restore the social and political order, it remained unable to refocus on its military missions as the overwhelming majority of its soldiers was occupied with police duties or assisting with manufacturing and agricultural production, while the officer corps' attention was absorbed by administrating the country.[162] Taking into account the PLA's preoccupation with internal affairs and its ongoing contributions to North Vietnam (around 170,000 troops were deployed abroad in March 1969), as well as the fact that "serious military training … had largely fallen into abeyance since the beginning of the Cultural Revolution,"[163] it seems more than appropriate to conclude that China's armed forces were not in a sufficient state of preparedness to open up a new front against the Soviet Union.

Logistical infrastructure

Second, the Soviet Union was clearly favored by its superior logistical infrastructure. As the Trans-Siberian Railway paralleled the entire length of the Sino-Soviet border and thereby connected key Soviet army and air bases, Moscow would have been easily able to transport vast amounts of material and reinforcements to the Far East.[164] Adding this advantage to the Red Army's distinctive air and ground mobility, the Soviet Union would have been able to concentrate and supply large forces on the spot within a relatively narrow time frame. China, on the other hand, lacked a similarly advanced infrastructure in its northern and northwestern provinces. Here, the railroad network was still underdeveloped and troops and material would have mainly depended on transportation by foot or on the relatively small number of available trucks.[165] In the case of large-scale military operations, Soviet troops would thus have enjoyed the greater sustainability in combat.

Assessing vulnerabilities: who had more to lose?

Third, in the case of escalation to a full-scale war, it was China that would have revealed the greater vulnerabilities: while the Soviet Far East and China's Inner Mongolia were (and remain) not known for outpourings of conviviality due to their sparse population, this did not hold true for the PRC's other northern provinces, as several population and industrial centers were located in this region. In 1950, Mao and other Chinese leaders had highlighted a pending security threat to the latter as the pretext for China's intervention in Korea. This time, however, no hot war in the periphery endangered China's territorial integrity, but the PRC's political and military systems were heavily struggling with internal fragility, chaos, and factionalism.[166] Even so, Mao ordered the 'harsh lessons' to take place at Zhenbao and thereby risked the outbreak of a full-scale war that would have placed the entire northern part of China under the threat of ground attacks, air assaults, and strikes with conventional or nuclear-tipped missiles.[167] Furthermore, since the conclusion of the Soviet–Mongolian defense treaty allowed the permanent stationing of Soviet forces on Mongolian soil, the Chinese capital had come under threat from a direct Soviet ground assault.[168] In the early 1960s, Soviet strategic planning for a potential escalation in Europe estimated that Soviet tank armies would advance against a defending NATO at an average speed of 100 kilometers per day, including the use of nuclear weapons on both sides.[169] Chinese military planners calculated that Soviet mechanized units could reach Beijing, located only around 500 kilometers from the Sino-Mongolian border, in less than two weeks.[170] Mao had clearly been aware of this threat before March 1969, as he perceived such an assault would be aimed at him personally, too:

> Mao had no effective defense against Soviet tanks, if they chose to target Peking. … But ever since [Soviet minister of defense Rodion] Malinovsky had sounded his close colleagues out about getting rid of him in late 1964, the idea of a quick Soviet thrust at his capital in coordination with his opponents had preyed on Mao's mind.[171]

His fears manifested in the order to "pile up some mountains if there aren't any" in the area around Beijing, in order to slow down or block the advance of attacking tanks: "Each of these [formations] was designed to be 20–40 meters high, 250–400 meters wide, and 120–220 meters deep. ... All who saw these 'mountains' ... concluded that they were completely useless."[172] On balance, it is more than obvious that the overall vulnerabilities were far greater on the Chinese side, and that China's leadership had been well aware of these vulnerabilities prior to the escalation of March 1969.

Mao's calculus on Soviet restraint

Last, and most remarkably, Mao's calculations on the expected Soviet restraint rested on the single and weak assumption that Brezhnev would not risk a war with China, probably not even a small one.[173] It seems as if Mao was simply convinced that Moscow would tolerate the Chinese provocation without strongly reacting to it. Counting "on the size of China and its population as insurance against anyone wanting to invade,"[174] the possibility and the grave implications of a serious Soviet military reaction appear to have been largely or even totally blanked out prior to the March 2 incident. While the Chinese leaders might have calculated for a limited Soviet retaliatory action, no alternative planning seemed to be at hand in the case of any large-scale Soviet military responses, and no preparations had been made for dissenting outcomes.[175] Apparently, Mao assumed that Moscow would simply back down after having received the Chinese 'lesson' at Zhenbao. In any case, the Chairman was convinced that the extent of a potential follow-up confrontation would be controllable and that the outbreak of violence between China and the Soviet Union would remain limited.

Only after the tension along the Sino-Soviet border unexpectedly reached a peak of intensity in late August 1969 did Mao order the northern military regions to the highest level of alert.[176] At this stage, however, Beijing had already lost control over the crisis. The Chinese leadership had greatly underestimated the Soviet Union's willingness to climb the ladder of escalation. Against this background, Thomas Robinson aptly questions whether "either Mao or his military planners [had] thought much beyond the Damansky/Zhenbao operation itself."[177] Mao's anticipation of Soviet restraint appears rather blue-eyed, and not only in retrospect: in 1969, the Soviet Union was in 'social imperialist' mode, as the invasion of Czechoslovakia evidently demonstrated, and had already concentrated combat-ready forces at the Sino-Soviet border. Furthermore, the Soviet armament and security policy under the Brezhnev administration had resulted in an evident and visible build-up of conventional capabilities, and had correspondingly led to a strategic re-thinking by the Soviet General Staff on the viability of conventional warfare.[178] The Chinese were definitely aware of these essentials, and therefore Beijing must have known that the potential for a substantial Soviet military reaction clearly existed. It is highly unlikely that Chinese political and military leaders did not discuss this possibility during the planning stage. However, the Chairman's strategic assessment apparently ruled out considerations on dissenting outcomes and implicated risks.[179]

Not before Mao had been reminded of the existence of these risks through increased Soviet conventional and nuclear pressure in the summer of 1969, a change in attitude followed. Then, China's policy became substantially risk-averse, with Beijing trying to regain control over the escalatory level of the crisis. In the end, the content of Mao's calculation – but not its logic – did prove true: due to the Soviet Union's dual approach of military pressure and diplomatic initiatives, the outbreak of a major war was avoided. However, this successful outcome actually reflected Moscow's forbearance and skilled crisis-management policies more than Beijing's deterrence capacity.

Interim conclusion: assessing the risks of challenging a superpower

Merging the respective findings of the two preceding analyses creates an apparently paradoxical result. On the tactical level, Beijing acted very sensitively to prevent the emergence of unknown quantities: by carefully selecting an highly advantageous battlefield and by setting explicit self-restraints concerning weaponry, deployed forces, timing, and the area of operations, China intended to keep the outbreak of hostilities deliberately limited, and in doing so, attempted to manage a priori the associated risks. This finding allows for two conclusions. First, at the tactical level, China was willing to engage in risk-taking up to a certain, in Beijing's view still controllable, degree. Second, in order to assess the most controllable degree of risk, Beijing's strategists and leaders must have considered the possibility of the worst-case scenario, which provides the rejoinder to the first question stated in the introduction to this section: Beijing had been obviously aware of the potential for a full-scale escalation, but as the Chinese calculations on the tactical level indicate, it was quite certain of its ability to assert control over the remaining risks.

At the strategic level, Beijing clearly accepted that this was a high-risk venture. Here, the Chinese calculations obviously rested on the single assumption that Brezhnev would not dare to wage war with China. However, besides all Chinese considerations and attempts at risk control and minimization, the choice of Zhenbao Island as the battlefield resulted in a tactical situation that actually forced upon the Soviet Union the decision whether to abandon the island or fight on Chinese soil. A priori, the outcome of this decision depended fundamentally on the Kremlin, and thus reveals itself as the only – but the most dangerous – imponderability that the Chinese could neither control nor influence. By basing their calculations on Mao's assessment that the Soviet Union would not risk an open war, the Chinese took a gamble in which the stakes could not have been higher. With regard to the overall political circumstances, the antagonism that had developed between the two nations, the force disposition that clearly favored the Soviet Union, China's disadvantages and vulnerabilities, and especially the fact that China had now proactively spilled Soviet blood, the question emerges: how could Mao expect that China would get away with it? Apparently, the potential outcome of all-out war had simply been dismissed, as the Chinese crisis-management policy in the aftermath of the clashes evidently demonstrates: as China had not considered an alternative scenario, there was no plan for dealing with the mounting Soviet military pressure at hand. In sum, it seems as if Beijing's leaders carefully considered the risks of their military adventure on the tactical level, but largely ignored its strategic implications. Assessing both dimensions reveals the incalculable risk arising from China's limited military adventure on a small island in the periphery.

Striking the balance for China's border clashes

Regarding the material issue at stake, i.e. sovereignty over Zhenbao Island, the island became de facto Chinese at the moment when Kosygin agreed to Zhou Enlai's proposal that the troops would stay where they were. De jure, the conflict remained unsettled until the conclusion of the Sino-Russian boundary agreement in 2004. In 2008, Russia agreed to transfer around 170 square kilometers of territory to the PRC, including the 0.74 square kilometers of Zhenbao Island.

China's de facto control over Zhenbao came at exceedingly high costs to its security: Beijing's obvious underestimation of Moscow's steadfast reaction resulted in a dramatic deterioration of China's security situation, as Beijing's leadership came to realize not only that the potential for a full-scale Sino-Soviet war existed, but also that it was now confronted with a latent threat to its vulnerable northern border. In the aftermath of the clashes, the Soviet high command created a self-sustaining fighting force on the Chinese flank, which functioned as an unmissable and permanent security threat to China's industrial and population centers.[180] For China, the threat of a full-scale, and possibly even nuclear, war was thus maintained for the following 15 years. Following the unprecedented war scare that had grasped China in autumn and winter 1969, Beijing attempted to counter the Soviet threat by strengthening its troop presence at the northern border and spent enormous sums in civil defense infrastructure, significantly setting back China's economy.[181] From a material perspective, Zhenbao Island came at a more-than-substantial price for China's economic and security situations.

When approached from a non-material perspective, however, Beijing's military adventure did actually pay off. Once again, the People's Republic had dared to challenge a superpower, and once again the PLA had shown surprising resilience and resolve against superior enemy forces. Even though opinions diverge as to which side can be actually credited with 'winning' the clashes at Zhenbao, Bruce Elleman's observation holds true that "[s]imply the existence of battles between the PLA and one of the world's great military powers added greatly to the reputation of the PLA."[182] Mao himself claimed that the battles broke the superstition "that the Soviet Union by virtue of its superior weaponry was invincible."[183] For sure, Mao's assessment is exaggerated, as Soviet troops were ambushed in the first clash and the second encounter was too negligible in scale to function as a genuine benchmark. However, Mao's judgment contains an element of truth: although the March 15 battle was not conclusive, the force disposition of both sides was balanced, and it was the PLA infantry that managed to achieve their military objective against superior Soviet forces. A trophy from this 'victory' – a captured Soviet T-62 tank – is displayed in the Military Museum of the Chinese People's Revolution to this day. In this sense, the Soviet forces' invincibility had taken more than a scratch, as the PLA successfully withstood the power of the vaunted Red Army.

The most important outcome of the Sino-Soviet border clashes, however, was that by deliberately provoking lethal encounters with Soviet troops, China demonstrated that it was absolutely unwilling to tolerate Moscow's attempts at military intimidation and to accept increasing Soviet influence in China's sphere of authority. The lesson the Chinese taught in spilling Soviet blood on the ice of the Ussuri thus had two recipients: The Soviet Union on the one hand, as China "directly challenged the 'Brezhnev' doctrine"[184] and Moscow's claim for leadership in the socialist movement; Moscow's client states on the other, to which Beijing sent a strong message through the clashes.

Conclusion: fighting to make a point

Having completed the empirical analysis, I will now summarize my central findings, provide an answer to the general research question, and evaluate the two theoretical models' explanatory capacity for the Chinese resort to force against the Soviet Union. Before doing so, I need to admit that as the complete methodological repertoire could not be utilized in this case study because of the sparse documentation of the decision-making process, a rigorous validation of the two competing hypothetical processes cannot be presented. Nevertheless, my partial analyses provided the following conclusive findings.

First, I was able to identify the People's Republic of China as the instigator of the border clashes. As my analysis demonstrated, the Chinese ambush of March 2 was a carefully prepared, politically intended, and proactive escalation of the level of violence at the Sino-Soviet border. The March 15 clash was the direct result of the ambush, as Soviet troops initiated this second battle in apparent retaliation. Beijing exercised direct command and control over the PLA's conduct of warfare at Zhenbao and had obviously anticipated Soviet military action in response. Instead of withdrawing, however, the Chinese forces stood their ground and showed great determination to remain in control of the island during the second encounter.

Second, it appears important to emphasize once more that the uninhabitable island had no material value for China or the Soviet Union. This indicates that China's resort to force was primarily intended as a symbolic military action; this also corresponds with my findings on China's general behavior at the border, which mirrored the overall deterioration of Sino-Soviet relations. Adding to this, I demonstrated that matters of principle rather than disagreement on substantial issues impeded a negotiated solution to the border dispute, as the subject was deeply linked to China's traumatic experiences during the Century of Shame.

Third, China's historical traumata eventually reemerged with Moscow's declaration of the Brezhnev Doctrine, which, in the eyes of the Chinese leadership, degraded the PRC once more to the status of a vassal by Moscow's grace. The Brezhnev Doctrine not only ran fundamentally contra to the self-conception of the New China but also functioned as the immediate trigger for Beijing's decision to resort to force, as it resulted in an evident change in China's border policy. Beijing primarily framed Moscow's policies as an openly stated challenge to China's ideological and political independence and a crude attempt to coerce China into submission.

Fourth, China's political and ideological emancipation from the Soviet Union functioned as the antecedent condition for the onset of the Sino-Soviet conflict, which evolved as an ideological, political, and regional rivalry for status, leadership, and loyalty. As my analysis revealed, China's desire to emancipate itself from the Soviet Union rested upon the conviction that Moscow had backstabbed China more than once, and was now about to betray the world revolutionary movement as a whole.

Fifth, Beijing was apparently willing to take high and even prohibitive risks in order to execute a limited military action against the Soviet Union, which in the end resulted in a substantial deterioration in China's security situation. As the investigation of China's risk behavior demonstrated, while Beijing had carefully calculated the risks of the ambush at the tactical level, the prohibitive strategic implications had been ignored, apparently based on Mao's personal assessment of the improbability of a large-scale military escalation.

Sixth, only after Beijing had comprehensively lost control over the escalatory level of the subsequent crisis did the Chinese leadership grasp the seriousness of the situation and backpedal. But even though Beijing's leaders were then willing to defuse the crisis by restarting negotiations with Moscow, priority was given to undertaking this step in a face-saving manner.

When taking these findings into account, the application of James Fearon's rationalist model struggles with the problem that China's specific risk behavior and Beijing's insistence on matters of principle collide with its basic assumptions. The negotiations during the Sino-Soviet border consultations of 1964 demonstrate that the territorial issue would indeed have been divisible, especially as the degree of adjustment was relatively small, which was also acknowledged by both sides. However, a negotiated solution, which was already in reach, was eventually impeded by non-material principles such as Beijing's insistence on a Soviet kowtow. As Fearon's explanatory model is not able to take these non-material factors into account, it cannot grasp the nature of the Sino-Soviet conflict and thus is unable to provide an explanation for its escalation. In line with this, none of my partial analyses generated any evidence that China's resort to force was the result of information asymmetries or was affected by a Chinese belief that Moscow would not keep its part of the bargain after the border dispute had been settled through negotiations.[185]

As I outlined above, the border issue can be regarded primarily as the stage on which the deterioration of relations between China and the Soviet Union materialized. The actual conflict is to be found in the Sino-Soviet rivalry for political and ideological leadership, and thus in the non-material dimension of international relations. Accordingly, Ned Lebow's Cultural Theory of International Relations offers a substantially better explanation for the onset, the specific evolution, and the final escalation of the Sino-Soviet conflict. The roots of the conflict are to be found in Moscow's repeated non-performance of its socialist obligations towards China, which eroded the legitimacy of the underlying *nomos*. In order to safeguard the world revolutionary movement, Beijing thus challenged the Soviet Union's leadership of the socialist society and put forward an alternative ideological model, which set off the Sino-Soviet ideological rivalry. Political rivalry then quickly followed as Beijing and Moscow competed over fellowship for their respective interpretations of the socialist *nomos*. The result was a regional rivalry over spheres of influence. China deeply resented Mongolia and North Korea's switches to the side of the Soviet Union, which might indicate that *spirit* then started to become the dominant motive among China's key leaders. In contrast, Moscow's hedging strategy reflected the ideal-type characteristics of a worldview dominated by *fear*, as the build-up of forces in the Far East, Moscow's alliance formations, and the strategic encirclement of China demonstrate. With the onset of the Cultural Revolution, Beijing finalized China's political and ideological emancipation from Moscow, the Soviet-led society, and its underlying *nomos*. But when the *nomos* is lost, the "competition for standing … is more unconstrained and possibly more violent."[186] This explains why the Brezhnev Doctrine was ambivalently received inside the Chinese leadership: while some leaders perceived the doctrine as a security threat (fear), others – including Mao – were infuriated as they framed it as a Soviet attempt to intimidate China into submission, and were thus the more determined to act resolutely (spirit).[187] Remarkably, the analyses of China's risk behavior and the actual use of force also reveal this ambivalence: Beijing acted in quite a risk-averse way (fear) at the tactical level, while the prohibitive risks at the strategic level were obviously blanked out (spirit). With regard to the actual use of force, the conclusion suggests itself that an ambush does not resemble the kind of honorable duel required by spirit-motivated warfare. Nevertheless, as China and the Soviet Union were then no longer restrained by a shared *nomos*, spirit-induced resorts to force can take on a no-holds-barred quality. The next change in motives is observable in the aftermath of the clashes. As the Soviet Union's mounting military pressure apparently cooled Beijing's temper, *reason* regained its restraining control over spirit, and Beijing showed willingness to negotiate with the Soviet Union, albeit in a face-saving manner.

Taken together, my analysis has shown that the PRC proactively instigated the border clashes of March 1969 in order to demonstrate China's resolve to stand against what was perceived as a Soviet attempt at intimidation. Accordingly, the motive *spirit*, and particularly its emotional effects, can be held responsible for Beijing's decision to spill Soviet blood on the ice of the Ussuri in a symbolic but limited military action. Moscow's declaration of the Brezhnev Doctrine functioned as the corresponding *trigger event* in this decision, while the Sino-Soviet split is identified as the *antecedent condition*.

Notes

1 Tai, Sung An, *The Sino-Soviet Territorial Dispute* (Philadelphia, PA: The Westminster Press, 1973), 91.
2 As Zhenbao Island is formally under the PRC's jurisdiction today, as officially accepted by Russia in 2008, I will use the Chinese name for the island in the following.
3 Maxwell, Neville, "How the Sino-Russian Boundary Conflict was Finally Settled: From Nerchinks 1689 to Vladivostok 2005 via Zhenbao Island 1969," in *Eager Eyes Fixed on Eurasia: Russia and Its Eastern Edge*, ed. Iwashita, Akihiro (Sapporo: Hokkaido University Press, 2007), 63.
4 Robinson, Thomas W., "The Sino-Soviet Border Conflict of 1969. New Evidence Three Decades After," in *Chinese Warfighting: The PLA Experience since 1949*, ed. Ryan, Marc A., Finkelstein, David M., and McDevitt, Michael A. (Armonk/London: East Gate Books, 2003), 204.

5 See Whiting, Allen S., "China's Use of Force, 1950–96, and Taiwan," *International Security* 26, no. 2 (2001): 118. Beijing maintains this version of the outbreak of hostilities to this day: see People's Republic of China, Ministry of Foreign Affairs, "Meeting between Zhou Enlai and Kosygin at the Beijing Airport."
6 Maxwell, Neville, "Report from China: The Chinese Account for the 1969 Fighting at Chenpao," *The China Quarterly* no. 56 (1973): 730.
7 See Ryabushkin, Dimitri S., "New Documents on the Sino-Soviet Ussuri Border Clashes of 1969," *Eurasia Border Review* vol. 3 – *Special Issue: China's Post-Revolutionary Borders* (2012): 163; Goldstein, Lyle J., "Return to Zhenbao Island: Who Started the Shooting and Why It Matters," *The China Quarterly* no. 168 (2001): 989. Even higher Soviet causality numbers are presented by Whiting, "China's Use of Force," 118; Barnouin, Barbara and Yu, Changgen, *Chinese Foreign Policy during the Cultural Revolution* (London: Kegan Paul International, 1998), 88. In modern warfare, the number of WIAs usually exceeds 2–4 times the number of KIAs: see Coupland, Robin M. and Meddings, David R., "Mortality Associated with the Use of Weapons in Armed Conflicts, Wartime Atrocities, and Civilian Mass Shootings: Literature Review," *British Medical Journal* 319 (1999): 407–10. Estimates of the number of Chinese casualties vary greatly, ranging from six KIA up to 100 casualties with 20–40 KIA: see Li, Xiaobing, *A History of the Modern Chinese Army* (Lexington, KY: The University Press of Kentucky, 2007), 227; Ryabushkin, "New Documents," 162.
8 See Robinson, "The Sino-Soviet Border Conflict," 199; Maxwell, "The Chinese Account for the 1969 Fighting," 734–35.
9 See the detailed account of the clash presented by Robinson, "The Sino-Soviet Border Conflict," 209.
10 See Maxwell, "How the Sino-Russian Boundary Conflict was Finally Settled," 731; Elleman, Bruce A., *Modern Chinese Warfare, 1795–1989* (New York: Routledge, 2001), 261.
11 See Ryabushkin, "New Documents," 166–69. However, "[a]llegations of vicious mutilation of Soviet corpses may have been exaggerated for East German consumption": Whiting, "China's Use of Force," 117, fn 52.
12 Shevchenko, Arkady N., *Breaking with Moscow: The Compelling Story of the Highest-Ranking Soviet Defector* (London: Grafton Books, 1985), 269–70.
13 Ryabushkin, "New Documents," 79.
14 See Robinson, Thomas W., "China Confronts the Soviet Union: Warfare and Diplomacy on China's Inner Asian Frontiers," in *The Cambridge History of China*, ed. McFarquhar, Roderick and Fairbank, John K. (New York: Cambridge University Press, 1991), 261–64.
15 See Maxwell, "The Chinese Account for the 1969 Fighting," 732–34. In general, readers should be careful with Maxwell's account on the events, as his "post-facto version conflicts with statements by the Chinese at the time of the events": Cohen, Arthur, "The Sino-Soviet Border Crisis of 1969," in *Avoiding War: Problems of Crisis Management*, ed. George, Alexander L. and Bar-Siman-Tov, Yacoov (Boulder, CO: Westview Press, 1991), 279.
16 Such an interpretation is presented as one of three explanations by Robinson, "China Confronts the Soviet Union," 261–64. Although the brutality might serve as evidence of an emotionally loaded mindset on the part of the Chinese soldiers, the argument is weakened when the method of killing is correlated with the victim's military rank: according to the autopsy report, in total 19 wounded soldiers were killed after the battle. While the overwhelming majority of the ordinary soldiers (10 out of 13) were

cruelly killed with bayonet stabs to the head or were beaten to death, the two officers and three of four non-commissioned officers received a more 'merciful' death by point-blank shots. These findings counter the intuitively expected higher degree of violence against enemy military leaders as perpetrator of the preceding humiliations: see Ryabushkin, "New Documents," 166–69.

17 See Elleman, *Modern Chinese Warfare*, 276–77; Ostermann, Christian F., "East German Documents on the Border Conflict, 1969," *Cold War International History Project Bulletin: The Cold War in Asia*, no. 6–7 (1995/96): 186–87.
18 Robinson, "The Sino-Soviet Border Conflict," 206. See also Gurtov, Melvin and Hwang, Byong-Moo, *China under Threat. The Politics of Strategy and Diplomacy* (Baltimore/London: The Johns Hopkins University Press, 1980), 202.
19 See Ostermann, "East German Documents," 189; Tai, *The Sino-Soviet Territorial Dispute*, 91.
20 See Whiting, "China's Use of Force," 117; Robinson, "The Sino-Soviet Border Conflict," 207.
21 Goldstein, "Return to Zhenbao Island," 990.
22 Maxwell, "The Chinese Account for the 1969 Fighting," 731.
23 Li, *A History of the Modern Chinese Army*, 227–28.
24 For revenge as Soviet motive, see Tai, *The Sino-Soviet Territorial Dispute*, 94; Elleman, *Modern Chinese Warfare*, 269; Robinson, Thomas W., "The Sino-Soviet Border Dispute: Background, Development, and the March 1969 Clashes," *The American Political Science Review* 66, no. 4 (1972): 1200. For deterrence, see Cohen, "The Sino-Soviet Border Crisis," 279–80; Yang, Kuisong, "The Sino-Soviet Border Clash of 1969: From Zhenbao Island to Sino-American Rapprochement," *Cold War History* 1, no. 1 (2000): 31; Chang, Jung and Halliday, John, *Mao – The Unknown Story* (New York: Anchor Books, 2006), 537. For the rivalry argument, see Robinson, "The Sino-Soviet Border Dispute," 1200.
25 See "The Sino-Soviet Border Conflict," 201.
26 For detailed accounts of the March 15 clash, see Cohen, "The Sino-Soviet Border Crisis," 279–80; Robinson, "The Sino-Soviet Border Conflict," 202–12. For estimates on the number of Chinese casualties, see Elleman, *Modern Chinese Warfare*, 269; Robinson, "The Sino-Soviet Border Dispute," 1190; Li, *A History of the Modern Chinese Army*, 228; Ryabushkin, "New Documents," 164.
27 Robinson, "The Sino-Soviet Border Conflict," 210–11. On April 3, a Soviet representative basically confirmed the Soviet abandonment of the island: see Cohen, "The Sino-Soviet Border Crisis," 281.
28 See Tai, *The Sino-Soviet Territorial Dispute*, 106.
29 See Elleman, *Modern Chinese Warfare*, 278; Chen, Jian, *Mao's China and the Cold War* (London, Chapel Hill: The University of North Carolina Press, 2001), 248; Whiting, "China's Use of Force," 118.
30 See Radchenko, Sergej, "Fehlwahrnehmungen in den chinesisch-sowjetischen Krisen 1966 bis 1969," in *Krisen im Kalten Krieg*, ed. Greiner, Bernd, Müller, Christian T., and Walther, Dierk (Bonn: Bundeszentrale für politische Bildung, 2009), 365–66; Yang, "The Sino-Soviet Border Clash," 32–33.
31 "A week [after the March 15 clash], the old hot line from Moscow unexpectedly came alive. It was the Soviet premier Aleksei Kosygin asking to speak to either Mao or Chou En-lai. ... The operator refused to put the call through, saying on the fourth attempt that they could not take a call for Chairman Mao from 'that scoundrel revisionist Kosygin'": Chang and Halliday, *Mao*, 538.
32 Cited in Whiting, "China's Use of Force," 118.

Sino-Soviet border clashes 181

33 Yang, "The Sino-Soviet Border Clash," 30.
34 Cohen, "The Sino-Soviet Border Crisis," 281.
35 See Li, *A History of the Modern Chinese Army*, 228.
36 Christensen, Thomas, "Windows and Wars: Trend Analysis and Beijing's Use of Force," in *New Directions in the Study of Chinese Foreign Policy*, ed. Johnston, Alastair and Ross, Robert S. (Stanford, CA: Stanford University Press, 2006), 71.
37 In mid-August, Beijing ordered the military regions bordering the Soviet Union and Mongolia to "enter the status of a general mobilization": Chen, *Mao's China*, 248. "The order ... was the culmination of a month of mounting fears of war": Khoo, Nicholas, *Collateral Damage. Sino-Soviet Rivalry and the Termination of the Sino-Vietnamese Alliance* (New York: Columbia University Press, 2011), 56–57.
38 Yang, "The Sino-Soviet Border Clash," 35.
39 See Robinson, "The Sino-Soviet Border Conflict," 189. In early September 1969, Foreign Minister Chen Yi informed Mao that "[q]uite recently [the Soviets] have voiced nuclear threats against us and plotted a sudden strike on our nuclear installations": Barnouin and Yu, *Chinese Foreign Policy*, 143. The timing of this report correlates with other sources used by the Soviet Union at the end of August to communicate its nuclear threat to Beijing. It seems plausible that the combined conventional and atomic threat, intentionally leaked via multiple and thus credible channels to Beijing, "was evidently credible enough to persuade Mao and his aides to curtail their actions and cool off the crisis": Cohen, "The Sino-Soviet Border Crisis," 287.
40 See Ryabushkin, "New Documents," 84; Maxwell, "How the Sino-Russian Boundary Conflict was Finally Settled," 68.
41 "The Chinese paranoia was such that it was feared that Kosygin's plane was a 'Trojan Horse'": Khoo, *Collateral Damage*, 57. However, it would not have been the first time that the Soviet Union had made use of this tactic: Soviet elite units had captured the airport of Prague in August 1968 in exactly the same way. For the content of the meeting, see Zhou, Enlai, "Letter to Alexei Kosygin" (September 18, 1969).
42 See Wishnick, Elizabeth, *Mending Fences. The Evolution of Moscow's China Policy from Brezhnev to Yeltsin* (Seattle, WA: The University of Washington Press, 2001), 7.
43 For the historical roots of the Sino-Soviet border issue, see ibid., 24–27.
44 Robinson, "The Sino-Soviet Border Dispute," 1176.
45 See Goncharev, Sergei N., Lewis, John W., and Xue, Litai, *Uncertain Partners – Stalin, Mao, and the Korean War* (Stanford, CA: Stanford University Press, 1993), 41, 62–65.
46 See Ryabushkin, Dimitri S., "Origin and Consequences of the Sino-Soviet Border Conflict in 1969," in *Eager Eyes Fixed on Eurasia: Russia and Its Eastern Edge*, ed. Iwishita, Akihiro (Sapporo: Hokkaido University, 2007), 347.
47 See Maxwell, "How the Sino-Russian Boundary Conflict was Finally Settled," 58.
48 "Many researchers consider the border dispute between the USSR and China as the main reason for the bloodshed ... However, it is sufficient only to cast a glance at a map to understand the inconsistency of the given statement. Practically, none of the islands [under dispute] had any important economic or military value, and, therefore, they could not serve as the reason for such serious confrontation ... Moreover, if the disputed islands had not existed at all, Mao Zedong and his colleagues in the Chinese leadership would have found other places for confrontation." Ryabushkin, "Origin and Consequences of the Sino-Soviet Border Conflict," 76.
49 Ostermann, "East German Documents," 186. "[T]he territorial issue between China and the Soviet Union is only a sidelight. It can be turned on or off as the overall political climate changes": Tai, *The Sino-Soviet Territorial Dispute*, 123.
50 See Robinson, "The Sino-Soviet Border Dispute," 1175–77.

51 See Cohen, "The Sino-Soviet Border Crisis," 271; Ostermann, "East German Documents," p. 186; Maxwell, "How the Sino-Russian Boundary Conflict was Finally Settled," 57–58.
52 See Ryabushkin, "Origin and Consequences of the Sino-Soviet Border Conflict," 75.
53 See Whiting, Allen S., *The Chinese Calculus of Deterrence: India and Indochina* (Ann Arbor: The University of Michigan Press, 2001), 72–75.
54 See Ryabushkin, "Origin and Consequences of the Sino-Soviet Border Conflict," 74.
55 Chen, Jian, *China's Road to the Korean War – The Making of the Sino-American Confrontation* (New York: Columbia University Press, 1994), 204.
56 Cohen, "The Sino-Soviet Border Crisis," 270–77.
57 See Gernet, Jacques, *Die chinesische Welt. Die Geschichte Chinas von den Anfängen bis zur Jetztzeit* (Frankfurt am Main: Suhrkamp, 1997), 555–56; Chang and Halliday, *Mao*, 450–56.
58 See Wishnick, *Mending Fences*, 7; Axelrod, Alan, *The Real History of the Cold War: A New Look at the Past* (New York: Sterling Publishing, 2009), 213.
59 See Ryabushkin, "Origin and Consequences of the Sino-Soviet Border Conflict," 74.
60 "Mao respected Stalin as the world Communist leader," but he certainly did not respect Khrushchev in this function: see Tai, *The Sino-Soviet Territorial Dispute*, 67.
61 Shevchenko, *Breaking with Moscow*, 202.
62 See Chang and Halliday, *Mao*, 445.
63 See Salisbury, Harrison E., *War between Russia and China* (New York: W.W. Norton & Company, 1969), 82; Chen, *Mao's China*, 240.
64 See Chang and Halliday, *Mao*, 451.
65 See Central Committee of the Communist Party of China, *A Proposal Concerning the General Line of the International Communist Movement, The Letter of the Central Committee of the Communist Party of China in Reply to the Central Committee of the Communist Party of the Soviet Union (March 30, 1963)*. Beijing: Foreign Language Press, 1963.
66 See Maxwell, "How the Sino-Russian Boundary Conflict was Finally Settled," 61.
67 This step was almost certainly provoked by Khrushchev's letter to the CCP of January 1963, in which the Soviet leader intentionally brought up the painful issue of China's lost territory by emphasizing that Beijing would follow "a double-standard approach" concerning the criticism of "peaceful coexistence" and the Chinese handling of still existing colonies (Taiwan, Hong Kong, Macao): see Tai, *The Sino-Soviet Territorial Dispute*, 75.
68 Paine, Sarah C.M., *Imperial Rivals: China, Russia and Their Disputed Frontier* (Armonk, NY: M.E. Sharpe, 1996), 9.
69 See Robinson, "The Sino-Soviet Border Dispute," 1179. Moscow's initiative revealed a 180-degree turn in the Soviet border policy: in November 1963, Khrushchev had still "rejected the Chinese position that a new, overall border agreement should be negotiation, stating that a historically formed boundary already existed [and] warned Mao against challenging long-existing Soviet dominance [and the status quo] at the border": Cohen, "The Sino-Soviet Border Crisis," 272.
70 Robinson, "The Sino-Soviet Border Dispute," 1180 [emphasis added].
71 See Wishnick, *Mending Fences*, 24.
72 Robinson, "The Sino-Soviet Border Dispute," 1180.
73 Lüthi, Lorenz, *The Sino-Soviet Split: Cold War in the Communist World* (Princeton, NJ: Princeton University Press, 2008), 292.
74 See Cohen, "The Sino-Soviet Border Crisis," 273.
75 See Whiting, "China's Use of Force," 116–17; Gurtov and Hwang, *China under Threat*, 212; Ostermann, "East German Documents," 186–87; Wishnick, *Mending Fences*, 24–30.

76 See Gomà Pinilla, Daniel, "Border Disputes between China and North Korea," *China Perspectives* no. 52 (2004).
77 See Bradsher, Henry S., "The Sovietization of Mongolia," *Foreign Affairs* 50, no. 3 (1972): 549; Ram, Rahul, "Mongolia between China and Russia," *Asian Survey* 18, no. 7 (1978): 660–63.
78 See Chen, Jian, "China's Involvement in the Vietnam War, 1964–69," *The China Quarterly* no. 142 (1995): 356–87.
79 See Whiting, "China's Use of Force," 117.
80 See Chen, "China's Involvement in the Vietnam War," 359.
81 See Gurtov and Hwang, *China under Threat*, 191; Christensen, "Windows and Wars," 70; O'Dowd, Edward C., *Chinese Military Strategy in the Third Indochina War: The Last Maoist War* (London, New York: Routledge, 2007), 40.
82 See Wishnick, *Mending Fences*, 7.
83 Cohen, "The Sino-Soviet Border Crisis," 274.
84 See Maxwell, "How the Sino-Russian Boundary Conflict was Finally Settled," 61; Ryabushkin, "Origin and Consequences of the Sino-Soviet Border Conflict," 75.
85 Cohen, "The Sino-Soviet Border Crisis," 274.
86 See Maxwell, "The Chinese Account for the 1969 Fighting," 732.
87 See Gurtov and Hwang, *China under Threat*, 214.
88 See Yang, "The Sino-Soviet Border Clash," 27; Goldstein, "Return to Zhenbao Island," 988.
89 See Ostermann, "East German Documents," 187.
90 See Gernet, *Die chinesische Welt*, 559.
91 Tai, *The Sino-Soviet Territorial Dispute*, 83.
92 See Scobell, Andrew, *China's Use of Military Force – Beyond the Great Wall and the Long March* (Cambridge: Cambridge University Press, 2003), 100.
93 See Wishnick, *Mending Fences*, 30.
94 Robinson, "The Sino-Soviet Border Dispute," 1176.
95 Whiting, "China's Use of Force," 117.
96 See Maxwell, "How the Sino-Russian Boundary Conflict was Finally Settled," 61.
97 See Cohen, "The Sino-Soviet Border Crisis," 276.
98 Brezhnev, Leonid, "Speech before the Fifth Congress of the Polish United Workers Party (November 12, 1968), Warszawa," *The Current Digest of the Soviet Press* 20, no. 46 (1968): 3–5.
99 See Khoo, *Collateral Damage*, 47.
100 O'Dowd, *The Last Maoist War*, 40. "It is important to notice that the sudden military invasion of the CSSR happened only after a wide propaganda campaign during which Soviet [media] inspired the idea that the problems in Czechoslovakia endangered socialism. Approximately the same expressions were being used by the Soviet mass media in their information about the situation in China": Ryabushkin, "Origin and Consequences of the Sino-Soviet Border Conflict," 79.
101 Gurtov and Hwang, *China under Threat*, 218. "Most importantly, [Mao] wondered out loud if the Soviet invasion [of Czechoslovakia] should be interpreted as the prelude to a more general war, which he believed might trigger 'revolution' and could only be prevented by 'revolution'. In any case, China had to be prepared": Chen, Jian and Wilson, David L., "'All under heaven is great chaos' – Beijing, the Sino-Soviet Border Clashes and the Turn Toward Sino-American Rapproachement, 1968–69," *Cold War International History Project Bulletin*, no. 11 (1998): 155.
102 See Wishnick, *Mending Fences*, 40; Chen, *Mao's China*, 240. Adding to the substantial buildup of Soviet military power at China's border, the "intrusion of Soviet military

aircraft into Chinese airspace [also] increased after the invasion of Czechoslovakia": Rea, Kenneth W., "Peking and the Brezhnev Doctrine," *Asian Affairs* 3, no. 1 (1975): 25. Apparently, the Soviet Union was undertaking reconnaissance missions on China's border-defense capabilities. In Beijing's view, this could be regarded as a prelude to a Soviet ground operation.
103 Robinson, "The Sino-Soviet Border Conflict," 206.
104 Cohen, "The Sino-Soviet Border Crisis," 273.
105 Ostermann, "East German Documents," 187.
106 See Christensen, "Windows and Wars," 70. According to the Report of the Four Marshals of March 1969, the Soviet Union was not ready to wage war against China as this would require the mobilization of at least three million troops: see Chen, *Mao's China*, 246.
107 Cohen, "The Sino-Soviet Border Crisis," 276.
108 Khoo, *Collateral Damage*, 47.
109 Rea, "Peking and the Brezhnev Doctrine," 24 [emphasis added].
110 Ibid., 22–23.
111 Cohen, "The Sino-Soviet Border Crisis," 276.
112 Maxwell, "How the Sino-Russian Boundary Conflict was Finally Settled," 59.
113 See Gurtov and Hwang, *China under Threat*, 226. Reinforcing the border with additional troops took some time, which may explain why the lesson Beijing sought to teach at Zhenbao was not seen until the following spring.
114 Yang, "The Sino-Soviet Border Clash," 28.
115 See Cohen, "The Sino-Soviet Border Crisis," 276.
116 See Robinson, "The Sino-Soviet Border Conflict," 206–07; Whiting, "China's Use of Force," 117.
117 See Ostermann, "East German Documents," 187.
118 See Robinson, "The Sino-Soviet Border Conflict," 207.
119 See Cohen, "The Sino-Soviet Border Crisis," 277–78. Moreover, Gurtov and Hwang observe that one week before the fighting broke out, "Radio Beijing issued a warning of forthcoming Soviet military maneuvers in Heilongjiang and signaled that the worsening situation along the Ussuri might erupt into a large-scale border war": *China under Threat*, 234.
120 See Robinson, "The Sino-Soviet Border Conflict," 207–08; Yang, "The Sino-Soviet Border Clash," 27–28.
121 See Whiting, "China's Use of Force," 117.
122 Robinson, "The Sino-Soviet Border Conflict," 207.
123 See Yang, "The Sino-Soviet Border Clash," 29; Christensen, "Windows and Wars," 69.
124 See Ryabushkin, "Origin and Consequences of the Sino-Soviet Border Conflict," 77.
125 Yang, "The Sino-Soviet Border Clash," 22.
126 See Goldstein, "Return to Zhenbao Island," 995.
127 Spence, Jonathan D., *The Search for Modern China* (New York: W.W. Norton & Company, 1991), 616.
128 See Yang, "The Sino-Soviet Border Clash," 31.
129 Robinson, "The Sino-Soviet Border Conflict," 208.
130 See Ryabushkin, "Origin and Consequences of the Sino-Soviet Border Conflict," 77.
131 According to Chang and Halliday, *Mao*, 523, Liu Shaoqi had already been imprisoned since late 1967, and Mao had given the order to "keep him alive until after the 9th Congress" to publicly expel Liu from the Party.
132 See Gernet, *Die chinesische Welt*, 560.
133 See Khoo, *Collateral Damage*, 45.
134 See Ostermann, "East German Documents," 186.

135 Goldstein, "Return to Zhenbao Island," 995.
136 This conclusion is shared by Gurtov and Hwang, *China under Threat*, 234.
137 For a similar assessment, see Khoo, *Collateral Damage*, 45.
138 Gurtov and Hwang, *China under Threat*, 234.
139 Elleman, *Modern Chinese Warfare*, 278.
140 The Central Military Commission issued the order that the battle should "be limited to our side of the channel course … be swift, that our forces not become tangled up with the enemy, be not carried away by the fighting, and after victory our forces should retreat to an advantageous place": Cohen, "The Sino-Soviet Border Crisis," 280.
141 See Robinson, "The Sino-Soviet Border Conflict," 207. The only exception was Chinese artillery fire that prevented the Soviets from recovering a disabled T-62 on the island: see Maxwell, "The Chinese Account for the 1969 Fighting," 735.
142 See Yang, "The Sino-Soviet Border Clash," 30.
143 See Ryabushkin, "Origin and Consequences of the Sino-Soviet Border Conflict," 83.
144 See Robinson, "The Sino-Soviet Border Conflict," 211.
145 "The topographical situation of Zhenbao is unusual, perhaps unique on the Ussuri at least": Maxwell, "How the Sino-Russian Boundary Conflict was Finally Settled," 66.
146 Cohen, "The Sino-Soviet Border Crisis," 275.
147 See Chang and Halliday, *Mao*, 537.
148 See Robinson, "The Sino-Soviet Border Dispute," 1187.
149 See Cohen, "The Sino-Soviet Border Crisis," 269.
150 See Robinson, "The Sino-Soviet Border Dispute," 1187.
151 See Maxwell, "How the Sino-Russian Boundary Conflict was Finally Settled," 66.
152 Cohen, "The Sino-Soviet Border Crisis," 277.
153 See Robinson, "The Sino-Soviet Border Conflict," 203.
154 See Gurtov and Hwang, *China under Threat*, 212; Robinson, "The Sino-Soviet Border Dispute," 1184–85.
155 See Wishnick, *Mending Fences*, 30; Robinson, "The Sino-Soviet Border Dispute," 1184.
156 Tai, *The Sino-Soviet Territorial Dispute*, 130.
157 See Gurtov and Hwang, *China under Threat*, 193.
158 See Chen, *Mao's China*, 248.
159 See Tai, *The Sino-Soviet Territorial Dispute*, 137.
160 Li, *A History of the Modern Chinese Army*, 234.
161 Scobell, *China's Use of Military Force*, 100.
162 Li, *A History of the Modern Chinese Army*, 235–36; Scobell, *China's Use of Military Force*, 101; Gurtov and Hwang, *China under Threat*, 195–96.
163 Chang and Halliday, *Mao*, 539.
164 See Robinson, "The Sino-Soviet Border Dispute," 1185.
165 With regard to the existing railroad capacities, the Cultural Revolution's "domestic turmoil made supplying the frontlines difficult – especially since the PLA relied heavily on the railways, a mode of transportation used heavily by Red Guards traveling around the country": Scobell, *China's Use of Military Force*, 114.
166 See U.S. Department of State, *Intelligence Note No. 665* (September 18, 1969), 2–3.
167 See Cohen, "The Sino-Soviet Border Crisis," 269; Elleman, *Modern Chinese Warfare*, 278; Whiting, "China's Use of Force," 118.
168 See Robinson, "The Sino-Soviet Border Conflict," 206.
169 See Uhl, Matthias, *Krieg um Berlin? Die sowjetische Militär- und Sicherheitspolitik in der zweiten Berlinkrise 1958–1962* (München: Oldenbourg Wissenschaftsverlag, 2008), 54, 166; "'Jederzeit gefechtsbereit' – Die NVA während der Kuba-Krise," in *Vor dem*

         Abgrund: Die Streitkräfte der USA und der UdSSR sowie ihre deutschen Bündnispartner in der Kubakrise, ed. Filippovych, Dimitrij N. and Uhl, Matthias (München: Oldenbourg Wissenschaftsverlag, 2005), 112–19.
170   See Zhang, Xiaoming, *Deng Xiaoping's Long War: The Military Conflict between China and Vietnam, 1979–1991* (Chapel Hill, NC: The University of North Carolina Press 2015), 29.
171   Chang and Halliday, *Mao*, 538.
172   Ibid.
173   See Cohen, "The Sino-Soviet Border Crisis," 276; Elleman, *Modern Chinese Warfare*, 278; Chen, *Mao's China*, 248.
174   Chang and Halliday, *Mao*, 538.
175   See Yang, "The Sino-Soviet Border Clash," 36.
176   See Robinson, "The Sino-Soviet Border Conflict," 206.
177   Ibid., 210.
178   See Stone, David R., *A Military History of Russia: From Ivan the Terrible to the War in Chechnya* (Westport: Praeger Publishing, 1995), 230.
179   See Cohen, "The Sino-Soviet Border Crisis," 288.
180   See Li, *A History of the Modern Chinese Army*, 229.
181   See Robinson, "The Sino-Soviet Border Conflict," 204.
182   Elleman, *Modern Chinese Warfare*, 278.
183   Robinson, "The Sino-Soviet Border Conflict," 204.
184   Elleman, *Modern Chinese Warfare*, 278.
185   Shortly before the Chinese ambush at Zhenbao took place, the Soviet newspaper of record *Izvestia* quoted General Losik, Soviet Far East Military Commander, "as saying that military maneuvers had taken place in the eastern part of the Soviet Union. It had also quoted General Losik's reference to the Sino-Soviet border conflict in 1929 and his claim that should a similar incident take place again in the future, the Soviet army would relentlessly crush the enemy": Gurtov and Hwang, *China under Threat*, 233.
186   Lebow, Richard N., *A Cultural Theory of International Relations* (Cambridge: Cambridge University Press, 2008).
187   See Ostermann, "East German Documents," 187; Cohen, "The Sino-Soviet Border Crisis," 276; Ryabushkin, "Origin and Consequences of the Sino-Soviet Border Conflict," 79.

Bibliography

Axelrod, Alan. *The Real History of the Cold War: A New Look at the Past*. New York: Sterling Publishing, 2009.

Barnouin, Barbara, and Yu, Changgen. *Chinese Foreign Policy during the Cultural Revolution*. London: Kegan Paul International, 1998.

Bradsher, Henry S. "The Sovietization of Mongolia." *Foreign Affairs* 50, no. 3 (1972): 545–53.

Brezhnev, Leonid, "Speech before the Fifth Congress of the Polish United Workers Party (November 12, 1968), Warszawa," *The Current Digest of the Soviet Press* 20, no. 46 (1968): 3–5.

Central Committee of the Communist Party of China, *A Proposal Concerning the General Line of the International Communist Movement, The Letter of the Central Committee of the Communist Party of China in Reply to the Central Committee of the Communist Party of the Soviet Union*, (March 30, 1963). Beijing: Foreign Language Press, 1963.

Chang, Jung, and Halliday, John. *Mao – The Unknown Story*. New York: Anchor Books, 2006.

Chen, Jian. *China's Road to the Korean War – The Making of the Sino-American Confrontation.* New York: Columbia University Press, 1994.

Chen, Jian. "China's Involvement in the Vietnam War, 1964–69." *The China Quarterly* no. 142 (June 1995): 356–87.

Chen, Jian. *Mao's China and the Cold War.* London, Chapel Hill: The University of North Carolina Press, 2001.

Chen, Jian, and Wilson, David L. "'All under heaven is great chaos' – Beijing, the Sino-Soviet Border Clashes and the Turn toward Sino-American Rapproachement, 1968–69." *Cold War International History Project Bulletin* no. 11 (1998): 155–75.

Christensen, Thomas. "Windows and Wars: Trend Analysis and Beijing's Use of Force." In *New Directions in the Study of Chinese Foreign Policy*, edited by Alastair Johnston and Robert S. Ross, 50–85. Stanford, CA: Stanford University Press, 2006.

Cohen, Arthur. "The Sino-Soviet Border Crisis of 1969." In *Avoiding War: Problems of Crisis Management*, edited by Alexander L. George and Yacoov Bar-Siman-Tov, 269–89. Boulder, CO: Westview Press, 1991.

Coupland, Robin M., and Meddings, David R. "Mortality Associated with the Use of Weapons in Armed Conflicts, Wartime Atrocities, and Civilian Mass Shootings: Literature Review." *British Medical Journal*, vol. 319 (August 1999): 407–10.

Elleman, Bruce A. *Modern Chinese Warfare, 1795–1989.* New York: Routledge, 2001.

Gernet, Jacques. *Die chinesische Welt. Die Geschichte Chinas von den Anfängen bis zur Jetztzeit.* Frankfurt am Main: Suhrkamp, 1997.

Goldstein, Lyle J. "Return to Zhenbao Island: Who Started the Shooting and Why It Matters." *The China Quarterly* no. 168 (December 2001): 987–97.

Gomà Pinilla, Daniel. "Border Disputes between China and North Korea." *China Perspectives* no. 52 (March 2004). Accessed at https://chinaperspectives.revues.org/806 (August 2, 2016).

Goncharev, Sergei N., Lewis, John W., and Xue, Litai. *Uncertain Partners – Stalin, Mao, and the Korean War.* Stanford, CA: Stanford University Press, 1993.

Gurtov, Melvin, and Hwang, Byong-Moo. *China under Threat. The Politics of Strategy and Diplomacy.* Baltimore/London: The Johns Hopkins University Press, 1980.

Khoo, Nicholas. *Collateral Damage: Sino-Soviet Rivalry and the Termination of the Sino-Vietnamese Alliance.* New York: Columbia University Press, 2011.

Lebow, Richard N. *A Cultural Theory of International Relations.* Cambridge: Cambridge University Press, 2008.

Li, Xiaobing. *A History of the Modern Chinese Army.* Lexington, KY: The University Press of Kentucky, 2007.

Lüthi, Lorenz. *The Sino-Soviet Split: Cold War in the Communist World.* Princeton, NJ: Princeton University Press, 2008.

Maxwell, Neville. "Report from China: The Chinese Account for the 1969 Fighting at Chenpao." *The China Quarterly* no. 56 (December 1973): 730–39.

Maxwell, Neville. "How the Sino-Russian Boundary Conflict was Finally Settled: From Nerchinks 1689 to Vladivostok 2005 via Zhenbao Island 1969." In *Eager Eyes Fixed on Eurasia: Russia and Its Eastern Edge*, edited by Akihiro Iwashita, 42–72. Sapporo: Hokkaido University Press, 2007.

O'Dowd, Edward C. *Chinese Military Strategy in the Third Indochina War: The Last Maoist War.* London, New York: Routledge, 2007.

Ostermann, Christian F. "East German Documents on the Border Conflict, 1969." *Cold War International History Project Bulletin: The Cold War in Asia* no. 6–7 (1995/96): 186–90.

Paine, Sarah C.M. *Imperial Rivals: China, Russia and Their Disputed Frontier.* Armonk, NY: M.E. Sharpe, 1996.

People's Republic of China, Ministry of Foreign Affairs. "Meeting between Zhou Enlai and Kosygin at the Beijing Airport." Accessed at www.fmprc.gov.cn/mfa_eng/ziliao_665539/3602_665543/3604_665547/t18005.shtml (August 2, 2016).

United States of America, Department of State. *Intelligence Note No. 665.* (September 18, 1969). Accessed at http://nsarchive.gwu.edu/NSAEBB/NSAEBB49/sino.sov.21.pdf (August 2, 2016).

Radchenko, Sergej. "Fehlwahrnehmungen in den chinesisch-sowjetischen Krisen 1966 bis 1969." In *Krisen im Kalten Krieg*, edited by Bernd Greiner, Christian T. Müller, and Dierk Walther, 343–68. Bonn: Bundeszentrale für politische Bildung, 2009.

Ram, Rahul. "Mongolia between China and Russia." *Asian Survey* 18, no. 7 (1978): 659–65.

Rea, Kenneth W. "Peking and the Brezhnev Doctrine." *Asian Affairs* 3, no. 1 (1975): 20–30.

Robinson, Thomas W. "The Sino-Soviet Border Dispute: Background, Development, and the March 1969 Clashes." *The American Political Science Review* 66, no. 4 (1972): 1175–202.

Robinson, Thomas W. "China Confronts the Soviet Union: Warfare and Diplomacy on China's Inner Asian Frontiers." In *The Cambridge History of China*, edited by Roderick McFarquhar and John K. Fairbank, 218–304. New York: Cambridge University Press, 1991.

Robinson, Thomas W. "The Sino-Soviet Border Conflict of 1969. New Evidence Three Decades After." In *Chinese Warfighting: The PLA Experience since 1949*, edited by Marc A. Ryan, David M. Finkelstein, and Michael A. McDevitt, 198–216. Armonk/London: East Gate Books, 2003.

Ryabushkin, Dimitri S. "Origin and Consequences of the Sino-Soviet Border Conflict in 1969." In *Eager Eyes Fixed on Eurasia: Russia and Its Eastern Edge*, edited by Akihiro Iwishita, 73–91. Sapporo: Hokkaido University, 2007.

Ryabushkin, Dimitri S. "New Documents on the Sino-Soviet Ussuri Border Clashes of 1969." *Eurasia Border Review* 3 – Special Issue: China's Post-Revolutionary Borders (Spring 2012): 161–74.

Salisbury, Harrison E. *War between Russia and China*. New York: W.W. Norton & Company, 1969.

Scobell, Andrew. *China's Use of Military Force – Beyond the Great Wall and the Long March*. Cambridge: Cambridge University Press, 2003.

Shevchenko, Arkady N. *Breaking with Moscow: The Compelling Story of the Highest-Ranking Soviet Defector*. London: Grafton Books, 1985.

Spence, Jonathan D. *The Search for Modern China*. New York: W.W. Norton & Company, 1991.

Stone, David R. *A Military History of Russia: From Iwan the Terrible to the War in Chechnya*. Westport, CT: Praeger Publishing, 1995.

Tai, Sung An. *The Sino-Soviet Territorial Dispute*. Philadelphia: The Westminster Press, 1973.

Uhl, Matthias. "'Jederzeit gefechtsbereit' – Die NVA während der Kuba-Krise." In *Vor dem Abgrund: Die Streitkräfte der USA und der UdSSR sowie ihre deutschen Bündnispartner in der Kubakrise*, edited by Dimitrij N. Filippovych and Matthias Uhl, 99–120. München: Oldenbourg Wissenschaftsverlag, 2005.

Uhl, Matthas. *Krieg um Berlin? Die sowjetische Militär- und Sicherheitspolitik in der zweiten Berlinkrise 1958–1962*. München: Oldenbourg Wissenschaftsverlag, 2008.

Whiting, Allen S. "China's Use of Force, 1950–96, and Taiwan." *International Security* 26, no. 2 (Fall 2001): 103–31.

Whiting, Allen S. *The Chinese Calculus of Deterrence: India and Indochina*. Ann Arbor, MI: The University of Michigan Press, 2001.

Wishnick, Elizabeth. *Mending Fences. The Evolution of Moscow's China Policy from Brezhnev to Yeltsin*. Seattle, WA: The University of Washington Press, 2001.

Yang, Kuisong. "The Sino-Soviet Border Clash of 1969: From Zhenbao Island to Sino-American Rapproachement." *Cold War History* 1, no. 1 (2000): 21–52.

Zhang, Xiaoming. *Deng Xiaoping's Long War: The Military Conflict between China and Vietnam, 1979–1991*. Chapel Hill, NC: The University of North Carolina Press, 2015.

Zhou, Enlai. "Letter to Alexei Kosygin" (September 18, 1969). Accessed at Wilson Center Digital Archive, http://digitalarchive.wilsoncenter.org/document/110475.pdf?v=ecf7033df6a63 b2220eaae4fc20528cc (August 2, 2016).

6 China's Vietnam War, 1979

On February 17, 1979, China launched a massive ground assault on the Socialist Republic of Vietnam (SRV). Beijing's intention behind this very special form of a socialist brotherly kiss was, as China's Vice Premier Deng Xiaoping explained, to teach Vietnam's wild ambitions some necessary lessons.[1] Unfortunately, the PRC's de facto leader abstained from further clarifying the concrete reasons for, and the particular content of, China's punitive lesson. As a result, existing analyses of the Sino-Vietnamese War traditionally struggle with at least four potential issues that might qualify as catalysts for the outbreak of violence: Hanoi's alliance with the Soviet Union; Vietnam's invasion of Cambodia; the systematic mistreatment and expulsion of ethnic Chinese from Vietnam; and the emergence of territorial disputes between Beijing and Hanoi.[2] Evidently, all of these issues added their relative share to the further deterioration of relations between China and Vietnam, but given "the complexity of the conflict, finding definite answers to the fundamental questions of causation and responsibilities is not an easy task."[3] In the following chapter, I attempt to provide an answer by highlighting the emotional dimension of Sino-Vietnamese relations. As Andrew Scobell has found, the Chinese "decision to attack Vietnam was made not only within the context of the geopolitical environment, it was influenced also by the sense of outrage at what Beijing felt was Hanoi's deceitful betrayal of a steadfast friend."[4] In order to comprehensively explain why China resorted to force against "a fellow Communist country, recent ally, and longtime beneficiary of Chinese economic and military support,"[5] it thus appears highly relevant to take Beijing's emotional perspective on the conflict into account. In doing so, I am able to demonstrate that a bitter sense of Hanoi's ingratitude toward China's loyal and crucial contributions to North Vietnam's independence and survival preceded the emergence of *realpolitik* in driving Beijing and Hanoi apart. The Soviet factor played a crucial role in both dimensions of the conflict. Only after the bilateral relationship had significantly cooled off due to Hanoi's increasingly noticeable turn to Moscow, did Beijing start to worry about the geopolitical implications of a pro-Soviet and unified Vietnam. However, it was Hanoi's ever more arrogant and disloyal behavior toward China that opened the route to conflict, culminating in Vietnam's formal defection to the Soviet Union in late 1978, which in turn affronted the Chinese leadership to such an extent that a military punishment of Vietnam was then considered indispensable.

Outline of the chapter

The chapter is organized into five parts. In the first section, I focus on the formation of the Sino-Vietnamese conflict and analyze the interplay of emotions and interest-based *realpolitik* in the social structure of the bilateral relationship. My investigation unfolds in three analytical steps, each covering a specific phase in Sino-Vietnamese relations, and examines the respective drivers and their impact on the deteriorating relationship. In doing so, I will demonstrate that emotions played a decisive role in steering Beijing and Hanoi toward conflict. My analysis does not reveal a single trigger event that sparked-off the Chinese decision to resort to force, but instead highlights the increasingly emotionalized perspective of the Chinese leadership and how this framed the three principal issues under contestation between China and Vietnam at the peak of the crisis in 1978. In the second section, I analyze the Chinese decision-making process and show that the decision to teach Vietnam a lesson was primarily induced by emotional considerations, specifically a strong desire on behalf of the Chinese leadership to exercise revenge. In the third section, I analyze China's risk calculations and demonstrate that Beijing was well aware of two strands of risk inherent in the Chinese campaign against Vietnam, namely the risks of military failure and of a Soviet military intervention. Even though these risks reveal themselves as prohibitive, the Chinese leadership nonetheless willingly took them in order to exercise their desired revenge on Hanoi. In the fourth section, I examine how the Chinese lesson unfolded on the battlefield. A brief assessment of the outcomes of China's Vietnam campaign follows. The concluding section provides a summary of my central findings, identifies the motivation for China's use of force against Vietnam, and evaluates the two competing theoretical models' explanatory capacity for the case at hand.

The formation of the conflict

"What was particularly surprising about the war," David Dreyer notes, "was that China and Vietnam had previously appeared to have been close allies."[6] Not even four years earlier, Beijing and Hanoi had been brothers-in-arms during the Second Indochina War. Now, they were engaged in the Third Indochina War, but this time they took up arms against one another. Even though a border conflict had emerged, the Chinese invasion of Vietnam did not aim at conquering territory under dispute. Neither was the attack driven by ideological reasons, as the Soviet-led intervention in Czechoslovakia had been. At the bilateral level, security considerations did not play a determining role, as Vietnam did not pose a substantial threat to China's territorial or sociopolitical security. Instead, I argue in the following that Beijing's invasion was launched to take revenge for what the Chinese leadership perceived as Vietnamese ingratitude and lack of loyalty toward the PRC. In the eyes of the Chinese leaders, their decades of steadfast and loyal contributions to Vietnam were rewarded by Hanoi with backstabbing and defection to the Soviet Union. In this chapter, I trace the evolution of Sino-Vietnamese conflict in order to show why Beijing felt so betrayed by Vietnam. Covering a period of three decades, the analysis also reveals the specific causes that turned the brotherly comradeship into bitter enmity.

Phase I: Brotherly comradeship

For almost 20 years, the relations between the PRC and the Vietnamese Communists were a textbook example of what Ho Chi Minh once described as 'brotherly comradeship.' During this period, "the Chinese state and party were by far the closest allies that the new Vietnamese government had."[7] Contacts between Chinese and Vietnamese leaders, as well as party-to-party relations, had traditionally been close.[8] The PRC was among the first countries to diplomatically recognize the Democratic Republic of Vietnam and had extensively supported the Viet Minh in their struggle for independence. Immediately after Stalin transferred to China the duty to safeguard the revolutionary movements in Asia, Beijing began to provide its Vietnamese comrades with substantial military assistance.

China's crucial assistance in the First and Second Indochina Wars

China's assistance was of decisive importance for the outcome of the First Indochina War, as the arrival of Chinese weaponry and advisors turned the tide in favor of the Viet Minh.[9] Beijing's leadership was well aware that the PRC's involvement in Indochina

> would further intensify China's confrontation with the United States as well as complicate Beijing's relationship with Paris. But they were determined to go their own way, because Indochina was to them a test case for the promotion of the new China's international prestige and influence.[10]

Even though the Korean War was then absorbing the lion's share of China's military resources, Beijing did not forget its obligations and provided continual financial assistance and military support to Vietnam. Adding to this, the Chinese territory also functioned as a valuable sanctuary for the Viet Minh, as well as an important base for logistics and training. A steadily growing number of Chinese advisors participated as unit commanders in all relevant campaigns of the war.[11] Most remarkably, and as acknowledged by all parties, it was China's assistance that enabled the presti-gious victory of the People's Army of Vietnam (PAVN) at Dien Bien Phu in 1954, which set an end to Vietnam's colonial status: all weaponry and ammunition, communication devices, and supplies used in this campaign, and even the idea to encircle and resolutely annihilate the French garrison by massively concentrating artillery on the surrounding heights, had been provided by the Chinese.[12]

In contrast to the PRC, which selflessly "executed its socialist international duty"[13] and thereby not only spent enormous sums in support of the Viet Minh but also accepted confrontation with the United States, Moscow was highly reluctant to become involved in the First Indochina War. In early 1950, Ho Chi Minh had tried to solicit Soviet assistance, but Stalin – unwilling to provide more than moral support – had forwarded Ho's request to Beijing.[14] When the Geneva Agreement of 1954 ended the First Indochina War with the provisional partition of Vietnam, Beijing could aptly claim that China's support had fundamentally enabled the Viet Minh to achieve independence as a sovereign state. Besides, the Geneva Conference resulted in another and, for the historical mission of the New China, even more important outcome: the crucial role China played at the conference "implied that for the first time in modern history ... China had been accepted by the international society – friends and foes alike – as a real world power."[15]

Soon, however, the Geneva Agreement turned out to be an unsound basis for preserving the peace in Vietnam. The plebiscite expected to reunify the country, initially scheduled for 1956, did not take place. Anticipating that Washington's interference would keep Vietnam indefinitely divided, the Democratic Republic of Vietnam (DRV) opted to liberate the South through revolutionary struggle. In mid-1958, Hanoi formally approached Beijing for advice: the Chinese leadership, then preoccupied with the country's recovery while facing external pressure from Taiwan and the United States, showed neither great enthusiasm nor opposition for Hanoi's plans. Nonetheless, when the revolution in South Vietnam finally erupted through the Vietcong's nationwide insurgency, Beijing again expansively honored its socialist obligations to the DRV.[16] This time, Beijing's extensive assistance not only safeguarded the very existence of the DRV but also enabled Hanoi to achieve victory in the Second Indochina War: "without the [Chinese] support, the history, even the outcome of the Vietnam War might have been different."[17] The promptness and extent of Beijing's assistance over the entire course of the war is all the more remarkable as China simultaneously faced severe domestic problems caused by the failure of the Great Leap Forward and the turmoil of the Cultural Revolution. In order to contribute their share to North Vietnam's survival, the Chinese thus had to tighten their own belts. Moreover, Beijing once again accepted the risk of a 'Korean-style confrontation' with the United States by becoming proactively involved in the Vietnam War.[18]

Notwithstanding these difficulties and risks, Beijing was willing to demonstrate its solidarity to Hanoi, which materialized in three ways. First, Beijing provided substantial material support. Even before 1963,

> China offered substantial military aid [totaling] 320 million yuan. China's arms shipment ... included 270,000 guns, over 10,000 pieces of artillery, 200 million bullets of different types, 2,02 million artillery shells, 15,000 wire transmitters, 5,000 radio transmitters, over 1,000 trucks, 15 planes, 28 naval vessels, and 1,18 million sets of field uniforms.[19]

These numbers further increased dramatically after 1965, and by the end of 1968 China was Vietnam's main supplier of military and civilian assistance. Over the entire course of the war, Beijing continued to spend enormous sums on military and economic support for Hanoi, which was of vital importance for the North's war efforts.[20] Second, Beijing deployed about 320,000 PLA engineering and anti-aircraft troops to the DRV between 1965 and 1970.[21] The main task of the Chinese People's Volunteer Engineer Force (CPVEF) was to provide air defense for strategically important rear areas and to build infrastructure in North Vietnam, which allowed Hanoi to use its own military capacities for more essential tasks. Third, Beijing also provided North Vietnam with far-reaching security commitments.[22] These guarantees can be regarded as China's most important contribution, because they functioned – together with the Chinese force detachment deployed to North Vietnam – as a credible detterent to an American ground invasion.[23] Beginning in 1963, Beijing assured Hanoi that in the case of a U.S. attack China would provide support "by all possible and necessary means," and declared in the aftermath of the Gulf of Tonkin incident that "America's aggression against the Democratic Republic of Vietnam is also an aggression against China, and that China will never fail to come to the aid of the Vietnamese."[24] At that point, Beijing's contingency planning incorporated the prospect of a military confrontation with the United States, and the PLAAF began to intercept and down U.S. aircraft in Chinese airspace. In spring 1965, Zhou Enlai communicated to Washington China's most explicit warning so far:

> China would not initiate a war with the United States, but China would definitely offer all manner of support to the Vietnamese; if the United States retaliated against China by starting an all-out war, China would meet it; even though the United States might use nuclear weapons against China, China was sure that the Americans would be defeated.[25]

From the first day of the Second Indochina War, China thus committed itself in word and deed to the cause of the North Vietnamese. In doing so, China not only mobilized massive efforts and resources, but also again risked an open confrontation with Washington.

The growing Soviet factor in Sino-Vietnamese relations

Following Khrushchev's ousting in October 1964, the new Soviet government under Leonid Brezhnev sought to improve the ties between Moscow and Hanoi, which had lain idle up to that point. As outlined in the preceding chapter, the reasons for the Kremlin's new impetus in strengthening Soviet relations with Asian countries were to be found in the ideological and political rivalry following the split between Moscow and Beijing, and in Soviet attempts to strategically encircle China. With regard to the ideological rivalry, assisting Vietnam in its struggle against the class enemy also became a litmus test for the two rivals' standing in the socialist movement.[26] However, Moscow could not pressure Hanoi into openly changing sides, as the ongoing war and China's vital contributions to North Vietnam impeded such a radical move.[27] Instead, Moscow decided to amplify the Soviet factor in Vietnam by increasing cooperation and material assistance in order to slowly but steadily separate Hanoi from Beijing. In other words, Moscow started to buy off Hanoi's loyalty to China, and as the Soviet Union had the better selling-points with regard to state-of-the-art weaponry, North Vietnam's dependency on Moscow constantly grew.[28]

Beginning in 1965, Moscow began to provide substantial support for Hanoi, and simultaneously called upon the socialist countries to adopt a unified position in support of Vietnam. This maneuvered China into an uncomfortable position: from Beijing's point of view, the rationale behind the new Soviet engagement in Vietnam was to drive back China's influence and isolate the PRC internationally.[29]

If Beijing accepted Moscow's proposal, China would lose on the ideological frontline, as the PRC would thereby acknowledge the Soviet Union's lead in the socialist movement. On the other hand, Beijing was well aware that it could not compete with the quality of Moscow's military assistance. The only option left was thus to appeal to the Vietnamese comrades not to accept Moscow's support, or otherwise, as Zhou Enlai explained to Ho Chi Minh in March 1965, the bilateral relationship "may turn from good to bad."[30] Confronted with this decision, Hanoi apparently decided that, for the sake of Moscow's support, it could afford to alienate a long-standing ally. Even though the Vietnamese leadership carefully avoided openly taking sides until Ho Chi Minh's death in 1969, the distance between Hanoi and Beijing constantly grew.

In order to contextualize this development, King C. Chen's study on the North Vietnamese position in the Sino-Soviet rivalry provides a valuable reference point. At the onset of the Sino-Soviet split, North Vietnam had maintained a neutral stance and had tried to mediate between Moscow and Beijing. By mid-1963, however, Hanoi had sided openly with Beijing.[31] Writing in 1964, Chen concluded his analysis with the following findings:

> Since last fall, Hanoi has sided ever closer to Peking. ... There are two fundamental reasons for the shift to China. First, geographical contiguity is a vital force. The geographic position of North Vietnam makes China too near to be ignored, while Russia is too far away to serve as an effective balance. ... The second basic factor determining Hanoi's present position is revolutionary strategy. ... Hanoi has decided that the Chinese revolutionary strategy is more suitable than that of Russia.[32]

With regard to this positive development in Sino-Vietnamese relations, Chen noted that there was only one question left: "How far will Hanoi go with Peking? It is likely that the more serious the Sino-Soviet disputes becomes, the stronger Hanoi will support China. ... [Vietnam] cannot and will not openly offend China."[33] In short, at that point in time, Beijing could assume that the Vietnamese were undoubtedly on China's side in the struggle against 'Soviet revisionism.' Only two years later, however, the exact development ruled out by Chen took place: as relations between Hanoi and Moscow intensified, Vietnam dared to offend its loyal ally:

> Beijing's leaders ... noted with surprise that Vietnamese media began to use China's invasion of Vietnam in the past to spur patriotism among ordinary Vietnamese people. Convinced that the Vietnamese were in fact inclined toward Moscow, Beijing's leaders were genuinely offended.[34]

Moreover, when Vietnam's then de facto leader Le Duan declared in March 1966 that the Soviet Union would be his 'second motherland' – a gesture of respect he had never shown China – the Chinese leadership was "angrily shocked."[35]

The Soviet strategy of buying off Hanoi's loyalty thus apparently worked out. It soon became apparent that the relationship between China and Vietnam was about to crack under the increasing weight of the Soviet factor.[36] In early 1968, friction between Hanoi and Beijing arose, as Moscow now exercised considerable influence on the North Vietnamese conduct of warfare and Hanoi not only stood on the Soviet side when it came to operative and strategic decisions, but even accused China of interfering in Vietnam's sovereignty. As the CPVEF's subsequent withdrawal from Vietnam indicates, Beijing was surely affronted by Vietnam's attitude, which it regarded as ungrateful and increasingly disrespectful.[37] Even set against these severe setbacks and the substantial cooling-off in Sino-Vietnamese relations, however, Beijing remained committed to supporting Hanoi until the fall of Saigon in 1975. Nonetheless, the brotherly comradeship between China and Vietnam was not to survive the Second Indochina War.

Phase II: Drifting apart

By 1969 it had become clear that China had suffered a loss in Vietnam, while the Soviet Union had scored a gain. As a result, Sino-Vietnamese relations entered an intermediary phase that lasted until the end of the Vietnam War. Although the relationship could no longer be characterized as being "as close as lips and teeth,"[38] it had not yet turned into open enmity. Beijing still hoped to prevent Hanoi's complete absorption into the Soviet orbit, and thus massively increased the assistance it provided. However, the quarrels between Beijing and Hanoi had already caused a gap of mutual mistrust and suspicion, which in turn allowed external factors to widen it to an unbridgeable extent. As China and Vietnam drifted further apart, the final years of the Vietnam War witnessed the full metamorphosis of the Sino-Vietnamese alliance into the Sino-Vietnamese split. Even before the war came to an end, China and Vietnam were already acting as proverbial enemies, with the occurrence of military clashes and the emergence of serious border disputes: "In a sense, the Third Indochina War began before the troops of the Second Indochina War had even exited the scene."[39]

The predominance of the Soviet factor in Vietnam

During the final phase of the Vietnam War, North Vietnam's conduct of warfare underwent a comprehensive Sovietization. As Hanoi's dependency on Moscow increased, the Soviet factor was further strengthened and Vietnam moved away from the Chinese positions on military and diplomatic strategies. Finally, after Ho Chi Minh, who had never ceased to emphasize the importance of socialist unity, passed away on September 2, 1969, his successor, Le Duan, headed an entirely pro-Soviet government.[40] In view of this, it was not surprising that Hanoi now openly sided with the Soviet Union even on non-Vietnamese issues, starting with Hanoi's support for the Soviet-led invasion of Czechoslovakia. To the great discontent of Beijing, increased Chinese assistance had not reversed this development.

China's strategic realignment: The United States and Cambodia

The year 1969 provided the Chinese leadership with two important insights. First, the Sino-Soviet border clashes not only finalized Beijing's split with Moscow, but also drastically revealed China's vulnerabilities *vis-à-vis* the Soviet Union. Second, Moscow was about to complete its strategic encirclement of the PRC, as Hanoi was moving substantially closer to the Soviet Union. In order to counter the looming threat to China's northern flank and to prepare for the completion of Vietnam's move to the Soviet side, Beijing's leadership had to reconsider China's global and regional strategies.[41] In doing so, geopolitical considerations gained priority over ideological zeal.

With Moscow having replaced the United States as China's primary enemy and Washington seeking a honorable exit from Vietnam, the famous report of the Four Marshals of September 1969 reached the conclusion that a window of opportunity had opened up to pursue a pragmatic step: China's rapprochement with the United States.[42] In secrecy, Beijing began to put out feelers to Washington. Over the course of the next two years, an informal framework of contact was established between China and the United States. The Sino-American rapprochement was kept private until July 1971, when President Nixon's visit to Beijing was announced.

At the same time, however, the Chinese leadership still had a genuine interest in preserving at least the status quo in Sino-Vietnamese relations. Beijing was well aware that improving ties between China and the United States might steer Hanoi into alignment with Moscow even more swiftly. In order to convince Hanoi that a Sino-American rapprochement would not come at the expense of the DRV, Beijing thus demonstrated increased impetus in supporting Vietnam. In 1970, Beijing therefore re-intensified its assistance to Vietnam, and in the following two years, Chinese provision of military and economic supplies to Hanoi reached record highs: despite the fact that Beijing needed to prepare itself for an expected Soviet invasion, the PRC spent more than nine billion yuan on military assistance to Hanoi.[43] Adding to this, the quality of China's supplies was also increased, as the assistance now included substantial numbers of tanks, naval vessels, and military vehicles, which were often directly transferred from the PLA to the North Vietnamese and played a crucial role in the success of the PAVN's Easter offensive in March 1972. With regard to the course of Hanoi's negotiations, Beijing switched its position from harsh criticism to formal support, and publicly endorsed the DRV's Seven Point Peace Plan of 1971.[44] Most remarkably, even with the evolving Sino-American rapprochement in the background, China resiliently reaffirmed its security commitments when the United States intensified the bombing of North Vietnam in 1970, and issued a series of stern warnings when U.S. troops invaded Laos in 1971.[45] Sino-Vietnamese joint communiqués "once again used strong language, which had been missing for eight years. … China was determined to take all necessary measures to support the Indochinese peoples, 'not flinching even from the greatest national sacrifices.'"[46] However, Beijing's attempt to re-intensify and strengthen the 'China factor' failed to lessen the impact of Nixon's visit in February 1972, which came as a shock to Hanoi. Even though the U.S. President also visited Moscow shortly afterwards, the Vietnamese, deeply offended, expressed much stronger bitterness toward China than toward the Soviet Union.[47] In order to limit the damage, Zhou Enlai flew twice to Hanoi to offer explanations, but Sino-Vietnamese relations had hit a low point. In Hanoi's perspective, China had betrayed Vietnam for a second time, after Beijing had already traded away the unity of Vietnam at the Geneva Conference.[48]

Chinese and Vietnamese interests then started to collide at the regional level. In order to hedge for the prospect of a unified and pro-Soviet Vietnam, as well as to prevent Hanoi's looming predominance over the whole Indochina region, China sought closer ties to Cambodia.[49] Historically, Cambodia had more than once been subdued by Vietnam, resulting in a strong anti-Vietnamese sentiment that could not even be bridged by shared ideology.[50] This made Cambodia a natural ally for Beijing's regional interests, which, however, ran contra to Hanoi's long-standing desire for its own sphere of influence: as Ho Chi Minh had outlined in his political testament, Vietnam should become the "paramount power that should, in effect, inherit the French mantle to exercise hegemony in Indochina."[51] Consequently, China and Vietnam competed rather than cooperated in Indochina: while Hanoi became the patron of Laos, Cambodia sided with Beijing.[52] When the Khmer Rouge seized power in April 1975, "the Chinese became the most trusted and powerful friends to them, whereas the Russians were treated like hated adversaries"[53] – and the Vietnamese as bitter enemies. Immediately after the end of the Second Indochina War, the Khmer Rouge began to act out this enmity by launching assaults deep into Vietnamese territory.[54] Beijing thus found itself indirectly entangled in an unwanted conflict with Vietnam.

Phase III: Ingratitude with Vietnamese characteristics

In April 1975, the Chinese leadership "greeted Hanoi's victory in the Second Indochina War with warm congratulations, looking forward to a future in which the Chinese people would 'continue unswervingly to unite and fight together with the Vietnamese peoples.'"[55] While it would be another four years before China and Vietnam eventually took up arms against each other, the 'unswerving unity' between Beijing and Hanoi was then already a relic of the past. Released from the burden of the war, blessed with unprecedented self-confidence as a new regional power, and backed by the Soviet Union, Hanoi assessed that the time was ripe to strike a balance with Beijing. The Vietnamese leadership now charged China with a long list of severe wrongdoings:

> It accused China of forcing Vietnam to accept the policy of prolonged ambush in order to prevent Vietnam from stepping up armed struggle in the South, and of turning on the green light for the United States to invade Vietnam. It also charged China with undermining the Soviet united action proposal, opposing Vietnam's negotiations … and preventing Hanoi from completely liberating South Vietnam. It further accused China of negotiating with the United States behind Vietnam's back.[56]

The Chinese leadership, greatly disturbed by the ungrateful behavior with which Hanoi repaid China's steadfast contribution, "lamented the loss of Chinese lives and the expenditure of so many resources for so little in return."[57] Beijing then opted for restraint and a wait-and-see policy. However, what the Chinese leadership then had to witness added furious anger to the already existing deep sense of Vietnamese ingratitude, as "the Cuba of the East"[58] now dared to openly challenge the People's Republic.

Territorial disputes

Beginning in 1975, territorial issues emerged as a source of friction between Hanoi and Beijing.[59] In particular, three bones of contestation existed: the course of the common land boundary, the jurisdiction over the Gulf of Tonkin, and the question of sovereignty over the Spratly and Paracel archipelagos in the South China Sea. In large part, existing scholarly analyses conclude that the territorial dispute played only a minor role in the bilateral conflict and thus did not function as a direct cause of the Sino-Vietnamese War's escalation.[60] However, as it was the Vietnamese side that reopened, in an almost revanchist manner, what in Beijing's perspective were already solved issues, the territorial dispute certainly added some bitterness to the resentment China already felt toward Hanoi. With regard to the demarcation of the land boundary, Beijing could aptly claim that in 1957 and 1958, China and Vietnam had agreed to respect the border as delineated by China and France in 1887. Concerning ownership of the Spratly and Paracel Islands, China had issued a declaration in September 1958 that explicitly stated the islands were Chinese territory. In contrast to Saigon, which had fundamentally denied this claim, the North Vietnamese government had been prompt in recognizing and supporting Beijing's declaration. Nor did Hanoi issue a formal claim in response when the PRC seized control of the Paracel Islands in 1974. Accordingly, Beijing assumed that the DRV – in line with the previous declarations – also accepted the legitimacy of China's claim.[61]

However, Hanoi reversed its policy on territorial issues after 1974. Hanoi then declared its sovereignty over the Paracels and refused to hand over to China the Spratly Islands, which had been occupied by South Vietnam in 1973.[62] Adding to this, apparently Vietnamese-initiated incidents along the Sino-Vietnamese border which had started to occur in the aftermath of Nixon's visit to China increased markedly after 1975 and came to a head in 1978, resulting in at least 300 Chinese military and civilian casualties.[63]

The expulsion of the Hoa-Chinese from Vietnam

The same year saw the mass exodus of the Hoa-Chinese from Vietnam. As King C. Chen has assessed, for China's leadership, the mistreatment and expulsion of ethnic Chinese by Vietnamese authorities then became the "most explosive and emotional issue"[64] in Sino-Vietnamese affairs. Traditionally, ethnic Chinese minorities existed in North and South Vietnam, but in contrast to the 300,000 Hoa in the DRV, the 1.2 million overseas Chinese in South Vietnam were an economically important and well-organized minority that publicly maintained their cultural heritage.[65] As they were not integrated into society but were economically better off than most Vietnamese, the Hoa maintained a complex position in post-war Vietnam. Accordingly, the Hoa were among those that had suffered most from the socio-economic reforms that were introduced from 1975 to 1978, as the majority then lost the basis of their lives literally overnight. In addition, the wealthy Chinese business families also became convenient targets for increasingly heated Vietnamese nationalist and anti-Chinese sentiments.[66] Even though Beijing was certainly aware of and concerned by Vietnamese authorities' mistreatment of Hoa-Chinese, it was in no position to interfere in Vietnam's internal affairs. Consequently, the PRC did not raise the Hoa issue until 1978.

Once the boundary had become a source of conflict between Beijing and Hanoi, in late 1977 the Vietnamese introduced a policy of 'purifying' the border, and all non-Vietnamese residents of the disputed areas became subject to deportation. Hanoi's rationale for this action was that China's claim would lose substance if only ethnic Vietnamese populated the disputed territories. Moreover, as Vietnam and China were then increasingly beginning to view each other as enemies, Hanoi was worried that the PRC might utilize the Hoa as a 'fifth column' in order to undermine Vietnam's authority and control in the disputed areas. This perception contributed to the harsh measures taken against the Hoa.[67] In March 1978, the Vietnamese authorities systematically intensified the pressure, confiscating at least 50,000 Chinese businesses and relocating 320,000 Hoa to rural areas of Vietnam, which finally led to the mass exodus of ethnic Chinese.[68] China vociferously condemned the Vietnamese action, cut down aid projects, and warned "the Vietnamese Government [that it would] bear full responsibility for all the consequences arising from these unwarranted measures."[69] Beijing dispatched two ships in order to evacuate the overseas Chinese who were willing to leave the country. Hanoi, however, refused permission for port entry, and China's evacuation mission failed. As Beijing thus had to stand idly by, watching hundreds of thousands of Chinese being driven out of the country and being systematically mistreated by Vietnamese authorities, emotions started to run high in China, and not only among the political and military leaders: many Chinese thought that Hanoi "was ungrateful for [China's] aid and sacrifice. There was a public outpouring of anger against Vietnam."[70]

Vietnam's invasion of Cambodia

On December 25, 1978, Vietnam launched a military offensive against Cambodia. In fewer than 14 days, the PAVN captured Phnom Penh and overthrew the Chinese-supported Khmer Rouge. Hanoi's attack was the result of a reciprocal increase of violence at the Vietnamese–Cambodian border, which had started in 1975 with naval clashes and raids on Vietnam's border outposts. In 1977, Pol Pot's Khmer Rouge then had set off a spiral of escalation by killing hundreds of Vietnamese civilians in numerous incursions into Vietnamese territory.[71] Vietnam retaliated, but even massive counterattacks failed to deter the Khmer Rouge. The rapid deterioration of the situation convinced Hanoi that only decisive military action would restore security along the border and enable Vietnam's predominance over the Indochina region. Accordingly, Hanoi decided to impose regime change in Phnom Penh.[72] When the Cambodian capital fell, Beijing lost its only remaining ally in Indochina; more than that, however, Vietnam's military action compromised the PRC, which "infuriated China's top civilian and military leaders."[73] Despite issuing sharp warnings and angry condemnations, China had not been able to stop the Khmer Rouge falling victim to Hanoi's offensive. China thus had lost face and was now "faced with a credibility problem. It was under tremendous pressure to do something to show that it was not soft and helpless."[74] However, at this time the decision to punish Vietnam had already been made, as foreshadowed in Deng Xiaoping's statement of January 6: "China must one day be obliged to take measures contrary to its wishes for peace."[75]

The common denominator: the Soviet Union

By late 1968, Sino-Vietnamese tensions had developed into a full-fledged crisis. In search of the rationale for Hanoi's increasingly provocative and assertive attitude toward the PRC, the Chinese leadership identified a common denominator that revealed itself in all three issues under contestation: the ever more visible hand of the Soviet Union on Hanoi's shoulder.[76]

When the border situation worsened, Vietnam had promptly received diplomatic backing, expressions of support, and military backup from Moscow. The Soviet Union had also strengthened its naval presence in the South China Sea and openly supported Hanoi's maritime claims. Furthermore, the Chinese leadership was convinced that "the Soviet Union was behind the expulsion of Chinese residents from Vietnam,"[77] as the director of the department for Overseas Chinese Affairs publicly declared in June 1978. Last, it was the Soviet Union that had encouraged Vietnam's ambitions for regional hegemony by providing a carte blanche for Hanoi's attack on Cambodia: in November 1978, Moscow and Hanoi concluded a treaty of friendship and cooperation that included a mutual defense agreement.[78] The Chinese leadership well understood that the new Soviet–Vietnamese military alliance was aimed against China, and that it spurred Vietnam's dreams of hegemony: "Vietnam," as Deng Xiaoping bluntly stated at the peak of the crisis, "is leaning towards the Soviet Union, which is the enemy of China."[79]

In Beijing's perception, Hanoi had become actively involved in the Soviet Union's global strategy, or, in less polite words, had revealed its true face as the Soviet Union's "running dog"[80] in Southeast Asia. With Vietnam's open defection to Moscow, tensions between Beijing and Hanoi escalated and the Sino-Vietnamese split was finalized. For Beijing, it was thus no coincidence that the clashes on the Sino-Vietnamese border, Vietnam's mistreatment and expulsion of overseas Chinese, and Hanoi's military action against Cambodia peaked in late 1978, when the Soviet–Vietnamese alliance was concluded. As Li Xiaobing observes, "[i]n the Chinese view, North Vietnam [had then become] an ingrate challenging China under Soviet protection."[81]

Interim conclusion: from comradeship to enmity

Over the course of three stages, Sino-Vietnamese relations underwent a complete metamorphosis: what had started as brotherly comradeship ended in bitter enmity. In essence, two strands of reason are responsible for this transformation. On the one hand, Chinese and Vietnamese strategic interests collided, as Vietnam's ambitions for its own sphere of influence in Indochina ran contra to China's interest: facing the Soviet ring of encirclement's closure by a pro-Soviet Vietnam, Beijing sought to keep a balance in Indochina. In doing so, however, the PRC soon found itself unintentionally entangled in the Vietnamese–Cambodian conflict. However, it was only after the Soviet Union took the Vietnamese side in this conflict that "China increasingly decided to commit itself to Cambodia and started sending military supplies and advisors to Cambodia."[82] As a result, China and Vietnam found themselves engaged in a regional conflict. At the international level, the Sino-American rapprochement drove the two actors further apart. Despite Beijing comprehensively fulfilling its commitments to Hanoi in order to prevent the widening of the existing gap in bilateral relations, Moscow was swift in exploiting this opportunity and increased the Soviet factor in Vietnam. Consequently, Beijing and Hanoi finally stood on two antagonistic sides in the Sino-Soviet rivalry.

On the other hand, my analysis has demonstrated that the emergence of these geopolitical considerations was clearly preceded, and thus affected, by an evident variation in the social structure of the bilateral relationship. Given its decisive assistance to Vietnam in both Indochina Wars, Beijing could aptly claim that Hanoi owed its independence and survival to the PRC. In committing itself to Vietnam's struggle for independence and unification, China also prioritized its socialist obligations over national interests, as Beijing's comprehensive security guarantees evidently demonstrate. However, the harmony in Sino-Vietnamese relations was noticeably disturbed by the increased Soviet factor in Vietnam. Against this background of Sino-Soviet rivalry, the established narrative that the Second Indochina War was a proxy war between capitalism and a united Communist front is thus highly questionable. Rather, the Vietnam War discloses itself as a battleground for the Sino-Soviet rivalry that materialized in competition for influence in Hanoi, while North Vietnam fought a war for national unification. In this line of argument, the United States and China both lost the Vietnam War: the former on the battlefield, and the latter with regard to Hanoi's loyalty. When the Soviet factor then became predominant and Hanoi increasingly moved in opposition to China, Vietnam's ingratitude and lack of loyalty caused deep resentment in Beijing, because "[t]he Chinese viewed the Vietnamese as ingrates who reciprocated decades of Chinese aid and sacrifice with backstabbing."[83] In the post-war phase, Vietnam's ingratitude then materialized into what Beijing perceived as arrogant, disrespectful, and provocative Vietnamese policies against the People's Republic that were instigated and backed by the Soviet Union. Moreover, the analysis of this crucial phase in Sino-Vietnamese relations has revealed that each of the three issues under contestation, and particularly the mistreatment of the overseas Chinese, added frustration, bitterness, and anger to the Chinese leadership's already emotionally loaded state of mind. Eventually, the bilateral relationship hit the rocks with Vietnam's open defection to the Soviet Union. As I will show in the following section, the Chinese leadership had then already decided it would be necessary to teach Vietnam a punitive lesson in return for the arrogance it had shown.

For the sake of completeness, it should be noted that I was not able to single out a specific event that triggered China's decision to resort to force, as existing accounts on the decision-making process provide several, partly conflicting dates for its onset.

This might indicate that the Chinese leadership "debated again and again the issue of war against Vietnam,"[84] possibly beginning in mid-1978.[85] In view of this, it seems reasonable to argue that as all three issues under contestation showed a dramatic peak in intensity by 1978, their accumulation, combined with the conclusion of the Soviet–Vietnamese alliance in late 1978, apparently helped the Chinese leadership to arrive at the decision that "they could not tolerate the rampage of the small and ungrateful brother in the south"[86] any longer.

The decision: China takes revenge

According to King C. Chen and Andrew Scobell, the decision to resort to force against Vietnam was essentially made during the Central Work Conference that ran from November 15 to December 15, 1978, the most important CCP meeting in the post-Mao era to that date. "It was at the later session of the [conference] in December that the Chinese leadership tentatively decided to wage a 'punitive' war."[87] In early December, the CMC also started to specify the operative considerations for the upcoming campaign. Instructions were issued to the Kunming and Guangzhou Military Region to prepare for combat operations in Vietnam. The order clarified

> that the war would be strictly limited, conducted within 50 kilometers from the border and lasting two weeks. It then emphasized the core tenets of the PLA's traditional operation doctrine requiring the two regional commanders to "concentrate superior force to envelope the enemy force from flanks, to destroy the enemy forces one by one with quick-decision battles of annihilation, and then to withdraw immediately."[88]

Accordingly, China's decision to teach Vietnam a lesson pre-dated the Vietnamese invasion of Cambodia of December 25, 1978.

On New Year's Eve, Deng Xiaoping formally introduced before the Chinese leadership the idea of a punitive campaign against Vietnam. When Deng's proposal was approved, the decision to go to war against Vietnam had been basically taken. From then on, Deng elaborated operative considerations in private meetings and rushed to the capitals of Thailand, Japan, and the United States to disclose and clarify China's intentions with regard to the upcoming campaign.[89] Washington provided more than moral support for China, as the United States offered valuable intelligence information on the crucial Soviet troop deployments along the Sino-Soviet border.[90] Eventually, on February 16, just hours before the onset of the invasion, a briefing on the upcoming attack took place in Beijing. Even though Chairman Hua Guafeng officially headed the meeting, it was Deng Xiaoping's responsibility to outline the characteristics of the lesson China intended to teach Vietnam. According to Deng, the military action should unfold as a limited, 'self-defense counterattack' similar to the Chinese offensive against India in 1962. The extent of the outbreak of violence was to be kept deliberately limited, and thus no air or naval forces would be involved. The objective of China's invasion was, as Deng summarized, to give Vietnam a lesson. Vietnam had become extremely arrogant, boasting to be the third strongest military power in the world. Apart from invading Cambodia and expelling Chinese residents, Vietnam had also made repeated border incursions in China and killed Chinese soldiers as well as civilians. China had to fight back but would not take an inch of Vietnamese territory. As soon as Chinese forces had achieved the objectives, they would unilaterally withdraw.[91]

When compared with the other cases of China's use of force investigated in this book, the decision-making process for China's military campaign against Vietnam reveals three specific characteristics. First, it was the first major foreign-policy decision made after the two most senior Chinese leaders, Mao Zedong and Zhou Enlai, passed away in 1976. The position of paramount leader was then still vacant, even though Deng was getting ready to occupy it. Thereby, the Sino-Vietnamese crisis played a crucial role. The PRC's Vice Premier and Chief of the PLA General Staff had not only been the first Chinese leader to openly convey to Hanoi China's displeasure over Vietnam's behavior, but was also a strong proponent of answering the arrogance shown by Vietnam with a military blow. As Zhang Xiaoming observes, Deng's

> annoyance with Vietnam's ungracious attitude towards China's aid can be traced back to the mid-1960s. As animosity between the two countries intensified in the late 1970s, he became increasingly sentimental, even once calling Vietnam the *wangbadan* [translated literally as "tortoise eggs" but, when contextualized, as "S.O.B."] in front of a foreign leader.[92]

Deng exercised great influence over the decision-making, for several reasons. He occupied a crucial position at the interface between civilian and military leadership. In addition to this, of the CCP's contemporary leadership triumvirate of Chairman Hua Guafeng and Vice-Chairmen Ye Jianying and Deng Xiaoping, Deng enjoyed the most seniority, especially in foreign-policy issues, and also had solid backing in the CCP Politburo. After the power struggle between Deng and Hua in late 1978, it was Deng that had become China's de facto leader and thus the PRC's principal decision-maker on Vietnam.[93]

The second characteristic of the decision-making process is that opposition to a military action against Vietnam was virtually absent. Those inside the leadership "who had assisted the Vietnamese communists in their wars against the French and Americans felt particularly betrayed and were eager to 'teach Vietnam a lesson'."[94] When disagreement emerged, it basically concerned the concrete extent of China's military campaign. While some leaders argued for a heavier blow to Hanoi, others – including Deng – were in favor of keeping the outbreak of hostilities decidedly limited.[95]

Third, the relatively long-simmering Sino-Vietnamese crisis had enabled the Chinese leadership to consider the whole range of political and military options before the crisis sharpened in late 1978. However, even though the decision to resort to force was thus carefully thought out, it revealed foremost an emotional response to Vietnam's all-around "anti-China" (*fan-Hua*) actions. The phrase "teach Vietnam a lesson" is itself filled with emotion. ... The contempt and venom for Hanoi among Beijing's leaders was patently evident in the way they spoke about Vietnam to officials from other countries.[96]

These three characteristics indicate that the final decision to resort to force against Vietnam was heavily affected by the emotional dimension of the Sino-Vietnamese dispute: "China's clearly stated desire to 'teach Vietnam a lesson' conveyed its foremost war objective to be an 'act of revenge'."[97]

China's Vietnam War: assessing the risks

Although the decision to resort to force against Vietnam was apparently the result of careful considerations, two major strands of risk were nonetheless incorporated in China's punitive campaign: the possibility of a debacle on the battlefield and the risk of Soviet retaliation. The analysis in the following section demonstrates that these risks were clearly known to Beijing. Although the Chinese leaders were notably concerned with the question whether their forces had enough time to prepare adequately for the invasion, they nevertheless were apparently willing to accept the implicated risks. In the following, I provide an assessment of the PLA's state of preparedness in 1979. I then present and discuss the Chinese leadership's assessment of the anticipated risks and Deng Xiaoping's evaluation. Finally, I examine the Chinese calculations of risk concerning a Soviet military response to China's punitive lesson to Vietnam. I conclude by assessing China's overall risk behavior.

The state of combat-readiness of China's armed forces in 1979

Almost ten years after the Sino-Soviet border clashes of 1969, there had been no substantial improvement in the PLA's inadequate level of preparedness for conducting combat operations abroad under the conditions of modern warfare. On the contrary, the PLA was in an embarrassing condition at that time, as three factors further undermined the PLA's combat-readiness: the repercussions of the Sino-Soviet split, which had blocked China's access to modern weaponry and technology; the still noticeable deficits in China's armament industry; and, probably most important, the reversion of Peng Dehuai's military reforms in the aftermath of the Great Leap Forward. The two former factors were discussed in the previous case study; this analysis focuses on the impact of Lin Biao's counter-reforms and on the specific shortcomings of the PLA, which surfaced just before the offensive against Vietnam was about to take place.

The impact of Lin Biao's military reforms

When Peng Dehuai became a victim of the Cultural Revolution, his military reforms, which had enabled the PLA's crushing victory over India in 1962, were also swiftly abandoned. Instead, his successor Lin Biao introduced a primarily ideologically based military doctrine, and the PLA subsequently took a fatal step backwards. Lin's conception rested on three key points. First, he strongly argued in favor of a massive concentration of troops as a prerequisite for offensives. Second, his reforms significantly curtailed autonomous decision-making in the lower ranks, as he was convinced that only senior commanders should issue orders on the battlefield. Third, Lin glorified the frontal assault, denigrating technical equipment as only an aid to, never a substitute for, bravery.[98] Accordingly, the bloody and ineffective human-wave assaults quickly reentered the PLA's tactical inventory. "Lin's tactical guidance, the return to the doctrine of massed attacks, set the PLA on the route to the disaster it was to experience twenty years later in battle against the disciplined, hardened soldiers of the PAVN."[99] Most importantly, however, Lin Biao's counter-reform closed a large number of military schools and significantly curtailed military training for PLA soldiers. Instead of combat training, the soldiers received intensive ideological education in order to form a loyal force dispositive for the CCP. As Edward O'Dowd observes, the "results were disastrous. Some soldiers had been in the armed forces for several years without ever touching a rifle, and some cadres could not lead troops."[100] Lin's military counter-reforms thus even amplified the Cultural Revolution's already negative effects on the PLA's state of preparedness. The product was politicized but unprofessional soldiers throughout the rank and file of the PLA, who lacked the technical education and leadership skills necessary for combat operations in modern warfare. It is thus not surprising that "many officers reported that they were unsure about the fighting capability of their troops"[101] when their units underwent intensive military training for virtually the first time: from late December to January 1979, the Chinese units earmarked for the pending campaign rushed into combat training, as many of the soldiers had only recently been conscripted, or had been assigned to non-military duties. Especially with regard to China's opponent, which was fielding soldiers who for decades had done nothing other than to successfully withstand seemingly superior enemy forces, this

> frantic last-minute effort [of remilitarizing the PLA] was, though helpful, definitely insufficient. Training was largely concentrated on basic soldier skills such as shooting and grenade throwing, with few units able to carry out any meaningful tactical training or exercise at regiment and division level.[102]

Deficits in leadership

In the years before China's war against Vietnam, two demobilization campaigns had swept through the ranks of the PLA that had extensively thinned out the numbers of experienced veterans. Consequently, the PLA had great difficulty in manning the crucial leadership positions at company and platoon level.[103] Shortly before the onset of the campaign, an army-wide search for replacements began and soldiers with less than two years of service were hurriedly promoted into commanding functions without having received proper training or preparation.

A typical platoon leader in 1978 would probably have had eight or ten years of military service. But in 1979, the situation was no longer typical, and the use of these younger men in key leadership positions created problems. They lacked the technical and leadership experience ... and sometimes they were defeated by basic military tasks.[104]

The same pragmatic solution was employed to fill vacant commands at battalion and regiment level. To illustrate the extent of these measures, the case of China's 41st Army might serve as a telling example: one week before the offensive, half of the unit's 11 regiments received new commanding officers, and about one quarter of the 4,500 cadres were fresh on duty.[105] Beijing was clearly aware of these striking deficits in the leadership of the Chinese troops. Furthermore, as around 80 percent of the cadres would directly participate in combat operations, it was thus obvious that replacements would be required for losses that occurred. However, as no replacements were available, the Chinese leadership thus tolerated the prospect of waging a war without a sufficient number of adequately qualified and prepared military leaders at hand.

Low morale across the rank and file

The PLA's last-minute attempt to patchwork units and commanders resulted in a further decrease in the troops' morale, which had already been remarkably low, as many soldiers could not grasp the political rationale behind their mission.[106] The longer-serving soldiers in particular could barely understand why they were now ordered to lead their units against their former brothers-in-arms. The political dimension of the campaign also affected the morale of the ordinary soldiers, among them a remarkably high number of just recently conscripted recruits, as a war between two socialist brother states heavily contradicted the ideological worldview into which they had been socialized.[107] To make matters worse, these soldiers were not only ordered to fight a war they did not understand and for which they felt inadequately prepared, but also marched to battle under commanders with whom they were unfamiliar. All this degraded the troops' morale. The PLA leadership, in continuation of its military tradition, then made extensive use of political mobilization in order to raise morale and improve combat efficiency. However, while propaganda might have convinced the soldiers of the political necessity to wage a war against Vietnam, it was obviously not an adequate measure to increase the troops' self-confidence and trust in their military commanders, and vice versa.[108] Despite intensive political indoctrination, the "political officers of the deployed PLA units [thus] faced enormous problems in readying their troops for combat."[109]

Obsolete weaponry

Quantitatively, the Chinese forces had a decisive edge over the PAVN in terms of heavy weaponry. However, the majority of the PLA's 10,000 tanks and 20,000 artillery pieces and rocket launchers were not only outdated but also in poor condition. In contrast, the Vietnamese forces could draw on a large amount of modern Soviet weaponry and on armaments left behind by the United States.[110] China's air-warfare capabilities were also drastically limited, as the PLAAF's inventory still resembled the state-of-the-art of the 1950s. Of a total of 4,100 interceptors, China's most advanced jets were 80 domestically produced MiG-21, but even these aircraft were no match for the Vietnamese MiG-23 and MiG-25, because China's industry lacked the capacity to produce reliable jet engines. Edward O'Dowd argues that China's shortcomings in air power probably played a role in Beijing's decision to limit the campaign against Vietnam to ground operations only. Even though China had amassed a large number of planes, the PLAAF did not engage in a single air-to-air combat encounter or in tactical ground support during the war.[111] The "real reason" for China's reluctance to commit air-force units to battle is thus "probably found in the sober calculation of the possibility of winning."[112] China's MiG-19 pilots were highly skeptical about their ability to compete with their experienced and capable Vietnamese counterparts, who had shot down three times as many U.S. planes during Operation 'Rolling Thunder' as were lost. In view of this, the conclusion may have suggested itself that the battle against the superior Vietnamese MIGs was one better to be avoided.

Last, the PLA's logistics also revealed striking deficits. Even though the area of operation lay only a few kilometers outside China, supplies did not reach the frontline in sufficient quantities during the whole course of the campaign.[113] The principal reasons for this shortcoming are to be found in the PLA's overall lack of preparedness and its systematically deficient organization. One particular episode provides an illustrative example of the twofold nature of the PLA's supply problem. Shortly after the onset of the campaign, a PLA artillery regiment reported that over a third of its transport vehicles had failed, not because of combat losses but due to technical problems: "If this was the case with a piece of equipment that the unit could reasonably be expected to have used frequently during peacetime, the mechanical problems found with little-used or stored equipment must have been daunting."[114]

The PLA en route to Vietnam: the leadership's assessment

In summing up the PLA's encompassing deficits, the conclusion suggests itself that the Chinese forces were definitely not in a sufficient state of preparedness to successfully launch a decisive offensive against a battle-hardened, well-prepared, and well-equipped enemy that had already forced the French army and the United States' armed forces into inglorious retreats. Even though the Chinese leadership was quite aware of the obvious inexperience and low morale in the ranks of the PLA, as well as the deficits in leadership and weaponry, the implications arising from this were not regarded as overly problematic, as Beijing heavily underestimated Vietnam's military power.[115] In December 1978, Deputy Defense Minister Su Yu assessed that the PLA

> could take Hanoi in one week with only partial strength of the Guangzhou and Kunming Military Regions. In fact, it took the PLA 16 full days to capture Lang Son (85 miles to Hanoi) with a strength of 10 divisions drawing from six

military regions – a strength almost as much as that of the Guangzhou and Kunming MR combined.[116]

Nonetheless, the military's apparent deficits in terms of conducting large-scale operations could not be so easily dismissed, especially as they became more pronounced as the onset of the campaign approached. On January 22, Deng Xiaoping received an alarming report on the PLA's overall lack of combat-readiness, which included a proposal to postpone the invasion for a month.[117] The Chinese leadership thus agreed to delay the offensive until mid-February. On this occasion, Deng put forward an assessment of the situation that may best depict the Chinese risk calculations: in his view,

> the war would bring China neither a great victory, nor a disaster. In dispelling the fear of a military failure, Deng argued that China might achieve about 70 percent of its war objectives. The 30 percent failure would serve as a stimulus for military improvement. It would actually help China's military modernization.[118]

In other words, while Beijing's leadership could see that the PLA was not in a sufficient state of preparedness to achieve all operative objectives, Deng regarded the campaign as a valuable exercise under live-fire conditions, and the risk of a military failure was more than apparent even before the first shot was fired. Against a substantial record of the PLA's shortcomings, the Chinese leadership was obviously willing to take this risk in order to execute China's revenge.

The threat to the north: the Soviet factor in Beijing's risk calculation

In considering the upcoming campaign, the Chinese leadership had to worry not only about the PLA's performance on the battlefield, but also about the possibility of Soviet military action in response to China's invasion. As demonstrated in the previous case study, China had revealed serious vulnerabilities *vis-à-vis* the Soviet Union, and Moscow's military pressure in the aftermath of the border clashes had provided the Chinese leaders with a foretaste of its military might. In the following, the Soviet Union had further strengthened its force posture in the Far East, so that in the mid-1970s about one million Soviet troops were deployed near the Sino-Soviet border, equipped with conventional and nuclear weaponry far superior to China's.[119] Consequently, as the threat of a full-scale Soviet invasion was not to vanish until the mid-1980s, the Chinese leadership had to take this eventuality into account when preparing an attack on a formal Soviet military ally.[120]

Considerations related to the Soviet response to China's invasion thus revealed themselves as the most worrisome obstacle during the decision-making process. The Chinese leadership anticipated three possibilities:

> a massive armed incursion including a direct attack on Beijing; instigation of the armed ethnic minority personnel, who were exiled in the Soviet Union, to attack China's outposts in Xinjiang and Inner Mongolia; or use of skirmishes to mount border tensions between the two countries.[121]

While the latter two scenarios incorporated a rather tolerable amount of risk, because the PLA would have been capable of handling these threats effectively, the former variant clearly implied the potential for open war between China and the Soviet Union.[122] In mid-1969, this prospect had forced Mao to abandon China's confrontational course and give in to Moscow's pressure. Ten years later, under virtually the same preconditions regarding the balance of forces and China's latent vulnerabilities in the north, the possibility of a large-scale invasion of Soviet armored forces heading toward Beijing under cover of superior air power had to be reconsidered. This time, however, the realization of this worst-case scenario would have meant that China found itself engaged in a two-front war, and on the northern frontline the enemy's military superiority was well known to Beijing.[123] Consequently, the risk of a Soviet military reaction could not be dismissed.

Before the onset of the campaign, Beijing thus evacuated about 300,000 inhabitants from the most exposed provinces and ordered the entire northern front to maximum alert.[124] These measures were evidently taken as precautions against a possible Soviet strike, and as their extent indicates, the Chinese leadership apparently calculated for more than just border clashes. However, while Beijing's contingency planning thus incorporated a Soviet military response, Deng Xiaoping's personal assessment of the unlikelihood of large-scale military action ruled out this obviously prohibitive risk during the decision-making process. Based on U.S. intelligence reports, which indicated that the Soviet Union had deployed only 430,000–450,000 soldiers to the Chinese border, Deng reached the conclusion that "with so few troops the Soviet forces could not drive rapidly toward Beijing. [Accordingly,] it was thus unlikely that the Soviet Union would launch a large-scale attack on China."[125] This does not mean, as Andrew Scobell observes, "that Deng threw caution to the wind; he was very concerned about the conflict escalating into a larger conflagration involving the Soviet Union."[126] In order to prevent the conflict from escalating uncontrollably, Deng advocated for a decisive but short campaign. He was convinced that by limiting the outbreak of hostilities in time and extent and by communicating this intent to Moscow and Hanoi, the possibility of Soviet intervention could be minimized. Immediately after the onset of the war, Beijing thus stated repeatedly that the campaign was strictly limited and that the PLA would be withdrawn after achieving China's war objectives.[127] Apparently, these measures proved capable of substantially reducing the danger of a Soviet intervention: even though Moscow responded with strong words, emphasizing its treaty obligations to Hanoi and warning China to "take its hands off Vietnam" and "stop before it is too late," no action followed on the Sino-Soviet border.[128]

Ex post facto, Deng Xiaoping's assessment did prove true. But when approached from the *ex ante* perspective, these sober considerations were nonetheless a quite risky gamble – one the Chinese leadership was obviously willing to take. In particular, Beijing could not be certain about the extent of Moscow's reaction, as China's military attack on Vietnam simultaneously brought the Soviet Union's credibility as a military ally under fire.[129] As my case study of China's intervention in Korea demonstrated (Chapter 3), the Chinese leadership should have been quite familiar with the necessity to weigh obligations against particular interests – and the corresponding outcomes. China's attack on Vietnam now forced Moscow into the same appreciation of values. With regard to the already tense situation between China and the Soviet Union, Beijing thus could not have been certain that the Kremlin would not feel it necessary to teach China a lesson in order to preserve Moscow's credibility as an alliance partner, and the Soviet Union's standing in Asia.

Interim conclusion: gambling with high stakes

As my analysis has shown, the Chinese leadership was apparently willing to take substantial risks in order to teach Vietnam a lesson. By knowingly deploying insufficiently prepared and equipped troops to battle, Beijing risked a military debacle on its southern front. Moreover, by proactively attacking one of Moscow's treaty allies, China risked becoming entangled in an open confrontation with the Soviet Union on its northern front, too. China was barely prepared to cope with the materialization of just one of these prospects, as each of them revealed itself as a gamble with some serious unknowns for Beijing. However, the Chinese leadership, and particularly Deng, were obviously willing not only to accept the risks incorporated in each single prospect but also to take into account the possibility of their combined materialization at the same time: the latter clearly incorporated a prohibitive amount of risk, but in order to take their revenge on Hanoi, Deng and the other Chinese leaders were apparently willing to shoulder this worst-case prospect. While China could assert control over the level of escalation on the southern battlefield, Beijing's calculations transferred to the Kremlin the crucial decision whether or not to set aflame the Sino-Soviet border. Although the Chinese leadership made attempts to control this risk, Beijing's calculation was nonetheless a high-risk venture that could have easily had dramatic consequences.[130] Beijing, however, "was spoiling for a fight"[131] and, as Deng Xiaoping told Japanese journalists on February 26, had "no fear of the Soviet Union."[132]

Revenge with Chinese characteristics: China's lesson in the field

On February 15, 1979 – exactly 24 hours after the 1950 Sino-Soviet Alliance Treaty could be legally terminated – Beijing announced its intention to attack Vietnam in a limited campaign. Adding to this, Beijing warned the Kremlin on the following day that China was prepared to wage a full-scale war if the Soviet Union dared to attack the PRC.[133] The next day, China and Vietnam were at war.

> The opening of hostilities on February 17 came as no surprise. In addition to the many incidents in preparation for the PLA attack, military preparations were massive. Ten of China's eleven military regions contributed forces. These included some 20 divisions, 300,000 troops, 700–1000 aircraft, 1,000 tanks, and 1,500 pieces of artillery.[134]

With regard to this massive concentration of military power, Edward O'Dowd aptly assesses the offensive against Hanoi as "similar in scale to the assault with which China made such an impact on its entry into the Korean War",[135] which highlights the punitive element inherent in China's use of force against Vietnam. The PLA theatre commander, General Xu Shiyou, "responded to the central leadership's war requirements with an approach known as *niudao shaji* (using a butcher's knife to kill a chick)"[136] – an approach suggestive of massive violence. By assembling an attack force that outnumbered the defenders by at least six to one, Beijing aimed for a quick, decisive, and painful blow: in a nutshell, the "Chinese wanted to demonstrate that their military force could wreak heavy damage on Vietnam at little relative costs to China, that the Vietnamese could not guarantee their own security, and that the Soviets would not come to Vietnam's defense."[137]

I now turn to analysis of the course of China's campaign, which can be divided into three phases. The initial phase (February 17–26) consisted in a fiercely conducted attack on two separate fronts, aiming for the three capitals of Vietnam's border provinces. During the second phase (February 27–March 4) the offensive primarily focused on Lang Son, a strategically important city for the defense of Hanoi. Eventually, after Beijing's objectives were achieved, the Chinese forces began withdrawing from Vietnam on March 5, concluding the third and final phase of China's Vietnam War.

The initial offensive: China's tanks against Vietnamese punji stakes

In the morning hours of February 17, Beijing unleashed its offensive on Hanoi. The opening of hostilities unfolded as a massive, fiercely executed, and powerful attack along three main axes: in the west, the Chinese attack aimed at Lao Cai, while in the east the PLA's primary targets were the provincial capitals Cao Bang and Lang Son. However, even though the PLA enjoyed overwhelming numerical superiority and the Chinese offenses were supported by intensive artillery barrages and spearheaded by tanks, a swift burst through the relatively weak Vietnamese defenses failed to materialize. Besides the unexpectedly strong Vietnamese resistance, the numerous deficits of China's armed forces were revealed markedly even at this early stage of the campaign, and significantly curtailed the PLA's combat effectiveness.[138]

First, the topographical setting in the area of operation reduced to absurdity Lin Biao's dictum that operations should only be commanded by senior officers: as "[t]he rugged terrain of the mountainous border area was substantially unfavorable to the movement of division-sized forces, [t]he Chinese were compelled to divide and re-divide their forces from the division to company and even platoon level."[139] This meant that the burden of command now rested primarily on the shoulders of junior and non-commissioned officers, a task for which they had not been educated and one with which they were unfamiliar.[140] Second, the PLA's overall lack of preparedness was revealed most drastically in terms of logistics. Even though the battlefield was located just beyond the border, the Chinese supply lines swiftly collapsed. Within days, the invading force ran short of supplies and ammunition. Communication equipment was also lacking or broke down, so that Chinese units occasionally had to rely on runners, flags, bugles, and sirens to exchange orders.[141] Third, the "PLA's tactics were not a Chinese strongpoint,"[142] as the previously noted deficits in combat training and military education were all the more pronounced on the battlefield. As PLA units of different branches had not been trained to conduct joint operations, coordination among artillery, infantry, and armored units was poor, and combined attacks thus lacked efficiency. Artillery troops "fired their guns with little awareness of the exact location of their targets. Their fire direction on occasion was simply based on observations of where the infantry appeared to be shooting."[143] The Chinese tanks, attacking without infantry support, swiftly found themselves stopped by the Vietnamese infantry and their skillful use of anti-tank weaponry.[144] In adherence to Lin's tactical principles, the Chinese infantry made extensive use of human-wave assault "to attain even the most minor of tactical objectives."[145] However, as the PLA's experiences in the Korean War had already demonstrated, the human wave is arguably the worst assault tactic against a well-prepared enemy in fortified positions. Consequently, the Chinese suffered considerably high casualties even in the very first days of the war – without achieving noteworthy territorial gains.

Hence, it was not until February 22 that the PLA finally managed to capture Lao Cai, which lay only one kilometer away from the border and had been defended by approximately 20,000 Vietnamese troops against 125,000 Chinese.[146] Cao Bang then fell three days later. Long columns of disabled tanks and skyrocketing Chinese casualty numbers revealed that the "men of the PLA had [had] the wrong idea of what to expect from their foe."[147] Accordingly, the already low morale of the Chinese troops dropped further. One PLA intelligence officer remembered:

> The war was incredible bloody and savage ... Those of us who had not been in Korea or India and who had never seen war before – we never believed that it would be like that ... We were really upset by the huge costs of the victory. ... We believed, we really believed, that if we applied the full force of the PLA that the Vietnamese would be shattered in a matter of hours, that we would be in Hanoi and Haiphong within a day or two.[148]

Instead of approaching Vietnam's capital, some Chinese units had by this point only managed to advance two kilometers into Vietnamese territory, but had already suffered high losses. The deepest Chinese advance at that time was only about 15 kilometers, while most of the available regular PAVN units were still held in reserve.[149] At the end of this initial phase, the fog of war had cleared: on the battlefield, the Chinese forces unexpectedly faced severe problems and had suffered dramatic losses. On the political frontline, Beijing publicly declared on February 25 that it had no intention to advance on Hanoi.[150] Adding to this, the Chinese leadership further explicated that the campaign would continue for approximately ten days, after which the Chinese troops would be withdrawn.

The battle for Lang Son and China's withdrawal

Against the series of setbacks in the first ten days, Beijing pushed the attack further. Fresh units were deployed to the frontline in order to enable the PLA's capture of Lang Son, which was apparently the central objective of China's campaign. As the city was of strategic importance for the defense of the Vietnamese capital, its "seizure ... would add to the significance of the lesson that Beijing planned to teach the

Vietnamese by exposing the vulnerability of Hanoi. For China, speedy success on this front was critical."[151]

The swift capture of Lang Son had failed to materialize, however, as a single Vietnamese division had managed to successfully defend the city and its surrounding heights against nine Chinese divisions. Hence, the Vietnamese resistance did not decrease until, on February 27, a second PLA army was deployed to support the attack. But it took another five days to completely surround the city, and the battle for Lang Son did not end until March 5. When the city finally fell to the PLA, however, the road to Hanoi had been opened. This was an important psychological victory for China, even though it seems highly unlikely that the PLA could have actually reached Hanoi without committing its entire strength and absorbing prohibitive losses.[152]

As the fall of Lang Son completed Beijing's war objectives, the Chinese govern-ment announced the end of the offensive and the PLA's withdrawal from Vietnam.[153] "Ironically, the Vietnamese government called, on the same day, for a nationwide general mobilization for the war."[154] Beijing warned Hanoi not to undertake any military action during the withdrawal. In response, Hanoi declared that in order to show Vietnam's good will and desire for peace, the PAVN would allow the Chinese invaders to withdraw. However, as Harlan Jencks observed, during the ten days of the withdrawal, "the [PAVN] followed just closely enough, and fired just enough artillery at the Chinese rear guard, to make a good show of it."[155] The Chinese forces left behind scorched earth. Apparently intended as one final punishment, the PLA destroyed and looted Vietnamese infrastructure during its withdrawal.[156] On March 17, when the last Chinese soldiers left Vietnamese territory, the Sino-Vietnamese War ended.

Striking the balance for China's Vietnam War

When evaluated from a military perspective, the lesson the Chinese wished to teach Hanoi turned into a debacle: "The PLA had amassed an enormous force and planned a war of 'quick decision', but it had failed utterly to make progress against the better-trained and more experienced PAVN."[157] It took the PLA three weeks to advance merely 20 kilometers into Vietnamese territory and seize the three provincial capitals. Against heavily outnumbered Vietnamese militia forces, the Chinese troops performed much more poorly than had been expected by Beijing's leadership, and also suffered far higher losses in men and material.[158] China's 'painful, little war' came at a toll of about 63,000 PLA casualties.[159] Militarily, it was China that had received an impressive lecture on the art of war. Hanoi appeared less impressed by China's military lesson: Vietnam neither withdrew from Cambodia nor refrained from the use of military force at the border. Over the following decade, a low-intensity border war took place between China and Vietnam, including frequent ground clashes and extensive artillery duels.[160] In the long-term perspective, Beijing's lesson for Vietnam thus came at the expense of China's security, but also forced Hanoi to station large PAVN contingents on its northern flank.[161]

In the final account, neither China nor Vietnam can aptly claim to have won the war. Even so, the war had an 'ultimate loser': the non-participating Soviet Union.[162]

While the Chinese leadership had initially framed the military lesson it wished to teach Vietnam primarily in terms of a "localized inter-state conflict rather than as part of China's global anti-hegemonic strategy,"[163] Beijing was swift to capitalize on Moscow's unwillingness to intervene and "publicly proclaimed that the USSR had broken its numerous promises to assist Vietnam."[164] Intended or not, China's attack against Vietnam greatly compromised the Soviet Union's credibility as an alliance partner. Before the eyes of the world, China had demonstrated that it did not fear attacking a Soviet ally and that it could get away with it unpunished. As Henry Kissinger observed, this bold move had historic consequences:

> A Soviet ally had been attacked by the Soviet Union's most vocal and strategically most explicit adversary, which was openly agitating for a containment alliance against Moscow – all this within a month of the conclusion of the Soviet-Vietnamese alliance. In retrospect, Moscow's relative passivity in the Third Vietnam War can be seen as the first symptom of the decline of the Soviet Union.[165]

When evaluated in terms of China's international strategy and standing, China's war against Vietnam can thus be regarded as a success.[166] In revealing the impotence of the Soviet 'paper polar bear,' China achieved a momentous political victory over Moscow.

Conclusion: warfare between comrades

I will now summarize the case study's central findings and approach the task of evaluating my two competing theoretical models' explanatory capacities in search of Beijing's motivation for its Vietnam War of 1979.

First, my analysis was able to furnish proof that China invaded Vietnam as a punishment. Beijing's declared intention was to 'teach Vietnam a lesson,' best understood as a strong Chinese desire to take revenge for Hanoi's slights against it. As the investigation of the decision-making process revealed, the Chinese leaders, with Deng Xiaoping taking the lead, were highly affronted by the arrogance Hanoi showed toward China. This collective and highly emotionalized state of mind apparently played the decisive role in fostering a strong consensus inside the Chinese leadership about the necessity to launch a military campaign against Vietnam.

Second, the underlying cause of China's resort to force is to be found in the breakdown of Sino-Vietnamese relations through the involvement of the Soviet Union. When Moscow and Beijing started to compete for Hanoi's loyalty in the wake of the Sino-Soviet split, the previously harmonious relationship between Beijing and Hanoi evolved into a triangular one and took a turn for the worse. As Hanoi moved closer to the Soviet Union, the social structure of Sino-Vietnamese relations was affected. My examination of the three phases in Sino-Vietnamese relations demonstrated that the negative developments in the social structure, i.e. the emotional dimension of Sino-Vietnamese relations, clearly preceded, and thereby affected, the emergence of strategic considerations that, in turn, drove Hanoi and Beijing further apart.

Third, Vietnam's increasingly provocative and disrespectful attitude toward China, which culminated in late 1978 with Hanoi's open alignment with the Soviet Union, revealed itself as the immediate cause for China's punitive campaign. As my analysis of the three contested issues has shown, these (material) bones of contention affected the way in which the Chinese leadership emotionally framed the bilateral conflict, and added strong resentment to what was perceived by the Chinese leadership as Vietnam's ingratitude toward China's steadfast contributions.

Fourth, Deng's outspoken bitterness toward Hanoi and his dominant position in the decision-making process show that personality played a significant role in China's decision to resort to force against Vietnam, as well as affecting the course of the overall Sino-Vietnamese conflict.[167] One might question whether China and Vietnam would have clashed in a war if the old guard – Mao Zedong, Zhou Enlai, and Ho Chi Minh – had still been in charge.[168]

Fifth, China went to war against Vietnam even though Beijing's leadership had arrived at the conclusion that Hanoi did not pose a substantial threat to China's territorial integrity and national security. While the bilateral territorial conflict had already escalated into violent clashes between Chinese and Vietnamese forces, these encounters were in no way substantial enough to be met with the sort of forceful and extensive military response that China eventually delivered on February 17, 1979. Security considerations only played a role in the Chinese decision to punish Hanoi militarily when it came to assessing the risks involved in the upcoming 'lesson.' As Vietnam had concluded a viable military alliance with the Soviet Union, the prohibitive risk of Soviet retaliation against China had to be taken into account. However, based on Deng's assessment, this significant strand of risk was essentially ruled out. In order to exert revenge on Vietnam, the Chinese leadership was not only prepared to gamble with high stakes, but also willingly accepted a substantial – potentially even disastrous – deterioration in China's security situation. Moreover, Beijing's leaders sent troops into battle that were neither adequately equipped nor sufficiently prepared to successfully fight a major war. The Chinese leaders were vividly aware of the PLA's many shortcomings and deficits but accepted them in order to punish Hanoi, and thus risked a military debacle for China on the battlefield.

Ned Lebow's Cultural Theory of International Relations is clearly at home with regard to these findings: China's relationship to Vietnam almost perfectly mirrored the patron–client relation of *spirit-based worlds*. Beijing, as a high-status actor, comprehensively fulfilled its social obligations – based on the shared *nomos* of socialist solidarity – to Hanoi during times of crisis, and thereby prioritized the common cause over China's immediate needs and particular interests. Accordingly, Beijing expected Hanoi's allegiance and support in return. But when Beijing was in need of Vietnam's loyalty, Hanoi decided to prioritize parochial interests by accepting Soviet support. This decision was apparently motivated by *appetite*, as it reflected a clear-cut cost–benefit calculation of weighting the Soviets' unconditional support and modern armaments against Beijing's conditional support. This development would not have been as problematic if the three actors of the triangle could have reached agreement on two points: the delineation of a status-hierarchy among them, and the outlining of an agreed-upon *nomos*. However, these two fundamental characteristics of a spirit-dominated society were then highly disputed, as China and the Soviet Union not only disagreed on the true interpretation of Communism, but were also rivals for the leadership position in the international socialist society. This explains why the Chinese leaders were so angrily affronted to learn that the Soviet Union's standing in Hanoi had grown. Nevertheless, they decided to continue to exercise China's social obligations, and competed with the Soviet Union in protecting and providing for Vietnam. As Hanoi's movement toward Moscow increased, the Chinese leadership started to anticipate the negative implications of an entirely pro-Soviet Vietnam for Beijing's regional strategic positioning, and eventually decided to employ an *appetite*-motivated hedging strategy. At the same time, however, my analysis has shown that Beijing was still genuinely interested in avoiding a collapse of the bilateral relationship, and thus intensified its support to Vietnam. This explains China's seemingly contradictory behavior in approaching the United States while simultaneously pouring enormous resources into the Vietnam War. Nevertheless, the breakdown of Sino-Vietnamese relations swiftly followed as Hanoi redefined its position *vis-à-vis* Beijing and increasingly challenged China's status in the aftermath of the Second Indochina War.

As the analysis of the contested issue demonstrated, the Chinese leadership framed Vietnam's provocations not in material terms, but primarily as arrogant slights and affronts against China. In late 1978, Vietnam even dared to show China up, infuriating the Chinese leaders – in particular, Deng Xiaoping. As Lebow reminds us, "such ... slight[s] can issue from equals, but provoke ... even more anger when [they come] from an actor who lacks the standing to challenge or insult us."[169] In Beijing's perspective, its small and ungrateful neighbor was certainly not in a position to allow itself such provocative behavior. As a result, the spirit-induced desire for revenge emerged and finally broke the ground with Vietnam's open and formal defection to the side of the Soviet Union. As Vietnam was then no longer a member of the same society as China, Beijing's military action did not reflect that of a duel; neither was it rule-guided. China's military punishment followed swiftly, was obviously not well prepared, and incorporated high risks, which nevertheless were willingly taken by Beijing's leaders. China was eager to fight, regardless of risks, costs, and casualties. The findings of my partial analyses unambiguously and strongly indicate that spirit was the dominant motive behind the punitive lesson China sought to teach Vietnam.

In contrast, Fearon's model is unable to generate any explanatory power for the case at hand, for three reasons. First, China acted in a highly risk-taking manner regarding its choice of strategy. Second, even though the conflict involved a divisible material issue, China did not resort to force in order to conquer the territory under dispute. Third, neither the commitment problem nor the existence of information asymmetries revealed itself as the central problem impeding a non-violent solution of the conflict, because China's stated desire for revenge collides by definition with the predominant interest in conflict resolution by non-violent means that is assumed by Fearon's rationalist explanation.

In sum, the analysis could not generate any evidence for the explanatory power of Fearon's model, and thus could not validate its hypothetical process. On the contrary, the findings of all partial analyses strongly confirm the process of escalation as outlined by Ned Lebow: imbalances at the individual level (Deng Xiaoping) were followed by imbalances on the collective level,[170] which then enabled the decision to resort to force. In addition, the analyses demonstrated the independent effect of emotions on the course of the Sino-Vietnamese relations and on its deterioration, as well as on China's decision to resort to force against its former ally. Accordingly, the breakdown of the brotherly comradeship functioned as the *antecedent condition*, while the *immediate cause* for China's spirit-motivated punitive invasion is to be found in Hanoi's provocative policies toward China, culminating in late 1978 with Hanoi's formal defection to the Soviet Union.

Notes

1 See Zhang, Xiaoming, *Deng Xiaoping's Long War: The Military Conflict between China and Vietnam, 1979–1991* (Chapel Hill, NC: The University of North Carolina Press, 2015), 1; Kissinger, Henry, *On China* (New York: The Penguin Press, 2011), 340; Khoo, Nicholas, *Collateral Damage. Sino-Soviet Rivalry and the Termination of the Sino-Vietnamese Alliance* (New York: Columbia University Press, 2011), 127–28; Zhai, Qiang, *China and the Vietnam Wars, 1950–1975* (Chapel Hill, NC: University of North Carolina Press, 2000), 214.
2 See Womack, Branly, *China and Vietnam: The Politics of Asymmetry* (Cambridge: Cambridge University Press, 2006), 192; Zhang, Xiaoming, "China's 1979 War with Vietnam: A Reassessment," *The China Quarterly* no. 184 (2005): 853; Chen, King C., *China's War with Vietnam, 1979: Issues, Decisions, and Implications* (Stanford, CA: Hoover Institution Press, 1987), xi; Dreyer, David R., "One Issue Leads to Another: Issue Spirals and the Sino-Vietnamese War," *Foreign Policy Analysis* 6, no. 4 (2010): 297–98. In contrast to that, other studies singled out specific factors such as changes in China's security environment – see Ross, Robert S., *The Indochina Tangle* (New York: Columbia University Press, 1988); Zhang, *Deng Xiaoping's Long War*, 5 – or Hanoi's invasion of Cambodia: see Mulvenon, James, "The Limits of Coercive Diplomacy: The 1979 Sino-Vietnamese Border War," *Journal of Northeast Asian Studies* 14, no. 3 (1995): 68–89.
3 Elliot, David W. P., "The Third Indochina Conflict: Introduction," in *The Third Indochina Conflict*, ed. Elliot, David W.P. (Boulder, CO: Westview Press, 1981), 2.
4 Scobell, Andrew, *China's Use of Military Force: Beyond the Great Wall and the Long March* (Cambridge: Cambridge University Press, 2003), 120.
5 Kissinger, *On China*, 368.
6 Dreyer, "One Issue Leads to Another," 279.
7 Westad, Odd Arne, "Introduction: From War to Peace in Indochina," in *The Third Indochina War. Conflict between China, Vietnam and Cambodia, 1972–79*, ed. Westad, Odd Arne and Quinn-Judge, Sophie (London, New York: Routledge, 2006), 4.
8 See Chen, Jian, "China and the First Indo-China War, 1950–1954," *The China Quarterly* no. 133 (1993): 86.
9 See Chen, Jian, *Mao's China and the Cold War* (London, Chapel Hill, NC: The University of North Carolina Press, 2001), 124–27.
10 Chen, Jian, *China's Road to the Korean War: The Making of the Sino-American Confrontation* (New York: Columbia University Press, 1994), 105.
11 See Li, Xiaobing, *A History of the Modern Chinese Army* (Lexington, KY: The University Press of Kentucky, 2007), 212.
12 See Duiker, William J., *China and Vietnam: The Roots of Conflict* (Berkeley, CA: Institute

13 Chen, *China's War with Vietnam*, 10.
14 Chen, "China and the First Indo-China War," 88; Zhang, *Deng Xiaoping's Long War*, 15.
15 Chen, *Mao's China*, 143.
16 See Westad, "From War to Peace in Indochina," 4.
17 Chen, Jian, "China's Involvement in the Vietnam War, 1964–69," *The China Quarterly* no. 142 (1995): 380.
18 See Kissinger, *On China*, 204; Chen, "China's Involvement in the Vietnam War," 362 fn. 23: "[T]here is little doubt from the Chinese documents that have been released that a US invasion of North Vietnam would have led to a war with China"; Westad, "From War to Peace in Indochina," 4.
19 Chen, "China's Involvement in the Vietnam War," 359.
20 See Garver, John W., "Sino-Vietnamese Conflict and Sino-American Rapproachment," *Political Science Quarterly* 96, no. 3 (1981): 447; Zhang, *Deng Xiaoping's Long War*, 27; Li, *A History of the Modern Chinese Army*, 251.
21 See Zhang, *Deng Xiaoping's Long War*, 22.
22 As early as March 1963, PLA Chief of Staff Luo Ruiqing declared that if the United States were to attack the DRV, "China would come to its defense." Following the expansion of the U.S. role in the war, Mao offered China's "unconditional support" in June 1964: see Chen, "China's Involvement in the Vietnam War," 359–60.
23 See Whiting, Allen S., *The Chinese Calculus of Deterrence: India and Indochina* (Ann Arbor, MI: The University of Michigan Press, 2001), 194–95; Khoo, Collateral Damage, 27.
24 Chen, "China's Involvement in the Vietnam War," 360–61, 65.
25 Cited in ibid., 367.
26 See Li, *A History of the Modern Chinese Army*, 222; Chen, *China's War with Vietnam*, 17.
27 Although the Soviet Union may have been able to compensate for cessation of China's material contribution, Moscow was nonetheless dependent on the Chinese railway system to transport such huge amounts of material to North Vietnam.
28 See Nguyen, Lien-Hang T., "The Sino-Vietnamese Split and the Indochina War, 1968–1975," in *The Third Indochina War: Conflict between China, Vietnam and Cambodia, 1972–79*, ed. Westad, Odd Arne and Quinn-Judge, Sophie (London/New York: Routledge 2006), 12–13; O'Dowd, Edward C., *Chinese Military Strategy in the Third Indochina War: The Last Maoist War* (London, New York: Routledge, 2007), 40; Gaiduk, Ilya V., *The Soviet Union and the Vietnam War* (Chicago, IL: Ivan R. Dee-Publishers, 1996), 216–17.
29 See Westad, Odd Arne *et al.*, "77 Conversations between Chinese and Foreign Leaders on the Wars in Indochina, 1964–1977," *Cold War International History Project, Working Paper No. 22* (Washington, D.C., 1998), 56 fn 82; Zhang, *Deng Xiaoping's Long War*, 24–25.
30 Cited in Westad *et al.*, "77 Conversations," 56.
31 See Garver, "Sino-Vietnamese Conflict," 447; Westad, "From War to Peace in Indochina," 4.
32 Chen, King C., "North Vietnam in the Sino-Soviet Dispute," *Asian Survey* 4, no. 9 (1964): 1035–36.
33 Ibid., 1036.
34 Chen, "China's Involvement in the Vietnam War," 382.
35 Ibid.
36 See Nguyen, "The Sino-Vietnamese Split," 13; Dreyer, "One Issue Leads to Another,"

303.
37 See Khoo, *Collateral Damage*; Nguyen, Manh Hung, "The Sino-Vietnamese Conflict: Power Play among Communist Neighbors," *Asian Survey* 19, no. 11 (1979): 1038; Garver, "Sino-Vietnamese Conflict," 450.
38 Womack, *China and Vietnam: The Politics of Asymmetry*, 162–63.
39 Nguyen, "The Sino-Vietnamese Split," 26.
40 See Chen, *China's War with Vietnam*, 23–26.
41 See Garver, "Sino-Vietnamese Conflict"; Nguyen, "The Sino-Vietnamese Split," 19–20.
42 See Kissinger, *On China*, 212.
43 See Zhang, *Deng Xiaoping's Long War*, 32; Chen, "China's Involvement in the Vietnam War," 379.
44 See Nguyen, "The Sino-Vietnamese Split," 22.
45 See Garver, "Sino-Vietnamese Conflict," 451–52.
46 Chen, *China's War with Vietnam*, 19.
47 See Dreyer, "One Issue Leads to Another," 303. "Soviet diplomats in Hanoi stressed to their Vietnamese counterparts that China's foreign policy effectively constituted both a 'betrayal' and an 'abandonment' of Vietnam, encouraging the DRV's leaders to assume a more independent course toward Beijing and to rely on Soviet support to stand firm against China's pressure": Zhang, *Deng Xiaoping's Long War*, 28.
48 See Chen, *China's War with Vietnam*, 21.
49 See O'Dowd, *The Last Maoist War*, 41; Zhang, *Deng Xiaoping's Long War*, 36–37; Kissinger, *On China*, 343.
50 See Nguyen, "The Sino-Vietnamese Split," 15.
51 Kenny, "Vietnamese Perceptions of the 1979 War," 218.
52 See Sutter, Robert G., "China's Strategy toward Vietnam and Its Implications for the United States," in *The Third Indochina Conflict*, ed. Elliot, David W.P. (Boulder, CO: Westview Press, 1981), 170.
53 Chen, *China's War with Vietnam*, 31.
54 See O'Dowd, *The Last Maoist War*, 35.
55 Ibid., 40.
56 Chen, *China's War with Vietnam*, 21.
57 Li, *A History of the Modern Chinese Army*, 252.
58 Scobell, *China's Use of Military Force*, 121.
59 See Dreyer, "One Issue Leads to Another," 304.
60 See Nguyen, "The Sino-Vietnamese Conflict," 1039; Burton, Bruce, "Contending Explanations of the 1979 Sino-Vietnamese War," *International Journal* 34, no. 4 (1979): 706; Kenny, "Vietnamese Perceptions of the 1979 War," 227; Womack, *China and Vietnam: The Politics of Asymmetry*, 199.
61 See Elleman, Bruce A., "China's 1974 Naval Expedition to the Paracel Islands," in *Naval Power and Expeditionary Warfare. Peripheral Campaigns and New Theatres of Naval Warfare*, ed. Elleman, Bruce A. and Paine, S.C.M. (Oxon: Routledge, 2011), 144; Nguyen, "The Sino-Vietnamese Split," 25; Nguyen, "The Sino-Vietnamese Conflict," 1039; Garver, "Sino-Vietnamese Conflict," 445.
62 See Fravel, Taylor M., *Strong Border, Secure Nation: Cooperation and Conflict in China's Territorial Disputes* (Princeton, NJ: Princeton University Press, 2008), 278.
63 See Zhang, *Deng Xiaoping's Long War*, 41; O'Dowd, *The Last Maoist War*, 41–42; Khoo, *Collateral Damage*, 96.
64 Chen, *China's War with Vietnam*, 39.
65 See Kenny, "Vietnamese Perceptions of the 1979 War," 224.

66   See Scobell, *China's Use of Military Force*, 121–22.
67   See Dreyer, "One Issue Leads to Another," 306; Chang, Pao-min, *The Sino-Vietnamese Territorial Dispute* (Washington, D.C.: The Center for Strategic Studies, 1986), 45.
68   See Chen, *China's War with Vietnam*, 65; Nguyen, "The Sino-Vietnamese Conflict," 1043.
69   Chen, *China's War with Vietnam*, 65.
70   Zhang, "China's 1979 War with Vietnam," 855. The expulsion of the Hoa "enraged Beijing's leaders who saw it as a direct affront to China": Scobell, *China's Use of Military Force*, 122.
71   See Quinn-Judge, Sophie, "Victory on the Battlefield; Isolation in Asia: Vietnam's Cambodia Decade, 1979–1989," in *The Third Indochina War: Conflict between China, Vietnam and Cambodia, 1972–1979*, ed. Westad, Odd Arne and Quinn-Judge, Sophie (London, New York: Routledge, 2006), 211.
72   See Khoo, *Collateral Damage*, 121.
73   Scobell, *China's Use of Military Force*, 123.
74   Nguyen, "The Sino-Vietnamese Conflict," 1049. See further Scobell, *China's Use of Military Force*, 136; Kenny, "Vietnamese Perceptions of the 1979 War," 221.
75   Cited in Chen, *China's War with Vietnam*, 37.
76   "If the Soviet factor were to removed from the equation, there was no reason why, with a little skillful diplomacy, a modus vivendi could have been worked out between Beijing and Hanoi": Khoo, *Collateral Damage*, 96.
77   Cited in Nguyen, "The Sino-Vietnamese Conflict," 1044.
78   See Kenny, Henry J., *Shadow of the Dragon: Vietnam's Continuing Struggle with China and the Implications for U.S. Foreign Policy* (Washington, D.C.: Brassey's, 2002), 66; Dreyer, "One Issue Leads to Another," 304–07; Scobell, *China's Use of Military Force*, 121.
79   Cited in Khoo, *Collateral Damage*, 125.
80   Zhang, "China's 1979 War with Vietnam," 862.
81   Li, *A History of the Modern Chinese Army*, 252.
82   Nguyen, "The Sino-Vietnamese Conflict," 1047.
83   Scobell, *China's Use of Military Force*, 120.
84   Chen, *China's War with Vietnam*, 68.
85   See Scobell, *China's Use of Military Force*; Zhang, "China's 1979 War with Vietnam."
86   Chen, *China's War with Vietnam*, 80.
87   Ibid., 87; Scobell, *China's Use of Military Force*, 125; Zhang, *Deng Xiaoping's Long War*, 43, 50; Jencks, Harlan W., "China's 'Punitive War' on Vietnam: A Military Assessment," *Asian Survey* 19, no. 9 (1979): 805.
88   Zhang, "China's 1979 War with Vietnam," 857.
89   See Kissinger, *On China*, 367.
90   Zhang, *Deng Xiaoping's Long War*, 62.
91   Chen, *China's War with Vietnam*, 94.
92   Zhang, "China's 1979 War with Vietnam," 855; see Zhang, *Deng Xiaoping's Long War*, 33, 46–48; Vogel, Ezra F., *Deng Xiaoping and the Transformation of China* (Cambridge: Harvard University Press, 2011), 528.
93   See Zhang, *Deng Xiaoping's Long War*, 33.
94   Zhang, "China's 1979 War with Vietnam," 855; *Deng Xiaoping's Long War*, 47.
95   See Scobell, *China's Use of Military Force*, 124; Zhang, *Deng Xiaoping's Long War*, 43.
96   Scobell, *China's Use of Military Force*, 125.
97   Zhang, "China's 1979 War with Vietnam," 861; see Chen, Jian, "The Sino-Soviet Alliance and China's Entry in the Korean War," *Cold War International History Project, Working Paper No. 1* (Washington, D.C. 1992), 150–51.
98   See Zhang, "China's 1979 War with Vietnam," 856–57; Scobell, *China's Use of Military*

Force, 125–42.
99 O'Dowd, *The Last Maoist War*, 150.
100 Ibid., 151.
101 Ibid., 150.
102 Zhang, "China's 1979 War with Vietnam," 862.
103 See O'Dowd, *The Last Maoist War*, 52.
104 Ibid., 119.
105 See ibid., 115.
106 See Zhang, *Deng Xiaoping's Long War*; O'Dowd, *The Last Maoist War*, 126.
107 See Zhang, "China's 1979 War with Vietnam," 859–62.
108 See O'Dowd, *The Last Maoist War*, 129.
109 Ibid., 52.
110 See Kenny, "Vietnamese Perceptions of the 1979 War," 228; Chen, King C., "China's War against Vietnam, 1979: A Military Analysis," *Contemporary Asian Studies (Occasional Papers/Reprints Series)* 85, no. 5 (1983): 10.
111 See Turley, William S. and Race, Jeffrey, "The Third Indochina War," *Foreign Policy* 38 (1980): 105.
112 O'Dowd, *The Last Maoist War*, 67.
113 See Kenny, "Vietnamese Perceptions of the 1979 War," 231.
114 O'Dowd, *The Last Maoist War*, 118.
115 See Chen, "China's War against Vietnam," 27.
116 Ibid.
117 See Zhang, *Deng Xiaoping's Long War*, 59.
118 Chen, *China's War with Vietnam*, 88.
119 See Cohen, Arthur, "The Sino-Soviet Border Crisis of 1969," in *Avoiding War: Problems of Crisis Management*, ed. George, Alexander L. and Bar-Siman-Tov, Yacoov (Boulder, CO: Westview Press, 1991), 269; Elleman, Bruce A., *Modern Chinese Warfare, 1795–1989* (Routledge: New York, 2001), 278; Zhang, *Deng Xiaoping's Long War*, 49.
120 See Scobell, *China's Use of Military Force*, 120; Robinson, Thomas W., "The Sino-Soviet Border Conflict of 1969. New Evidence Three Decades After," in *Chinese Warfighting: The PLA Experience since 1949*, ed. Ryan, Marc A., Finkelstein, David M., and McDevitt, Michael A. (Armonk/London: East Gate Books, 2003), 213.
121 Zhang, "China's 1979 War with Vietnam," 859.
122 As Deng noted, a "medium-scale intervention would mean an attack in Xinjiang, Inner Mongolia, or Heilongjiang, similar to the 1969 conflicts. A small-scale attack would be border harassment or clashes. They would not be serious. China was prepared for them": Chen, *China's War with Vietnam*, 87.
123 See Elleman, *Modern Chinese Warfare*, 290.
124 See Zhang, "China's 1979 War with Vietnam," 859; Chang, Pao-min, *Kampuchea between China and Vietnam* (Singapore: Singapore University Press, 1985), 88–89; Jencks, "China's 'Punitive War' on Vietnam," 806.
125 Chen, *China's War with Vietnam*, 87.
126 Scobell, *China's Use of Military Force*, 129.
127 See Whiting, Allen S., "China's Use of Force, 1950–96, and Taiwan," *International Security* 26, no. 2 (2001): 120; O'Dowd, *The Last Maoist War*, 46.
128 See Zhang, *Deng Xiaoping's Long War*, 58; Li, *A History of the Modern Chinese Army*, 258.
129 See Ross, Robert S., *The Indochina Tangle* (New York: Columbia University Press, 1988), 225; Elleman, *Modern Chinese Warfare*, 285.
130 See Kissinger, *On China*, 376; Zhang, *Deng Xiaoping's Long War*, 71.

131 Scobell, *China's Use of Military Force*, 134.
132 Cited in Jencks, "China's 'Punitive War' on Vietnam," 803.
133 See Elleman, *Modern Chinese Warfare*, 291.
134 Kenny, "Vietnamese Perceptions of the 1979 War," 229. Bruce Elleman notes that China gradually built up the invasion force. Initially, around 30,000 PLA troops crossed the Sino-Vietnamese border but "by 25 February, this number had risen to 75,000 Chinese troops out of a total of 180,000 troops deployed along the border. Finally, by early March, an estimated 120,000 Chinese faced an equal number of Vietnamese": *Modern Chinese Warfare*, 291.
135 O'Dowd, *The Last Maoist War*, 45.
136 Zhang, "China's 1979 War with Vietnam," 861 [emphasis in original].
137 Turley and Race, "The Third Indochina War," 104.
138 Besides minor contingents of the regular PAVN, about 75,000 to 100,000 militia engaged in the fighting. These troops were well equipped and highly disciplined, and could rely on an extensive network of fortified defense positions and underground tunnels: see Kenny, "Vietnamese Perceptions of the 1979 War," 230.
139 Chen, *China's War with Vietnam*, 106.
140 O'Dowd, Edward C. and Corbett, John F. Jr., "The 1979 Chinese Campaign in Vietnam: Lesson Learned," in *The Lessons of History: The Chinese People's Liberation Army at 75*, ed. Burkitt, Laurie, Scobell, Andrew, and Wortzel, Larry M. (Carlisle: Strategic Studies Institute: U.S. Army War College, 2003), 367.
141 See Kenny, "Vietnamese Perceptions of the 1979 War," 231; O'Dowd, *The Last Maoist War*, 80; Zhang, "China's 1979 War with Vietnam," 871.
142 Kenny, "Vietnamese Perceptions of the 1979 War," 80.
143 O'Dowd, *The Last Maoist War*, 87.
144 See Li, *A History of the Modern Chinese Army*, 256.
145 O'Dowd, *The Last Maoist War*, 63.
146 See Li, *A History of the Modern Chinese Army*, 254–55.
147 O'Dowd, *The Last Maoist War*, 140.
148 Cited in ibid., 141.
149 See Li, *A History of the Modern Chinese Army*, 255.
150 See Chen, *China's War with Vietnam*, 109.
151 O'Dowd, *The Last Maoist War*, 55–56.
152 See Jencks, "China's 'Punitive War' on Vietnam," 813–14; Li, *A History of the Modern Chinese Army*, 259.
153 See Zhang, *Deng Xiaoping's Long War*, 112.
154 Chen, "China's War against Vietnam," 22.
155 Jencks, "China's 'Punitive War' on Vietnam," 811.
156 See Chen, "China's War against Vietnam," 26; Li, *A History of the Modern Chinese Army*, 255.
157 O'Dowd, *The Last Maoist War*, 73.
158 See Scobell, *China's Use of Military Force*, 127.
159 See O'Dowd and Corbett, "The 1979 Chinese Campaign," 354; O'Dowd, *The Last Maoist War*, 45. Several sources state that the PLA suffered at least 25,000 KIAs: see Zhang, "China's 1979 War with Vietnam," 866; Kenny, "Vietnamese Perceptions of the 1979 War," 231; Womack, *China and Vietnam: The Politics of Asymmetry*, 200.
160 See Clodfelter, Michael, *Vietnam in Military Statistics: A History of the Vietnam Wars, 1772–1991* (London: McFarland & Co, 1995), 288.
161 See Zhang, *Deng Xiaoping's Long War*, 141–68.
162 See Kissinger, *On China*, 374.

163 Zhang, "China's 1979 War with Vietnam," 856.
164 Elleman, Bruce A., "Sino-Soviet Relations and the February 1979 Sino-Vietnamese Conflict" (Vietnam Symposium 1966: After the Cold War: Reassessing Vietnam, Texas Tech University 1996), 1.
165 Kissinger, *On China*, 374.
166 "Indeed, on March 30, 1979, Deng claimed that the conflict had enhanced China's 'international prestige'": Scobell, *China's Use of Military Force*, 137.
167 See Zhang, "China's 1979 War with Vietnam," 869.
168 See Chen, *China's War with Vietnam*, 153.
169 Lebow, Richard N., *A Cultural Theory of International Relations* (Cambridge: Cambridge University Press, 2008), 69.
170 Even though the military commanders were not content with Deng's vaguely defined operative considerations and objectives, they "nevertheless subjected themselves to the desires of the central leadership. Once the decision was made to wage a punitive invasion of Vietnam, PLA generals were eager to undertake their missions with preference to employment of maximum force": Zhang, "China's 1979 War with Vietnam," 869.

Bibliography

Burton, Bruce. "Contending Explanations of the 1979 Sino-Vietnamese War." *International Journal* 34, no. 4 (1979): 699–722.

Chang, Pao-min. *Kampuchea between China and Vietnam*. Singapore: Singapore University Press, 1985.

Chang, Pao-min. *The Sino-Vietnamese Territorial Dispute*. Washington, D.C.: The Center for Strategic Studies, 1986.

Chen, Jian. "The Sino-Soviet Alliance and China's Entry in the Korean War." *Cold War International History Project, Working Paper no. 1*. Washington, D.C., 1992.

Chen, Jian. "China and the First Indo-China War, 1950–1954." *The China Quarterly* no. 133 (March 1993): 85–110.

Chen, Jian. *China's Road to the Korean War: The Making of the Sino-American Confrontation*. New York: Columbia University Press, 1994.

Chen, Jian. "China's Involvement in the Vietnam War, 1964–69." *The China Quarterly* no. 142 (June 1995): 356–87.

Chen, Jian. *Mao's China and the Cold War*. London, Chapel Hill: The University of North Carolina Press, 2001.

Chen, King C. "North Vietnam in the Sino-Soviet Dispute." *Asian Survey* 4, no. 9 (September 1964): 1023–36.

Chen, King C. "China's War against Vietnam, 1979: A Military Analysis." *Contemporary Asian Studies (Occasional Papers/Reprints Series)* 85, no. 5 (1983): 1–32.

Chen, King C. *China's War with Vietnam, 1979: Issues, Decisions, and Implications*. Stanford, CA: Hoover Institution Press, 1987.

Clodfelter, Michael. *Vietnam in Military Statistics: A History of the Vietnam Wars, 1772–1991*. London: McFarland & Co, 1995.

Cohen, Arthur. "The Sino-Soviet Border Crisis of 1969." In *Avoiding War: Problems of Crisis Management*, edited by Alexander L. George and Yaacov Bar-Siman-Tov, 269–89. Boulder, CO: Westview Press, 1991.

Dreyer, David R. "One Issue Leads to Another: Issue Spirals and the Sino-Vietnamese War." *Foreign Policy Analysis* 6, no. 4 (2010): 297–315.

Duiker, William J. *China and Vietnam: The Roots of Conflict*. Berkeley, CA: Institute of East

Asian Studies, University of California, 1986.

Elleman, Bruce A. "Sino-Soviet Relations and the February 1979 Sino-Vietnamese Conflict" (Vietnam Symposium 1966: After the Cold War: Reassessing Vietnam, Texas Tech University 1996).

Elleman, Bruce A. *Modern Chinese Warfare, 1795–1989*. Routledge: New York, 2001.

Elleman, Bruce A. "China's 1974 Naval Expedition to the Paracel Islands." In *Naval Power and Expeditionary Warfare. Peripheral Campaigns and New Theatres of Naval Warfare*, edited by Bruce A. Elleman and S.C.M. Paine, 141–51. Oxon: Routledge, 2011.

Elliot, David W.P. "The Third Indochina Conflict: Introduction." In *The Third Indochina Conflict*, edited by David W.P. Elliot, 1–21. Boulder, CO: Westview Press, 1981.

Fravel, Taylor M. *Strong Border, Secure Nation: Cooperation and Conflict in China's Territorial Disputes*. Princeton, NJ: Princeton University Press, 2008.

Gaiduk, Ilya V. *The Soviet Union and the Vietnam War*. Chicago, IL: Ivan R. Dee-Publishers, 1996.

Garver, John W. "Sino-Vietnamese Conflict and Sino-American Rapproachment." *Political Science Quarterly* 96, no. 3 (1981): 445–64.

Jencks, Harlan W. "China's 'Punitive War' on Vietnam – A Military Assessment." *Asian Survey* 19, no. 9 (1979): 801–15.

Kenny, Henry J. *Shadow of the Dragon: Vietnam's Continuing Struggle with China and the Implications for U.S. Foreign Policy*. Washington, D.C.: Brassey's, 2002.

Kenny, Henry J. "Vietnamese Perceptions of the 1979 War with China." In *Chinese Warfighting: The PLA Experience since 1949*, edited by Mark A. Ryan, David M. Finkelstein, and Michael A. McDevitt, 217–40. Armonk/London: East Gate Books, 2003.

Khoo, Nicholas. *Collateral Damage: Sino-Soviet Rivalry and the Termination of the Sino-Vietnamese Alliance*. New York: Columbia University Press, 2011.

Kissinger, Henry. *On China*. New York: The Penguin Press, 2011.

Lebow, Richard N. *A Cultural Theory of International Relations*. Cambridge: Cambridge University Press, 2008.

Li, Xiaobing. *A History of the Modern Chinese Army*. Lexington, KY: The University Press of Kentucky, 2007.

Mulvenon, James. "The Limits of Coercive Diplomacy: The 1979 Sino-Vietnamese Border War." *Journal of Northeast Asian Studies* 14, no. 3 (1995): 68–89.

Nguyen, Lien-Hang T. "The Sino-Vietnamese Split and the Indochina War, 1968–1975." In *The Third Indochina War: Conflict between China, Vietnam and Cambodia, 1972–79*, edited by Odd Arne Westad and Sophie Quinn-Judge, 13–32. London/New York: Routledge 2006.

Nguyen, Manh Hung. "The Sino-Vietnamese Conflict: Power Play among Communist Neighbors." *Asian Survey* 19, no. 11 (1979): 1037–53.

O'Dowd, Edward C. *Chinese Military Strategy in the Third Indochina War: The Last Maoist War*. London, New York: Routledge, 2007.

O'Dowd, Edward C., and Corbett, John F. Jr. "The 1979 Chinese Campaign in Vietnam: Lesson Learned." In *The Lessons of History: The Chinese People's Liberation Army at 75*, edited by Laurie Burkitt, Andrew Scobell, and Larry M. Wortzel, 353–78. Carlisle: Strategic Studies Institute: U.S. Army War College, 2003.

Quinn-Judge, Sophie. "Victory on the Battlefield; Isolation in Asia: Vietnam's Cambodia Decade, 1979–1989." In *The Third Indochina War: Conflict between China, Vietnam and Cambodia, 1972–1979*, edited by Odd Arne Westad and Sophie Quinn-Judge, 206–30. London/New York: Routledge, 2006.

Robinson, Thomas W. "The Sino-Soviet Border Conflict of 1969: New Evidence Three Decades After." In *Chinese Warfighting: The PLA Experience since 1949*, edited by Marc A. Ryan, David M. Finkelstein, and Michael A. McDevitt, 198–216. Armonk/London: East

Gate Books, 2003.
Ross, Robert S. *The Indochina Tangle*. New York: Columbia University Press, 1988.
Scobell, Andrew. *China's Use of Military Force: Beyond the Great Wall and the Long March*. Cambridge: Cambridge University Press, 2003.
Sutter, Robert G. "China's Strategy Toward Vietnam and Its Implications for the United States." In *The Third Indochina Conflict*, edited by David W.P. Elliot, 163–92. Boulder, CO: Westview Press, 1981.
Turley, William S., and Race, Jeffrey. "The Third Indochina War." *Foreign Policy* no. 38 (Spring 1980): 92–116.
Vogel, Ezra F. *Deng Xiaoping and the Transformation of China*. Cambridge: Harvard University Press, 2011.
Westad, Odd Arne. "Introduction: From War to Peace in Indochina." In *The Third Indochina War: Conflict between China, Vietnam and Cambodia, 1972–79*, edited by Odd Arne Westad and Sophie Quinn-Judge, 1–11. London, New York: Routledge, 2006.
Westad, Odd Arne, Chen, Jian, Stein, Tonnesson, Nguyen, Vu Tung, and Hershberg, James G. "77 Conversations between Chinese and Foreign Leaders on the Wars in Indochina, 1964–1977." *Cold War International History Project, Working Paper no. 22*. Washington, D.C., 1998.
Whiting, Allen S. "China's Use of Force, 1950–96, and Taiwan." *International Security* 26, no. 2 (Fall 2001): 103–31.
Whiting, Allen S. *The Chinese Calculus of Deterrence: India and Indochina*. Ann Arbor, MI: The University of Michigan Press, 2001.
Womack, Branly. *China and Vietnam: The Politics of Asymmetry*. Cambridge: Cambridge University Press, 2006.
Zhai, Qiang. *China and the Vietnam Wars, 1950–1975*. Chapel Hill, NC: University of North Carolina Press, 2000.
Zhang, Xiaoming. "China's 1979 War with Vietnam: A Reassessment." *The China Quarterly* no. 184 (December 2005): 851–74.
Zhang, Xiaoming. *Deng Xiaoping's Long War: The Military Conflict between China and Vietnam, 1979–1991*. Chapel Hill, NC: The University of North Carolina Press 2015.

7 Conclusion

More than 35 years have passed since China last resorted to the use of large-scale military force in foreign affairs. During this period, the PRC underwent a complete metamorphosis from a poor peasant society to the world's second-largest economy, and it seems it is only a matter of time before China eventually makes its greatest 'Leap Forward' and overtakes the United States in terms of economic power. Deng Xiaoping's political reforms and open-door policy have not only allowed the PRC "to achieve a number of remarkable accomplishments and to consolidate China's standing and role in world politics"[1] during the past decades, but have also transformed the once revolutionary China into an integral and well-respected member of the international community of states.[2] As indicated by the PRC's permanent seat in the UN Security Council, China has even been promoted into the elite of the current international society. It seems as if the once backward country has successfully managed to re-emerge as a leading political power in Asia and in world affairs, a status China should rightfully always have occupied according to its self-image and worldview.[3] However, does this imply that status-seeking no longer fuels Chinese foreign policy and thereby affects Beijing's behavior in international conflicts? The answer to this crucial question will be provided in the last part of this concluding chapter. In the following two sections, I first summarize the central findings of my four case studies, on the basis of which I then evaluate the explanatory capacities of the two competing theoretical models under investigation. This concludes my twofold research objective.

Empirical findings

My primary research interest consisted in identifying the concrete motivation as the immediate cause of China's large-scale resort to military force. In this section, I summarize the central findings of my four case studies and explicate the specific motive in each instance. My results strongly confirm Ned Lebow's observation that states "frequently go to war for reasons that have little, if anything to do, with security."[4] This insight seems to hold especially true for the four cases under investigation, as I could not generate empirical evidence for considerations of national security (or the corresponding motive, *fear*) as the rationale for China's resort to force.

Instead, I found that China went to war four times for reasons that are closely associated with Lebow's ideal-type motive *spirit*. As I will outline in more detail in the following, the People's Republic of China resorted to military force in order to enhance and preserve its standing and status by fulfilling its societal obligations toward the international socialist movement, to punish slights and revenge affronts against it, to clarify that China should be taken seriously, and to make the point that China was not to be bullied into submission.

Merely one year after he had proclaimed the People's Republic, Mao Zedong led China into the Korean War. As the case study demonstrates, there is little to question Mao's assessment that going to war in Korea was decided by himself and, to a lesser extent, by Zhou Enlai. All my partial analyses strongly confirm the decisive role Mao played in enabling and executing China's intervention even against serious internal opposition, in awareness of the enormous risks entailed, and in disregard of the costs to China's security that arose. Moreover, the investigation of the actual use of force in Korea revealed that China's conduct of war was extensively determined by Mao and was thus primarily oriented by political objectives rather than strategic necessities. Just as it was Mao's determination that set the course toward intervention, it was also primarily the Chairman's motives that functioned as the causes of China's military engagement in Korea. Thereby, however, considerations of China's national security played only the minor role of a pretext in order to bring the reluctant Chinese leadership into line. Rather, my analysis demonstrates that the underlying causes of China's intervention are to be found in Mao's eagerness to fulfill the social obligation to safeguard the revolutionary movements in Asia, which had been transferred to the PRC by Stalin's Soviet Union. The findings of all my partial analyses clearly depict *spirit* as Mao's dominant motive, and the Chairman's statement in the critical Politburo session of October 4, 1950 can be regarded as a 'smoking gun.' On that occasion, Mao agreed that the arguments against a military engagement abroad put forward by other Chinese leaders were reasonable, but simultaneously lectured his colleagues that "it would be *shameful* for us to stand by seeing our neighbors in perilous danger without offering any help"[5] and, if China were to decide to just stand idly by, "we [would] feel terrible inside, no matter what we may pretend."[6] Mao's statement reveals the central components of spirit's effects on social behavior, as defined by Ned Lebow: in order to avoid internal shame and public disgrace, actors will risk life and limb for an endeavor that others regard as highly unreasonable. Or, to use Lebow's words, when "the spirit is dominant, when actors seek self-esteem through honor, standing or autonomy, they are often willing to risk, even sacrifice, themselves or their political units in pursuit of these goals."[7] Apparently, this was the case with regard to China's (or, better, Mao's) intervention in the Korean War. The results of my partial analyses strongly disconfirm the established narrative of a security-induced Chinese intervention. Instead, my findings point unambiguously to spirit as the dominant motive behind the Chinese intervention that Mao wanted so eagerly, regardless of the costs and risks to the PRC's national security.

In 1962, China resorted to force against India in order *to create the conditions the Chinese leadership regarded as necessary for negotiating peace*. This may sound paradoxical, but as my findings show, in the eyes of the Chinese leadership, India's 'fixed and final' policy on the territorial dispute fundamentally impeded a resolution by compromise. Beijing, on the other hand, had been genuinely interested in solving the bilateral territorial dispute through a mutually acceptable and negotiated settlement on the basis of the status quo. At its core, the Sino-Indian conflict was the result of a collision between two fundamental approaches toward the settlement of the territorial issue. However, while the material issue under contestation would have been divisible, as indicated by Zhou Enlai's proposal for a swap of demands, New Delhi instead continued its 'fixed and final' policy on the ground with the implementation of the forward policy. Convinced that its claims were established beyond any doubt and that it was morally superior in this conflict, New Delhi then started to systematically infiltrate Chinese-controlled territory with military forces, and thereby changed the 'rules of the game' at least three times. Confronted with India's increasingly assertive and provocative policy, Beijing showed remarkable restraint and forbearance, unilaterally employed several measures in order to contain the conflict from escalating, and actively worked toward its non-violent resolution. As India showed no willingness to change its course toward confrontation even after Beijing had gradually climbed the ladder of escalation with regard to warnings and signaling, China's patience evaporated. Finally, when India changed the 'rules of the game' one last time with the Dhola incident, the Chinese leadership reached the conclusion that the Nehru administration simply *refused to take China seriously*. Consequently, in the eyes of the Chinese leaders, it then became essential to teach the Indian government a 'fierce and painful lesson' as to why China ought to be taken seriously. As demonstrated in my analysis of the decision-making process and the operative considerations for the PLA's Himalayan campaign, *spirit* had then become the dominant motive among China's leaders, and once again it was Mao who was taking the lead. However, even though spirit had become China's dominant motive, it was still held in check by reason, because one of the objectives of the war was to force Nehru back to the negotiating table. The punitive element of China's military campaign was significantly more pronounced in the final phase of the Sino-Indian War: only after New Delhi had rejected China's proposal for a resumption of negotiations in word and deed did the PLA extend the offensive, and the humiliation of India's armed forces followed.

In 1969, China resorted to force against the Soviet Union in order *to make the point that the PRC would not be bullied into submission* by either the Soviet show of force along the Sino-Soviet border or Moscow's declaration of the Brezhnev Doctrine. In degrading China to the rank of a vassal by Moscow's grace, the Doctrine collided strongly with the self-conception of the New China, resulted in an emotional flashback to China's traumatic historical experience of a status of 'limited sovereignty' during the 'Century of Shame,' and thus greatly affronted the Chinese leadership. Moreover, as the PRC had then already emancipated itself ideologically and politically from the Soviet Union, the declaration of the Brezhnev Doctrine was also perceived as a crude attempt to coerce China back into a position of subordination. With Moscow's openly stated challenge, fear and spirit became the competing motives inside the Chinese leadership. But as China's paramount leader was in favor of reacting in a resolute manner, spirit eventually became dominant and thus functioned as the motive for the Chinese ambush at Zhenbao Island, which in turn resulted in a further and more substantial engagement between Chinese and Soviet forces. Apparently, the Chairman's personal assessment of the improbability of further escalation to open war had led the Chinese leaders to blank out this prohibitive risk. My analysis was not only able to prove that China deliberately and proactively instigated these clashes, but also revealed that the material issue under contestation – the border dispute, and in particular the 0.74 square kilometers of Zhenbao Island – were a stage for China's swelling ideological and political conflict with the Soviet Union rather than the actual source of the eventual escalation of violence. The evolution of China's conduct at the border evidently mirrored the stages of the developing Sino-Soviet rivalry for ideological leadership and political influence. In sum, the case study shows the interplay between the three motives spirit, fear, and reason in affecting China's decision-making, risk behavior, and the use of force, whereby spirit clearly functioned as the dominant motive for China's resort to force against the Soviet Union on the ice of the Ussuri.

China's military campaign against Vietnam in 1979 reveals the characteristics of *spirit-induced punitive action* to their full extent. In the eyes of the Chinese leadership – and particularly for Deng Xiaoping – decades of Chinese steadfast loyalty and extensive assistance had been reciprocated by Vietnam with open backstabbing. To make things even worse, the small and ungrateful neighbor to the south then also started to challenge China on several fronts and with obvious disrespect for the status of the Middle Kingdom: in Beijing's perspective, Hanoi had dared to forcefully contest China's territorial integrity, systematically mistreated its ethnic-Chinese minority, and embarrassed China by laying hands on Beijing's regional ally, Cambodia. Finally, Vietnam openly defected to the declared enemy and rival of the People's Republic, the Soviet Union. As my analysis demonstrates, these issues decidedly affected the Chinese leadership's emotional state of mind by adding furious anger to the already existing bitterness about Hanoi's ingratitude. As emotions ran high inside China's elite, it is thus not surprising that the political decision-making and actual use of force extensively reflected the distinct *emotionalization* of the bilateral conflict. In order to swiftly *avenge* Vietnam's slights, the Chinese leadership was willing to take high risks, as Beijing was well aware of the PLA's striking deficits and the potential for Soviet military action in retaliation to China's invasion of Vietnam. In this, I identified spirit as the Chinese leadership's dominant motive.

Theoretical reflection

My secondary research interest consisted in evaluating the applicability and explanatory capacity of Ned Lebow's Cultural Theory of International Relations for a non-Western actor. To do so, I confronted the theory with the task of providing explanations for the four empirical cases investigated in this book. As the "plausibility of an explanation is enhanced to the extent that alternative explanations are considered less consisted with the data, or less supportable by available generalizations,"[8] I decided to introduce James Fearon's well-established 'rationalist explanation for war' as the competing explanatory model. In a nutshell, and as already outlined in the concluding sections of the case studies, I found that Fearon's rational choice-based approach proved unable to generate explanatory power for the cases at hand, while Lebow's theory demonstrated the capacity to arrive at comprehensive and convincing explanations well beyond its Western-centric core domain.

With regard to the specific characteristics of the Chinese culture, and taking China's unique historical experience into account, it should not come as a surprise that the Chinese society and its leaders are traditionally highly attuned to matters of status, standing, and respect. Accordingly, Ned Lebow's theory is at home when tasked with explaining the causes for the four cases of China's use of force investigated in this book. As my findings illustrate, not only did Lebow's model enable me to arrive at solid results in each case but, in addition, the theory-informed re-reading of well-accepted narratives allowed me to expose and solidify several causal relationships underlying China's use of force that – as far as I know – had not previously been comprehensively identified or explicated. My empirical findings strongly correspond with the theory's assumptions and postulated mechanisms with regard to the three analytical categories of cooperation, conflict, and risk behavior. My analysis was also able to furnish proof for the independent effects of the four motives *appetite*, *spirit*, *reason*, and *fear* on the Chinese leadership's decisions and actions during the process leading up to the conflict, during the decision-making itself, and during the actual use of military force. I was also able to demonstrate that not all of the Chinese leaders were affected by the occurrence of a trigger event to the same extent, or showed the same motives after the event had taken place. The Chinese leadership's deliberations on the question whether or not to send troops to Korea provide a telling example: while Gao Gang highlighted the imperative of economic reconstruction (appetite) and Lin Biao stressed the uncertainty of military success (fear) as impediments to an intervention, Mao was strongly determined to become militarily involved in the Korean War for the sake of China's status and standing inside the socialist international society (spirit). Each leader's argument rested on a specific, self-contained conception of rationality, and because of that, Gao, Lin, and Mao could agree to disagree when confronted with one and the same issue, and while holding the same level of information on it. In three of my four case studies, I was also able to comprehensively verify the hypothetical process as deduced from the Cultural Theory. My analyses demonstrate that imbalances on the individual level occurred first, and were most pronounced, among China's key leaders, Mao Zedong, Zhou Enlai, and Deng Xiaoping. The expected crosscutting effect between the individual and the collective levels was then observable during the decision-making processes that led up to China's intervention in Korea, to the Sino-Indian War, and to the Sino-Vietnamese War, as the Chinese leadership as a whole eventually arrived at a collective decision to resort to the use of military force. Unfortunately, this process step could not be verified for the Sino-Soviet border clashes because of the lack of available data on the Chinese decision-making in this case. Even so, it seems probable that the decision-making in this instance also followed the same pattern observable for the three other cases. Taken together, my findings strongly confirm that Lebow's theory is applicable to a non-Western actor. Moreover, I was also able to comprehensively validate the Cultural Theory's logical coherence and explanatory capacity for a crucial test case (China's intervention in Korea), as well as for two other most-likely cases (China's punitive campaigns against India and

Vietnam) and one least-likely case (the Sino-Soviet border clashes) of China's use of large-scale military force in foreign affairs.

In contrast, my alternative explanatory model was not able to generate explanatory capacity for these cases, because Fearon's 'rationalist explanation for war' was confronted with three insurmountable empirical problems. First, in each of the four cases, at least one of the two opponents decided to gamble with high stakes and thus acted against Fearon's assumption that "leaders do not like gambling when the downside risk is losing a war."[9] In three of the four cases, it was the Chinese leadership that decided to act in a high-risk-taking manner, the single exception being the Sino-Indian War. In this case, Beijing's leaders could not engage in high-risk-taking behavior, as there were simply no significant risks to shoulder. However, this aspect was comprehensively executed by New Delhi in its implementation and continuation of the forward policy as a high-risk strategy. Second, I was unable to substantiate the two postulated causal mechanisms – information asymmetries and the commitment problem – as central problems that impeded non-violent resolution of the given conflicts. With the possible exception of the Sino-Soviet border clashes, Beijing gradually escalated its warnings and signals in each instance before resorting to force. However, as the United States, India, and Vietnam failed to take heed of these warnings and thus crossed China's pre-announced red lines, Fearon's argument of deliberately created information asymmetries hardly applies as a resilient explanation for these cases. Nor did the commitment problem reveal itself as the central obstacle that prevented a non-violent resolution of those conflicts in which a material issue was contested. The bilateral consultations on the demarcation of the Sino-Soviet border failed to yield a result not because one of the two disputants anticipated that the other would not adhere to a negotiated settlement in the future, but because of China's insistence on matters of procedure and principle. The same conclusion can basically be drawn for the Sino-Indian territorial dispute, as there is no reason to doubt that Beijing or New Delhi would have reopened the territorial question once a mutually acceptable solution had been achieved. In these two cases, conflict resolution through negotiations failed for reasons that are not associated with uncertainty regarding the future under the structural conditions of anarchy, as proposed by Fearon's theoretical model. Third, rational-choice explanations for conflict escalations in general are fundamentally dependent on the existence of a material bone of contention in order to function. But when conflicts escalate from the material to the non-material dimension or exclusively take place in the latter, the rationalist logic is unable to take into account matters of principle, cultural sensitivities, or emotional issues. In such cases, the actors' specific risk behavior is then also oriented on the specific appreciation of values and no longer adheres to the rationalists' generalized logic of (objective) consequences. As my findings show, the causes of escalation in the four conflicts under investigation are primarily to be found in the non-material dimension of international relations. As a consequence, it is difficult to address them with rational choice-based approaches and their analytical repertoire. Herein lies a striking deficit of rational-choice approaches, which enjoy noteworthy popularity especially among political practitioners and advisors.

Back to the future: today's Middle Kingdom, conflicts, and status

It is obvious that contemporary China differs eminently, and in many regards, from the revolutionary Middle Kingdom it was during the heyday of Mao Zedong's leadership. Domestically, China has evolved into what Ned Lebow would describe as a profoundly appetite-driven society, in which material welfare and display have become the predominant markers of social status. Externally, the People's Republic has integrated itself into the international community as an elite member and has also adopted its *nomos*. Since the PLA's invasion of Vietnam in 1979, Beijing has refrained from using large-scale military force as an instrument for shaping its external affairs. When comparing the findings of my four case studies, three variables reveal themselves that could potentially have contributed to China's restraint.

One of these variables is the absence of the Soviet factor. With the demise of the Soviet Union, a major point of friction for the PRC dissolved. As my analysis has shown, Moscow was directly or indirectly entangled in all four cases I investigated in this book, and in none of these instances did the Kremlin's involvement contribute to Beijing's reluctance to resort to military force. In the case of the Korean War, Stalin executed a textbook example of John Mearsheimer's bait-and-bleed/bloodletting strategy for gaining power at the advantage of (actual and potential) rivals by dragging China into the war while keeping the Soviets out, and by carefully containing the conflict from spreading uncontrollably. Moscow's moral and material support also contributed its share to New Delhi's conviction that India's claims in the Sino-Indian dispute were legitimate and established beyond any sense of doubt, which in turn resulted in the erroneous forward policy.[10] In 1969, the Soviet Union itself became the target of China's aggression, and ten years later the Soviet factor played a decisive role in the Chinese decision to launch a punitive campaign against Vietnam. The multifaceted rivalry between China and the Soviet Union included competition for primacy on the ideological, political, and regional levels, while the common denominator for the bilateral rivalry on all of these levels reveals itself as the competition for relative status. With regard to the current relationship between China and Russia, it seems that the question of ordering status ranks appears to have been clarified, which in turn contributes positively to the non-continuation of the traditional rivalry between Moscow and Beijing.

A second variable that might have affected Beijing's restraint reveals itself through a look at the targets of China's use of force. In three of the four cases, China resorted to military force against former allies or friends. As my findings indicate, the establishment of close relations or even friendship with the People's Republic was apparently a double-edged sword, as Beijing obviously demanded high standards with regard to reciprocal loyalty in bilateral affairs, and the Chinese leadership resented it deeply when its expectations were not met. With North Korea as the single exception, today's China has no military allies, and it seems as if Pyongyang's continuous nuclear defiance and its policy of instigating crises in China's immediate periphery is increasingly wearing on Beijing's patience and goodwill. Pyongyang is heavily dependent on China's continuing support and assistance: without the vital support provided by China's in the past, the DPRK would not exist today, and without

China's contemporary assistance it seems very likely that North Korea would be bound to collapse. However, North Korea's actions and its behavior *vis-à-vis* China do not necessarily reflect the DPRK's fundamental dependency on its single remaining sponsor. Quite the contrary, it is hard to find another state actor that has dared to publicly humiliate Beijing as many times as North Korea has done in the recent past. Nonetheless, Beijing still keeps the line of preserving "minimal stability"[11] of the North Korean system, even though the bilateral relationship comes at a significantly negative expense to China's international reputation.[12] Beijing's impetus for continuing the disadvantageous bond with its pathetic and ungrateful little ally, however, is hardly found in shared ideological convictions or in the declining strategic relevancy of the DRPK as a buffer zone;[13] rather, it seems as if Beijing's leadership has not yet found a viable way out of China's North Korea dilemma, and thus continues to muddle through in order to preserve at least some influence in Pyongyang and avoid the anticipated negative implications for China of a collapse in the DRPK system. As Victor Cha aptly summarized Beijing's dilemma,

> the problem today is that China is both omnipotent and impotent in North Korea. It has great material influence as the North's only patron. Yet, as the sole patron, if Beijing shut down its assistance to punish Pyongyang for its bad behavior even temporarily, it could precipitate an unraveling of the regime, which would be even more threatening to China.[14]

Even so, discontent and annoyance seem to be on the rise within China's political and military elites.[15] As a Chinese diplomat recently told me, China cannot indefinitely put up with being compromised in the eyes of the world by North Korea's provocative policies and brinkmanship. One day, China's patience will likely come to an end.

The third variable that might be relevant to Beijing's contemporary restraint reveals itself with substantial effect in all four cases of China's past resorts to force: in each instance, personality played a significant role in shaping the course of China's relations with its respective opponents. My analysis also demonstrated that the individual determination of Mao Zedong, Zhou Enlai, and Deng Xiaoping was of substantial importance in setting the course for China's resort to military force in each of the four cases. However, since Deng Xiaoping's demise, the position of paramount leader is vacant, and it is unlikely that this function will be reactivated in China's contemporary political system.[16] The effects of individual motivations or emotions on China's foreign-policy decision-making are therefore now tempered by institutional arrangements.

Does this mean, however, that status-seeking and its associated emotions no longer affect China's foreign policy and its behavior in international conflicts? Quite the contrary: today's China is, as Yong Deng and others have found, arguably the most status-conscious state actor on the globe.[17] Beijing has never ceased its attempts to fulfill its historical mission to restore China's lost status as Asia's Middle Kingdom.[18] In line with this, issues of specific sensitivity to China – particularly the indivisible ones, such as Taiwan, Tibet, and territorial integrity – reveal a remarkable consistency in their importance to China's leadership, from Mao Zedong until today. The findings of my previous analyses have shown that layers of ideology were unable to conceal the fundamental conviction of Chinese exceptionalism in China's national identity. In view of that, it is also highly likely that layers of capitalism will fail to do so. As a consequence, status-seeking and preservation are still defining elements and core motivations of Chinese foreign policy. To signal its status aspirations, contemporary China has utilized a variety of markers that include a sophisticated space program, a range of technological innovations, the hosting of the 2008 Olympic Games, and the establishment of new regional organizations and forums such as the Shanghai Cooperation Organization.[19] Besides these rather innovative indicators, China also employs more traditional markers to underline its desired status in international relations, such as the build-up of a blue-water navy including an aircraft-carrier program, expanding areas of interest, and the demand for *droit de regard* in China's immediate periphery.[20] In today's China, however, international status is not only an end in itself but has become an important source of regime legitimacy, too. With popular nationalist sentiment on the rise in Chinese society while ideology is losing its appeal, the Communist Party "must be even more Chinese."[21] In practice, this means that making "China prosperous, strong and *respected in the world* is now the most important source of the CCP's domestic legitimacy."[22] For the Chinese leadership, increased popular nationalism is a double-edged sword: on the one hand, it has become a convenient substitute for the ideological justification of the CCP's rule; on the other, it has also become a template for the Chinese people to judge the performance of the CCP government against.[23] As Thomas Christensen has observed, the days when the Chinese leadership could ignore the nationalist demands of public opinion are gone, because

> nationalist pundits and bloggers in China find allies in high places. … The result has been the creation of a dangerously stunted version of a free press, in which a Chinese commentator may more safely criticize government policies from a hawkish, nationalist direction than from a moderate, internationalist one.[24]

Beijing's leaders thus increasingly face domestic pressure to forcefully safeguard China's interests and international status in the numerous conflicts involving the PRC, which in turn shrinks the leeway Beijing has for pragmatic policies.[25] This development should be alarming for the United States and its Asian allies, because

> if this type of nationalism prevails in shaping the foreign policy of a rising China, it would make compromise extremely difficult if not impossible on issues that China deems as its core interest and thereby push China to adopt increasingly bellicose foreign policies.[26]

This shifting pattern – and with it the transition from elite to more popular Chinese status demands in international affairs – is already observable in the three most crucial conflicts involving the PRC.

Chinese–Japanese rivalry in the East China Sea

In September 2012, the long-standing conflict between China and Japan over the ownership of the Senkaku/Diaoyu Islands in the East China Sea gained dramatic momentum.[27] For long, both governments had pragmatically sidelined the dispute for the sake of preserving cooperative relations.[28] However, when Tokyo decided to purchase three of the contested islands, tensions flared up to such an extent that observers predicted military confrontation between the countries.[29] Short of resorting to the use of military force, China then climbed the ladder of escalation in reaction to Japan's unilateral move: besides condemnation of Tokyo's action, Beijing issued a governmental statement declaring a baseline around the island for the first time and dispatched coast-guard and law enforcement vessels, as well as surveillance drones and planes, near the islands in order to patrol the disputed area. Jet fighters of the two opponents also tailed each other in the airspace above the islands.[30] Finally, Beijing established an Air Defense Identification Zone (ADIZ) in November 2013 to counter Japan's territorial claims.[31]

Two observations of the 2012–13 Senkaku–Diaoyu Crisis seem worth emphasizing, and both depart from the insight that the dispute is directly relevant to China's domestic politics and international status.[32] First, Beijing's handling of the island crisis basically resembled its approach to the Sino-Indian territorial dispute. Only after Japan changed the status quo by purchasing the islands and declaring the intention to renationalize them did Beijing react, by climbing the ladder of escalation in order to signal the seriousness of the situation and emphasize its discontent with Tokyo's unilateral action.[33] Moreover, similar to New Delhi's position, Tokyo had long refused to acknowledge the existence of a territorial dispute over Senkaku/Diaoyu between Japan and the PRC, and because of that, the Japanese government saw no need for resolution. Tensions in the East China Sea only declined after Tokyo accepted the existence of the territorial dispute, which in turn paved the way for a meeting between Japan's Prime Minister Shinzo Abe and PRC President Xi Jinping during the APEC summit in January 2014. Up to that point, the crisis had come at great costs for both opponents. As Tokyo was finally willing to give in to China's precondition for talks, i.e. to acknowledge the existence of the territorial dispute, it was China that scored a gain with regard to the bilateral status-hierarchy, even though this gain came at a cost to China's national economy.

Second, at the height of the crisis, large anti-Japanese protests erupted throughout the country, including in first-tier cities such as Beijing, Shanghai, and Guangdong.[34] The extent of the public outpouring of anger against Japan at these demonstrations was unprecedented, even against the historical record of anti-Japanese protests in China: Japanese businesses were vandalized, Japanese-made cars were set aflame, and people of (seemingly) Japanese origin were harassed in the streets on several occasions before the Chinese authorities were able (or willing) to restore order.[35] Japan's purchase of the three islands had hit China, as one Ministry of Foreign Affairs official described it, like an atomic bomb.[36] This observation holds especially true with regard to the strained emotional dimension of China's relationship with Japan, in which the Japanese occupation and wartime atrocities traditionally emerge as trouble-spots. Taken together with the Chinese government's past efforts to promote official nationalism as a means to legitimize the CCP's claim for leadership through patriotic history education, this problematic mélange has opened the gate to a flood of anti-Japanese popular nationalist sentiment inside China. As He Yinan observes,

> the general public has developed enormous grievances as well as a strong sense of entitlement with regards to Japan. Whenever there is a conflict of interest with Japan, the Chinese people always expect Japan to make concessions because it owed China so much throughout history.[37]

Such emotionally fueled and highly popular sentiments significantly curtail China's political leeway vis-à-vis Tokyo, because if the Chinese government wants to compromise, the angry public may "quickly turn against the 'traitorous' government"[38] and its legitimacy could be challenged.[39] With regard to the task of maintaining cooperative relations with Japan, Beijing's strategy of bolstering the CCP's claim to power through nationalism is likely to result in a dilemma, and the Chinese society's rising consciousness for matters regarding China's international status will almost certainly add its share to the further aggravation of this already precarious situation. Finding a solution acceptable to all will thus become even more challenging in the future.

The South China Sea: a Chinese sphere of influence?

As a major maritime crossroad for commerce and trade, the South China Sea is of global relevancy. Virtually every state involved in international trade thus has an interest in maintaining peace, stability, and the freedom of navigation in this area, including the claimants to the territorial dispute (Brunei, the PRC, the Republic of China on Taiwan, Malaysia, the Philippines, and Vietnam). Currently, the task of maintaining these common interests rests upon the United States, and particularly on the U.S. Navy, which regularly conducts so-called 'freedom of navigation patrols' in the disputed waters of the South China Sea.

Among the six claimants to the dispute, the People's Republic attracts the most attention because of its expansive claim, its growing naval capabilities, and its past use of military force.[40] In 1974, South Vietnamese and Chinese naval forces clashed near the Crescent Islands, resulting in a Chinese victory. In what followed, China gained control over the Crescent Group and completed its seizure of the strategically important Paracels. A second military engagement, this time involving China and the Socialist Republic of Vietnam, occurred in 1988 in the Spratly Islands over Johnson South Reef. Again, Chinese force prevailed and Beijing gained control over six reefs and atolls in the area. While it remains unclear which side fired the first shots in the respective skirmishes, China's military presence in the area and its provocative actions prior to the engagements certainly contributed their share to the occurrence of these clashes.[41] Besides these two violent episodes, China has basically opted to take what Taylor Fravel describes as a delaying strategy, "which involves maintaining a state's claim to a piece of land but neither offering concessions nor using force. In essence, a delaying strategy is premised on maintaining existing claims in a dispute."[42] By strengthening its own claims while deterring other claimants from doing so, China's approach of preserving the status quo – including its extensive territorial claim that encompasses almost the entire South China Sea[43] – through military, diplomatic, and economic means has raised enormous obstacles for any compromise. More recently, observers have found that China is employing this strategy more assertively, self-confidently, and proactively, including a "markedly increased willingness to use threats and displays of force on issues relating to the control of waters, air space, surface features, and resources off China's coast."[44] In contrast, other scholars, such as Alastair Johnston, doubt that China's foreign policy in general has become more assertive and thus argue that if China has on occasion acted in a more assertive or forceful manner, this was the result of provocation by others.[45] However, even Johnston agrees that when it comes to China's conduct in the South China Sea dispute, Beijing's "diplomatic rhetoric and practice" has moved "fairly sharply in a more hard-line direction."[46] In search of the rationale for this shift, most arguments point to the change in the overall balance of power in China's favor, the expansion of China's national interests and security needs, the impact of China's growing naval capabilities, and, as already outlined above, the rise of popular nationalism within China.[47] Taken together, these lines of argument cumulate in the observation that China, carried on the wings of its economic success, is asserting its claimed status rank as Asia's Middle Kingdom more self-confidently and robustly *vis-à-vis* the other claimants in the South China Sea dispute. In view of this, it is no coincidence that China's former Foreign Minister, Yang Jiechi, emphasized to his colleagues during an ASEAN foreign-minister meeting in 2010 that "China is a big country and other countries are small, and that's just a fact."[48]

It seems that a rising and increasingly self-confident China expects other states to show greater deference to its interests and wishes in this crucial area, and that the "changing Chinese posture towards assertiveness is [thus] a reflection of its growing discontent with the actions of other regional states,"[49] as Li Mingjiang notes. For China, the South China Sea is not only an area that can support its growing demands for energy, nutrition, and security. It also functions as a symbol compensating for the perceived historical injustices China had to suffer during the Century of Shame, and as an arena for affirming China's status ambitions through demonstrations of its increased economic weight and military might in the region.[50] Since March 2010, Beijing has referred to the South China Sea as belonging to China's 'national core interests.'[51] These 'core interests' are matters of principle and essentially non-negotiable in nature, as they are directly related to China's sovereignty, security, and dignity.[52] As with other 'core interests' such as Tibet and Taiwan, Beijing does not tolerate any foreign interference and is willing to defend them. In Xi Jinping's words, China "will never give up" its legitimate rights or sacrifice its national core interests: "no country should presume that we will engage in trade involving our interests or that we will swallow the 'bitter fruit' of harming our sovereignty, security or development."[53] Beijing seems poised to foster a claim on the South China Sea as a zone of exclusive influence and a marker of China's great-power status.[54]

The United States and China: the gathering storm?

Despite China's impressive economic and military rise, the United States is still the predominant power and principal guarantor of peace and stability in the Asia-Pacific region. As indicated by Washington's 'pivot' or 'rebalancing' toward Asia during the presidency of Barack Obama, the United States is also willing and ready to assume this crucial role in the future. With regard to the maritime disputes in the East and South China Seas, Washington and Beijing find themselves on opposing sides because of the United States' reaffirmed commitments to allies and friends in the region. However, this makes up a highly delicate, problematic, and worrisome situation in which the maritime disputes have become focal points in a larger rivalry between China and the United States for power, status, and influence in the Asia-Pacific region.[55] This not only complicates the Herculean task of finding acceptable solutions to the regional disputes but also stimulates the emergence of new problems and frictions in U.S.–China relations, which could easily and inadvertently take on features of the "historical model of a clash between the status quo power and the emerging power."[56] In Beijing, the U.S. pivot and related policy initiatives nurture the impression that the United States has opted for a more clear-cut strategy of counterbalance in order to contain and stifle China's rise "by strengthening its military presence in the western Pacific, expanding and deepening security ties with regional members, and fanning the flames of dispute in the South China Sea, among other ways."[57] On the other side of the Pacific, China's self-confident, more robust, and occasionally assertive approach toward the maritime disputes has further substantiated the perception of the PRC as a strategic challenge to Washington's security interests and to the U.S.-led order in the Asia-Pacific region.[58] In addition, both actors are "locked in a very interactive pattern of military modernization where each side takes the other as its most likely 'demanding security threat' and develops its own responses with the other in mind."[59] As mutual trust has become a scarce resource in U.S–China relations, it seems as if the most important bilateral relationship of the twenty-first century is heading toward a one-way street of intense strategic competition and rivalry that could unnecessarily result in serious arms races, antagonism, and a Cold War-like confrontation, with the potential to even end in war.[60]

Fortunately, such an outcome is far from inevitable, as there is still a chance to peacefully integrate China into the current international system as a genuine Asia-Pacific stakeholder. This is a demanding task for sure, particularly with regard to the lack of trust and mutual understanding and the conflicting perceptions that have manifested between Washington and Beijing over the past decades. Nonetheless, China and the United States still have major common interests in the Asia-Pacific region – including the preservation of peace and stability, freedom of navigation, the promotion of economic growth, and the liberalization of trade and investment – which could function as the stabilizing nucleus for the bilateral relationship in the future, in addition to the unprecedented degree of comprehensive interdependence that already characterizes China–U.S. relations.[61] If both sides are really interested in preserving peace and stability by keeping their relationship afloat, then the only viable method is to meet each other halfway, probably in the form of a U.S.–China 'grand bargain': as Charles Glaser argues, such a

> grand bargain, in which the United States ends its security commitment to Taiwan and China reaches diplomatic solutions to its sovereignty and maritime disputes in the South China and East China Seas, while officially recognizing a

long-term security role for the United States in East Asia, is currently the United States' best option for dealing with China's rise.[62]

However, a sound and reliable 'grand bargain' would not only require mutual strategic reassurance and a tacit agreement concerning the rules of the game – especially when it comes to the 'core interests' of both parties in the region – but would also require meeting China's demands international status, which are likely to increase further with China's growing weight in world politics.[63] It remains questionable whether Washington is willing and/or able to acknowledge Chinese status claims, because this would not only affect the United States' prestige as a superpower but might also come at the expense of regional allies, and eventually compromise the credibility of U.S. security commitments worldwide.[64] As a consequence, a mutually acceptable compromise for the non-material status dimension of the Sino-American rivalry is likely to be the hardest bone of contention and thus may function as a major impediment to the success of a 'grand bargain' – especially at a time when the slogan 'Making America Great Again' is enjoying considerable popularity in the American society.

A well-established argument in the current debate over the future of the Asia-Pacific region and China's strategic intentions can be summarized as follows: as Beijing faces immense domestic challenges in the decades to come, there is good reason to assume that it is not interested in altering the balance of power in the Asia-Pacific region or asserting its claims in the numerous territorial conflicts by resorting to the use of military force. Of course, this argument is logically consistent and valid. However, my findings show that China faced even more momentous internal challenges and crises while intervening in the Korean War (post-Civil War agenda), fighting a war against India (Great Leap Forward), and confronting the Soviet Union on the ice of the Ussuri River (Cultural Revolution).[65] The more recent Senkaku/Diaoyu Crisis between China and Japan showed that Chinese matters of principle and aroused public sentiment could easily become an explosive mixture and may spiral out of control.

Future research should thus pay attention to the independent role of emotions in the formation of foreign policy in general, and systematically clarify how processes of collective emotionalization affect states' behavior during international crises and conflicts. As I have shown above, emotional situations such as perceived humiliation and the quest for revenge can become powerful motivations for the resort to military force. When considering the potentially problematic mélange of historical trauma, public nationalism, and status-related sentiments inside Chinese society and its elites, it appears all the more relevant, necessary, and appropriate to conduct further research on the emotional dimension of international relations.

This book demonstrates that the politics of status-seeking and status preservation have had some very real implications for China's conduct of foreign relations. At four times in the past, China has resorted to the use of military force for reasons that are directly related to status, standing, and respect. In order to preserve peace and stability in the Asia-Pacific region, policymakers in Washington and in the capitals of East Asia would thus be well advised to take the Middle Kingdom's status-consciousness seriously.

Notes

1 Kindermann, Gottfried-Karl, *Der Aufstieg Ostasiens in der Weltpolitik 1840–2000* (München: Deutsche Verlags Anstalt, 2001), 544 [own translation].
2 See Deng, Yong, *China's Struggle for Status: The Realignment of International Relations* (Cambridge: Cambridge University Press, 2008), 46; Peng, Yuan and Hachigan, Nina, "Global Roles and Responsibilities," in *Debating China: The U.S.–China Relationship in Ten Conversations*, ed. Hachigan, Nina (New York: Oxford University Press, 2014), 92–93.
3 See Kallio, Jyrki, "Dreaming of the Great Rejuveniation of the Chinese Nation," *Fudan Journal of Humanities and Social Sciences* 8, no. 4 (2015): 521; Sutter, Robert G., *Chinese Foreign Relations: Power and Policy Since the Cold War* (Plymouth: Rowman & Littlefield Publishers, 2008), 38; Wolf, Reinhard, "Auf Kollisionskurs: Warum es zur amerikanisch-chinesischen Konfrontation kommen muss," *Zeitschrift für Politik* 59, no. 4 (2012): 396–97.
4 Lebow, Richard N., *Why Nations Fight: Past and Future Motives for War* (Cambridge: Cambridge University Press, 2010), 12.
5 Cited in Sheng, Michael, "The Psychology of the Korean War: The Role of Ideology and Perception in China's Entry into the War," *The Journal of Conflict Studies* 22, no. 1 (2002) [emphasis added].
6 Cited in Li, Xiaobing, *A History of the Modern Chinese Army* (Lexington, KY: The University Press of Kentucky, 2007), 84 [emphasis added].
7 Lebow, Richard N., *A Cultural Theory of International Relations* (Cambridge: Cambridge University Press, 2008), 19. "The active pursuit of honor and standing by individuals and states is often costly; vast sums of money have been spent in colonies, national airlines and space exploration, often with no expectation of material net gain. Foolhardy feats in battle, *accepting war under unfavorable circumstances* or building battle fleets that needlessly provoke a conflict with another major power indicate that honor and standing are not infrequently pursued at significant costs to security": ibid., 509 [emphasis added].
8 George, Alexander L. and Bennett, Andrew, *Case Studies and Theory Development in the Social Sciences* (Cambridge/London: MIT Press, 2005), 91.
9 Fearon, James D., "Rationalist Explanation for War," *International Organization* 49, no. 3 (1995): 388.
10 See Liegl, Markus B., "Status, Prestige, and Emotions: The Social Dimension of the Sino-Indian Territorial Dispute." Paper presented at the Annual Convention of the International Studies Association, New Orleans, February 18–21, 2015, 18; Lüthi, Lorenz, "Sino-Indian Relations, 1954–1962," *Eurasia Border Review* 3 (2012), 111–12; Calvin, James B., "The China–India Border War (1962)" (Quantico, VA: Marine Corps Command and Staff College, 1984), 16.
11 Cha, Victor, *The Impossible State: North Korea, Past and Future* (New York: HarperCollins Publishers, 2012), 332, 42. See also Wu, Xinbo and Green, Michael, "Regional Security Roles and Challenges," in *Debating China: The U.S.–China Relationship in Ten Conversations*, ed. Hachigan, Nina (New York: Oxford University Press, 2014), 199–200.
12 See Blancke, Stephan and Rosenke, Jens, "Blut ist dicker als Wasser. Die chinesisch-nordkoreanische Militär- und Geheimdienstkooperation," *Zeitschrift für Außen- und Sicherheitspolitik* no. 4 (2011): 264; Cha, *The Impossible State*, 344.
13 "There is a growing conviction that, as China is no longer in serious danger of a military invasion, she no longer needs a buffer state and could come to accept a unified Korea under Seoul's control if it could take place gradually and well into the future": Beukel, Eric, "The Last Living Fossil of the Cold War. The Two Koreas, the Dragon, and the

Eagle: Towards a New Regional Security Complex in East Asia?" *Danish Institute for International Studies Report* no. 10 (2012).
14 Cha, *The Impossible State*, 344.
15 See Perlez, Jane, "China's Annoyance With North Korea Bubbles to the Surface," *New York Times*, December 21, 2014, A24; Cha, *The Impossible State*, 331; Taylor, Brendan, "Does China Still Back North Korea?" *Survival* 55, no. 5 (2013): 85–86.
16 See Zhao, Suisheng, "Foreign Policy Implications of Chinese Nationalism Revisited: The Strident Turn," *Journal of Contemporary China* 22, no. 82 (2013): 544.
17 Deng, *China's Struggle for Status*, 8. As William Wohlforth observes, "rising China seeks the status of a great power second to none in a multipolar world": "Status Dilemmas and Interstate Conflict," in *Status in World Politics*, ed. Paul, T.V., Welch-Larson, Deborah, and Wohlforth, William C. (Cambridge: Cambridge University Press, 2014), 115.
18 See Welch-Larson, Deborah and Shevchenko, Alexei, "Status Seekers: Chinese and Russian Responses to U.S. Primacy," *International Security* 34, no. 4 (2010): 66.
19 See Pu, Xiaoyu and Schweller, Randall L., "Status Signaling, Multiple Audiences, and China's Blue Water Navy," in *Status in World Politics*, ed. Welch-Larson, Deborah, and Wohlforth, William C. (Cambridge: Cambridge University Press, 2014), 147.
20 See Glosny, Michael A. and Saunders, Phillip C., "Debating China's Naval Nationalism," *International Security* 35, no. 2 (2010), 166; Buszynksi, Leszek, "The South China Sea: Oil, Maritime Claims, and U.S.–China Strategic Rivalry," *The Washington Quarterly* 35, no. 2 (2012): 145.
21 Christensen, Thomas J., "Chinese Realpolitik," *Foreign Affairs* 75, no. 5 (1996): 46.
22 Deng, *China's Struggle for Status*, 66 [emphasis added].
23 See Zhao, "Foreign Policy Implications of Chinese Nationalism Revisited," 541.
24 Christensen, Thomas J., "The Advantages of an Assertive China: Responding to Beijing's Abrasive Diplomacy," *Foreign Affairs* 90, no. 2 (2011).
25 See He, Yinan, "History, Chinese Nationalism and the Emerging Sino-Japanese Conflict," *Journal of Contemporary China* 16, no. 50 (2007): 3.
26 Zhao, "Foreign Policy Implications of Chinese Nationalism Revisited," 553.
27 For a historical overview on the bilateral conflict, see Pan, Zhongqi, "Sino-Japanese Dispute over the Diaoyu/Senkaku Islands: The Pending Controversy from a Chinese Perspective," *Journal of Chinese Political Science* 12, no. 1 (2007): 73–75.
28 See Fravel, Taylor M., "Explaining Stability in the Senkaku (Diaoyu) Islands Dispute," in *Getting the Triangle Straight: Managing China–Japan–US Relations*, ed. Curtis, Gerald, Kokubun, Ryosei, and Wang, Jisi (Tokyo: Japan Center for International Exchange, 2010), 157; He, "History, Chinese Nationalism and the Emerging Sino-Japanese Conflict," 4.
29 See Harry, R. Jade, "A Solution Acceptable to All? A Legal Analysis of the Senkaku-Diaoyu Island Dispute," *Cornell International Law Journal* 46, no. 3 (2013): 654.
30 See "Dangerous Shoal," *The Economist*, January 19, 2013; Fravel, Taylor M., "China's Assertiveness in the Senkaku (Diaoyu) Island Dispute," *MIT Political Science Research Paper* no. 19 (2016): 11–12; Harry, "A Solution Acceptable to All?" 663.
31 See Dutton, Peter A., "China's Maritime Disputes in the East and South China Seas," *Naval War College Review* 67, no. 3 (2014): 13.
32 See Pan, "Sino-Japanese Dispute," 72.
33 See Wu and Green, "Regional Security Roles and Challenges," 203.
34 See Fravel, "China's Assertiveness in the Senkaku (Diaoyu) Island Dispute," 10.
35 See Wallace, Jeremy and Weiss, Jessica Chen, "The Political Geography of Nationalist Protest in China: Cities and the 2012 Anti-Japanese Protests," *The China Quarterly* no. 222 (2015).

36 See Fravel, Taylor M., "Things Fall Apart: Maritime Disputes and China's Regional Diplomacy," in *China's Challenges*, ed. deLisle, Jacques and Goldstein, Avery (Philadelphia, PA: University of Pennsylvania Press, 2015), 216.
37 He, "History, Chinese Nationalism and the Emerging Sino-Japanese Conflict," 10.
38 Ibid., 11.,
39 "Given the strong connection of the Diaoyu/Senkaku Islands dispute with nationalism, both the Chinese and the Japanese governments link their stance and attitude with their respective legitimacy in domestic politics. Nationalism serves as [a] wild card that might constrain the ability of both Japanese and Chinese leaders to pursue compromise." Pan, "Sino-Japanese Dispute," 86.
40 See Fravel, Taylor M., "China's Strategy in the South China Sea," *Contemporary Southeast Asia* 33, no. 3 (2011): 292–93.
41 See Hayton, Bill, *The South China Sea: The Struggle for Power in Asia* (New Haven, London: Yale University Press, 2014), 75–76, 83; Garver, John W., "China's Push Through the South China Sea: The Interaction of Bureaucratic and National Interest," *The China Quarterly* no. 132 (1992): 1002–03; Fravel, Taylor M., *Strong Border, Secure Nation: Cooperation and Conflict in China's Territorial Disputes* (Princeton, NJ: Princeton University Press, 2008), 281–82, 95; Elleman, Bruce A., "China's 1974 Naval Expedition to the Paracel Islands," in *Naval Power and Expeditionary Warfare. Peripheral Campaigns and New Theatres of Naval Warfare*, ed. Elleman, Bruce A. and Paine, S.C.M. (Oxon: Routledge, 2011), 141–49.
42 Fravel, "China's Strategy in the South China Sea," 297.
43 See Simon, Sheldon W., "Conflict and Diplomacy in the South China Sea: The View from Washington," *Asian Survey* 52, no. 6 (2012): 996.
44 Friedberg, Aaron L., "The Sources of Chinese Conduct: Explaining Beijing's Assertiveness," *The Washington Quarterly* 37, no. 4 (2015): 133.
45 See Johnston, Alastair I., "How New and Assertive Is China's New Assertiveness?" *International Security* 37, no. 4 (2013): 7–38; Jerdén, Björn, "The Assertive China Narrative: Why It Is Wrong and How So Many Still Bought into It," *The Chinese Journal of International Politics* 7, no. 1 (2014): 47–88; Twomey, Christopher P. and Xu, Hui, "Military Developments," in *Debating China. The U.S.–China Relationship in Ten Conversations*, ed. Hachigan, Nina (Oxford/New York: Oxford University Press, 2014), 173.
46 Johnston, "How New and Assertive Is China's New Assertiveness?" 19.
47 See Yahuda, Michael, "China's New Assertiveness in the South China Sea," *Journal of Contemporary China* 22, no. 81 (2013): 446–59; Pham, Derek, "Gone Rouge? China's Assertiveness in the South China Sea," *Journal of Politics & Society* 22, no. 1 (2011): 139–64.
48 Pomfret, John, "U.S. Takes Tougher Tone with China," *Washington Post*, July 30, 2010.
49 Li, Mingjiang, "Reconciling Assertiveness and Cooperation? China's Changing Approach to the South China Sea Dispute," *Security Challenges* 6, no. 2 (2010): 58.
50 See Bräuner, Oliver, "'Wenn du einen Schritt machst, dann mache ich zwei' – Chinas maritime Strategie im Ost- und Südchinesischen Meer," *Zeitschrift für Außen- und Sicherheitspolitik* 7, no. 4 (2014): 443; Dutton, "China's Maritime Disputes in the East and South China Seas," 9.
51 See Li, "Reconciling Assertivness and Cooperation?" 61; Mearsheimer, John J., "The Gathering Storm: China's Challenge to US Power in Asia," *The Chinese Journal of International Politics* 3, no. 4 (2010): 389.
52 See Lee, Walter, "China's Unassertive Rise: What Is Assertiveness and How We Have Misunderstood It?" *International Journal of China Studies* 4, no. 3 (2013): 513–15; Zeng,

Jinghan, Xiao, Yuefan, and Breslin, Shaun, "Securing China's Core Interests: The State of Debate in China," *Foreign Affairs* 91, no. 2 (2015): 245–46.
53 Zhang, Yunbi, Li, Xiang, and Zhang, Chunyan, "Xi Vows No Surrender on "Legitimate Rights, Core Interests'," *China Daily*, January 30, 2013.
54 See Holmes, James R., "China's Monroe Doctrine," *The Diplomat*, June 22, 2012; Mearsheimer, "The Gathering Storm," 389. As early as 2007, a Chinese naval officer reportedly proposed splitting the Pacific into two zones of influence. According to Admiral Timothy Keating, then commander of the United States Pacific Command (USPACOM), this 'deal' "envisaged that the Pacific region could be divided into two areas of responsibility, with China handling the western Pacific and Indian Ocean region and the United States taking care of the eastern Pacific": Kumar, Satish, *India's National Security: Annual Review 2010* (New Delhi/Oxon: Routledge, 2011), 67.
55 See Buszynksi, "The South China Sea: Oil, Maritime Claims, and U.S.–China Strategic Rivalry," 139–40.
56 Peng and Hachigan, "Global Roles and Responsibilities," 103. See also Goldstein, Avery, "First Things First. The Pressing Danger of Crisis Instability in U.S.–China Relations," *International Security* 37, no. 4 (2013): 54.
57 Wu and Green, "Regional Security Roles and Challenges," 201. See also Xiang, Lanxin, "China and the 'Pivot'," *Survival* 54, no. 5 (2012): 113–28; Goldstein, Lyle J., *Meeting China Halfway: How to Defuse the Emerging U.S.–China Rivalry* (Washington, D.C.: Georgetown University Press, 2015), 330.
58 See Ross, Robert S., "U.S. Grand Strategy, the Rise of China, and U.S. National Security Strategy for East Asia," *Strategic Studies Quarterly* 7, no. 2 (2013): 24–25; Dobbins, James, "War with China," *Survival* 54, no. 4 (2012): 7.
59 Twomey and Xu, "Military Developments," 159.
60 See Wolf, "Auf Kollisionskurs," 392, 405–06; Foot, Rosemary, "China and the United States: Between Cold War and Warm Peace," *Survival* 51, no. 6 (2009): 123.
61 See Wu and Green, "Regional Security Roles and Challenges," 204.
62 Glaser, Charles L., "A U.S.–China Grand Bargain? The Hard Choice between Military Competition and Accomodation," *International Security* 39, no. 4 (2015): 89.
63 See Wolf, "Auf Kollisionskurs," 397–99; Jacques, Martin, *When China Rules the World. The Rise of the Middle Kingdom and the End of the Western World* (London: Allen Lane, 2009), 380–82.
64 See Wolf, "Auf Kollisionskurs," 399–400.
65 Even though the conclusion might suggest itself that divisionary theories of conflict and crisis behavior (i.e. that states deliberately create or utilize an external crisis for domestic purposes) may generate explanatory power in these cases, Alastair Johnston found that "there is no relationship between domestic unrest and China's use of force externally": "China's Militarized Interstate Dispute Behavior 1949–1992: A First Cut at the Data," *The China Quarterly* no. 153 (1998): 18.

Bibliography

Beukel, Eric. "The Last Living Fossil of the Cold War. The Two Koreas, the Dragon, and the Eagle: Towards a New Regional Security Complex in East Asia?" *Danish Institute for International Studies Report*, no. 10 (2012). Accessed at www.files.ethz.ch/isn/150951/RP2012-10-Last-living-fossil_web.jpg.pdf (September 1, 2016).

Blancke, Stephan, and Rosenke, Jens. "Blut ist dicker als Wasser. Die chinesisch-nordkoreanische Militär- und Geheimdienstkooperation." *Zeitschrift für Außen- und Sicherheitspolitik* no. 4 (2011): 263–94.

Bräuner, Oliver. "'Wenn du einen Schritt machst, dann mache ich zwei' – Chinas maritime Strategie im Ost- und Südchinesischen Meer." *Zeitschrift für Außen- und Sicherheitspolitik* 7, no. 4 (2014): 441–50.

Buszynksi, Leszek. "The South China Sea: Oil, Maritime Claims, and U.S.–China Strategic Rivalry." *The Washington Quarterly* 35, no. 2 (2012): 139–56.

Calvin, James B. "The China–India Border War (1962)." Quantico, VA: Marine Corps Command and Staff College, 1984.

Cha, Victor. *The Impossible State: North Korea, Past and Future*. New York: HarperCollins Publishers, 2012.

Christensen, Thomas J. "Chinese Realpolitik." *Foreign Affairs* 75, no. 5 (1996): 37–52.

Christensen, Thomas J. "The Advantages of an Assertive China: Responding to Beijing's Abrasive Diplomacy." *Foreign Affairs* 90, no. 2 (2011). Accessed at www.foreignaffairs.com/articles/east-asia/2011-02-21/advantages-assertive-china (September 2, 2016).

"Dangerous Shoal." *The Economist*, January 19, 2013. Accessed at www.economist.com/news/leaders/21569740-risks-clash-between-china-and-japan-are-risingand-consequences-could-be (September 1, 2016).

Deng, Yong. *China's Struggle for Status: The Realignment of International Relations*. Cambridge: Cambridge University Press, 2008.

Dobbins, James. "War with China." *Survival* 54, no. 4 (2012): 7–24.

Dutton, Peter A. "China's Maritime Disputes in the East and South China Seas." *Naval War College Review* 67, no. 3 (2014): 7–18.

Elleman, Bruce A. "China's 1974 Naval Expedition to the Paracel Islands." In *Naval Power and Expeditionary Warfare. Peripheral Campaigns and New Theatres of Naval Warfare*, edited by Bruce A. Elleman and S.C.M. Paine, 141–51. Oxon: Routledge, 2011.

Fearon, James D. "Rationalist Explanation for War." *International Organization* 49, no. 3 (1995): 379–414.

Foot, Rosemary. "China and the United States: Between Cold War and Warm Peace." *Survival* 51, no. 6 (2009): 123–46.

Fravel, Taylor M. *Strong Border, Secure Nation: Cooperation and Conflict in China's Territorial Disputes*. Princeton, NJ: Princeton University Press, 2008.

Fravel, Taylor M. "Explaining Stability in the Senkaku (Diaoyu) Islands Dispute." In *Getting the Triangle Straight: Managing China–Japan–US Relations*, edited by Gerald Curtis, Ryosei Kokubun, and Jisi Wang, 144–64. Tokyo: Japan Center for International Exchange, 2010.

Fravel, Taylor M. "China's Strategy in the South China Sea." *Contemporary Southeast Asia* 33, no. 3 (2011): 292–319.

Fravel, Taylor M. "Things Fall Apart: Maritime Disputes and China's Regional Diplomacy." In *China's Challenges*, edited by Jacques deLisle and Avery Goldstein, 204–26. Philadelphia, PA: University of Pennsylvania Press, 2015.

Fravel, Taylor M. "China's Assertiveness in the Senkaku (Diaoyu) Island Dispute." *MIT Political Science Research Paper* no. 19 (2016). Accessed at http://papers.ssrn.com/sol3/Delivery.cfm/SSRN_ID2807084_code1609318.pdf?abstractid=2788165&mirid=1 (September 2, 2016).

Friedberg, Aaron L. "The Sources of Chinese Conduct: Explaining Beijing's Assertiveness." *The Washington Quarterly* 37, no. 4 (2015): 133–50.

Garver, John W. "China's Push Through the South China Sea: The Interaction of Bureaucratic and National Interest." *The China Quarterly* no. 132 (1992): 999–1028.

George, Alexander L., and Bennett, Andrew. *Case Studies and Theory Development in the Social Sciences*. Cambridge/London: MIT Press, 2005.

Glaser, Charles L. "A U.S.–China Grand Bargain? The Hard Choice between Military Competition and Accomodation." *International Security* 39, no. 4 (2015): 49–90.

Glosny, Michael A., and Saunders, Phillip C. "Debating China's Naval Nationalism." *International Security* 35, no. 2 (2010): 161–75.

Goldstein, Avery. "First Things First. The Pressing Danger of Crisis Instability in U.S.–China Relations." *International Security* 37, no. 4 (2013): 49–89.

Goldstein, Lyle J. *Meeting China Halfway: How to Defuse the Emerging U.S.–China Rivalry.* Washington, D.C.: Georgetown University Press, 2015.

Harry, R. Jade. "A Solution Acceptable to All? A Legal Analysis of the Senkaku-Diaoyu Island Dispute." *Cornell International Law Journal* 46, no. 3 (2013): 653–82.

Hayton, Bill. *The South China Sea: The Struggle for Power in Asia.* New Haven, London: Yale University Press, 2014.

He, Yinan. "History, Chinese Nationalism and the Emerging Sino-Japanese Conflict." *Journal of Contemporary China* 16, no. 50 (2007): 1–24.

Holmes, James R. "China's Monroe Doctrine." *The Diplomat*, June 22, 2012. Accessed at http://thediplomat.com/2012/06/chinas-monroe-doctrine/ (September 1, 2016).

Jacques, Martin. *When China Rules the World: The Rise of the Middle Kingdom and the End of the Western World.* London: Allen Lane, 2009.

Jerdén, Björn. "The Assertive China Narrative: Why It Is Wrong and How So Many Still Bought into It." *The Chinese Journal of International Politics* 7, no. 1 (2014): 47–88.

Johnston, Alastair I. "China's Militarized Interstate Dispute Behavior 1949–1992: A First Cut at the Data." *The China Quarterly* no. 153 (March 1998): 1–30.

Johnston, Alastair I. "How New and Assertive Is China's New Assertiveness?" *International Security* 37, no. 4 (2013): 7–48.

Kallio, Jyrki. "Dreaming of the Great Rejuveniation of the Chinese Nation." *Fudan Journal of Humanities and Social Sciences* 8, no. 4 (2015): 521–32.

Kindermann, Gottfried-Karl. *Der Aufstieg Ostasiens in der Weltpolitik 1840–2000.* München: Deutsche Verlags Anstalt, 2001.

Kumar, Satish. *India's National Security: Annual Review 2010.* New Delhi/Oxon: Routledge, 2011.

Lebow, Richard N. *A Cultural Theory of International Relations.* Cambridge: Cambridge University Press, 2008.

Lebow, Richard N. *Why Nations Fight: Past and Future Motives for War.* Cambridge: Cambridge University Press, 2010.

Lee, Walter. "China's Unassertive Rise: What Is Assertiveness and How We Have Misunderstood It?" *International Journal of China Studies* 4, no. 3 (2013): 503–38.

Li, Mingjiang. "Reconciling Assertiveness and Cooperation? China's Changing Approach to the South China Sea Dispute." *Security Challenges* 6, no. 2 (2010): 49–68.

Li, Xiaobing. *A History of the Modern Chinese Army.* Lexington, KY: The University Press of Kentucky, 2007.

Liegl, Markus B. "Status, Prestige, and Emotions: The Social Dimension of the Sino-Indian Territorial Dispute." Paper presented at the Annual Convention of the International Studies Association, New Orleans, February 18–21, 2015.

Lüthi, Lorenz. "Sino-Indian Relations, 1954–1962." *Eurasia Border Review* 3 (Spring 2012): 95–120.

Mearsheimer, John J. "The Gathering Storm: China's Challenge to US Power in Asia." *The Chinese Journal of International Politics* 3, no. 4 (2010): 381–96.

Pan, Zhongqi. "Sino-Japanese Dispute over the Diaoyu/Senkaku Islands: The Pending Controversy from a Chinese Perspective." *Journal of Chinese Political Science* 12, no. 1 (2007): 71–92.

Peng, Yuan, and Hachigan, Nina. "Global Roles and Responsibilities." In *Debating China: The U.S.–China Relationship in Ten Conversations*, edited by Nina Hachigan, 88–110. New York:

Oxford University Press, 2014.

Perlez, Jane. "China's Annoyance with North Korea Bubbles to the Surface." *New York Times*, December 21, 2014, A24.

Pham, Derek. "Gone Rouge? China's Assertiveness in the South China Sea." *Journal of Politics & Society* 22, no. 1 (2011): 139–64.

Pomfret, John. "U.S. Takes Tougher Tone with China." *Washington Post*, July 30, 2010. Accessed at www.washingtonpost.com/wp-dyn/content/article/2010/07/29/AR201007 2906416.html (September 2, 2016).

Pu, Xiaoyu, and Schweller, Randall L. "Status Signaling, Multiple Audiences, and China's Blue Water Navy." In *Status in World Politics*, edited by Deborah Welch-Larson and William C. Wohlforth, 141–62. Cambridge: Cambridge University Press, 2014.

Ross, Robert S. "U.S. Grand Strategy, the Rise of China, and U.S. National Security Strategy for East Asia." *Strategic Studies Quarterly* 7, no. 2 (2013): 20–40.

Sheng, Michael. "The Psychology of the Korean War: The Role of Ideology and Perception in China's Entry into the War." *The Journal of Conflict Studies* 22, no. 1 (2002). Accessed at https://journals.lib.unb.ca/index.php/jcs/article/view/367/580 (30 October 2016).

Simon, Sheldon W. "Conflict and Diplomacy in the South China Sea: The View from Washington." *Asian Survey* 52, no. 6 (2012): 995–1018.

Sutter, Robert G. *Chinese Foreign Relations: Power and Policy since the Cold War*. Plymouth: Rowman & Littlefield Publishers, 2008.

Taylor, Brendan. "Does China Still Back North Korea?" *Survival* 55, no. 5 (2013): 85–91.

Twomey, Christopher P., and Xu, Hui. "Military Developments." In *Debating China: The U.S.–China Relationship in Ten Conversations*, edited by Nina Hachigan, 152–75. Oxford/New York: Oxford University Press, 2014.

Wallace, Jeremy, and Weiss, Jessica Chen. "The Political Geography of Nationalist Protest in China: Cities and the 2012 Anti-Japanese Protests." *The China Quarterly* no. 222 (2015): 403–29.

Welch-Larson, Deborah, and Shevchenko, Alexei. "Status Seekers: Chinese and Russian Responses to U.S. Primacy." *International Security* 34, no. 4 (2010): 63–95.

Wohlforth, William C. "Status Dilemmas and Interstate Conflict." In *Status in World Politics*, edited by T.V. Paul, Deborah Welch-Larson, and William C. Wohlforth, 115–40. Cambridge: Cambridge University Press, 2014.

Wolf, Reinhard. "Auf Kollisionskurs: Warum es zur amerikanisch-chinesischen Konfrontation kommen muss." *Zeitschrift für Politik* 59, no. 4 (2012): 392–408.

Wu, Xinbo, and Green, Michael. "Regional Security Roles and Challenges." In *Debating China: The U.S.–China Relationship in Ten Conversations*, edited by Nina Hachigan, 198–220. New York: Oxford University Press, 2014.

Xiang, Lanxin. "China and the 'Pivot'." *Survival* 54, no. 5 (2012): 113–28.

Yahuda, Michael. "China's New Assertiveness in the South China Sea." *Journal of Contemporary China* 22, no. 81 (2013): 446–59.

Zeng, Jinghan, Xiao, Yuefan, and Breslin, Shaun. "Securing China's Core Interests: The State of Debate in China." *Foreign Affairs* 91, no. 2 (2015): 245–66.

Zhang, Yunbi, Li, Xiang, and Zhang, Chunyan. "Xi Vows No Surrender on 'Legitimate Rights, Core Interests'." *China Daily*, January 30, 2013. Accessed at http://europe.chinadaily.com.cn/china/2013-01/30/content_16185789.htm (August 20, 2016).

Zhao, Suisheng. "Foreign Policy Implications of Chinese Nationalism Revisited: The Strident turn." *Journal of Contemporary China* 22, no. 82 (2013): 535–53.

Index

Abe, Shinzo, 236
Afghanistan, 114
Aksai Chin 107–17, 122f., 134, 140
Alliance: China–North Korea 86, 234; China–Soviet Union 59ff., 86, 211, 215; Soviet–Mongolian 163; Vietnam–Soviet Union 190, 20ff., 215f.
Alliance formation 33, 38, 42, 59, 178
Amur River 153
Anarchy 27–31, 232
Armed Coexistence 117–21, 123
Arunachal Pradesh 107, 109f., 134, 136
Asia–Pacific 2, 4, 8, 9, 13, 29, 238ff.
Association of Southeast Asian Nations (ASEAN) 238

Bargaining theories 30f.
Bennett, Andrew 19, 44
Berlin Crisis 13
Bhutan 107, 109
Bluff 30, 68, 126, 136
Brahmaputra Valley 134
Brezhnev–Doctrine: Chinese reactions to 156, 187; concept of limited sovereignty 162; impact on China 163f., 167, 178
Brezhnev, Leonid 154, 159, 173f., 194
British India: colonial boundary drawing 107, 122
Brunei 237
Burma 114

Cambodia 196, 230; aggression against DVR 200; relations to China 198, 202; Vietnamese invasion of 190, 200ff., 214
Cao Bang 212f.
Carter, James Earl 'Jimmy' 6

Central Military Commission (CMC) 10, 65, 69, 117, 124, 126, 133, 152, 161, 165, 203
Century of Shame 109, 238; collective trauma 158, 164, 176, 229; national identity 60; Opium War 59f.; unequal treaties 60, 158
Chen Xilian 166
Chen, King C. 195, 199, 203
Chen Yi 120
Chiang Kai-Shek 123
China: armament industry 171, 205; assertiveness 2, 238; assistance to Vietnam 61, 160, 192f., 197, 202, 230; border guards 112, 151f., 164; foreign policy 9, 61, 155, 167, 204, 227, 234f., 238; glory 57, 60, 68, 78, 108; military power 2, 12, 132f.; new type of great power relations 2; non–interference 68; peaceful development 2; political system 108, 172, 234; popular nationalism 235, 238; post–Civil War agenda 63, 240; proclamation of 3, 58, 60; revolutionary commitment 57; rise in world politics 2, 4, 8, 238ff.; security 92, 135, 172, 178, 216, 228, 238; sovereignty 61, 68, 109, 123, 167, 175, 199, 238f.; sphere of influence 60, 160f., 237; stakeholder 2, 239; status 6, 12, 40f., 58, 68, 82, 92, 106, 109, 126, 164, 176, 217, 230, 233; international status of 6, 57, 91, 227f., 231, 235ff., 240; restoration of lost international status 60, 63; rank of 6, 89, 91, 137, 216, 233, 238; sensitivity of 231, 234f., 240; strategic challenge 2, 8, 239; strategic orientation 2, 63; U.S.

Index 249

containment of 2f., 8, 239; worldview 60, 227
China–foreign relations:
 China–Cambodia relations 198, 202, 230
 China–DPRK relations 68, 86, 233f.
 China–India relations (see also Sino–Indian territorial conflict; see also Sino–Indian war); border agreements 114; friendship 12, 106, 111f., 122, 124, 137f.; honeymoon–period 108f., 137; territorial concessions 114; territorial conflict 136, 137; Tibet–issue 108ff., 122, 129
 China–Japan relations 1, 236f., 240
 China–Soviet Union relations (see also Sino–Soviet border clashes; see also Sino–Soviet boundary conflict; see also Sino–Soviet split); alliance 59ff., 86, 211, 215; economic assistance 59, 157; military balance 170f.; patron–client relationship 88f.; security guarantees 61; Soviet 'betrayal' of China 75, 156; strategic partnership 60; Treaty of Friendship and Mutual Assistance 60, 155
 China–U.S. relations: economic interdependence 8; new Cold War 8; rapprochement 197, 202; rivalry 1, 8, 239f.; security dilemma 3
 China–Vietnam relations (see also: First Indochina War; see also Second Indochina War; see also Sino–Vietnamese border conflict; see also Sino–Vietnamese war); brotherly comradeship 13, 191f., 196, 201, 218; Chinese assistance to North Vietnam 61, 160, 192f., 197, 202, 230; impact of Sino–American rapprochement 197, 202; regional competition 198, 201f.; Sino–Vietnamese split 196, 201; Soviet–factor 160, 190, 194ff., 202, 233; Vietnamese arrogance and disrespect 202, 204
China's intervention in the Korean War: air power 73f., 76; armistice agreement 78, 82ff., 89f.; battlefield situation 64, 67, 81, 85; cease–fire negotiations 82, 85, 89; decision–making 64, 67, 69ff., 77, 89f.; deliberations 61, 67, 70; fifth Chinese offensive 81f.; first Chinese offensive 79, 82; fourth Chinese offensive 80f.; intervention force (see Chinese People's Volunteers (CPV)); Kaesong 82; Mao-Zhou collaboration 64, 71, 90; military balance 83, 85; negotiation positions 87f., 91; North Eastern Border Defense Army (NEBDA) 65ff., 71; operative planning 76, 78; opposition to 69, 71, 228; Panmunjom 58, 83, 85f., 89; postponement of the intervention 75; preconditions 77; pretext 57, 172, 228; prisoner-of-war (POW) issue 88ff.; red line for 67; risk-assessment 72ff., 77; second Chinese offensive 79f., 82; Soviet air force detachment 74, 76; Soviet military assistance 72; Soviet renegade on air support 71, 76; Stalin's death 58, 78, 87ff.; state of military capabilities 57, 65, 77, 91; third Chinese offensive 80f.; voluntary repatriation of POW 83; warnings 67f., 91
China-Threat theory 2
Chinese Civil War 57–63, 65, 72, 107, 109, 162
Chinese Communist Party (CCP) 57–60, 63, 91, 203f., 206, 235, 237; 9th CCP Congress 165f.; Politburo 10, 64, 69, 124, 163; pro-Soviet faction 166; theory of the intermediary zone 59
Chinese Nationalist Party 59, 72–4, 111, 114, 135
Chinese People's Volunteer Engineer Force (CPVEF) 193, 196
Chinese People's Volunteers (CPV) 71–85, 88ff.
Classical Realism 25–27, 31
Cold War 1–5, 8, 29, 59, 63, 151, 159, 239; détente 88
Colonialism 108
Commitment Problem 26, 30f., 42f., 45, 91, 137, 217, 232
Communism 157, 217
Communist Party of the Soviet Union (CPSU): 23rd CPSU Congress 161
Cuba Crisis 106, 158
Cultural Revolution 151f., 161, 171, 178, 240: anti–Soviet programmatic 155, 162; China's ideological emancipation 177f.; domestic turmoil 162, 165ff., 193; impact on PLA 152, 171, 205f.

Cultural Theory of International Relations 4f., 12f., 26, 32ff., 44, 46, 91, 137f., 177, 216, 230f.; ideal-types 38; international society 39; motives 33; risk-behavior 36f., 40ff., 46, 232ff.
Czechoslovakia (CSSR): Soviet intervention 162

Dalai Lama 190
Damansky Island 149, 151, 166, 173 (*see also* Zhenbao Island)
Decision-Making: Korean War 64, 69ff.; Sino–Indian War 107, 116, 127ff.; Sino–Soviet border clashes 165; Sino–Vietnamese War 202–206, 209f., 215f.
Democratic People's Republic of Korea (DPRK) 1, 57, 62, 68, 82–86, 233
Democratic Republic of Vietnam (DRV) 192ff., 197–199
Deng Hua 84
Deng Xiaoping 6, 190, 201–205, 209ff., 215–218, 227, 230f., 234
Department for Overseas Chinese Affairs 201
Deterrence failure 29f., 57
Dhillon, Joginder Singh 126
Dien Bien Phu 192
Disgrace 34, 158, 228
Disrespect 12, 90, 106, 125f., 136f., 154, 164, 196, 202, 216, 230
Diversionary theories of conflict 6
Dreyer, David 191
Duel 36, 41, 137, 178, 217
Dulles, John Foster 86

East China Sea: maritime territorial dispute 1, 236, 239 (*see* also Senkaku/Diaoyu Islands)
Eisenhower, Dwight D. 86; Chance-for-Peace initiative 88
Elleman, Bruce 175
Emotions: in IR theorizing 4, 7, 32, 39, 240; in Sino–Vietnamese relations 191, 200, 218

Fearon, James 12f., 26, 29ff., 42ff., 91, 137, 130, 177, 217, 230, 232
First Indochina War 192ff.
First Kashmir War 108

Five Principles of Peaceful Coexistence 106, 108, 112, 137
Forward Policy 12, 115, 118–121, 129, 136, 229, 232f.; Chinese reactions to 119 (*see also* Armed Coexistence); Indian calculus 123
France 199
Fravel, Taylor 113f., 135, 237
Friendship 8, 12, 36, 41, 106, 111f., 233

Gao Gang 66, 69, 82, 231
Geneva Agreement 192f.
Geneva Conference 120, 192, 198
George, Alexander L. 44
Glaser, Charles 239
Goldstein, Lyle 152, 167
Gongsi 165
Great Britain 111
Great Leap Forward 114, 157, 193, 205, 240
Grieco, Joseph 25
Guangzhou Military Region 203, 208f.
Gulf of Tonkin–incident 194
Guomindang (GMD) (*see* Chinese Nationalist Party)

Heilongjiang Military Region 165
Ho Chi Minh 154, 160, 192, 195f., 198, 216
Hoa-Chinese: expulsion from Vietnam 199; Vietnamese mistreatment of 200
Honor 33–36, 40, 63, 137, 228
Hua, Guafeng 203f.
Humiliation 36, 40f., 115, 133, 135, 151, 229, 240

Inchon-Landing 12, 58, 64, 66f., 90
India: 3–6, 12, 87, 106–138, 156, 159, 203, 205, 213, 228f., 231ff., 240; armed forces 112, 117–122, 129–134; relations to Tibet 108f.; victimization 135
Indochina 13, 160, 191–202, 217
Information asymmetries 30, 42, 137, 177, 217, 232; private information 26, 30, 43, 45
Inner Mongolia 172, 209
Interdependence: in US–China relations 8, 239
International Order 2
International Relations: theory of 3f., 7, 12, 25ff., 33

Japan 1, 5, 132, 164, 203, 236f., 240
Johnston, Alastair 6, 238

Kashmir 107f.
Kaul, Brij Mohan 116, 133
Khmer Rouge 198, 200f.
Khrushchev, Nikita 113, 156–159,163, 166,194; policy of 'peaceful coexistence' 158
Kim Il-sung 61, 82, 159; military ambitions 61f.; request for Chinese intervention 68f.; Stalin–Kim collaboration 63; visit to Beijing 62
Kissinger, Henry 215
Korea Crisis of 2013 1
Korean Peninsula 1, 3, 62, 70, 74f., 80, 91
Korean People's Army 61, 66ff., 75f., 79f., 84; collapse of organized resistance 76
Korean War: armistice negotiations 78, 82; demilitarized zone (DMZ) 82f.; Inchon-Landing 64, 66ff., 90; Kaesong 82; military demarcation line (MDL) 82f.; Panmunjom 83, 85f., 89; prisoner-of-war (POW) issue 86ff.; Pusan Perimeter 66, 85; ROK crossing of the 38th parallel 80, 86; stalemate 78; U.S. aerial bombing 85f.; U.S. nuclear coercion 86
Korean Worker's Party (KWP) 68
Kosygin, Alexei, N. 154, 175
Kunming Military Region 203, 208f.

Ladakh 107f., 113, 126
Lang Son 208, 212ff.
Lao Cai 212f.
Laos 114, 197f.
Le Duan 195f.
Leaning-to-one-side policy 59, 108, 157
Lebow, Richard Ned 4f., 12f., 26, 32,ff., 37–40, 43f., 91f., 137, 177, 216ff., 227f., 230f., 233
Levy, Jack S. 31
Li Keqiang 135
Liberalism 6, 33
Lijphart, Arend 10
Lin Biao: 69, 123, 163, 166, 212, 231; military reforms 205f.
Liu Shaoqi 60, 166
Liu Bocheng 125
Logic of appropriateness 40f.

Logic of consequences 5, 25, 29, 42f., 232 (see rationality)
Long March 129

MacArthur, Douglas 77, 79
Malaysia 237
Malinovsky, Rodion 172
Manchuria 66
Mao Zedong 9, 57, 59, 61ff., 66–79, 80–92, 112ff., 118, 123ff., 135f., 152ff., 157–163, 171–178, 203, 210, 216, 228f., 231, 233ff.; determination 58; doctrine on nuclear warfare 86; interference in CPV command 79ff.; leaning-to-one-side speech 59f.; military ambitions in Korea 81; men-over-weapons doctrine 73; patron-client relationship 88; personal discrepancies with Stalin 59, 89; visit to Moscow 60f.; status 57
Maxwell, Neville 116, 149f.
McMahon Line 107, 109f., 112ff., 121f., 131, 134
Mearsheimer, John J. 26–29, 88, 233
Menon, Krishna 116, 120
Middle Kingdom (see China)
Military balance 5, 83, 85, 26, 130
Mongolia 114, 159f., 162, 172, 178, 209; Soviet–Mongolian Alliance 160, 163, 172; Soviet stationing of nuclear missiles and troops 172
Morgenthau, Hans J. 26f.
Mountain warfare 128ff.
Myanmar 107

Nam Il 82
NEBDA 65ff., 71, 74
Nehru, Jawaharlal 106, 109–116, 120–133, 136f., 229
Neorealism 6, 9, 25–29, 31
Nepal 107, 114
New China: historical mission 58ff., 91, 109, 192f.; self conception 63, 176, 229
Nie Rongzhen 69
Nixon, Richard 197, 199
North Atlantic Treaty Organization (NATO) 171f.
North Korea (see DPRK)
North Vietnam (see Democratic Republic of Vietnam (DRV))

252 Index

Nuclear weapons 1, 86, 172, 194; nuclear deterrence 170

Obama, Barack 8, 239

Pakistan 114
Panch Sheel (*see* Five Principles of Peaceful Coexistence)
Paracel Islands 199
Peng Dehuai 70f., 76f.; commander of CPV 70f., 76–86; military reforms 130, 205; singing of Korean War armistice agreement 89f.
People's Army of Vietnam (PAVN) 192, 197, 200, 206f., 213f.
People's Liberation Army (PLA) 2, 6, 10f., 29, 58, 61, 65, 69, 109ff., 119ff., 125–135, 152, 160f., 193, 197, 205ff., 208–214, 229f.; General Staff 62, 66, 69, 118, 124, 133
People's Liberation Army Air Force (PLAAF) 73f., 194, 208
People's Republic of China (*see* China)
Personality 136, 157, 216, 234
Philippines 237
Pol Pot 200
Politburo 10, 64, 69, 70f., 75, 124, 126, 151f., 163, 204, 228
Power Transition 2
Prestige 58, 81, 84, 89, 125, 157, 192, 240
Pusan Perimeter 66

Qiliqin Island incident 161, 168

Rationalist explanation for war 12, 26, 31, 42, 44ff., 230, 232
Rationality 30; ontology 7, 30; rational deterrence theory 5; rationalist theories of war 5; rational–choice assumption 3, 5, 30, 32, 38
Realism: Anarchy 27–31, 232; Balance of Power 6, 8, 27f., 238, 240; Classical Realism 25ff.; Defensive/Structural (Neo) Realism 26, 28; Offensive (Neo) Realism 28, 32; Polarity 27ff.
Realpolitik 59, 190f.
Red Army: combat effectiveness 170f.; mobile warfare 171; offensive capacity 163
Red Guards 162

Report of the Four Marshalls 197
Republic of Korea (ROK) (*see* South Korea)
Republic of Vietnam (*see* South Vietnam)
Reputation 7, 70, 84, 111, 175, 234
Resentment 199, 202, 216
Retaliation 5, 152ff., 166, 176, 205, 216, 230
Revenge 13, 36, 151f., 191, 203, 205, 209, 211, 215ff., 228, 240
Rhee, Syng-man 84f., 90
Risk behavior 36f., 40ff., 46; Chinese risk–behavior 90, 129, 138, 168, 177f., 205, 230ff.
Rivalry: China–Soviet Union 156, 159–163, 167, 177, 195, 202, 230, 233; U.S.–China 1, 8, 239f.

Scobell, Andrew 70, 171, 190, 203, 210
Second Indochina War: Chinese involvement in 193; Chinese security commitments to DVR 194; CPVEF 193, 196; Sino–Soviet competition in assisting Vietnam 202; U.S. involvement in 160
Security 3ff., 26ff., 33, 38ff.; security myth 9
Security dilemma 3, 37; Self–fulfilling prophecy 9
Senkaku/Diaoyu Islands 1, 236, 240 (*see also* East China Sea)
Seventeen–Point–Agreement 109
Shame 34, 70, 91, 228
Shastri, Lal Bahadur 133
Shenyang Military Region 165
Shevchenko, Arkady 151
Shu Zhi 62
Simla Convention 110, 137
Sino–Indian territorial conflict: armed clashes 112; battle at Thag La ridge 126; boundary dispute 109; casualties 117ff.; conflicting strategies 113; Dhola–Incident 121; historical roots 122; intensification of violence 112; militarization of 112; Namka Chu River 122; negotiations 122; rules of the game 121, 123
Sino–Indian War: cease–fire 132, 134; China's initial offensive 125, 131; Chinese negotiation offer 131f., 136;

Chinese withdrawal 134f.; collapse of Indian defense 134; combat at high-altitudes 127ff. (*see* also Mountain Warfare); Chinese decision for 123f.; duel 137; humiliation of India's armed forces 133f.; Indian counterattack 133; military balance 126, 130, 133; military preparations 136; objectives 112, 128, 131f., 135; operative considerations 124f.; outcome 135; punitive element 136; risk-assessment 130; second offensive 134; winter season 128, 131

Sino–Soviet border clashes: aftermath 168, 174f., 178; Chinese ambush 150, 152, 165f.; Chinese attempts of crisis management 174; Chinese casualties 150, 153; Chinese decision-making 165, 176; Chinese risk-calculations 168ff.; Chinese trophy 175; nuclear threats 174; Soviet causalities 150, 153; Soviet diplomatic initiatives 153, 174; Soviet retaliation 154, 176

Sino–Soviet boundary conflict: border consultations 158f.; Chinese incursions into Soviet territory 156, 161, 165; historical roots 155, 164; intensification of violence 165; unequal treaties 158

Sino–Soviet Split 156f., 162, 167, 195, 205, 215; boundary as mirror for 157; political rivalry 156; regional rivalry 159

Sino–Vietnamese territorial conflict 199 (*see also* Spratly Islands; *see also* Paracel Islands)

Sino–Vietnamese War: act of revenge 205, 209, 216; Battle for Lang Son 212ff.; casualties 199, 213f.; Chinese decision-making 203ff.; Chinese risk-calculations 205ff.; emotions 190f., 199f., 202, 205, 215f., 218; logistics 208, 212; morale of Chinese soldiers 207f., 213; punitive campaign 205, 216, 231; scorched earth 214; threat of Soviet retaliation 205, 216, 230; U.S. intelligence assistance 210; withdrawal 213f.

Smith, Adam 36

Socialist international society: 91, 231; China's entry into 63; China's sphere of influence and responsibility 160f. (*see* also Sino–Soviet Split); social obligations 57, 90, 216f.

Socialist Republic of Vietnam (SRV): alliance with Soviet Union 190, 201ff., 215f.; Chinese invasion of (*see*: Sino–Vietnamese War); invasion of Cambodia 200f.; hegemonic ambitions 201; support for Soviet intervention in Czechoslovakia 196

South China Sea 1ff., 199, 201, 237ff.

South Korea 1, 57, 62, 82, 84

South Vietnam 114, 193, 198f., 237

Soviet Union (Union of the Soviet Socialist Republics, USSR): agenda of interests 88; alliance with Vietnam 190, 201ff., 215f.; armed forces 170f. (*see* Red Army); credibility as ally 210f., 215; détente with the United States 132; de-Stalinization 157, 'pivot' to Asia 159; military posture in Far East 159; strategic encirclement of China 178, 197

Spratly Islands 199, 237

Stalin, Joseph: bait-and-bleed strategy 88, 233; bloodletting-strategy 88; death 87ff.; dedication of an own sphere of responsibility to China 60; green light for DPRK's invasion 62; influence on Beijing 87; realpolitik 59; rejection of Kim Il-sung's invasion plans 61; renegade on promise to provide air support for CPV in Korea 75f.; support for CCP 59

Standing 6, 33ff., 41, 47, 178, 217, 227f., 231, 240

Status: conflicts 7; emotional implications of 7f.; hierarchy 36; international politics 6, 8; for war 32, 35, 89, 126; social implications of 6, 8, 34; status seeking 7f., 227, 234f., 240

Strategic Trust 3

Su Yu 208

Sun Yat-sen 59

Taiwan 3, 11, 62, 69, 114, 234, 237

Tawang 131

Territorial Conflicts 136, 240

Tezpur 134

Thailand 203

Third Indochina War (*see* Sino–Vietnamese War)

Thompson, William R. 31
Tibet Military Region 117, 126, 137
Tibet 11, 109f., 120ff., 124, 127, 130, 133, 234, 237; autonomy 109; Chinese annexation of 11, 108; Tibetan rebellion 111f., 122
Trauma 60, 68, 135, 158, 164, 167, 229
Truman, Harry S. 68, 86
Trust 3, 31, 36f., 207, 239

United Nations (UN): 44, 57, 66, 83; Security Council 108, 227
United States (U.S.): containment of China 8; intervention in Korean War 62f.; invasion of Laos 197; involvement in Second Indochina War 160; leadership role in Asia–Pacific 2; pivot to Asia 3, 8, 239; strategic engagement 8
USSR (*see* Soviet Union)
Ussuri River 13, 149, 154, 156, 165, 169, 176, 178, 230, 240

Viet Minh 61, 129
Vietcong 193
Vietnam War (*see* Second Indochina War)
Vietnam 3, 6, 9, 160, 190ff., 230ff., 237; independence 190, 202; partition of 192; unification 202

Walong 131, 133

Waltz, Kenneth N. 26–29
War: as power-maximization strategy 28; as result of miscalculation 29–30 (*see* also deterrence failure); ex post inefficiency of 26, 30; non-material incentives for 32; trigger event 32, 40, 45, 47, 155, 178, 191, 231; theories of interstate warfare 25ff.
Weber, Max 38
Wendt, Alexander 8
Whiting, Allen S. 110, 121, 132f.

Xi Jinping 236, 238
Xinjiang 110, 130, 209
Xu Shiyou 212

Yalu River 58, 66–68, 71, 75, 84
Yang Jiechi 238
Ye Jianying 204

Zero-sum game 8, 38
Zhang, Xiaoming 204
Zhenbao Island 5, 29, 149–152, 161, 164–178, 229f.
Zhou Enlai 62, 64, 67f., 71, 74, 84, 86, 92, 110f., 122–124, 131, 134, 154, 159, 166, 175, 194f., 197, 204, 216, 229, 231; facilitating role 65, 234; proponent of China's intervention 64, 71, 90f., 228; visit to Moscow 88f.; visit to New Delhi 113–115

Made in United States
Orlando, FL
11 October 2025